ORU Journal of Theology

Vol 9, Nos 1 & 2 (2024)

Spiritus: ORU Journal of Theology
Vol 9, Nos 1-2 (2024)

ISSN: 2573-6345

ISBN: 978-1-950971-35-0

This print edition of this compilation consists of both Nos 1 & 2 of Vol 9, released originally in 2024.

Copyright © 2024 Oral Roberts University; published by ORU's College of Theology and Ministry and the Center for Spirit-empowered Research.

All rights reserved. To reproduce by any means any portion of this journal, one must first receive the formal consent of the publisher. To request such consent, write *Spiritus* Permissions – ORU COTM, 7777 S. Lewis Ave., Tulsa, OK 74171 USA. *Spiritus* hereby authorizes reproduction (of content not expressly declared not reproducible) for these non-commercial uses: personal, educational, and research, but prohibits re-publication without its formal consent.

Each issue is available at no cost for authorized uses at www.oru.edu/spiritus .

Spiritus: ORU Journal of Theology is published semi-annually in Spring and Fall.

Annual volumes comprising Spring and Fall issues (or "Numbers") will be available for sale in print through online resellers, such as Amazon and Barnes & Noble (and globally, wherever Ingram distributes Print On Demand titles; see https://bit.ly/GobalConnect). We expect Volumes 1–9 to be published in this way throughout 2025 and then annually, after the Number 2 of a Volume is released. Spiritus will continue to be available freely online at https://digitalshowcase.oru.edu/spiritus/.

Spiritus: ORU Journal of Theology is indexed through the Digital Commons (https:// www.bepress.com/impact-analytics/) and in the ATLA Religion Database published by the American Theological Library Association, 5600 South Woodlawn Avenue, Chicago, IL 60637. *Spiritus* contents may be searched at www.oru.edu/spiritus and through any web search engine. (Because another "Spiritus" journal is published by The Johns Hopkins University Press, searches for contents from ORU's *Spiritus* may succeed better by using the full title and subtitle.)

Cover designer: ORU design by Prof. Jiwon Kim.

Compositor: Daniel Isgrigg

ORU JOURNAL OF THEOLOGY

EDITOR

Jeffrey S. Lamp, Senior Professor, New Testament & Instructor, Environmental Science

ASSOCIATE EDITORS

Wonsuk Ma, Distinguished Professor of Global Christianity and Executive Director, Center for Spirit-empowered Research

Daniel D. Isgrigg, Associate Professor, College of Theology and Ministry

REVIEWS EDITOR

Robert D. McBain, Research Coordinator, Center for Spirit-empowered Research

EDITORIAL ADVISORY BOARD

Allan Anderson, University of Birmingham, UK
Candy Gunther Brown, Indiana University
Kwabena Asamoa-Gyuadu, Trinity Theological Seminary, Ghana

UNIVERSITY ADMINISTRATION

William M. Wilson, President
Kathaleen Reid-Martinez, Provost
Adrian E. Hinkle, Dean, College of Theology and Ministry

Spiritus: ORU Journal of Theology . . .

- Publishes studies from all disciplines pertaining to Spirit-empowered Christianity, from established and emerging scholars

- Emphasizes theological and cognate studies and works from and about Christianity in the Majority World

- Reviews pertinent scholarly works and some professional and popular works of merit

- Publishes scholarship to benefit especially Spirit-empowered Christian communities globally.

Find instructions for submitting articles and reviews for consideration at http://DigitalShowcase.ORU.edu/Spiritus/. This site receives all submissions leading to publishing decisions.

Views expressed in *Spiritus* are those of the contributors only.

Their publication in *Spiritus* does not express or imply endorsement by Oral Roberts University.

Correspondence (not related to submissions or subscriptions) is welcomed at <Spiritus@ORU.edu> or

Spiritus — ORU
Center for Spirit-empowered Research
7777 S. Lewis Ave.
Tulsa, OK 74171 USA.

CONTENTS (NUMBER 1)

Editorial

What is Spirit-empowered Scholarship?
Jeffrey S. Lamp 1

Essays

"Study to Show Thyself Approved": An Analysis of Oral Roberts' Personal Copy of the Commentary on Exodus by Umberto Cassuto
Daniel D. Bunn, Jr. 5

A Proposed Pentecostal *Quadrilectic:* Explorations for Asian Pentecostal Hermeneutics
Lora Angeline E. Timenia..23

The Prayer Tongue and the Jesus Prayer: The Witness of Abbot David Geraets
Clyde Glandon 39

Holiness as Wholeness in Afro-Pentecostal Tradition: A Theological Perspective
Ivan Hartfield..57

Managing Financial Sector Crisis: Do "Faith" and "Leave It to God" Matter?
Rebecca Attah, Christine Avortri, Emmanuel Appah, and Alexander Preko...............81

Pentecostalism and Current Development in West Africa: Reimagining the Pentecostal Landscape, Politics, and Vision
Fred Cudjoe Adadey and Barnabas Yisa 99

COVID-19 and Church Attendance Behavior Trends: Evidence from Ghanaian Pentecostal-Charismatic Churches
Justice A. Arthur and Lydia Andoh-Quainoo...117

Reviews

Pentecostal Orthodoxy: Toward an Ecumenism of the Spirit. By Emilio Alvarez.
S. Slade Hogan 135

Tongues of Fire: A Systematic Theology of the Christian Faith. By Frank Macchia.
Michael Young...138

A Pneumatology of Race in the Gospel of John. By Rodolfo Estrada.
Harold Gutierrez 141

Oneness Pentecostalism: Race, Gender, and Culture. By Lloyd D. Barba, Andrea S. Johnson, and Daniel Ramírez.
Peter Althouse...143

CONTENTS (NUMBER 2)

Editorial

Editorial: Most Likely You Go Your Way…
Jeffrey S. Lamp 147

Essays

PCCNA and USCCB Historic Exploratory Dialogue: From Mass to the Vatican then "Little Rome."
Harold D. Hunter 151

A Catholic Perspective on the New Relationship Between the Pentecostal Charismatic Churches of North America and the United States Conference of Catholic Bishops
Walter F. Kedjierski 157

Initiation Sacraments and Directions for Catholic-Pentecostal Dialogue: An Essay for the Exploratory USCCB/PCCNA Dialogue
Kimberly Hope Belcher 173

Initiation (Water Baptism) in North American Pentecostalism
Frederick L. Ware 187

Response to Frederick L. Ware
Kimberly Hope Belcher 201

Response to Kimberly Hope Belcher
Frederick L. Ware 205

Varieties of Healing: A Catholic Perspective
Andrew Prevot 207

Healing in the Pentecostal Tradition
David Han 229

Response to David Han's "Healing in the Pentecostal Tradition"
Andrew Prevot 245

A Pentecostal Appreciation of Andrew Prevot's "Varieties of Healing: A Catholic Perspective"
Harold D. Hunter 247

A Brief Consideration of the Sacrament of Marriage from a Catholic Perspective for Pentecostal Christians
Walter F. Kedjierski 253

Lex Orandi, Lex Serviendi: Roman Catholic Theology of Ordained Ministry in Select Texts from the Rites of Ordination
Leonardo J. Gajardo 273

Called: A Pentecostal Theology of Vocation
Martin W. Mittelstadt 295

Response to Martin Mittelstadt
Leonardo J. Gajardo 319

Response to Walter Kedjierski and Leonardo Gajardo
Martin W. Mittelstadt 323

Reviews

Pentecostal Prophets: Experience in Old Testament Perspective. By Stephen D. Barkley.
Wonsuk Ma 326

Phenomenal Phenomena: Biblical and Multicultural Accounts of Spirits and Exorcism. By Joy L. Vaughan.
Daniel D. Isgrigg 329

Christ Centered: The Evangelical Nature of Pentecostal Theology. By Robert Menzies.
Michael Young 332

Follow the Healer: Biblical Foundations for Healing Ministry. By Stephen Seamands.
Sam M. Barsoum 335

The Kaleidoscopic City: Hong Kong, Mission, and the Evolution of Global Pentecostalism. By Alex R. Mayfield.
Van Hnuai Kim 338

Soon and Very Soon: A Biblical and Theological Study of the Events Surrounding Jesus Christ's Second Coming. By David K. Hebert.
Cletus L. Hull, III 341

Editorial: What is Spirit-Empowered Scholarship?

Jeffrey S. Lamp, Editor

In my now eight years of serving as lead editor of *Spiritus*, I have had opportunity to consider articles submitted by Spirit-empowered scholars that cover a broad spectrum of topics. Many times, these articles appear in the pages of the journal; others are not accepted, but still demonstrate the breadth of interests among these scholars. In the past year, Oral Roberts University (ORU), the institutional home of *Spiritus*, has undergone an organizational reordering that has resulted in the formation of the Center for Spirit-empowered Research (C4SER). Under the direction of Wonsuk Ma, the C4SER is tasked with facilitating the university's scholarly efforts to serve the worldwide Spirit-empowered Movement through efforts to support faculty, students, and friends of the university in their scholarly work. *Spiritus* and other publishing activities are often the fruits of such scholarly enquiry. My role as editor of this journal has occasioned me to consider with increasing frequency just what we mean by "Spirit-empowered research." Is it research that focuses only on topics of interest to the Spirit-empowered Movement? Certainly it includes this focus, but is the term sufficiently expansive to include topics that may be of interest to Spirit-empowered believers and communities, but may also be of interest to those who would not self-identify as Spirit-empowered believers? It often appears that "Spirit-empowered" is simply a synonym for "Pentecostal" or "Charismatic." But does the term "Spirit-empowered" also lend itself to an understanding that it applies to the totality of the work of the Holy Spirit that does not exclusively entail the experiences typical of Pentecostal-Charismatic Christianity? Surely traditions that appeal to the work of the Spirit apart from *charismata* are covered under the heading "Spirit-empowered," aren't they?

Of course, there is nothing inappropriate about an entity that seeks to focus on what might be described as the purview of believers who would identify as Pentecostal or Charismatic. Scholarship undertaken from this specific orientation is a relatively recent phenomenon, embodied, though not exclusively, by the formation of the Society for Pentecostal Studies (SPS). It is reasonable that scholars in this group would conduct research into biblical, theological, and historical topics that are of particular interest to Pentecostal-Charismatic believers. For the first several decades following the Azusa Street revival, it appears that more generic evangelical scholarship provided the scholarly context for Pentecostal-Charismatic believers as they focused on their missional efforts viewed largely as evangelism. As the movement has matured, it has grown to view scholarship as an appropriate expression of its faith. And I have been privileged to contribute to this effort in my role as editor of *Spiritus*.

What I often bristle at is the implication, conscious or not, that the only audience that may be labeled "Spirit-empowered" is one that self-identifies with church communities that are of more traditional Pentecostal-Charismatic stripes. In 1980 I became a Christian through the efforts of adherents of the Word of Faith Movement. I owe the beginnings of my spiritual journey to this particular Charismatic tradition. I spent the first three or so years of my journey in such churches. I eventually moved to the United Methodist Church (UMC), particularly to a church in Tulsa that was formed by ORU seminary professors who sought to form a community that held to the best of Wesleyan and Charismatic spirituality, and I pursued ordination in the UMC while I attended the seminary at ORU during the time it was an accepted institution for the training of UMC ministerial candidates. Over the course of my time in the UMC, which consisted of nine years of pastoral ministry and many years on faculty at ORU, I self-identified as a "charismatic," lower-case "c," United Methodist. And for the past almost nine years, I have identified confessionally as an Eastern Orthodox Christian. I still include those original moorings of my Christian walk in Charismatic Christianity as part of my spirituality to this day. I consider myself charismatic. But I have often encountered the charge that I am not "Spirit-empowered" due to this identification. As an aside, I am more convinced now that Eastern Orthodox and Pentecostal expressions of Christianity have much in common and that this may serve as an impetus for these two strands of Christianity to engage in dialogue. I have often participated in SPS conferences, and in the present I have been invited by many traditional Pentecostal-Charismatic scholars to contribute to studies concerning Pentecostalism and popular culture and ecological engagement. Certainly this community of "Spirit-empowered" believers considers me one of their own. I fear that the moniker "Spirit-empowered" may become rather parochial, when it actually opens this movement to see itself as a vital contributor to the larger Christian community as it also serves its own constituency. If I recall correctly the history of the Pentecostal Movement I learned as a seminary student at ORU, this is how the earliest Pentecostals saw themselves.

This issue consists of seven articles that explore a broad range of topics, and in a couple of instances, it explores topics that extend beyond a narrow definition of "Spirit-empowered." The issue opens with a rather serendipitous study by Daniel Bunn of Oral Roberts' use of a scholarly biblical commentary. As he was giving his students a tour of the library at ORU, he happened across a commentary on Exodus by Israeli scholar Umberto Cassuto that had previously been owned by Roberts in which he underlined and wrote margin notes on various passages in the commentary. Bunn places Roberts' reading of the commentary in the tumultuous period of Roberts' life in which he owned and studied the commentary. He explores Roberts' engagement with the commentary in order to discern how Roberts' own reading habits of this work were later incorporated into a sermon published in the periodical *Abundant Life* in 1985. The resulting study is a revealing insight into how one of the giants of twentieth-century Spirit-empowered Christianity availed himself of the insights of biblical scholarship.

Lora Angeline E. Timenia follows with a hermeneutical proposal for Asian Pentecostal hermeneutics that builds upon the triadic models developed by Kenneth Archer and Amos Yong. The result is a *quadrilectic* model that she argues is more appropriate for Asian hermeneutical contexts, adding consideration of the Asian context to the triad of Spirit, Scripture, and tradition. Clyde Glandon contributes a study of the work of Charismatic Roman Catholic Abbot David Geraets in bringing together the Pentecostal practice of *glossolalia* with the Eastern Orthodox Jesus Prayer. Geraets argued that *glossolalia* and the Jesus Prayer mutually enhance the practice of these two modes of prayer. Glandon argues that this often overlooked figure provides a crucial contribution that would greatly benefit the spiritual lives of Spirit-empowered believers who seek a deeper experience of prayer. Ivan Hartsfield contributes a study that examines the concept of holiness as wholeness in Afro-Pentecostal tradition, drawing on the example of the Church of God in Christ (COGIC). Drawing on the thought of C. H. Mason, Hartsfield argues that the COGIC understands holiness as entailing the "human flourishing of the total person," resulting in an experience of holiness that is available to all people, not just those considered "saints."

The issue concludes with three studies that focus on African Christianity. First, Rebecca Attah, Christine Avortri, Emmanuel Appah, and Alexander Preko present the findings of a qualitative research study that examined the responses of religious persons following the financial sector clean-up efforts by governmental agencies in Ghana designed to alleviate corruption in the country's financial system. The results of this effort caused significant distress to individuals. The study addresses two religious responses to the suffering experienced by people—"faith" and "leave it to God"—coping mechanisms that customers employ to address circumstances that lay outside their ability to influence directly. The authors suggest that these two responses, largely ignored by financial management literature, may be profitably considered in future studies. Though not explicitly focused on Spirit-empowered believers, the study is an example of how Spirit-empowered researchers may contribute to research on topics that involve Spirit-empowered believers in the larger social context. Fred Cudjoe Adadey and Barnabas Yisa follow with a study of the contribution that African Pentecostals may make in the area of development in Western Africa. Drawing on research conducted in two large churches—the Redeemed Christian Church of God, Nigeria, and the Church of Pentecost, Ghana—the authors demonstrate how these Pentecostal groups contribute to the social and political landscape in light of the growing sense that Pentecostal mission entails engagement in social arenas. In the final article, Justice A. Arthur and Lydia Andoh-Quainoo examine how the COVID-19 pandemic has influenced church attendance in Pentecostal-Charismatic churches in Ghana. Employing the concept of religious economy, the authors employ a survey of church leaders and attendees to gauge the attitudes and practices regarding church attendance in terms that view church leaders as marketers of religious products and attendees as consumers of these products. The study looks at how participants in the survey viewed church attendance in the pre-COVID-19, COVID-19, and post-COVID-19 periods, observing how the pandemic has affected church attendance behaviors, both in negative and positive ways.

Four book reviews close out the issue.

The scope of these articles demonstrates the breadth of topics available for research for Spirit-empowered scholars. Many times the topics are specific to the Spirit-empowered Movement; other times they exemplify how these scholars might participate in studies that address concerns of the larger Christian community. In each case, the results are fruitful contributions to Spirit-empowered scholarship.

Jeffrey S. Lamp (jlamp@oru.edu) is Senior Professor of New Testament and Instructor of Environmental Science at Oral Roberts University, Tulsa, Oklahoma, USA.

"Study to Show Thyself Approved"

An Analysis of Oral Roberts' Personal Copy of the Commentary on Exodus by Umberto Cassuto

Daniel D. Bunn, Jr.

Keywords *Oral Roberts, Exodus, Moses, miracle, seed faith, City of Faith*

Abstract

> Having happened upon what was previously Oral Roberts' personal copy of the commentary on Exodus by Umberto Cassuto, I observed his active interaction with the volume by way of notes and underlines. I determined to analyze his interaction with it. This essay shares the results of the analysis of that book. It begins with a brief overview of his personal life during the time in which he possessed the commentary. Then, it makes observations about his interaction, showing specific examples. Finally, it will look more intently at a sermon in which his use of the commentary is made explicit.

Introduction

On a biennial basis, I teach a class on the book of Exodus. The culmination of this class is an analytical paper on a selected passage from the book. In preparing the students for that process, I often take them to the library to acquaint them with some of the most valuable resources. This usually involves pointing out the many exemplary commentaries that have been written over the centuries on this momentous book of the Bible.

On one such occasion, I opened for them the distinguished volume written by the late Umberto Cassuto, Professor of Bible at the Hebrew University in Jerusalem. The volume—a translation of the original Hebrew in which he wrote it—is a staple in close investigation of the book of Exodus. As I flipped open the cover to show the students, I was surprised by the signature of a familiar figure: Oral Roberts. This particular volume was at one time a part of his personal library. As I flipped further, I was surprised to see detailed notes, underlining, and other markings throughout the book. As someone who has been significantly shaped by the life and ministry of Oral Roberts, I sensed that I was peering through the window to see Oral himself, at work in his study. I decided to sit with this volume in order to see what might emerge from it.

In this article, I wish to share some of the results of that process. I will begin by considering the timeframe in which Oral Roberts possessed the volume so as to situate his engagement with the text within his own life's context. I will then synthesize observations made about his interaction with the commentary, looking at examples along the way. Finally, I will consider in depth a sermon in which his use of this commentary is made explicit, thereby exploring some of the ways in which he moved from study to sermon.

A Tumultuous Decade

When did Oral Roberts possess and use this commentary? Being able to situate the volume chronologically might help us to plumb its significance for him. As I moved further into my investigation, I observed two key pieces of data in this regard. First, below Roberts' signature inside the cover, he included a date: "1–78." This, then, is the *terminus a quo*—January 1978.

Figure 1

Also on the cover is a stamped sticker with the following: Presented to Oral Roberts University Library/Theology Library by President Roberts, April 6, 1990. That provides the *terminus ad quem*.

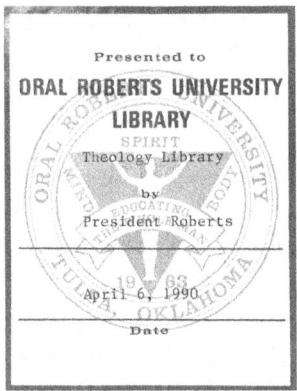

Figure 2

I want to consider what took place during this timeframe in the life of Oral Roberts. I want to proceed with caution, though. On the one hand, such an effort to situate the commentary within his life might help to offer further insight into the ways in which he was engaging the volume. On the other hand, the attempt could falsely lead to unsubstantiated conclusions about particular comments that he writes in the commentary and their possible connection to real-life events. I offer the summary of this time period in his life with the intent of staying closer to the former while avoiding the latter.

The beginning of this time period is enshrouded with heavy burdens. A consideration of this time period must begin with an event that took place nearly one year before Roberts received the book. On February 11, 1977, Roberts endured what no parent should: his eldest child, Rebecca Roberts Nash, 37, was tragically killed with five other people as their plane crashed in a storm over Kansas.[1]

With that loss not even one year in behind him, another significant event happened in the life of Roberts, one that would cause ripples for years to come. On January 24, 1978—which also happened to be his sixtieth birthday—ground was broken for the City of Faith. Cathy Carothers of *Communiqué*—a publication for Oral Roberts University (ORU) alumni, at the time—captured Roberts' statements at the event:

> "Today is dreary and overcast," said President Roberts, as he celebrated his 60th birthday by breaking ground, "and that's the condition that millions of people are in. They have depressed minds, sick bodies, spirits that are down, and they're

---

[1] "Daughter of Oral Roberts Is Killed with 5 Others in Crash of Airplane," *The New York Times*, February 13, 1977, https://www.nytimes.com/1977/02/13/archives/daughter-of-oral-roberts-is-killed-with-5-others-in-crash-of.html.

looking for the sun to break through the clouds. And the Bible says, 'The Son of Righteousness will rise with healing in His wings.'"[2]

The years following this event would be marked by active efforts to see the project through to completion.

Famously, it was during this period that Roberts indicated that he had experienced a vision of Jesus. In the September 1980 issue of *Abundant Life*, he included a letter to donors that described the event.[3] In a section entitled, "I'VE SEEN JESUS," he says:

> He came to me five times in a period of an hour and a half as I stood up close in front of the CITY OF FAITH structure, beginning at 7:00 p.m., May 25. The CITY OF FAITH is over 600 feet tall. I saw Jesus appear, and He looked like He stood at least 900 feet tall. I saw Him bend down and put His hands UNDER the unfinished CITY OF FAITH structure and lift it and say, "**See how easy it is for Me to lift it?**" (emphasis original)

His depiction of his experience would be the source of ridicule for decades to come. Certainly in the years immediately following, many were skeptical that his vision was an elaborate ruse to get the money needed to fund the building project.

The City of Faith was dedicated on November 1, 1981. In some ways, the event represented the hard-won victory of the dream Roberts had for this facility. Sue Smith, with *The Oklahoman*, reported that approximately 12,000 people filled the Mabee Center. Included among that number were "television evangelists Rex Humbard and Pat Robertson, Tulsa Mayor Jim Inhofe, Gov. George Nigh, Congressman Jim Jones, former football player and television performer Rosie Grier, country-western singer Barbara Mandrell [who sang the National Anthem] and a delegation from the government of Kenya."[4] The event brought national attention. At the ceremony, Congressman Jones read a letter of congratulations from an unnamed sender. At the conclusion of the letter, he announced the sender's name: President Ronald Reagan.[5]

What followed in subsequent years, however, casts a shadow back over the dedication festivity. Though not immediately related to the City of Faith project, tragedy again struck the Roberts family as their eldest son, Ronald, died by suicide in 1982. One knows that such a loss for anyone would be devastating. But in Oral Roberts' case, it was compounded. First, as was mentioned above, he lost his daughter

---

[2] Cathy Carothers, "Ground Broken for City of Faith," *Communiqué*, Spring 1978, https://digitalshowcase.oru.edu/cof/2.

[3] *Abundant Life*, 34:8 (1980), 10.

[4] Sue Smith, "Evangelist Oral Roberts Dedicates City of Faith," *The Oklahoman*, November 2, 1981, https://www.oklahoman.com/story/news/1981/11/02/evangelist-oral-roberts-dedicates-city-of-faith/61314137007/.

[5] Smith, "Evangelist Oral Roberts Dedicates City of Faith," n.p.

in 1977. Thus, the entire process from groundbreaking to dedication was bookended by the tragic loss of two of his children. Second, the public scrutinized Ronald's death—its nature, his life leading up to it, and the reality that he was Oral Roberts' son. For example, Bob Bonebrake, reporting during the aftermath in *The Oklahoman*, said, "Growing up, Ronald Roberts watched as thousands of the sick and desperate came searching for help. . . . It might have surprised many of those searchers to know the younger Roberts was also searching for something, something he apparently never found."[6] Implied in this reporting is that Oral Roberts was able to help many, yet he could not help his own son.

Insufficient funding for the City of Faith likewise complicated the celebration of the dedication of the complex. Entire issues of *Abundant Life* would be dedicated to pleading with donors to send in support in order to fund the remainder of the project. The cover of the special issue from February 1982 includes a picture of Roberts preaching over a yellow background.[7] At the top, in large, red letters, it says, "EMERGENCY." Down the side, it says, "HELP KEEP THIS MINISTRY ALIVE." The issue indicates that at the time of the opening of the City of Faith, the interior of the buildings still remained about 80% incomplete.[8] Roberts expresses the direness of the situation, from his perspective:

> This is a very, very special sermon. I hurt as I write it. I am facing the worst crisis I've faced in my 35 years in this ministry of God's Word. THE DEVIL IS TRYING TO DESTROY THIS ENTIRE MINISTRY. And, partner, I need you to keep it alive. Unless we get a continuous miracle—a breakthrough from heaven for your life and mine—this ministry is gone. The City of Faith, where thousands are being healed through the merging of medicine and prayer, will be closed. The 4,200 young people at Oral Roberts University will have to go home. Our television and radio outreach . . . will end. If this ministry dies, your letters to me will not be answered. There'll be no more ABUNDANT LIFE. . . . The Prayer Tower will close. Millions of hurting people will not be helped. We're in that kind of financial crisis, and I'm here to tell you about it.[9]

Readers can sense the desperation that Roberts felt at that moment.

This desperate situation culminated with another notorious moment, as Roberts claimed that if he did not raise necessary funding, then his life would end. In the January–February 1987 issue of *Abundant Life*, he opened with the following: "As I

---

[6] Bob Bonebrake, "Reasons Behind Suicide of Evangelist's Troubled Son Are Still a Mystery," *The Oklahoman*, June 20, 1982, https://www.oklahoman.com/story/news/1982/06/20/reasons-behind-suicide-of-evangelists-troubled-son-are-still-a-mystery/62881106007/.

[7] *Abundant Life*, 36:2 (1982), 1.

[8] *Abundant Life*, 36:2 (1982), 13.

[9] *Abundant Life*, 36:2 (1982), 1.

have shared with you since last March, God gave me a mandate at that time to turn the ORU medical school into a total missionary outreach to the nations. He gave me one year to do it. And he said if I didn't do it, my work would be done and He would call me home."[10] As the end of March drew near, Roberts planned to enter and remain in the Prayer Tower, fasting and praying, until the remaining money had been raised. Spokeswoman Jan Dargatz, quoted in the *Los Angeles Times*, said, "When Oral does this, it's almost like a marathon, but he has trained for it. He prays every day."[11] The event drew heavy criticism from those inside and outside the church.

Two years later, in September 1989, eleven years after ground was broken for the City of Faith, Roberts announced that it would be closing. Whereas the issues of *Abundant Life* during those eleven years were replete with updates about the City of Faith, those issues that arrived in the months leading up to the announcement were notably silent on the building complex. Focus shifted to other ministry efforts and the university. The publication, which by this time had moved to every other month rather than monthly, did not even produce what would have been a September–October issue in 1989. The last headline related to the City of Faith came in the January–February 1989 issue: "A Neurosurgeon Joins the Staff of Spirit-filled Physicians at the City of Faith."[12]

After the events of the previous decade, Roberts unsurprisingly came under further scrutiny as he announced the closing of the City of Faith. Robby Trammell and Jim Killackey, in an article in *The Oklahoman* entitled, "Roberts Urged Not to Build City of Faith Hospital in '78," said:

> Tulsa State and local authorities tried to tell evangelist Oral Roberts in 1978 that his proposed City of Faith hospital was not feasible, that it would be a monumental mistake. But nothing seemed capable of stopping the high-rolling national television minister's ambitious plans. . . . A more humbled Roberts announced Wednesday that the financially plagued hospital where God's miracle healing power would be combined with the wonders of modern medicine would close by Jan. 1, affecting 600 employees.[13]

Writing in the *Washington Post*, Arnold Hamilton quoted a medical student who was attending the medical school at the time that the closing was announced:

---

[10] *Abundant Life*, 41:1 (1987), 3.

[11] "Oral Roberts to Climb Tower, Pray for Money," *Los Angeles Times*, March 21, 1987, https://www.latimes.com/archives/la-xpm-1987-03-21-me-4582-story.html.

[12] *Abundant Life*, 43:1 (1989), 17.

[13] Robby Trammell and Jim Killackey, "Roberts Urged Not to Build City of Faith Hospital in '78," *The Oklahoman*, September 15, 1989, https://www.oklahoman.com/story/news/1989/09/15/roberts-urged-not-to-build-city-of-faith-hospital-in-78/62601125007/.

Medical student Pat Rice, 30, . . . said he was not surprised by the decision . . . "I've been here two and a half years and kind of watched things fall apart," Rice said. "I've watched doctors leave in droves. I've watched classmates leave in droves. . . . I frankly don't have a lot of confidence in the leadership here from what I've seen and experienced. You get told one thing and other things happen."[14]

The general time period during which Roberts possessed the commentary that is the subject of this article, then, was marked by some of the most extreme experiences of his career and personal life. Personally, he experienced severe tragedies. Professionally, he pursued perhaps his most ambitious plan to date. Though he would see some success along the way with the City of Faith, on the whole, the plan did not end as he had hoped it would. By fall 1989, the project had come to an end. Within a few months of the closing, Roberts would donate the commentary to the university.

Oral Roberts Reads Umberto Cassuto

I now want to look at Roberts' engagement with the commentary. As noted above, the volume is filled with personal notes and interaction with the text. Roberts regularly marks the text itself and writes notes in the margins. In this section, I will examine the specific ways in which Roberts interacts with the commentary. In particular, I will focus on the three main ways he interacts with it: he repeats points made in the commentary; he summarizes points, often doing so through his own theological framework; and he reflects on pastoral implications of the points. I will suggest that these three methods of engagement, when taken together, indicate Roberts' posture as an active learner.[15] I will focus on his interaction with Exodus 1–2.[16]

He is especially keen on numbers in these chapters. He underlines and rewrites a comment about the number 70: "70/indicates perfection of a family blessed with offspring."[17] He draws attention to the commentary's discussion of "Seven expressions of increase"; he calls them "7 phases of increase," and he lists them out in order.[18] He highlighted the commentary's observation of uses of *seven* in Exodus: "7 is found often

---

[14] Arnold Hamilton, "Oral Roberts to Shut Down Hospital and Medical School at Tulsa," *Washington Post*, September 16, 1989, https://www.washingtonpost.com/archive/local/1989/09/16/oral-roberts-to-shut-down-hospital-and-medical-school-at-tulsa/16a43a8a-cb9c-4fa1-8762-1d850d59fd69/.

[15] As the notes in the commentary are handwritten, they can be difficult to determine clearly at points. When the text is in doubt, I will not attempt to conjecture. Emphasis added by capitals and underlining are original.

[16] All citations will be from Umberto Cassuto, *A Commentary on the Book of Exodus*, trans. Israel Abrahams (Jerusalem: The Magness Press, 1976).

[17] Cassuto, *Exodus*, 8.

[18] Cassuto, *Exodus*, 9.

in Exodus."[19] An example that stood out to him was the word *child*: "child — occurs 7 times."[20]

He also seems drawn to discussions of *multiply/increase*. He wrote out a phrase from the commentary, "multiplied exceedingly," and added a parenthetical gloss: "an overflowing measure."[21] He focused on the aforementioned "7 phases of increase," writing out the details provided by the commentary.[22] In reflecting on the commentary's note about the affliction imposed on the Israelites in Exodus 1, he adds, "Satanic in origin—to stop them from growing."[23] He writes out the note from the commentary that "the more the latter [the Israelites] continued to multiply," and adds: "very important." He writes out from the commentary, "and the people multiplied and grew very mighty despite efforts of enemies."[24]

He paid special attention to the commentary's discussion of the birth of Moses, speaking of the "miracle" of this event and the "seeds" that had been planted through faithfulness. He is first drawn to the example of the midwives. Summarizing a point made in the commentary, Roberts says, "Midwives of Pharaoh feared King of the Universe, not King of Egypt."[25] Being regularly drawn to steps and patterns, he paid special attention to the midwives: "Midwives helped Hebrews and were blessed for it— and the people multiplied and grew very mighty despite efforts of enemies."[26]

Roberts is likewise drawn to the demonstration of the faith of Moses' mother. He shares the note from the commentary that Moses' mother had placed Moses' sister in a position to watch what would happen with the baby once he was placed in the river. He comments: "She expected a miracle! ([. . .] of what she did—her seed planted)."[27] He lists eight steps in the miracle of Moses, which involved Pharaoh's daughter, Moses' mother, Moses' sister, and Moses' own crying. All converged to enable the rescue. The results would be blessing beyond what would have previously been possible, as Moses' own mother will now raise him for pay. Roberts adds, "Get a Hebrew wet nurse FOR YOU (planted a seed here)."[28]

---

[19] Cassuto, *Exodus*, 17.

[20] Cassuto, *Exodus*, 21.

[21] Cassuto, *Exodus*, 9.

[22] Cassuto, *Exodus*, 9.

[23] Cassuto, *Exodus*, 10.

[24] Cassuto, *Exodus*, 15.

[25] Cassuto, *Exodus*, 14.

[26] Cassuto, *Exodus*, 15.

[27] Cassuto, *Exodus*, 19.

[28] Cassuto, *Exodus*, 20.

The miracle, for Roberts, would continue into Moses' adulthood. He asks of the text, "How did Moses know that Hebrews were his brethren?"[29] He follows with his hypothesis: "Jochebed." Though neither the text of Exodus nor the commentary are explicit, Roberts sees in every one of the mother's actions intentionality that flowed out of her trust in and relationship with God.

He observes the commentary's description of what motivates the adult Moses. He states from the commentary, "He LOOKED on their burdens just as his mother and Pharaoh's daughter took pity on him, so he felt compassion on his brethren—their burden."[30] Roberts reflected also on the role of the cries in the people in motivating the Lord's response. He underlined the text of the commentary that said, "And God remembered." He elaborated: "Listen: Are you groaning inside for deliverance?/Are you crying to God/Are you asking him to help you."[31] He rewrote the following as a summary of the commentary's point: "1. God heard 2. God remembered 3. God saw 4. God remembered . . . stage by stage God's response to the groaning of the Ch. of Isr. and finally He decides to intervene on their behalf."[32]

One can sense, based on what he has selected to write out from the commentary, his theological concerns. His concern with multiply/increase occurred throughout his ministry. The language of miracles and planting seeds also stood center stage for much of his life.[33] These dimensions of his own theological reflection came together concretely in his hope to see the funding for the City of Faith to come to fruition. One does not have to probe too deeply to consider that during these years of his life, Roberts found in the story of Moses—the faith demonstrated in the women surrounding him, the miraculous nature of his early life, God's use of him to deliver the people, the blessing that follows seemingly insurmountable trials—a template for his own longed-for success with the vision he saw for the City of Faith. This connection will be demonstrated explicitly in what follows.

Sermon on Exodus 3

During the research for this project, I sought a tangible demonstration of Roberts' use of this commentary in his writings. I searched especially through the issues of *Abundant Life*,

---

[29] Cassuto, *Exodus*, 22.

[30] Cassuto, *Exodus*, 22.

[31] Cassuto, *Exodus*, 28.

[32] Cassuto, *Exodus*, 29.

[33] See, e.g., Oral Roberts, *The Miracle of Seed-Faith* (Tulsa, OK: Oral Roberts Evangelistic Association, Inc. 1970); Oral Roberts, *Expect a Miracle* (Nashville: Thomas Nelson, 1998).

since this was one of Roberts' main forms of regular, public communication during the time at which he possessed the commentary. In most issues, he opened with a sermon. As one might imagine, the sermons were often directed toward encouraging readers of the hope that God would bring the vision of the City of Faith to pass. To my joy, I eventually discovered an issue from 1985 that included a sermon on Exodus 3. In this section, I will explore the connections between that sermon and Roberts' engagement with the commentary. In particular, I will seek to accomplish two goals: (1) I will show how the sermon is more generally based on notes from the commentary, and (2) I will demonstrate specific moments at which Roberts explicitly uses the commentary.

On the cover of the November–December 1985 issue of *Abundant Life* are a Christmas tree background and two family photos—one of Richard and Lindsay Roberts and their child and the other of Oral and Evelyn Roberts. The caption reads, "From Our Hearts to Yours . . . Merry Christmas!" The opening page states: "Nearly 2,000 years ago this Christmas, Jesus Christ—the LIGHT of the world—was born into the world. Throughout the centuries, those who have followed him have carried that LIGHT to countless generations. If you are a follower of Jesus Christ this holiday season, remember that through our personal relationship with Him . . . ," followed by, "We Are a Lighted People"—which is the title of his sermon on Exodus 3.[34]

His sermon opens by setting the stage for discussing Moses as an example of someone being used by God. Summarizing Exodus 2, he says, "As a man, Moses was rejected by his people and forced to live a life of exile."[35] This note does not appear in the commentary; it appears to be Roberts' own interpretation. Following this summary comment, he expresses the main thesis: "From that encounter with God, Moses became a LIGHTED person. Through his obedience to God, he carried that LIGHT to countless generations to follow . . . so that you and I today, as followers of Jesus Christ, can also be a LIGHTED people."[36] The emphasis on *lighted* comes from the commentary, as will be demonstrated below. Following this introduction, he shares the text of Exodus 3:1–15.[37]

After sharing the Scripture, he aims to draw a parallel between readers and Moses, the elders of Israel, and what God had called them to do.[38] The basis of this parallel he expresses as follows: "Because you and I, as Christians, are also a *called* people, a *chosen*

---

[34] *Abundant Life*, 39:8 (1985).

[35] *Abundant Life*, 39:8 (1985), 3.

[36] *Abundant Life*, 39:8 (1985), 3.

[37] *Abundant Life*, 39:8 (1985), 3.

[38] *Abundant Life*, 39:8 (1985), 3.

people, a people who are sent out into this world with a mission of bringing those who are still in bondage today out of darkness into His marvelous LIGHT."[39]

He then returns to the opening chapters of Exodus and the factors leading up to the birth of Moses. He mentions the rise of a new Pharaoh who did not know Joseph and who "saw a fruitfulness among the Israelites that he was determined to stop."[40] This statement appears to be based on a combination of two notes that Roberts had written in the commentary. First, he underlines the commentary and states from it, "They 'multiplied exceedingly' (in overflowing measure)."[41] Second, as stated above, Roberts notes regarding the commentary's mention of Pharaoh's affliction of the people of Israel that it was "Satanic in origin—to stop them multiplying."[42]

He then reflects in his sermon further on the intentions of Pharaoh and the experience of the people of Israel. He states, "[Pharaoh] determined to lay heavy burdens upon the Israelites and to increase their burdens until he had reduced them to slave status in Egypt."[43] This sentence appears to derive from the commentary's discussion of the Hebrew word for *serve* as well as the name *Hebrew* itself. The commentary notes that the word for *serve* and the word for *rigor* occur seven times in total in Exodus 1:14 in order to drive home the servitude of the people.[44] Regarding the name *Hebrew*, the commentary says, "In the Bible the children of Israel . . . are called *Hebrews* particularly when the writer has in mind their relationship to the foreign environment in which they find themselves . . . , and more especially when they are in the position of slaves. . . ."[45] Roberts wrote out notes on both of these points. He wrote on the first point, "toil that breaks/that crushes."[46] On the second, he wrote, "1. Called chil (*sic*) of Israel when not slaves 2. Called Hebrews when in position of slaves."[47]

The next sentence in Roberts' sermon says, "Soon they felt the hammerlike blows of the king's burdens laid upon them."[48] In the commentary, he has written the note,

---

[39] *Abundant Life*, 39:8 (1985), 3.
[40] *Abundant Life*, 39:8 (1985), 3–4.
[41] Cassuto, *Exodus*, 9.
[42] Cassuto, *Exodus*, 10.
[43] *Abundant Life*, 39:8 (1985), 4.
[44] Cassuto, *Exodus*, 11–12.
[45] Cassuto, *Exodus*, 13.
[46] Cassuto, *Exodus*, 11.
[47] Cassuto, *Exodus*, 13.
[48] *Abundant Life*, 39:8 (1985), 4.

"Their work was like <u>hammer blows</u>."[49] This comment of his seems to be the basis of his statement in the sermon. This is interesting, though, in light of what the commentary actually says: "The words [related to the Hebrew word for *serve*] follow one another in these verses like hammer blows. . . ."[50] The author of the commentary is not talking about the nature of the work, but rather the use of words related to *serve*. Perhaps Roberts found in that metaphor useful language for reflecting on the experience of servitude; possibly he misunderstood what the author was communicating. In either case, his note in the commentary seems to be the basis for his statement in the sermon.

In the following paragraph in the sermon, Roberts seems to blend two moments in the Exodus narrative and their corresponding discussion in the commentary. First, he looks at Exodus 2 when he says, "When [the people of Israel were burdened by Pharaoh], the children of Israel *cried*, the Bible says. They cried brokenheartedly to the Lord for deliverance." The statement that "the children of Israel *cried*," including emphasis, appears to derive from the following in the commentary: "[T]he children of Israel *cry* out from their place of bondage."[51] The statement, "They cried brokenheartedly," seems to come from the following: "'From their bondage' . . . the children of Israel were groaning brokenheartedly and crying unto God. . . ."[52]

Second, he states from Exodus 1, "Yet they grew in their oppression. The more they were oppressed, the more they multiplied their numbers."[53] This statement seems to come from the following, which Roberts has underlined and labeled as "very important" in the commentary: "The more they sought to persecute the Israelites and to weaken them, the more the latter continued to multiply in increasing measure, as Scripture narrates: *But . . . the more they were oppressed, the more they multiplied . . . and the more they spread abroad.*"[54]

Later in his sermon, Roberts considers the act of Moses' mother constructing the basket and putting it in the river. He says, "I find it very interesting that the Word says that she 'placed' it upon the river. Because to me that one word indicates that God operates by a divine plan. He knows precisely what He's doing in this world . . . and in our lives."[55] In the commentary, the author highlights the use of the word *place*. He says, "The repetition of the word *placed* appears to imply that the mother put the ark

---

[49] Cassuto, Exodus, 12.

[50] Cassuto, *Exodus*, 12.

[51] Cassuto, *Exodus*, 29.

[52] Cassuto, *Exodus*, 29.

[53] *Abundant Life*, 39:8 (1985), 4.

[54] Cassuto, *Exodus*, 11.

[55] *Abundant Life*, 39:8 (1985), 4.

down very gently, with the same tender care with which she had put the child in the ark."⁵⁶ Alongside this point, Roberts notes, "placed the bassinet <u>carefully</u> in the water."

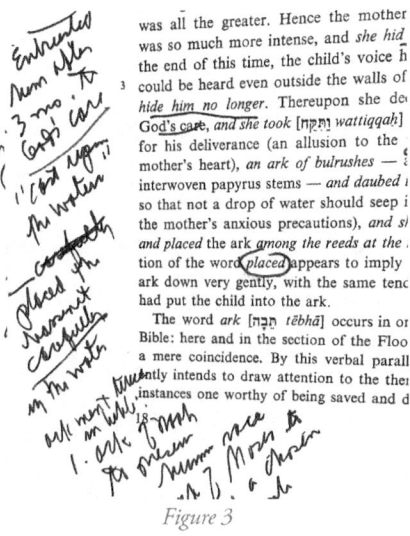

Figure 3

This seems to be the basis of Roberts' statement in the sermon here. Roberts saw in the commentator's words not only the care and intentionality of Moses' mother, but through her acts, the care and intentionality of God.

Next, Roberts considers in his sermon the coincidence of Pharaoh's daughter coming to the exact spot where Moses' mother had placed him. He says, "And while the princess was bathing, *the baby cried*. Now there's something very important here. When you read the Bible, you must remember that there's nothing *accidental* in it. It says, '. . . the baby cried.' He could have kept from crying until the princess had left, but he *cried* and she *heard* it."⁵⁷ In considering the scene involving Pharaoh's daughter, the commentary says, "The thing that immediately attracted her attention was his weeping. He is crying, therefore he is not dead, but is suffering and arouses compassion."⁵⁸ Roberts notes in the commentary, "Baby cried at precise moment to gain her attention . . . his crying got to her—was suffering, aroused her compassion."⁵⁹ He next considers in his sermon what resulted from the encounter: Moses' mother "not only got

---

⁵⁶ Cassuto, *Exodus*, 18.

⁵⁷ *Abundant Life*, 39:8 (1985), 4.

⁵⁸ Cassuto, *Exodus*, 19.

⁵⁹ Cassuto, *Exodus*, 19.

to nurse and raise her own baby—who would have been killed had she not listened to God—but she was paid to do it!"⁶⁰ In the commentary, Roberts had written out the following: "Paid to raise her own child, who had been condemned to death. No more anxious for his life."⁶¹

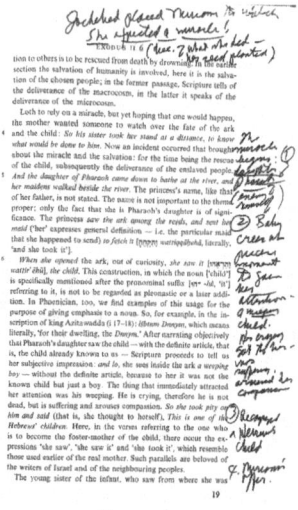

Figure 4

After ending his consideration of Exodus 1–2, he connects what he has observed to his readers' experiences. He asks, "Do you think that that was just an accident? Do you think *your life* today is just an accident? No. . . . Somebody planted a seed, somebody went to battle."⁶² As was noted above, the language of "planting a seed" is found in Roberts' notes in the commentary at just this point.

Roberts then moves into the main focus of the sermon, Exodus 3. He begins, "A bush on fire was not an uncommon sight on the mountain where Moses had gone with his sheep. But this one was different, and Moses could not turn his eyes away. For this bush burned, *but it was not consumed by the fire*. Its flame came up out of itself and lighted the bush and made it flame and shine to give a man a vision of God."⁶³ This appears to come from a note in the commentary: "Although the bush . . . is commonly found in steppe country, and it is no unusual phenomenon for a bush dried by the summer's heat to catch fire, yet the bush that Moses saw was not consumed in the

---

⁶⁰ *Abundant Life*, 39:8 (1985), 4.

⁶¹ Cassuto, *Exodus*, 20.

⁶² *Abundant Life*, 39:8 (1985), 4.

⁶³ *Abundant Life*, 39:8 (1985), 5.

flame. . . ."[64] Further, the commentary says, "On this mountain Moses was vouchsafed a vision of God," a note which Roberts has underlined.[65] In reflecting on the discourse between the Lord and Moses, Roberts states in his sermon, "It's interesting to me that the first thing God wanted Moses to do was to tell the people his testimony."[66] In a note written in the commentary, Roberts says, "Moses' personal testimony: God of Abraham, Isaac, and Jacob, has appeared to ME/the God of your father—has appeared to ME."[67]

Next, he comes in his sermon to what is perhaps the most intriguing connection between the sermon and the commentary. He says:

> I have more than fifty commentaries on the Old Testament written by Jewish rabbis. In one commentary I was reading recently, the author brought out a point that is very meaningful to us today. He said that THE LIGHT THAT WAS IN THE BUSH LIGHTED MOSES! That was part of Moses' testimony. In coming down to the elders of Israel, Moses said, in effect, "I am LIGHTED. I've been LIGHTED BY GOD and I'm bringing that LIGHT to you. You are now LIGHTED. And as LIGHTED PEOPLE we will now go to Pharaoh and say, 'Let God's people go.'" As I read that commentary, I bawled like a baby.[68]

The commentary under discussion says the following:

> Another point: Moses and the elders were to tell Pharaoh that God *lighted* . . . upon them (to be exact: upon one of them on behalf of all of them), that means, that He revealed Himself to them by chance; whereas in the narrative above (v. 2) the verb *appeared* . . . occurs; so, too, when Moses speaks to the elders (v. 16) he uses the term *has appeared* . . . . Also in this distinction between "appeared" and "lighted" there is discernible the intention to adapt the language to the Gentiles' way of thinking. For in the Canaanite tongue the verb [*lighted*] signified a theophany. . . . Consequently, the Bible also uses this verb in accounts of theophanies to non-Israelites. . . . The words *and now* introduce, as usual, the conclusion: since our God has lighted upon us, we request your permission to go forth. . . .[69]

---

[64] Cassuto, *Exodus*, 31.

[65] Cassuto, *Exodus*, 31.

[66] *Abundant Life*, 39:8 (1985), 5.

[67] Cassuto, *Exodus*, 41.

[68] *Abundant Life*, 39:8 (1985), 5–6.

[69] Cassuto, *Exodus*, 42–43.

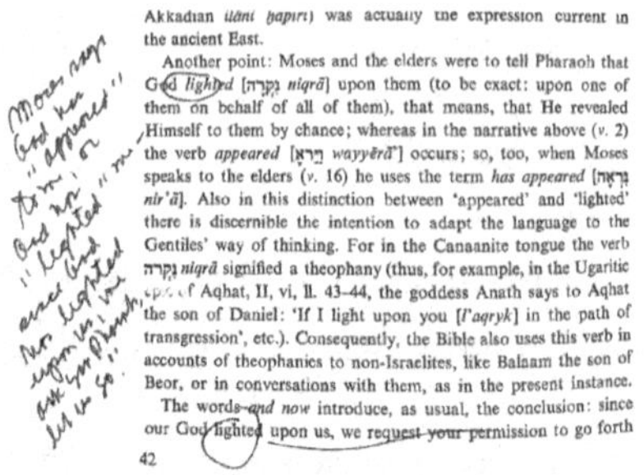

Figure 5

Readers can see the obvious connection here. The commentary to which Roberts refers is the commentary under discussion. The commentary's explication of *lighted* is the basis of Roberts' sermon. Roberts finds in the language a combination of experiential encounter with God followed logically by testimony to it. Further, we can thus safely say that Roberts interacted with this commentary toward the end of 1985.

Afterward, Roberts considers implications for readers. He says: "Recently a member of the American Medical Association was here on campus. And he let me know that prayer is no longer an issue in hospitals across this country. It all can be traced right here to this little spot of ground in Tulsa, Oklahoma, that's been LIGHTED with the LIGHT OF GOD . . . where the bush is still burning."[70] He ends by stating, "Just one little bush—this university or that City of Faith, *your* church or *your* Christian school—is burning with the flame that comes up out of its own flame, out of God who has engulfed us, and WE ARE LIGHTED."[71] He seeks to utilize Moses' experience to motivate his readers to acknowledge their similar experience and their vocation to extend that light into the world.

Roberts' sermon on Exodus 3 provided a unique opportunity to see how his thoughts could move from the latent state during his interaction with the Cassuto commentary to the actualized form found in that sermon. Often, he demonstrates his reliance on the expertise of the commentator. He even allows himself to be vulnerable in sharing how a section of the commentary moved him emotionally as he read it. Overall, he implicitly reveals his posture as an active learner. But he does not merely repeat what he has read there; he also engages it and interacts with it, plumbing its depths for pastoral implications.

---

[70] *Abundant Life*, 39:8 (1985), 6.

[71] *Abundant Life*, 39:8 (1985), 6.

Conclusion

In this essay, I have sought to reflect on Oral Roberts' use of the commentary on Exodus written by Umberto Cassuto. The impetus for this was my happenstance discovery of what was previously his personal copy of this commentary, filled with notes and interaction. I began by sketching important events from the time period during which he possessed this volume. I then made some broad-brush comments about the types of interaction found within the volume. Finally, I moved to a more substantial comparison and analysis of the commentary itself, his interaction within the commentary, and his sermon on Exodus 3.

As someone who has been deeply influenced by the life and ministry of Oral Roberts as well as someone who studies the Old Testament, I have benefited tremendously from this exercise. One does not often have the opportunity to access such a personal, intimate item from someone who lived such a public life. I have attempted to walk lightly into the journey. The result has been a deeper appreciation for the intentionality with which Oral Roberts studied Scripture. Throughout, he positions himself as someone who is willing and eager to learn from others. Especially crucial in that regard was witnessing the journey of his note in the commentary on God "lighting" on Moses to its presence in his sermon. It is apparent that this portion of the commentary truly moved him—academically and spiritually. My hope is that this essay can contribute, in some small way, to a deeper appreciation for Oral Roberts, a man whose life and testimony have influenced many.

In retrospect, we might consider the City of Faith a failed project. That story of Roberts' ministry did not end as he had expected. But from another vantage point, we might admire the vision Roberts had. At a time when many other pastors might have pushed for the separation of medicine and faith, Roberts insisted that medicine was a good gift from God for the healing of those who hurt. Likewise, his willingness to take up and read the commentary by Cassuto testifies to his belief that such resources can be gifts from God, and that we honor God and grow in our faith as *whole* people—spirit, body, and mind.

Daniel D. Bunn, Jr. (dbunn@oru.edu) is Assistant Professor of Old Testament, Undergraduate Theology Department, Oral Roberts University, Tulsa, Oklahoma, USA.

ORU

APPLY FOR THE FALL PROGRAM
PhD IN THEOLOGY

ORU's College of Theology & Ministry is excited to invite qualified applicants to be a part of the next Cohort. Renowned for its "globally positioned" orientation, this degree explores the contextual theologies of global Christianity and the phenomenal growth and emerging scholarship within the global Spirit-empowered movement. It aims to equip scholars and practitioners to engage, impact, and expand the Spirit-empowered ethos and faithfully serve the Kingdom of God.

Among the teaching faculty of world-renowned scholars in Pentecostal/Charismatic Studies are:

Dr. Wonksu Ma   Dr. Julie Ma   Dr. Eric Newberg   Dr. Peter Althouse

For more information contact: phdtheology@oru.edu or visit http://www.oru.edu/phd

A Proposed Pentecostal *Quadrilectic*

Explorations for Asian Pentecostal Hermeneutics

Lora Angeline E. Timenia

Keywords *Asian, Pentecostal, hermeneutics, quadrilectic, dialectic exegesis, contextual, contextualization, pneumatological lens*

Abstract

Developing a general framework for Asian Pentecostal hermeneutics is necessary for a continent where the Holy Bible is "Scripture among scriptures." Although Pentecostal Christianity in Asia is growing, interpreting Scripture in a manner relevant to local contextual realities is necessary to propagate grassroots theologies. As such, the current Pentecostal hermeneutical triad of Spirit-Scripture-Community (Archer) or Spirit-Word-Community (Yong) needs further articulations of a reader's tradition and cultural/ethnic contexts. The concept of an interpretive "Pentecostal community" needs clarification in the Asian setting where multiple interpretative communities exist. This study proposes a framework that recognizes the dialectical role of the text's context and the reader's context in biblical interpretation. The offered framework is a quadrilectic—a dialectic of Spirit-Scripture-Tradition-Context. Modifying Yung Suk Kim's critical contextual biblical interpretation with the pneumatological lens of Craig Keener's Spirit hermeneutics, the author suggests that Asian readers (in this study, Filipino Pentecostals) use a pneumatological lens (ala Keener) in their critical contextual biblical interpretation.

Introduction

The development of identity hermeneutics, in this case, Asian Pentecostal hermeneutics, owes its aegis to the prevailing realization that biblical interpretation is contextual and that no construal occurs without a reader's method or judgment. In his book, *Biblical Interpretation: Theory, Process, Criteria*, Yung Suk Kim writes, "Interpretation means explaining a text from a wide array of perspectives."[1] He does not mean that perspective trumps all in exegesis; perspective, in the form of contextual lenses, plays a vital role in the negotiation of meaning. Kim explains, "Biblical

---

[1] Suk Kim Yung, *Biblical Interpretation: Theory, Process, Criteria* (Eugene, OR: Pickwick Publications, 2013), 7.

interpretation involves three layers of difficulties (the text, translation, and interpretation) and three elements of interpretation (the text, the reader, and the theological lens)."[2] Accordingly, biblical interpretation must be both critical and contextual in that both the historical-literary context of the text and the fluid contexts of the actual or intended readers must be in a mutual dialogue.

Critical contextual interpretation is nothing new. The apostles in the New Testament practiced critical contextualization of Scripture as they entered new cultures in the propagation of the gospel. Andrew Walls explained it well:

> Theological activity arises out of Christian mission and Christian living, from the need for Christians to make Christian choices and to think in a Christian way. This compulsion to think in a Christian way becomes more powerful and more urgent whenever the gospel crosses a cultural frontier since the process of crossing cultural frontiers almost inevitably creates situations not previously encountered by Christians, and a different climate of thought poses intellectual questions not considered before.[3]

For example, in Acts 11:19–21, in the endeavor to introduce Jesus to the Gentiles in Antioch, evangelists used the word *kyrios* (Lord), a word customarily attributed to cultic deities, instead of the Jewish word, *messiah*.[4] Yet, *Kyrios Iesous* (Lord Jesus) effectively translated the Jewish concept and served its purpose in introducing the identity of Jesus to the Gentiles. History proved it to be effective as Acts 11:21 records, "The Lord's hand was with them, and a great number of people believed and turned to the Lord."[5]

As Christianity spread in the first century, Jesus' followers had to wrestle with how to live the Christian life amid a pluralistic and Hellenistic society; they wrestled with the tensions of the Jewish tradition, Jesus' Way, and grassroots realities. The Apostle to the Gentiles, Paul, spent much of his ministry responding to these interpretative issues, writing occasional and pastoral epistles to the toddling New Testament church. No wonder Jesus promised the empowerment of the Holy Spirit before the commencement of his disciples' witness (Acts 1:8), and glossolalia (speaking in other tongues) became the demonstrable sign of such empowerment (Acts 2:4). I propose that this promised pneumatic empowerment was crucial in the communication of Jesus' message and way of living to a world of diverse languages and contexts.

This point brings us back to the issue of developing an Asian Pentecostal hermeneutic. As Christianity advances with its sacred Scripture, the Bible, Christians in

---

[2] Yung, *Biblical Interpretation*, 11.

[3] Andrew Walls, "The Rise of Global Theologies," in *Global Theology in Evangelical Perspective: Exploring the Contextual Nature of Theology and Mission*, eds. Jeffrey P. Greenman and Gene L. Green (Downers Grove, IL: InterVarsity Press, 2012), 19–20.

[4] Walls, "The Rise of Global Theologies," 21.

[5] Unless otherwise noted, Scriptural verses are taken from the New International Version, 2011.

Asia face multitudinous contextual issues and competing interpretative communities. Early Christians' questions still bother Christians in Asia today: how does one contend for the faith in different contextual milieus? How does one live a Spirit-empowered life amid competing religious spirits? In the face of these queries, how an Asian Pentecostal interprets Scripture matters.

This article no longer concerns itself with answering the questions of necessity and significance. The fact that Christianity in Asia is still a minority and that Christian Scripture is one of the sacred texts in the continent provides the impetus for delving into critical contextual biblical interpretation. Perhaps a more appropriate question is: what elements are needed to develop an Asian Pentecostal hermeneutic?

At the outset, this article proposes that an Asian Pentecostal hermeneutic comprises the *quadrilectic* elements of Scripture, Spirit, tradition, and context. That is to say, in the process of critical contextual biblical interpretation, the Asian Pentecostal hermeneut holds in dialectical tension the mediation of the Holy Spirit, the historical-literary context of Scripture, Pentecostal tradition, and the reader's Asian context.

Delineating Concepts and Assumptions

Delineating Concepts

Loaded discussions and unclear definitions surround some of the terms or concepts used in this article. A few important terms will be delineated. The key terms to be defined here are Asian, Pentecostal, Asian Pentecostal, critical contextual biblical interpretation, and context.

Asian

The word "Asian" is a descriptive term that refers to people, languages, customs, religions, and cultures native to the Asian continent. Asia is vast and diverse as the world's largest and most populous continent.[6] It comprises five geopolitical identities: Western Asia, Central Asia, South Asia, Eastern Asia, and Southeastern Asia.[7] Because of its diversity, Asia cannot be viewed in monolithic terms; instead, it is a continent composed of polyvocal and plural civilizations.

Nevertheless, many scholars use the general term "Asia" about works with an Asian orientation. R. S. Sugirtharajah explains, "In a sense, the current usage of 'Asia' as

---

[6] Martha London, *Asia*, World Studies (Lake Elmo, MN: Focus Readers, 2020), https://search-ebscohost-com.oralroberts.idm.oclc.org/login.aspx?direct=true&db=nlebk&AN=2364869&site=eds-live&scope=site.

[7] "How Many Countries Are There in Asia?," *WorldAtlas*, March 11, 2021, https://www.worldatlas.com/articles/how-many-countries-are-in-asia.html.

a continental unity is a combination of two factors—the Western habit of naming the 'other' and the Asian strategy of invoking Asian values to withstand Western materialism."[8] On the one hand, Asia is a Western naming; on the other hand, it is the agreed-upon strategy for maintaining traditional values and a somewhat loose sense of identity.

Asian values and shared traits have also been used to develop theologies or hermeneutics. Some traits shared by the Asian community include collectivism or group-oriented cultures, honor-shame practices, patron-client systems, ritual purity, suffering and persecution, the embeddedness of religion in culture, spiritual worldviews (or folk religiosity), preference for stories or storytelling, and the non-dichotomization of the sacred and the secular.[9] These traits, values, and socio-religious realities allow for the development of pan-Asian Christian theologies.

Pentecostal

"Pentecostal" describes a believer belonging to the fourth major Christian tradition in World Christianity: Pentecostalism. Pentecostals owe their name to the Pentecostal outpouring in Acts 2. Classically, a Christian believer who affirms a pneumatic (Holy Spirit) experience akin to that of the disciples at Pentecost and identifies oneself as belonging to a family of believers who espouse the continuity of a Pentecostal outpouring in prophetic and missiological terms were called Pentecostals.[10] However, this definition has become less espoused today since Pentecostalism has widened its streams to include Charismatics, Neocharismatics, and other Pentecostal-like groups. Allan Anderson argues that there cannot be exact definitions of "Pentecostal" and "Pentecostalism" because it is a diverse global movement emphasizing "experience and spirituality rather than in formal theology or doctrine."[11]

The difficulty in defining exact terms is understandable. However, for this article, "Pentecostal" will be defined in both broad and narrow terms. Broadly, Pentecostals refer to believers who belong to the world Christian tradition of Pentecostalism, which

---

[8] R. S. Sugirtharajah, *The Bible and Asia: From the Pre-Christian Era to the Postcolonial Age* (Cambridge, Massachusetts: Harvard University Press, 2013), 3.

[9] Kar Yong Lim, "The New Testament and the Sociocultural and Religious Realities of the Asian Contexts," in *An Asian Introduction to the New Testament*, ed. Johnson Thomaskutty (Minneapolis, MN: Fortress Press, 2022), 10–26; Donald Leroy Stults, *Developing an Asian Evangelical Theology* (Manila, Philippines: OMF Literature, Inc., 1989), 33–35.

[10] William W. Menzies and Robert P Menzies, *Spirit and Power: Foundations for Pentecostal Experience* (Grand Rapids, MI: Zondervan, 2000), 109–19.

[11] Allan Anderson, *An Introduction to Pentecostalism: Global Charismatic Christianity* (Cambridge University Press, 2004), 6.

shares the core tenet, "God is still active in the world through the Holy Spirit, so that miracles and spiritual gifts are an expected component of the Christian life."[12]

Narrowly, Pentecostals affirm the classical doctrine of post-conversion Spirit baptism as pneumatic empowerment for prophecy and mission.[13] This study holds broad and narrow definitions in tension because the particular (or local) stream does not occur in a vacuum; it is best understood as part of a whole. Hence, the current study narrows the term to thoroughly understand one form in the cacophony of other forms within its global family.

Critical Contextual Biblical Interpretation

As explained by Yung Suk Kim in his book *Biblical Interpretation*, critical contextual biblical interpretation is an interpretative method that dialectically engages the reader, the text, and the contextuality of the text and the reader.[14] In his footnote, Kim explained that critical meant "examining biblical writings from a diversity of interpretive perspectives," while contextual meant "considering life contexts of the text and the readers alike."[15]

Adapting Daniel Patte's elements of interpretation,[16] Kim illustrates his three-element method as follows:[17]

Table 1. Three-Element-Interpretation

WE	Are READING	THE BIBLE
The Reader	The Theological Lens	The Text
Contextual/relational choice	Theological/hermeneutical choice	Analytical/textual choice
Why do we read?	*What do we read?*	*How do we read?*

First, Kim highlights the importance of the reader of the Bible, who reads from various social locations and diverse life settings. He echoes Hans George Gadamer's

---

[12] Douglas Jacobsen, *The World's Christians: Who They Are, Where They Are, and How They Got There* (Chicester, UK: John Wiley & Sons, Incorporated, 2011), xxvviii.

[13] William W. Menzies and Stanley Horton, *Bible Doctrines: A Pentecostal Perspective*, rev. ed. (Springfield, MO: Gospel Pub. House, 2012).

[14] Yung, *Biblical Interpretation*, 34.

[15] Yung, *Biblical Interpretation*, xivn3.

[16] Cristina Grenholm and Daniel Patte, "Overture: Reception, Critical Interpretations, and Scriptural Criticism," in *Reading Israel in Romans: Legitimacy and Plausability of Divergent Interpretations*, eds. Cristina Grenholm and Daniel Patte, vol. 1 (Harrisburg, PA: Trinity, 2000), 1–54.

[17] Yung, *Biblical Interpretation*, 35.

dialectic when he points out that "understanding is participation with the text."[18] Accordingly, Kim writes, "The view of the participatory reader is possible because God is not known only through the Bible. God is known through us too, and vice versa."[19]

Second, Kim recognizes that readers read from a theological lens or make choices concerning their theological view of the text. This second element "has to do with a viewing angle among many choices of theological interpretation."[20] Accepting that every reader makes interpretive choices, predominantly from their theological view of the text, is crucial.

Third, Kim points to the Bible as the written text. The Bible has a double character: historical writing and sacred text.[21] As a historical writing, it holds records of ancient cultures and religious experiences. Therefore, it calls for the need for critical textual methods. As a sacred text, the Bible is Scripture, and it affects its readers' faith and praxis. Affirming the Bible's double character enables readers to make proper choices concerning textual methods.

Using Kim's critical contextual biblical interpretation as one of the dialogue partners of this study is apt because his theory combines both critical and contextual approaches to the interpretative process. It also recognizes that understanding divine revelation comes with the dialectic of two horizons: the text's and the reader's horizons. This theory offers Asian Pentecostals the opportunity to interpret biblical texts from a critical textual angle and in conversation with their reading lens and their life contexts.

Context

Finally, the word "context," which is often used in this article, is defined as the complex combination of experience (either personal, communal, or contemporary-collective), culture (a system of inherited conceptions), social location, and social change.[22] Stephen Bevans explains that all theologies are contextual since they are products of their authors' contexts; the Bible itself is a collection of books written in/for particular contexts.[23]

The two contexts of the Bible assumed in this article are cultural-historical and literary contexts. Cultural-historical context refers to "the placement of a text against the

---

[18] Yung, *Biblical Interpretation*, 34; Hans George Gadamer, *Truth and Method* (New York: Seabury, 1975), 345–447.

[19] Yung, *Biblical Interpretation*, 39.

[20] Yung, *Biblical Interpretation*, 37.

[21] Yung, *Biblical Interpretation*, 15.

[22] Stephen B. Bevans, *Models of Contextual Theology*, Faith and Cultures Series, rev. and expanded ed. (Maryknoll, NY: Orbis Books, 2002), 5–7.

[23] Bevans, *Models of Contextual Theology*, 7.

cultural and historical background of its author and its first readers."²⁴ Literary context refers to the relationship of a word, phrase, sentence, or passage in the larger biblical literature that contributes to the meaning of a text. It can also be generally defined as information that elucidates the contextual meaning of a text.²⁵

Delineating Assumptions

Using the three questions Kim asked in his three-element-interpretative process, this article delineates the following assumptions.

Why Do We Read?

The first assumption is that readers (whether real or implied) are situated in a cultural and theological context. They come to the text with their theological lenses and read it for a reason. Some read for reflection, some read to teach, while others read to answer questions. Kim writes, "To critically, faithfully engage the ancient readers, we must know who we are as real readers."²⁶ Hence, readers should know their history, culture, theological affirmation, and life contexts because these influence the critical contextual interpretative process.

As such, the reader of this study is an Asian Pentecostal, specifically Filipino Pentecostal. Filipino Pentecostal theological identity, as argued in a journal article entitled "Bridging the Distance: A Microcosm of Filipino Classical Pentecostal Identity," is a spiral construct of the Filipino Christian consciousness with the classical Pentecostal theology of Spirit empowerment.²⁷ Moreover, the Filipino Pentecostal identity amalgamates many socio-religious factors: indigenous religious consciousness, Hispanic Roman Catholicism, Western Protestantism, and North American classical Pentecostalism. A Filipino Pentecostal reads the Bible to know God and to draw closer to him; in the process, the reader receives a restoration of identity, hope, dignity, and empowerment for participation in the ongoing story.²⁸

---

[24] James D. Hernando, *Dictionary of Hermeneutics: A Concise Guide to Terms, Names, Methods, and Expressions* (Springfield, MO: Gospel Publishing House, 2005), 17.

[25] Hernando, *Dictionary of Hermeneutics*, 17.

[26] Yung, *Biblical Interpretation*, 39.

[27] For a comprehensive discussion on the construct of a Filipino Pentecostal theological identity, see Lora Angeline Embudo Timenia, "Bridging the Distance: A Microcosm of Filipino Classical Pentecostal Identity," *Pentecostal Education* 7:1 (Spring 2022), 111–30.

[28] A proposed Filipino Pentecostal gospel was presented in the paper, "Bridging the Distance." In said proposal, the Bible becomes the means for Filipino Pentecostals to genuinely know God, his work in the world, and his participatory purposes for his people. Timenia, "Bridging the Distance," 125–28.

What Do We Read?

Second, this article assumes the double nature of the Bible as both historical writing and sacred text. As historical literature, the Bible includes genres written during different historical and cultural milieus. Although many scholars have argued that it is impossible to reconstruct *de facto* histories surrounding biblical texts, the truth remains that information and themes passed on and later transcribed are based on actual events, people, or situations. Hence, efforts should be made to understand biblical texts in their historical moorings.

Craig Keener points out that there is a concreteness to the settings in biblical writings, and these settings explain "the particularities in the shape of such writings."[29] For example, there was an apostle named Paul who wrote an occasional letter to the Christian community in Rome. Moreover, there was a historical Jesus whose life, message, and ministry were witnessed and passed on by devout followers.

The Bible, though, is not just historical literature. It is also a sacred text. Jürgen Habermas defined the Bible evocatively as "the linguistification of the sacred."[30] In most of Asia, there is no struggle to accept such linguistification. The Christian Scripture is one of the many scriptures in Asia. In explaining this "Scripture among scriptures" purview, Havilah Dharamraj outlines the features of Scripture as follows: "(1) Authoritative oral or written text; (2) often believed to be of divine origin and, therefore, considered sacred and powerful; (3) canonical and normative for a certain community of faith; (4) appropriated and perpetuated as teaching to the point that it becomes an 'obligatory touchstone for religious thinking.'"[31] In Asia, these scriptures could come in the form of the Hindu *Vēdas*, Islam's *Qur'an*, China's Confucian classics, or perhaps Sikhism's *Gŭrŭ Grănth*. For Christians, Scripture is known as the Holy Bible. It is authoritative because it is God's revelation mediated by the inspiration of the Holy Spirit (2 Tim 3:16). It stands out among other scriptures because it is uniquely relational, especially in the form of Jesus, who is not just God incarnate and the "Word made flesh" but also the fullness of divine revelation.

---

[29] Craig S. Keener, *Spirit Hermeneutics: Reading Scripture in Light of Pentecost* (Grand Rapids, MI: William B. Eerdmans Publishing Company, 2016), 2.

[30] Jürgen Habermas, *The Theory of Communicative Action*, trans. Thomas McCarthy, *Lifeworld and System: A Critique of Functionalist Reason* (Boston, MA: Beacon, 1984), 77–111.

[31] Havilah Dharamraj, "On the Doctrine of Scripture: An Asian Conversation," in *Asian Christian Theology: Evangelical Perspectives*, eds. Timoteo D. Gener and Stephen T. Pardue (Cumbria, UK/Manila, Philippines: Langham Global Library/Asia Theological Association, 2019), 40; Steven G. Smith, "What Is Scripture? Pursuing Smith's Question," *Anglican Theological Review* 90:4 (2008), 753–75.

How Do We Read?

Lastly, this article assumes that in the interpretative process, meaning is mediated by the Holy Spirit in both the text and the reader. Kim affirms the double character of the Bible as sacred text and historical writing. However, like other reader-oriented interpreters, Kim attributes meaning to the reader; for him, the reader decides the final meaning of the text.[32]

Contra Kim, this study prefers Keener's position in *Spirit Hermeneutics*, whereby meaning is generated by the Holy Spirit both in the text and in the reader.[33] Keener writes:

> The Spirit already generated meaning through the inspired human agents writing in their language and setting. The Spirit's role of illumination thus focuses on the text's perlocution, i.e., "the successful conclusion of the speech act:" normally understanding and response. . . . Perlocution is what identifies the expected response to a speech act. If the illocution is a command, the perlocution would be obedience . . . the Holy Spirit is largely involved at the perlocutionary level as we are enabled to understand the truthfulness of the text, recognize what it requires from us and then actually take the appropriate steps to actualize the intentions that the Holy Spirit initially delivered to the human instrument.[34]

On the one hand, there is meaning as intended by the Holy Spirit in the first context. On the other hand, there is contemporary meaningfulness that the same Holy Spirit mediates to readers in their respective contexts. When conversing in dialectical conversation, these two contextual horizons (text and reader) can produce a critical contextual biblical interpretation that is both faithful to the first context and relevant to the current reader's context.[35]

Spirit-mediated interpretation is contextual (especially as biblical messages continue to be interpreted globally), but not to the extent of disregarding what the text originally meant to communicate. Keener explains, "Part of our transcultural goal should be listening honestly to the texts. The more effectively we hear texts in their first contexts, the greater our confidence to recontextualize the principles for other settings. The greater our shared basis for dialoguing about what the texts say to us today."[36]

---

[32] Yung, *Biblical Interpretation*, xiv–1.

[33] Keener, *Spirit Hermeneutics*, 12.

[34] Keener, *Spirit Hermeneutics*, 12.

[35] Oliverio notes that Keener's dialectic of two horizons attends to the "critical both-and" in hermeneutical theory; it is a kind of hermeneutical realism that does not subsume either categories. L. William Jr. Oliverio, *Pentecostal Hermeneutics in the Late Modern World: Essays on the Condition of Our Interpretation* (Eugene, OR: Pickwick Publications, 2022), 226.

[36] Keener, *Spirit Hermeneutics*, 69.

Keener correctly states that the Bible comes to readers already contextualized and offers exemplars for ongoing critical contextual interpretations.

A Proposed Asian Pentecostal *Quadrilectic*

Having already clarified concepts and assumptions, it is right to discuss the proposed elements that make up an Asian Pentecostal hermeneutic. Unlike the *triadic* Pentecostal hermeneutics,[37] like Kenneth Archer's Spirit-Scripture-Community,[38] or Amos Yong's Spirit-Word-Community,[39] this hermeneutic offers a *quadrilectic*, or a dialectic of four elements, Spirit-Scripture-Tradition-Context, in the interpretative process.

This study proposes that in the process of critical contextual biblical interpretation, the Asian (Filipino) Pentecostal hermeneut submits to the mediation of the Holy Spirit both in the text and in the reader's context by holding in dialectical tension the historical-literary meaning of Scripture, Pentecostal tradition's theology of Spirit empowerment, and the reader's socio-religious history and cultural context.

Theoretically, this *quadrilectic* is like Archer's and Yong's *triad* in that all three consider Scripture and the Holy Spirit essential in the interpretative process. Yet it differs from the two because the word "community" is articulated as "tradition" (Pentecostal Christianity) and "context" (Asian/Filipino) to delineate the role and contribution of a reader's theological affirmation and cultural/ethnic lens in the interpretative process. This delineation is conducive to a multicultural and polyvocal continent like Asia. Asian (Indian) Pentecostal, Roji Thomas George comments:

> Despite the best intention of such [*triadic*] interpretive exercises, they only recognize voices emerging from many corners without acknowledging the visible marks of their unique accents, styles, and valid cultural expressions of the Spirit illuminated biblical insights. Merely lived experience of fissured migrant identity, sociocultural vulnerability, oppression, etc., as spaces of constructing contextual Pentecostal hermeneutics will be shallow and not beneficial to the native Pentecostals' theological reflection. Such a weakness is enormously experienced in a pluralistic context like India, where cultural discourses are soaked in religious and secular literary traditions. Without such an incarnation of Pentecostal

---

[37] A concise discussion on contextual Pentecostal hermeneutics can be read in Oliverio, *Pentecostal Hermeneutics in the Late Modern World*, 52–53.

[38] Kenneth J. Archer, *A Pentecostal Hermeneutic: Spirit, Scripture, and Community* (Cleveland, TN: CPT Press, 2009).

[39] Amos Yong, *Spirit-Word-Community: Theological Hermeneutics in Trinitarian Perspective* (Aldershot, UK: Ashgate, 2002).

hermeneutical practice in the native tongue and color, it will be estranged from developing a robust local shape and appearance.[40]

Indeed, there must be a critical dialectic with the reader's sociocultural context for Pentecostal hermeneutics to serve Asian constituents better. I suggest that a hermeneut clarifies which element of context is being dialogued with to avoid abstractions. In this study, for instance, the context dialogued with is the experience of Pentecostal outpouring (Spirit baptism) in the backdrop of a Filipino Christian's socio-religious history and culture.[41]

Including the reader's context in the hermeneutical process is a recognition of what Oliverio calls a "hermeneutical turn" or the reader's "traditioned and enculturated second nature" in interpreting the text.[42] Whether aware or not, human interpretations are contextual. A reader's religious experience, theological tradition, culture, and social location will, amid efforts of objectivity, affect interpretative choices. On a positive note, it also has the potential to facilitate the negotiation of meaning and meaningfulness.

Asian scholars have successfully pointed out that the Asian lens can be beneficial in interpreting biblical texts because the Bible is a product of West Asia and share many cultural and societal values with most of the continent. For example, one of the texts that causes significant discomfort among Asian Christians is Matthew 10:37, when Jesus said, "Anyone who loves their father or mother more than me is not worthy of me." The call to follow Jesus amid parental disagreement, as laid out in this verse, is a high price to pay for Asians. The virtue of filial piety in Taoism or Confucianism demands that children continue the tradition of ancestral worship.[43] Rejecting ancestral worship due to Christian conversion may result in being kicked out of the family or being shamefully labeled as "unfilial." In the Filipino context, dishonoring parents may result in one being labeled as *"walang utang na loob"* (ungrateful) or *"walang hiya"* (shameless).

So, an Asian Christian who follows Jesus in the face of being labeled unfilial, ungrateful, or shameless understands what it means to "count the cost." This interpretation is a prime example of how shared cultural values (or experiences) enrich exegetical processes and connect the current reader to the struggles of Jesus' followers in the first century. Hence, the *quadrilectic* proposed with its Spirit-Scripture-Tradition-Context offers opportunities for developing not just a Pentecostal hermeneutic but also

---

[40] Roji Thomas George, "Interpretive Communities of the Spirit in Multicultural Context: Reflections on Pentecostal Hermeneutics," *Asian Journal of Pentecostal Studies* 26:1 (February 2023), 92.

[41] For a microcosm of a Filipino Pentecostal's socioreligious history and culture, see Timenia, "Bridging the Distance," 111–30.

[42] Oliverio, *Pentecostal Hermeneutics in the Late Modern World*, 226.

[43] Lim, "The New Testament and the Sociocultural and Religious Realities of the Asian Contexts," 11.

an Asian Pentecostal hermeneutic that takes into consideration the reader's socio-religious and cultural milieu.

Spirit-mediated Interpretative Process

The proposed interpretative system is an adaptation of Kim's three-element-interpretative process but modified based on Keener's Spirit hermeneutics. The table below illustrates the process as follows:

Table 2. Spirit-meditated Interpretation

WE Contextual/relational choice	Are READING Theological/hermeneutical choice	The TEXT Analytical/textual choice
Asian (Filipino) Pentecostal	Pneumatological Lens	Dialectical-Contextual Exegesis
Context: Filipino Pentecostal identity is a construct of the Filipino religious consciousness with the Pentecostal experience of Spirit empowerment.	1. The Holy Spirit generates meaning in the original text through inspiration, inscripturation, and traditioning. 2. The Holy Spirit mediates meaning to the reader through illumination, experience, and perlocution.	1. First context: historical-literary criticism of the text to determine its nearest original meaning. 2. Second context: sociocultural exegesis to draw out elements from the reader's context that can bridge the first context to the second context. 3. Dialectical analysis: dialogue between the text's contextual meaning and the reader's cultural exegesis to arrive at contemporary contextual meaningfulness.

The table above outlines the interpretative process of this proposed Asian Pentecostal hermeneutic. The Asian context in this study is Filipino, and the Pentecostal tradition is narrowed down to classical Pentecostalism. The theological view of Scripture highlights the role of the Holy Spirit in interpretation (ala Keener's Spirit hermeneutics). At the same time, the analytical process is a dialectical-contextual exegesis of both the text and the reader's context.

WE (the Reader)

First, for this article, the reader is identified as a Filipino Pentecostal. A fuller description of the Filipino Pentecostal theological identity is available in the *Pentecostal Education Journal*, entitled "Bridging the Distance: A Microcosm of Filipino Classical Pentecostal Identity."[44] Due to space constraints, the current author describes the reader's socio-religious background as an amalgamation of indigenous religious consciousness, Hispanic Catholicism, Western Protestantism, and classical Pentecostalism. The reader affirms a personal experience of Spirit baptism, speaking in tongues, prophecy, and manifestation of signs and wonders. Overall, the current reader identifies with both the Filipino identity (with its colonial history) and Pentecostal spirituality (with its affirmation of Spirit empowerment).

Are READING (Theological Lens)

Second, the theological lens used to view the text is a pneumatological one. Keener is affirmed here in his recognition of the role of the Holy Spirit in the interpretative process in both the first context (the ancient sacred text) and the second context (the modern reader).[45] The Holy Spirit generates meaning in the text through inspiration (the Spirit synergistically enabled human communicators), inscripturation (the Spirit guided the production of the written form), and traditioning (the Spirit superintended the preservation and transmission of the text from generation to generation).

The Holy Spirit also mediates meaningfulness to contemporary readers of the ancient sacred text through exegesis (the Spirit guides the reader's cognitive functions in studying a text), illumination (the Spirit enlightens human understanding), experience (the Spirit facilitates pneumatic actualities like charismatic revelation or prophecy), and perlocution (the Spirit guides readers into appropriate response or application of the message).

The TEXT (Analytical Process)

Finally, the analytical procedure to be used in interpreting the text is a proposed process of dialectical-contextual exegesis. The process begins with historical-literary criticism,

---

[44] Timenia, "Bridging the Distance."

[45] Keener, *Spirit Hermeneutics*, 12; c.f. Oliverio, *Pentecostal Hermeneutics in the Late Modern World*, 226.

where the text's historical and literary contexts are reconstructed as best as possible. Keener explains:

> Of course, we cannot perfectly reconstruct the original meaning. We have access neither to everything the authors thought nor to the full original contexts that they assumed their ideal audiences shared, the information needed to fill lacunae in secondary communication. But whatever else a biblical text might mean, it usually means at least what it meant to the inspired author, who understood his own language, idioms, and cultural allusions better than we do. Offering historical reconstructions as responsibly as possible (given the limits of evidence and our own horizons) is a reasonable objective that need not be discounted simply because it cannot be perfectly achieved.[46]

Although historical-literary reconstruction cannot be perfectly achieved, it does not mean one should not try. As previously explained, the text is both historical writing (written in an original historical and cultural milieu) and sacred text. Efforts should be made to exegete what it was meant to say or mean in its original context. This endeavor protects readers from misinterpreting the meaning of the text.

After historical-literary criticism, the reader proceeds to cultural exegesis; that is, they must draw out elements in their culture that can serve as bridges between the first and the readers' contexts. Readers can use some elements of culture like language, norms, values, symbols, and artifacts to facilitate dialectical communication of meaning and help express the Spirit-mediated meaning of the text in "a robust local shape and appearance."[47] For example, in the recent offering of the Langham Global Library, Filipino theologians interpreted the Lord's Prayer by first translating it as "Ama Namin" (the Filipino translation of "Our Father"). Entitling it "Ama Namin (Our Father)" instead of "The Lord's Prayer" highlights the role of both the native tongue and Asian family values in facilitating the meaning of a text to a local context.[48]

One should also note that both horizons can potentially help exegete the other in this dialectic of two contexts. This does not mean that the reader's context determines the meaning of the text. It only means that the text can help enlighten readers of their culture (whether good or bad). At the same time, elements in the reader's culture can also help clarify what the author/speaker was trying to communicate (as seen in the example above about how Asians interpret the cost of following Jesus).

Throughout the interpretative process, one must endeavor to hold the proposed *quadrilectic* elements of Spirit, Scripture, tradition, and context in dialectical tension.

---

[46] Keener, *Spirit Hermeneutics*, 141.

[47] George, "Interpretive Communities of the Spirit in Multicultural Context," 92.

[48] Timoteo D. Gener and Jason Richard Tan, eds., *Ama Namin: The Lord's Prayer in Philippine Life and Spirituality* (Cumbria, UK: Langham Global Library, 2023), 1.

Such a hermeneutic is to interpret meaning bearing into account both horizons of text and reader in submission to the mediation of the Holy Spirit.

Conclusion

In conclusion, the proposed Asian Pentecostal hermeneutics offers a system of interpretation that takes into consideration the role of the Holy Spirit, the historical-literary context of Scripture, the theological spirituality of Pentecostal tradition, and the reader's context (which includes religious experience, culture, social location, and social change). The *quadrilectic* of Spirit-Scripture-Tradition-Context allows for a dialectical analysis of two horizons—text and reader. In this manner, meaning is mediated by the Holy Spirit as the two horizons dialectically interact to arrive at the text's original meaning and its contemporary meaningfulness.

The process adapts critical contextual biblical interpretation after all concepts and assumptions are clarified. Illustrated as WE are READING the TEXT, the reader is identified (at least for this article) as a Filipino Pentecostal, reading a pneumatological view of Scripture and interpretation and using a proposed dialectical-contextual exegesis.

Recommendation

As a recommendation for further study, an Asian Pentecostal hermeneut can use the hypothesis of an Asian Pentecostal hermeneutic with its *quadrilectic* of Spirit-Scripture-Tradition-Context. A case study using such a proposal may demonstrate its feasibility and contribute to the growing body of global Pentecostal hermeneutical studies.

Lora Angeline E. Timenia (lora.timenia@apts.edu) teaches Research and Pentecostal Studies at Asia Pacific Theological Seminary, Baguio City, Philippines..

BAYLOR UNIVERSITY PRESS

Alex R. Mayfield
The Kaleidoscopic City
Hong Kong, Mission, and the Evolution of Global Pentecostalism

$59.99 $47.99 Hardcover | 279 pages | 6 x 9
ISBN 978-1-4813-1897-6

"This groundbreaking and innovative study pushes the history of Pentecostalism in new, fresh, and compelling directions."

—**DANA L. ROBERT,** *William Fairfield Warren Distinguished Professor, Boston University*

The Holy Spirit and Higher Education
Renewing the Christian University
Amos Yong and Dale M. Coulter
Paperback | $49.99 $39.99 | 320 pages | 7 x 10
ISBN 978-1-4813-1814-3

The Holy Spirit before Christianity
John R. Levison
Hardcover | $44.99 $35.99 | 272 pages | 6 x 9
ISBN 978-1-4813-1003-1

Phenomenal Phenomena
Biblical and Multicultural Accounts of Spirits and Exorcism
Joy L. Vaughan
Hardcover | $69.99 $55.99 | 275 pages | 6 x 9
ISBN 978-1-4813-1836-5

Receive a 20% discount and free US shipping
Use code 17SPRING24 until 7/31/2024 at
www.baylorpress.com | 1.800.848.6224

The Prayer Tongue and the Jesus Prayer

The Witness of Abbot David Geraets

Clyde Glandon

Keywords *prayer tongue, Jesus Prayer, Pentecostal monastic community, Eastern Churches, spiritual direction, depth psychology, charismatic prayer meetings, spiritual journal, baptism of suffering, baptism in the Holy Spirit, contemplative prayer, Taboric light*

Abstract

To my knowledge Abbot David Geraets (1935–2012) of the Pecos Benedictine Monastery has been the only Christian witness and writer, past or present, to join the practice of the ancient Jesus Prayer and the prayer tongue. He simply says that "repeating the name of Jesus can become a masterful art of glossolalia prayer." Abbot David's statement is not found as such in the centuries of Eastern Orthodox literature about the Jesus Prayer. Nor is such a joining found among classical Pentecostal Christians who, while fully familiar with the prayer tongue and with life and power in Jesus' name, commonly have no particular awareness of the practice of the Jesus Prayer. Such a joining moves across the boundary between the ecclesiastical cultures that normally separates Eastern Christian communities and Western Pentecostal communities. It is a matter of spiritual practice.

Introduction

In this writing I am inviting readers who are Pentecostal Christians to consider a practice of prayer that may be new to many, the Jesus Prayer, especially as it may be related to one's praying in tongues. My observation is that there are virtually no Pentecostal prayer meetings today in which participants may experience a community that prays the Jesus Prayer together in the context of prayer tongues and singing in tongues among the gifts.

In this sense, what is offered in this article has little to do with theological argumentation, and more to do with pondering examples and witnesses—especially from Abbot David Geraets—that might inspire and encourage prayer, new practice, and its effects. I invite the reader to approach the contents of this article as an exercise itself in devotional reading, reading that might lead to prayer. Abbot David's personal witness in the excerpts included here, as well as the samples of classical teachers of the Jesus Prayer I include, come out of the experience of revelatory prayer. Ascetical theology is about prayer, arises from prayer, and is offered as a witness to inspire prayer. The Jesus Prayer tradition seeks to avoid scholastic theological intellectualism, but instead seeks to read, to pray, and to live *with the mind in the heart*. Pentecostal theology, if it remains Pentecostal, is not a scholastic exercise. Much theology, as David Geraets said repeatedly, becomes a "head trip."

It probably goes without saying that many Christian communities that are neither Eastern Orthodox nor Pentecostal—i.e., those that have been referred to in the West as "mainline" denominations, as well as Evangelical traditions—have had no emphasis upon either the Jesus Prayer or the prayer tongue.

What follows is a presentation of Abbot David Geraets' Pentecostal witness and ministry, and a brief introduction to the Jesus Prayer. I offer several excerpts from Abbot David's witness about his interpretation and practice. I close with examples of discussions of prayer in the classic and modern ascetical literature of the Eastern Churches, which Abbot David's integration may illumine. That is, I follow David Geraets in communicating, shall we say, a Pentecostal hermeneutic of the Jesus Prayer tradition as far back as the early writings in *The Philokalia*.

From my first exposure in 1981 to the Pentecostal community of the Pecos Benedictine Monastery, and since my co-founding of the ecumenical Fellowship of the Holy Name in 2010, I have been calling Pentecostal and non-Pentecostal Christians to see a ground for the "charismatic renewal"—the living contemporary experience of Pentecost—in the biblical and ascetical theology of the Desert and Christian East. This tradition lies deeply behind more recent movements that often are seen by some as new, and by others as simply passing. David Geraets discovered in his personal experience of the Jesus Prayer an unrecognized doorway to, and instance of, the prayer tongue. His contemporary George Maloney writes of the "baptism in the Holy Spirit" in introducing the fifth-century *Macarian Homilies*,[1] as well as describing Christians who prayed the Jesus Prayer in that era as "charismatics."[2] Here grace is a perceptible *energy* of God, beyond a doctrinal tenet. "Grace" is, after all, a translation of the word *charis*.

The combination of teachings and practices at the Pecos Monastery in its charismatic era is a combination that, in this writer's experience for over forty years, is unknown in practice, and one that deserves wider knowledge among Pentecostal

---

[1] George A. Maloney, "Introduction," in *Pseudo-Macarius: The Fifty Spiritual Homilies and the Great Letter*, ed. and trans. George A. Maloney (New York: Paulist Press, 1991), 19.

[2] George A. Maloney, *The Breath of the Mystic* (Danville, NJ: Dimension Books, 1974), 84.

Christians. David Geraets' leadership offered a specific and distinctive path for *discipleship* in Pentecost among individuals and communities.

David Geraets

David Geraets made his monastic profession at the St. Benedict's Abbey in Benet Lake, Wisconsin, in 1962. His doctoral thesis at Gregorian University in Rome was on music and catechetics. The charismatic renewal that had begun in Roman Catholicism in the United States in the late 1960s came to the community in Benet Lake and, as Abbot David says below, it split the community. He and his brothers who had come to know the baptism in the Holy Spirit moved to Pecos, New Mexico, to found Our Lady of Guadalupe Monastery as a charismatic monastery. He thus gave Pentecostal meaning, witness, and embodiment to the Benedictine vocation itself.

He served as abbot there from 1973 until 1992, when he and several brothers moved to a sister monastery, the Monastery of the Risen Christ, in San Luis Obispo, California, where he lived until his death. In 1974 he invited Morton Kelsey[3] to begin the integration of the Catholic charismatic renewal with Jungian depth psychology. The year 1978 marked the community's first school for charismatic spiritual directors. The Pecos community founded Dove Publications, which focused on Pentecostal subjects.

Abbot David's writings are few. His primary book was *Jesus Beads*.[4] A shorter piece is *Baptism of Suffering*.[5] He wrote the foreword to George Maloney's *Man the Divine Icon*[6] and the preface to *Exploring the Gift of Prophecy* by Arthur Labonte.[7] I transcribe below several excerpts from audiotapes of lectures he offered at the school for spiritual directors at Pecos, from my personal collection.[8] I also include short transcriptions from Abbot David's video interview with Bill O'Donnell in 2006 on the Roman Catholic television network EWTN.

---

[3] Morton Kelsey was an Episcopal clergyman and Jungian psychotherapist who wrote prolifically and taught for many years at Notre Dame. Among his writings are: *Encounter with God*; *God, Dreams, and Revelation*; *Dreams: A Way to Listen to God*; *Discernment: A Study in Ecstasy and Evil*; *The Other Side of Silence: A Guide to Christian Meditation*; *Tongue Speaking*; and *Adventure Inward: Christian Growth Through Journal Writing*.

[4] David Geraets, *Jesus Beads* (Pecos, NM: Dove Publications. 1973).

[5] David Geraets, *Baptism of Suffering* (Watching, NJ: Charisma Books, 1971).

[6] David Geraets, "Foreword," in *Man the Divine Icon: The Patristic Doctrine of Man Made according to the Image of God*, by George A. Maloney (Pecos, NM: Dove Publications, 1973), vii–x.

[7] David Geraets, "Preface," in *Exploring the Gift of Prophecy*, by Arthur LaBonte (Pecos, NM: Dove Publications, 1974), 1–7.

[8] Permission to use excerpts from Abbot David's lectures in 1981 has been granted by Abbot Aiden Gore of the Pecos Monastery.

The Pecos Community

It is realistic to say that few have known of such a thing as a Pentecostal monastic community. I attended their fourth school for charismatic spiritual directors in 1981–82. The community's life and mission combined the following elements: a Roman Catholic monastic community that included daily Eucharist and morning and evening community prayer with charismatic practice; a single residential community of celibate men and women, unique in Roman Catholicism; a ministry of charismatic retreats, with missions to many outside communities, including Tulsa, Oklahoma; a school for charismatic spiritual directors; the use of Jungian psychology and dream work in Christian spiritual direction and the life of sanctification; and the daily personal practice of the Jesus Prayer among its members.

Some Emphases

Prayer Meetings

Jesus Beads is David Geraets' integration of the Jesus Prayer and charismatic manifestations. In this book and in his lectures and organization of participants at the Pecos schools, he makes a strong emphasis upon the charismatic prayer meeting as a primary arena, and relatively safe context, in which to experience and practice the gifts of the Holy Spirit. That is, in an ongoing community of relationships, practice, and accountability. At this writing, I have been aware that charismatic prayer meetings have not been emphasized or practiced in Christian congregations for a long number of years. I see this as a strategically missing arena in Pentecostal Christian formation, practice, life, and ministry, given that the Wesleys, Smith Wigglesworth, and Azuza Christians, among others, proactively formed and continued prayer meetings as basic to Pentecostal life and mission. It is fair to say that for David Geraets prayer is fully as vital as Holy Scripture is for Christian discipleship.

Practicing into the Charismatic Gifts

He taught quite specifically that Christians can and do practice into the gifts of the Holy Spirit, that we are in fact called, for our part, to act and participate in moving into the gifts.

Discipline in Pentecost

Abbot David spoke of the problems of the "Shepherding Movement" as part of his reasons for seeking to raise up a cadre of spiritual directors who included journaling and "inner work" as part of their responsible participation in and leadership of charismatic prayer communities. It was at Pecos that I first heard the term "stewardship of consciousness," most especially as it applies to many of the excesses of so-called "charismania," as well as to personal misconduct among Christian leaders. In integrating Jungian depth psychology into charismatic Christian culture, he placed a strategic and well-developed psychology into the path of Christian sanctification. He placed spiritual direction, journaling, and dream work as defining elements of our participation in Pentecost. He said he would not continue to offer spiritual direction to anyone who did not take their spiritual life seriously enough to keep a journal.

The Three Baptisms

His writing on "the baptism of suffering" is in the context of his witness that there are three "small-b" baptisms in the one Christian baptism. That is, our conscious awakening to the risen Christ, our baptism in the Holy Spirit, and our baptism into the Father, or the laying down of our lives in a baptism of suffering, following Jesus, so that brothers and sisters may come to know the first two baptisms. As a Roman Catholic, he taught this from his view that sacramental infant baptism is theologically accurate, but often is not experientially or existentially dynamic in a maturing Christian's actual consciousness of God's perceptible life and activity.

A Sampler of David Geraets' Incisive Statements

In my experience of forty years, for most of the short excerpts here—like David Geraets' singular joining of the prayer tongue with the Jesus Prayer—I have not heard Pentecostal Christians, or other Christians, speak this way. That Jesus is the model charismatic. That charismatic renewal is a poor man's mysticism, said positively. That love is higher than truth. That if contemplative practice only leads to non-response and silence, no one will turn to the God we proclaim. That our actions matter and play a part—putting our foot out—in miracles of the Kingdom.

> Jesus is the model charismatic.[9]
>
> I got filled with the Holy Spirit, which is a kind of way of saying that you know God's love deeply. Charism means love, that you are filled with love, the overwhelming love of God's presence, which brings charismatic gifts.[10]
>
> Experience continues to teach us that this Divine Love is most effectively communicated through spontaneous shared prayer.[11]

---

[9] David Geraets, "Scripture and the Charismatic Renewal," Lecture 2 (lecture, Benedictine Monastery, Pecos, NM, January 6, 1981).

[10] David Geraets, interview by Bill O'Donnell, "Charismatic" Prayer Ministry, Pt. 1, EWTN, 2006.

[11] Geraets, *Jesus Beads*, 53.

[In regard to tongues] If you want to catch a squirrel, you have to climb up a tree and act like a nut.[12]

The Red Sea parted when someone put their foot out, and not before.[13]

Charismatic gifts must be present in a Christian community if it is to be a witness to the Divinity of Jesus, just as much as human compassion and social activity should evidently witness to His humanity.[14]

Love is higher than truth.[15]

Until our churches recapture this vision of the Holy Spirit's manifestation of signs and wonders of the Kingdom and in God-given loving community in this world, there will be mediocrity in Christendom.[16]

The charism is lost if you put someone in office who doesn't own the charism.[17]
If your God is deaf and dumb, who in the world is going to turn to Him?[18]
Shucks, when someone is healed, your evangelism is done for you.[19]
The charismatic renewal is a poor man's mysticism.[20]

The Jesus Prayer

There is a rich bibliography on the Jesus Prayer. Those unfamiliar with the Jesus Prayer will find most helpful practical wisdom in the anthology edited by Igumen Chariton of Valamo, *The Art of Prayer*,[21] and in Lev Gillet, *On the Invocation of the Holy Name*.[22] *The Art of Prayer* consists primarily of the writings of Theophan the Recluse (19th C.). The first book on the Jesus Prayer to become widely known in the West was *The Way of a Pilgrim*, in various editions now. I first learned of the Jesus Prayer in Anthony Bloom's

---

[12] David Geraets, "Basic Spirituality," Lecture 1 (lecture, Benedictine Monastery, Pecos, NM, January 13, 1981).

[13] David Geraets, "Scripture and the Charismatic Renewal," Lecture 1 (lecture, Benedictine Monastery, Pecos, NM, January 5, 1981).

[14] Geraets, *Jesus Beads*, 51–52.

[15] David Geraets, "Sexuality" (lecture, Benedictine Monastery, Pecos, NM, March 1, 1982).

[16] Geraets, "Scripture and the Charismatic Renewal," Lecture 1.

[17] David Geraets, "The Charismatic Gift of Discernment," (lecture, Benedictine Monastery, Pecos, NM, January 22, 1981).

[18] David Geraets, "Relationships," (lecture, Benedictine Monastery, Pecos, NM, January 15, 1981).

[19] Geraets, interview by Bill O'Donnell.

[20] David Geraets, "Christianity and Depth Psychology," (lecture, Benedictine Monastery, Pecos, NM, January 28, 1981).

[21] Igumen Chariton of Valamo, ed., *The Art of Prayer: An Orthodox Anthology*, trans. E. Kadloubovsky and E. M. Palmer (Boston: Faber and Faber, 1981).

[22] Lev Gillet, *On the Invocation of the Holy Name* (Springfield, IL: Templegate, 1985).

book *Beginning to Pray*.[23] Authors in the volumes of *The Philokalia* discuss the Jesus Prayer, notably Hesychios and Diadochos. Classically, its form is "Lord Jesus Christ, Son of God, have mercy upon me," taken from the blind man's cry from the side of the road in Mark 10:47–48. The practice is to pray this—or a shorter version, simply "Jesus"—repetitively, that is, as a way to pray without ceasing, to pray at all times in the Spirit, to make melody to God in our hearts, and to do everything in the name of Christ.

It is a prayer, not a mantra from the non-Christian East, but interestingly, many Westerners who are familiar with the mantra from Hinduism come home to the Jesus Prayer for the experience of Jesus' and Paul's teachings about our life in Christ. That is, Christ being formed in us, having the mind of Christ, God making God's home in us, opening the door of our hearts, our bodies being filled with light, what Jesus says his followers will do in his name, and the Holy Spirit's interceding for us with sighs too deep for words. Theophan especially offers counsel on the way of *descending with the mind into the heart*. In the language of Western Christian spirituality, this is a joining of mental with affective prayer. Theophan's words below about the name of Jesus becoming like a quietly-flowing inner stream as well as fanning a spark to flame in our hearts are easily associated with the prayer tongue.

One of the Fellowship of the Holy Name's mottos is: *The Name of Jesus brings Pentecost, inside and out.*

Excerpts from David Geraets' Witness

The Name of Jesus and Permeation in the Holy Spirit

In this excerpt, the Jesus Prayer is linked with baptism in the Holy Spirit, and is identified as a form of glossolalia prayer. Inviting people into this prayer is itself a form of evangelism.

> The immediate purpose of praying is to grow in communion with our Triune God.
>
> . . . One manner of making "head" knowledge (i.e., God exists) also become "heart" knowledge (i.e., I personally know He lives in me) is to practice repetition. It is precisely this "heartfelt prayer of a good man which works very powerfully" (James 5:16, Jerusalem Bible).

---

[23] Anthony Bloom, *Beginning to Pray* (New York: Paulist Press, 1970).

> Speaking the name of Jesus repeatedly with love, humility, and reverence creates a vacuum within our hearts which evidently draws down the living Presence of God's Spirit to permeate our entire being.[24]
>
> He who has not yet received a charismatic Gift from God need not feel abandoned or left out of the Pentecostal renewal. Repeating the name of Jesus can become a masterful art of glossolalia prayer, complete in itself.[25]

Revelatory Vision, the Jesus Prayer, and Vocational Commitment

In this section, Abbot David combines his experience of vision and being filled with light—what he calls the Taboric experience—with his witness about the Jesus Prayer and tongues. He calls it "The Jesus Prayer of tongues."

For some Christians, David Geraets' description of the Jesus Prayer below is another way of describing contemplative prayer. Fr. Rusty Shaughnessy, a member of the Pecos community at the time, said that the prayer tongue is "voiced contemplation." However, nearly all contemporary Western Christian teachers of contemplative prayer, in dozens of volumes—with the notable exception of Thomas Merton—do not discuss the Jesus Prayer. Merton says nothing of the prayer tongue, nor do they. Based in my experience a year after hearing this lecture—when I was again at Pecos and when, unlooked for, the light of the Holy Spirit filled me as I lay in bed at night—my witness is this: *Baptism in the Holy Spirit is our participation in Jesus' transfiguration.* Is not contemplative prayer an immersion in the Holy Spirit's revelation of Jesus the light of the world?

Abbot David says here he was "looking for a theological justification for tongues" and not finding it in the Western world. One might make the wry comment that, whether or not tongues are identified in Western *theology*, the New Testament itself might offer whatever justification Christians may seek.

> The most important thing in the life of a Christian is that you get a vision, that you know who you are and where you're going. I have a classical Pentecostal friend who says that there are three very important things in regard to the vision.
>
> First, if you don't have one for your life, pray that you get one. Everybody needs a burning bush like Moses. Needs a vocational call like Isaiah, or the wheels like Ezekiel, or some deep manifestation of God's presence in your life. Call, vocation.
>
> The second thing is that you move into that vision, once you've received it. I have known people who have had a call to move into Pentecost who didn't have

---

[24] Geraets, *Jesus Beads*, 6, 8–9, 14.
[25] Geraets, *Jesus Beads*, 83.

enough guts to move into it. That's the second stage. And that will cost you oftentimes.

And the third one is to last it out all the days of your life. That's the dimension of commitment. Either we have commitments or we have affairs. It is going toward a goal, believing in a future, having a hope. People without a vision perish.

The main function of prophecy is to give people a view of the Kingdom. Two thirds of Jesus' teaching is about the Kingdom.

And so: To move into the vision. That's so important. You're really going to have to have that reiterated many times in your life. Never lose your vision. Because then life is meaningless. Keeping the end in view. Jesus keeping his eyes on the cross and the resurrection.

When they began to move in charismatic circles in the abbey, the first thing it did was split the community right down the middle. Some went into the Baptism in the Spirit into the renewal, some couldn't go into it. And that was the hardest thing I ever suffered in my whole life. My deepest revelations in life have come when I have experienced the deepest pain.

Now I could have written those people off, and said, those people, well, they're just not Christian. That would have been pretty easy, but when you've lived with people and you know their sincerity and you know their practice, you can't write them off, but your great pain, my great pain is—I'm something of a musician—it's like trying to share my song with someone who can't sing. That's why, the experience for me, I try to share the experience of the Baptism in the Spirit with someone who can't open up to it. And so I was wondering whether I was supposed to go into the renewal or not.

I went into a real crisis on that, and I remember—I don't know if I would advise this, whether it would be prudent for your life—but I went on my knees and I said, *Lord, I am not moving off my knees until you talk to me. I want to know whether I'm supposed to be in this thing or not.*

And I remember the first evening, I don't know if I was awake or was sleeping, I am waiting in prayer, and I saw the map of the United States at that time, and I'll never forget these visions as long as I live—the interpretation changes, but the vision never changes—I saw little fires breaking out, different geographical locations, becoming one big fire. And the Lord speaking, saying, *that's how I'm going to renew my people. I'm going to have these little fires breaking out, and they'll become one big fire,* and I watched it into England and continental Europe and I saw parts of Latin America. I didn't see it in the Orient, parts where the Lord was going to take me later.

And the second night I was in prayer again, like that was not good enough, with the Lord saying that's how I'm going to renew my church, you know I'm going to bring these people into one big bonfire, and then he showed me a large river. See, the background to your visions and dreams frequently are the background of where you're raised. I'm raised fifteen miles from the Mississippi River, and I see this big river going, and the Lord said, *Do you see the river?* and I said, *Yes, Lord, I see the river.* And he said: *Now regarding the river, a person can do one of three of things. He can swim across it, ignore the current, he can swim with the current, or against the current, but that's not going to stop the flow of the river.* And then he went on to say, *Now that's how it's going to be these days with this renewal. I'll pour my Spirit out and some people will be like the one who chooses to ignore the current, swims across the current, and some will go against my Spirit, some will go with my Spirit, but,* He said, *they won't stop the outpouring of my Spirit.*

And that's how it's been, you know, these thirteen years. Beyond my fondest expectations I've seen this renewal when it wasn't kosher to even have it in a house, if you were Catholic, I've seen it just spread all over the world. And do you realize, in what a short time? In the Catholic church especially. Goodness, you know in the first years, when something happens, we normally say it's a heresy. Then after maybe about twenty-five years, we say, well, there's maybe a few good things in it. Then after a hundred years, we say, well, that's already in the writings of St Augustine! [laughter] But it's happened a little faster this time.

One reason is probably because we don't have that much time. I'm not talking end of times, but I'm talking the urgency of the gospel. Because without it, an awful lot of people are getting hurt, getting smashed up, aren't they? That's why I have an urgency to preach the gospel. I don't come from a place that *Jesus comes tomorrow, panic today*. I hope he comes tomorrow because since he's left, it hasn't been too good. I'm working and praying for it. But I have an urgency to preach the gospel, because without it I see young people on dope, frying their brains, I see them smashing into the mountains out here beside us, I see marriages falling apart, I see good families shattered. And that's the urgency for me to preach the gospel, because without that Word, God's people perish. That's why I'll go across the country, I'll go across the world, I told the Lord you can take me anywhere you want, because I sense the urgency of the gospel, because without it we don't make it, we just don't make it.

The third evening, as I was in prayer, I had no precedent for it, but I will never forget it as long as I live, and I've never had as powerful experience as this, maybe there'll be one down the line, I hope so. Because, having experienced God's light, there is nothing like it in this world, and I'd do anything to experience that light again, and I hope that isn't just selfish. It came to me at 2 o'clock in the morning, with a bright light that went straight through my whole body. And it was peaceful and it was loving and it was ecstatic. He didn't say much in words. I've never had the Lord be very verbose with me.

He didn't waste words. He said *Go, and I will be with you.* He didn't say very much, but He said everything, didn't he? What more do you need?

And then I heard, but this wasn't a voiceless voice. St Augustine talks about the voiceless voice, you hear down here, it's almost like your own imagination, it goes around and around, and then other times it gets so loud I'm afraid that somebody sitting beside me is going to listen in. And he said, *I want you within the church, and not outside the church.*

In those days it was very easy to get an invitation to speak outside the Catholic church settings. I couldn't get many on the inside.

And I want the witness in the core center where you are.

Now that's how I learned the Taboric experience. I went to my spiritual director, I went all over, I tried to find someone who could tell me what this light is. Went through all of them. They didn't know what the light was. So I had to go back in my Scriptures. And I went back in the writings of the Fathers. And I searched out the whole Eastern Church. I learned about the Jesus Prayer because I was looking for a theological justification for tongues. I can't find it in the Western world.

I found the best theological explanation of it in the Jesus Prayer. A prayer of abandonment. Where you don't go to God with preconceived notions in your head, or preconceived notions in your heart, but you go empty, and you say, you put in my head what you want, you put in my heart what you want. That's the essence of the Jesus Prayer of tongues, it's a prayer of abandonment, it's the apogee, the high point of abandonment, where you become totally feminine, totally receptive and you don't program anything between you and God but you receive God on God's own terms.

So I searched my Scriptures and I found some amazing things. I found Paul talking about that light that was on Moses' face being the light now in the heart of a Christian. Do you know that the early fathers and the Christian and the patristic writers and the Scriptures, expected that the Christian would have the light within the heart as well as the love within the heart. *See how they love one another*, was the sign of a Christian but they also were to have the glow of the Spirit on their face. You would be able to tell if they were a Christian by the way they were lit up, if you want. Have you ever had an experience like that? That's happened to me once. When I went to Japan for the first time, I came back through San Francisco, and I went up to the desk there to the man who was taking the tickets, and I looked at him, at his face, and I said, *Brother, are you baptized in the Holy Spirit?*—I've never done that before or since—and he said *Praise the Lord*, and here are all of these people around us. [laughter] And it's not like me to do that.

But you should be able to walk down the street and see Christians. I'm not putting a judgment on others, but if there's not something special about being a Christian, why would you want to be one? If it doesn't show, a light on your face.

And I looked in II Peter, and this is a gem. Chapter 1:16. He's talking about evangelization—*we were eyewitnesses of his majesty*. What we relate to you was an actual historical happening. *We ourselves heard this voice when we were with him on the sacred mountain. We have the word of prophecy made more certain. And you will do well to pay attention to it as a light shining in a dark place, until the day dawns and the morning star rises in your heart.* What's he saying? You keep your eyes focused on the revelation, you keep believing, until you have an experience where light comes into your heart. And that light will verify two things to you. The first one is that the gospel is real in a way that you never dreamt before.

And the second thing is, that you can lay your life down for it. I don't think you can put your life on the line without that type of revelation. I think it was necessary in the life of Jesus and I think it is necessary in the life of every Christian if they're to last out a commitment.[26]

The Jesus Prayer and Relationship with God

Abbot David speaks of our personal identity as grounded, and defined, in experiential knowledge of Jesus Christ. His witness is that the Jesus Prayer is a way into this relationship, in his experience and in the experience of others he has counseled. Again, living relationship with God is more vital than ideas about God.

> Nobody knows who they are until they know who Jesus is. The only way I know to get a deep knowledge of Jesus, like John the Baptist at the Jordan and Peter's Spirit-anointed recognition of Jesus, is to spend a lot of time with the Jesus Prayer. Until I can say the Name of Jesus 1,000 times without repeating myself, I think I'll begin to know a little bit about prayer. We are talking about relationship and the quality of relationship. The Holy Spirit is like the finger of God. I send a lot of people out into the mountains to pray among the pinons, walking, doing the Jesus Prayer, and the Lord touches them.[27]

Realization of Christian Initiation, Prayer Community, the Word, and Charismatic Gifts in Prayer and Worship

Here Geraets talks about several subjects in a brief space, saying that Christian initiation, indeed evangelism, is to bring baptism in the Holy Spirit, as well as Christian community. Again, there is a key emphasis upon the charismatic prayer meeting for Christian leaders to form. The gifts of the Spirit are to be part of the experience of the gospel if, as he says, the word and worship are to be real and personal. Without elaborating, he states how easily non-charismatic worship actually makes for *accidia*, or no living sense of God's activity among us.

> Catechesis [Christian formation, i.e., in Christian education or preparation for Confirmation] isn't complete until they know Jesus, until there's baptism in the Holy Spirit, and until there is some kind of solid community, solid relationship.

> I found myself when I was moving in that ministry, I went out to the various prayer groups—I get closer to those people in the prayer groups than I was to those in my own community.

---

[26] Geraets, "Scripture and the Charismatic Renewal," Lecture 2.

[27] Geraets, "Scripture and the Charismatic Renewal," Lecture 2.

I found myself saying: David, you've got to be real.

Either you get this type of spirituality in community or else you're going to have to step outside that community where it is.

I think everyone is going to have to ask that question sooner or later.

If you don't have a charismatic prayer meeting, you've got to form one.

I think a diocesan priest should be praying with his people, where we pray with one another. I mean daily, that's what the Liturgy of the Hours is. There should be a charismatic prayer meeting there; if it isn't, go form one.

Your own parish, your own neighborhood, I don't care, no one can keep you from praying. No one has the authority to do that.

The Word is not broken open by someone getting up and proclaiming the Word. That's one form, and I'm not putting that down. But the way the Word is really broken open, the way the powerful Word of God becomes personal, is when you have a movement of prophecy and tongues and inspiration in the assembly. That's how it becomes personal. That's why you need charismatic gifts.

Some people say, "Oh, what is the rationale for mumbling and tongues and prophecy, etc.?" That's how the power, the Word of God, with its power in the assembly, becomes personal, and it's not really worship until that happens.

The prayer meeting is the liturgy of the Word *par excellence*. It's a preparation for Eucharist and flows out of Eucharist.

You can go through the choreography of religious life without praying. It's called *accidia*. Holy indifference.[28]

Practicing into the Charismatic Gifts

Unlike some interpretations of Augustine in the Protestant Reformation, David Geraets does not believe that it is Pelagian to practice into the gifts of the Holy Spirit, that is, to put your foot out. That there is such a thing as a practicum in the gifts of the Spirit. It is striking that his counsel is not to let sin block us from aspiring to move in the gifts.

> I know some people who didn't fear to babble like an idiot, only to find Jesus in their heart, in a way they'd never dreamt of. You will never pray in tongues until you are willing to babble like an idiot. And you may need to babble like an idiot for maybe nine months before you get the gift of tongues. I don't know how long I bounced it off the wall before a breakthrough came. And when we start out, there's an awful lot of practice. When you start with tongues, I will wager that as high as 90% is not tongues. But it's a practicum, or praxis, *toward* tongues. And only if I continue in the practice does the gift break in.

---

[28] Geraets, "The Charismatic Gift of Discernment."

I share with you tonight, don't let any sin ever block you from your ministry, and don't let pride and deception block you from moving in and appropriating charismatic gifts, because an awful lot of people are doing that today, and what they really get hung up on is tongues.[29]

One Additional Reference in Christian Writing to the Prayer Tongue and the Jesus Prayer

I cite here Agnes Sanford in her book *The Healing Gifts of the Holy Spirit*, in her chapter "The Gift of Tongues and of Interpretation." This chapter, in my view, is well worth revisiting, especially in her emphasis upon moving from tongues, or other inspirations, into active charismatic ministry for others. "This gift is one of the tools with which we do our bit in building the Kingdom of God on earth. A good builder need not say, 'Look at my wonderful tools!' One looks instead at that which he has built."[30]

This is in consonance with David Geraets' chapter "The Kingdom of Heaven" in *Jesus Beads*. Repeating a statement found in his *Scripture and the Charismatic Renewal, Lecture 2*, that *Jesus is the model charismatic*, he writes:

> It will happen something like this. As the gift of swimming is given in and during the simulated action of splashing of water, so the Kingdom of Heaven will come when all God's people imitate the actions of their Master, Jesus. "The man who has faith in me will do the works that I do, and greater far than these" (John 14:12). Their doing these things will be the occasion if not the cause for Jesus to return physically and establish the Kingdom of Heaven in fullness. The effort can be fostered or frustrated by our free-will actions. No splashing, no gift of swimming; no charismatic action, no Kingdom. Therefore we pray and work eagerly that our Lord may return soon.[31]

Here is a conversation Sanford records about the Jesus Prayer and tongues—in effect, an independent aspiration toward David Gereats' experience, without ever knowing of him.

> A very holy man, Abbot Lazarus of the Greek Orthodox Church, author of books on the mysticism of this church once said to me, "I wish very much that I had the gift of tongues."
>
> "Why, Abbot Lazarus?" I inquired, surprised beyond measure that this most erudite, British-educated scholar should desire such a gift.
>
> "Because from my study in mysticism I have come to know that it would be a shortcut to contemplative prayer. We spend hours every day saying the Jesus

---

[29] Geraets, "Basic Spirituality," Lecture 1.
[30] Agnes Sanford, *The Healing Gifts of the Spirit* (New York: HarperCollins, 1966), 182.
[31] Geraets, *Jesus Beads*, 82.

Prayer ('Lord Jesus Christ, Son of God, have mercy on me') in an effort to make contact with God. If I could speak with tongues, this contact would be made instantly."[32]

Witnesses from the Eastern Churches

In the context of David Geraets' reports above, I read the following traditional excerpts as witnesses from personal experience of the Spirit rather than as products of speculative theology. The reader is invited to come to know the relationship between the Jesus Prayer and the prayer tongue through his or her own personal practice as well as among other Christians praying together. Gregory of Sinai's words in the fourteenth century are in resonance with the contemplative dynamics in contemporary charismatic worship. I interpret Hesychios' term "intellections" to mean vision as well as words of prophecy, knowledge, and wisdom, when alone and among others.

Theophan the Recluse (19th C.)

> What do we seek through the Jesus Prayer? We seek for the fire of grace to appear in our hearts, and we seek for the beginning of unceasing prayer which manifests a state of grace. When God's spark falls into the heart, the Jesus Prayer fans it into flame. . . . Try not to quench this fire, and it will become established in such a way that the prayer repeats itself; and then you will have within you a small murmuring stream. . . .[33]

Diadochos of Photike (5th C.)

> Knowledge: to lose awareness of oneself through going out to God in ecstasy.[34]

> Then the Lord awakens in the soul a great love for His glory; for when the intellect with fervor of heart maintains persistently its remembrance of the precious name, then that name implants in us a constant love for its goodness, since there is nothing now that stands in its way.[35]

---

[32] Sanford, *The Healing Gifts of the Spirit*, 182, 183. For an introduction to Abbot Lazarus, see Kalllistos Ware, "Foreword," in Ignatius Brianchaninov, *On the Prayer of Jesus*, trans. Fr. Lazarus (Boston: New Seeds Books, 2006).

[33] Theophan, "God's Spark" and "A Murmuring Stream" in *The Art of Prayer*, 108, 110.

[34] Diadochos of Photike, "On Spiritual Knowledge," in *The Philokalia*, vol. 1, ed. Nikodimos of the Holy Mountain, trans. G. E. H. Palmer, Philip Sherrard, and Kallistos Ware (London: Faber and Faber, 1979), 252.

[35] Diadochos of Photike, "On Spiritual Knowledge, 270–71.

Gregory of Sinai (14th C.)

In others it is manifest as an unconquerable love and peace, shown toward all, or as a joyousness that the fathers have often called exultation—a spiritual force and an implosion of the living heart that is also described as a vibration and sighing of the Spirit who makes wordless intercession for us to God (Rom. 8:26). Isaiah has also called this the "waves" of God's righteousness (cf. Isa. 48:18), while the great Ephrem calls it "spurring." The Lord Himself describes it as "a spring of water welling up for eternal life" (John 4:14)—He refers to the Spirit as water—a source that leaps up in the heart and erupts through the ebullience of its power.

You should know that there are two kinds of exultation or joyousness: the calm variety (called vibration or sighing or intercession of the Spirit), and the great exultation of the heart—a leap, bound, or jump, the soaring flight of the living heart towards the sphere of the divine. . . . This is also known as a stirring of the spirit—that is to say, an eruption or impulsion. . . .

Divine awe is accompanied by a tremulous sense of jubilation arising from the prayer of fire that we offer when filled with awe.

The energy of grace is the power of spiritual fire that fills the heart with joy and gladness, stabilizes, warms, and purifies the soul, temporarily stills our provocative thoughts, and for a time suspends the body's impulses. The signs and fruits that testify to its authenticity are tears, contrition, humility, self-control, silence, patience, self-effacement and similar qualities, all of which constitute undeniable evidence of its presence.[36]

Lev Gillet (20th C.)

To grow in the invocation of the Holy Name is to grow in the knowledge of the "Spirit of His Son" (Gal. 4:6).[37]

Hesychios the Priest (8th or 9th C.)

Truly blessed is the man whose mind and heart are so closely attached to the Jesus Prayer and to the ceaseless invocation of His name as air is to the body or flame to the wax. The sun rising over the earth creates the daylight; and the venerable and holy name of the Lord Jesus, shining continually in the mind, gives birth to countless intellections radiant as the sun.[38]

---

[36] Gregory of Sinai, "On How to Discover the Energy of the Holy Spirit" and "On Divine Energy," in *The Philokalia*, vol. 4 (London: Faber and Faber, 1995), 360, 361, 362.

[37] Gillet, *On the Invocation of the Holy Name*, 83.

[38] Hesychios the Priest, "On Watchfulness and Holiness," in *The Philokalia*, vol. 1, 197.

Thomas Merton (20th C.)

> ... the humble invocation of the Lord Jesus. . . . This simple practice is considered to be of crucial importance in the monastic prayer of the Eastern Church, since the sacramental power of the Name of Jesus is believed to bring the Holy Spirit into the heart of the praying monk.[39]

Conclusion

I have offered illustrations for a Pentecostal hermeneutic of the practice of the Jesus Prayer. That is, a grounding of Pentecostal renewal and ministry in the ancient practice of the Jesus Prayer. And David Geraets' virtually unique contemporary joining of the Jesus Prayer with permeation in the Holy Spirit. Accompanied—as only briefly mentioned—by such practices as journaling, dream work, and spiritual direction. That charismatic prayer groups are practicums for the gifts of the Holy Spirit. That baptism in the Holy Spirit is in the context of a conscious awakening to Jesus and of a baptism into the Father, a baptism of suffering, to bring brothers and sisters to Jesus and the Spirit. It is my hope that there will be a renewed interest among Pentecostal Christians to cultivate charismatic prayer meetings, to become some of the fires that Pentecost brings to the world, little fires becoming one big fire.

The Spirit-anointed and revelatory utterance of wisdom, knowledge, prophecy, tongues, interpretation, evangelical proclamation and witness, spiritual song, and words that bring God's healing, are all of a piece with the Spirit-anointed utterance, silently or out loud, of the name of Jesus. When Jesus and the Holy Spirit are active in prayer and worship and ministry, *a God-altered state of consciousness*, with perceptible effects among us, is set in motion. The name of Jesus brings Pentecost, inside and out. "O, that the Spirit of Pentecost would come and write within us the Name of Jesus in flame."[40]

Clyde Glandon (clyde.glandon@cox.net) is a retired Episcopal clergyman, former Executive Director of the Center for Counseling and Education in Tulsa, Oklahoma, USA, and co-founder of the Fellowship of the Holy Name.

---

[39] Thomas Merton, *Contemplative Prayer* (New York: Doubleday, 1969), 22.
[40] Gillet, *On the Invocation of the Holy Name*, 80.

Do you want to become part of something more?

At Oral Roberts University, we believe that our students were born to be leaders who impact the world. ORU students represent all 50 states and over 106 nations. They are visionaries and world-changers who become equipped through our whole-person approach to education, graduating empowered to invest in the world around them. Take your next step with ORU today by applying at apply.oru.edu!

>> Apply today! apply.oru.edu >>

Holiness as Wholeness in Afro-Pentecostal Tradition

A Theological Perspective

Ivan Hartsfield

Keywords *COGIC, C. H. Mason, holiness, social justice, exile, wholeness, sanctification, Afro-Pentecostalism*

Abstract

Using the Church of God in Christ (COGIC) as the exemplar, I explore the theological rationale that undergirds the COGIC priority of holiness as a prescription for human wholeness. By wholeness, I mean human flourishing of the total person. For the COGIC, "Salvation is a deliverance from dangers and enemies." Through the democratization of what was historically reserved for spiritual heroes, namely the designation of "saint," common people of little means were immediately uplifted. They grabbed ahold of this moniker, which redefined them and identified their new place of spiritual residence in Zion. By faith, they expected to experience a modicum of the blessing of Abraham, right now. Such personal and social uplift includes peace, provision, power, healing, deliverance, and victory over their natural and spiritual challenges and foes while in exile. As an exilic people, they created a way of being "in the world, but not of it." This created a holy space where they were not despised outcasts, but "a chosen generation, a royal priesthood, an holy nation, a peculiar people" (1 Pet 2:9, KJV). By inhabiting this space, their lowly status was washed away in the blood.

Introduction

Using the Church of God in Christ (COGIC) as the exemplar, I explore the theological rationale that undergirds the COGIC priority of holiness as a prescription for human wholeness. By wholeness, I mean human flourishing of the total person through spiritual, mental, emotional, material, and social prosperity. Since for the COGIC, "Salvation is a deliverance from dangers and enemies," immediate separation from the world, the flesh, and the devil is normalized COGIC soteriology.[1]

---

[1] O. T. Jones and J. E. Bryant, *Manual of the Church of God in Christ* (Memphis, TN: Church of God in Christ, 1940), 12.

Through the democratization of what had been historically reserved for spiritual heroes, namely the designation of "saint," common people of little means were immediately uplifted. They grabbed ahold of this moniker, which identified their new place of spiritual residence in Zion. As the saints persevere in holiness, they live in a "now, not-yet" tension. By faith, they expected to experience a modicum of the blessing of Abraham, right now. Such personal and social uplift includes peace, provision, power, healing, deliverance, and victory over their natural and spiritual challenges and foes while in exile. Despite Pentecostal distinctives, the COGIC is known, not as a Pentecostal church, but as the "sanctified church." According to Cheryl J. Sanders, members of this movement

> follow the holiness mandate in worship, in personal morality, and in society, based on a dialectical identity characteristic of the tradition: "in the world, but not of it." This dialectical identity reflects the social aspect of exilic consciousness, as manifested in the saints' awareness of alienation or separation from the dominant culture, based on racial differences and religious practices.[2]

As an exilic people, they created a way of being "in the world, but not of it" by employing holiness codes and prohibitions that rejected worldly pleasures and practices. This created an alternate world, a holy space where they were not despised outcasts, but "a chosen generation, a royal priesthood, an holy nation, a peculiar people" (1 Pet 2:9, KJV). By inhabiting this space, their lowly status was washed away in the blood.

To flesh out the notion of holiness as wholeness, I will review the historical development of holiness in the tradition as understood by the founder, C. H. Mason, as it relates to wholeness. Then, I will discuss how the complex historical distinctives and existential particularities of a marginalized people necessitated a quest for social resurrection. Next, I will engage Mason's own theological understanding of holiness as wholeness. After that, I will engage and exegete aspects of the 1931/40 COGIC articles of religion, taught and practiced as lived religion up until 1973 for insights into this holiness/wholeness dynamic. Lastly, I will provide a theological summary of holiness as wholeness from this Afro-Pentecostal tradition and suggest ways in which the broader Christian community can benefit from this theological construction.

The Development of Holiness as Wholeness in C. H. Mason

In 1891 Mason married Alice Saxton. Unfortunately, Alice was opposed to Mason's ministry pursuits and their marriage ended just two years later in 1893. The constant travel associated with the preaching lifestyle and lack of monetary gain were likely

---

[2] Cheryl J. Sanders, *Saints in Exile: The Holiness-Pentecostal Experience in African American Religion and Culture* (Oxford: Oxford University Press, 1996), 5–6.

contributors to the divorce.[3] This traumatic experience was so grievous to Mason that he contemplated suicide. Based on a 1994 interview of Mason's daughter, Lelia Mason Byas, Mason separated from his first wife in 1893 due to his wife's marital infidelity. According to Mason's daughter, Julia, Mason explained that God sanctified him during the separation from his first wife and healed him of his mental and physical distress, which enabled him to overcome the separation. By his daughter Mary Mason's account, the resistance of C. H. Mason's first wife to his call to preach was the source of his problems as he moved further and further away from God. She compares C. H. Mason's ordeal to that of Jonah and provides an insightful account.[4] As a result of this transformative experience, Mason overcame moral compromise and felt revitalized for ministry. It was after this experience that he preached his first message on sanctification entitled, "Endure Hardness as a Good Soldier" (2 Tim 3:12–13). After developing a zeal for, and commitment to, the doctrine of sanctification broadly construed, through his own personal crisis, Mason believed that sanctification brought spiritual renewal and social liberation.[5]

In November of 1893, Mason entered Arkansas Baptist College for the first time in search of help with his preaching. This was the first of two stints with Arkansas Baptist College. The second stint would be with the affiliated Minister's Institute. However, according to Mason's own testimony, during the first stint he was disillusioned with the school. Becoming suspicious of the curriculum, he believed that the institution had assimilated to the culture and its methods and would not be able to help him maintain the vitality of slave religion, albeit with the appropriate evangelical modifications:[6]

> I entered the Arkansas Baptist College November 1, 1893, and stayed about three months. I still entered the same so that an education would help me out in

---

[3] Calvin White, "In the Beginning, There Stood Two: Arkansas Roots of the Black Holiness Movement," *The Arkansas Historical Quarterly* 68 (Spring 2009), 7.

[4] Mary Mason, *The History and Life Work of Elder C. H. Mason Chief Apostle and His Co-Laborers* (Memphis, TN: The Church of God in Christ, 1987), 22–23.

[5] Elton Hall Weaver, "'Mark the Perfect Man': The Rise of Bishop C. H. Mason and the Church of God in Christ" (PhD diss., University of Memphis, 2007), 57–60.

[6] "During slavery Mason's parents adhered to a set of religious beliefs that emerged out of a blending of African Traditional Religions with white protestant [sic] Christianity. Slave religion was a set of spiritual and cultural beliefs created by the slaves. The sacred world views Africans brought to the Americas came from West and Central Africa, and included beliefs in a supreme god, spiritual energy, a hierarchy of good and evil spirits, witchcraft, life after death in an upper and lower world. They believed in a world of the living and a world for the dead. Slave religion appealed to enslaved Africans because it incorporated 'Africanisms' (the continual flow of African cultural beliefs) like spirit possession, adherence to herbal specialist and sacred funeral rites and rituals to honor the dead." Weaver, "Mark the Perfect Man," 38.

preaching. The Lord showed me that there was no salvation in schools and colleges; for the way they were conducted grieved my very soul. I packed my books, arose and bade them a final farewell to follow Jesus with the Bible as my sacred guide. I began to lift up Christ by word, example and preceipt [sic], in my ministry, the word drew the people from the streets, roadsides, and from the utmost part of the country. Very soon the word of God began to sanctify the people everywhere He sent me. Bless His holy name.[7]

According to Lelia Mason Byas, her father had very specific concerns. "My father did not like how blacks were mimicking whites, wanting to be like them, socially, politically, and religiously. He was searching for knowledge about the God who had liberated black Americans, the God of the slaves, and the God that healed the poor and afflicted. That God papa said was never mentioned."[8] From this episode, it seems clear that Mason was not so much in search of theological clarification, but spiritual manifestation sufficient to change the trajectory of his people.

Influence of William Christian

One of the most influential people in Mason's understanding of holiness was previously enslaved ex-slave William Christian with his restorationist theology. Having a similar trajectory to that of Mason, Christian started off as a Baptist preacher, but received a revelation that he was preaching the human doctrine instead of Christ. This changed his theology and message. Being accused of deviating from the Baptist faith, he withdrew from the Baptists to establish the Church of the Living God.[9] Mason's initial exposure to, and subsequent affiliation with, Christian and the Black Restorationist Movement coincides well with his personal pursuit of clean or holy living.[10] While definitive documented evidence is lacking, circumstantial evidence suggests that Mason's understanding of clean living was initially influenced by this movement in general, and William Christian in particular.[11] Importantly, Mason's yearning from his early childhood for the uplift of his people and the power of slave religion would imply that

---

[7] Mason, *The History and Life Work of Elder C. H. Mason*, 24–25.

[8] Weaver, "Mark the Perfect Man," 63.

[9] David D. Daniels, "The Cultural Renewal of Slave Religion: Charles Price Jones and the Emergence of the Holiness Movement in Mississippi" (PhD diss., Union Theological Seminary, 1992), 159–61.

[10] Daniels, "A More Excellent Way," 115.

[11] This assertion is based on Daniel's commentary in "A More Excellent Way: The Theological Journey of Bishop Charles Harrison Mason in the Theological Formation of the Church of God in Christ," in *With Signs Following: The Life and Ministry of Charles Harrison Mason*, ed. Raynard Smith (St. Louis, MO: Chalice, 2015), 114–15. Additional support for Christian's influence upon Mason may possibly be found in the archives of the Church of God (Christian Workers for Fellowship). However, further confirmation is beyond the scope of this effort.

Mason had some personal sense of racial equality as a righteous pursuit. Christian's polygenesis, appeal to Christianity, and love, certainly heightened Mason's insights and would have provided some scriptural support for his thinking.

In this polygenesis (i.e., the theory that different races have different origins), the gentiles or Caucasian, Asians, and blacks, also referred to as Ethiopians or black Jews, all have different origins. Adam and Eve, patriarchs and prophets, even Christ and his family and certain apostles were black. Furthermore, the curse of Cain would have been an intra-black and not interracial issue, as was commonly taught. This subverted the popular Hamitic curse theory based on the subjugation of the black race.[12] While Christian does not preach black superiority, according to his train of logic, with such a noble heritage, black folks need to open their eyes and recognize that they can be and are as good as any other people.[13] Whether one is better than another is based upon how well one lives, as Christian explains: "No man on earth is better than I am, unless he beats me doing right and everybody in this world that beats me doing right is better than I am and nobody's color or wealth makes them better than I am, and everybody in this world, regardless of their color or wealth, that I beat doing right, I am better than they are."[14] With holy living as the great equalizer, for Christian, social hierarchy was predicated upon how one lived before God, instead of economic or racial distinctives.

Although not a proponent of Christian's polygenesis, Christian's posture concerning his people resonated with Mason. Furthermore, Mason also preached and demonstrated a profound love for all people, as expressed in an account by his daughter, Mary Mason. While evidence reveals that Mason had a sense of racial parity and desire for social uplift before his exposure to the Black Restorationist Movement, it appears that William Christian's impact upon Mason at least heightened Mason's sensitivity to such matters, if not informed or taught him in some respects.

The Practical Theology of C. P. Jones

As practical theology for the social and political challenges of black people, holiness provided freedom from different types of bondage. This included not just immorality, but racism.[15] Concerning the efficacy of the gospel for everyday life, C. P. Jones commented, "Mind that God did not teach Israel to have religion apart from a political hope. They were combined. Christ was to reign in their hearts and over their affairs.

---

[12] William Christian, *Poor Pilgrim's Work* (Texarkana, AR: Joe Ehrlich's Pring, 1896), 1–7; Daniels, "A More Excellent Way," 115.

[13] Christian, *Poor Pilgrim's Work*, 4–7.

[14] Christian, *Poor Pilgrim's Work*, 20.

[15] Daniels, "The Cultural Renewal of Slave Religion," 199–200.

And so it is yet to be."[16] The realization of a better future for African Americans required a life of virtue, which would bestow "dignity, nobility, beauty, grace, and wisdom." The hindrance to this achievement was sin defined in relational, cause and effect terminology. For example, sin destroys reputations, and hamstrings the wealthy and powerful through the production of shame; the vicious and arrogant have their lives shortened; vices create conspicuous consumption that hinders virtue, even infecting the innocent, producing death.[17]

Although African Americans were plagued with profound socio-economic and political challenges, Jones was convinced that great opportunities were ahead. As a pan-Africanist (i.e., one who affirms the solidarity of people of African descent), Jones affirmed the historical contributions and nobility of African people.[18] Believing that nobility was oftentimes bestowed upon the marginalized by God, African Americans should have hope in the future. For Jones, character could overcome these challenges. Character was inclusive of self-respect and other virtues. In fact, character was developed through salvation and the teaching of Scripture.

Character was salvific or the means through which God's redemption manifested to save black people. In this respect, Jones proffered a list of virtues shaped by truth, courage, and compassion.[19] Key to social uplift were, "faith, indomitable will, dauntless courage, serpent-like wisdom, and dove-like disposition." In support of these virtues were the pursuit of "truth, knowledge, discretion, honesty, honor, integrity." These were integral to God's wishes to elevate, instruct, and guide his people for the spiritual and social salvation of others.[20] Jones' explication of holiness as liberation affected by character provided a theological foundation for Mason's own effort to preserve slave religion with his own view of holiness as freedom, and his efforts towards social uplift rooted in personal and communal sanctification.

Pentecostal Distinctives and Racial Diversity at Azusa

Inspired by the Welsh Revival of 1904, William J. Seymour, a black Holiness preacher from Louisiana, led a group of 100 "prayer warriors" into a ten-day fast for revival on Bonnie Brae Street in Los Angeles, California. Within three days, participants were being baptized in the Holy Spirit with the evidence of speaking in tongues, reminiscent of the Day of Pentecost in Acts 2:4. This resulted in an unprecedented and

---

[16] Daniels, "The Cultural Renewal of Slave Religion," 201.
[17] Daniels, "The Cultural Renewal of Slave Religion," 230–31.
[18] Daniels, "The Cultural Renewal of Slave Religion," 217.
[19] Daniels, "The Cultural Renewal of Slave Religion," 217.
[20] Daniels, "The Cultural Renewal of Slave Religion," 232–35.

unimaginable display of Christian unity. The revival would grow to include as many as twenty different races and nationalities from a myriad of ecclesiastical backgrounds worshipping together. The work grew so quickly, and the worship was so loud and lively, that Seymour decided to move into the old Stevens African Methodist Episcopal Church on 312 Azusa Street. This abandoned building with sawdust floors was more like a barn than a church. In egalitarian worship and fellowship, blacks and whites prayed for each other; men and women participated freely and preached in the services. From 1906 to 1909, the ministry conducted three services a day. These were non-liturgical gatherings designed to be Spirit-led. As a result of this newfound freedom, meetings were filled with fervent prayers, songs, testimonies, preaching, conversions, Spirit baptism, exorcisms, and healings. Despite these miraculous effects, the violation of social conventions concerning race and gender, along with the raucous worship experience, evoked condemnation by the media and others. Undisturbed by the rigorous schedule or social convention, those desperate to experience Spirit baptism headed upstairs to the Upper Room, reminiscent of Acts 2. This multicultural, multi-ethnic melting pot of people included blacks, whites, immigrants, and Mexicans, who also played an early role in the revival, along with Swedish, Irish, English, Russian, Armenian, Chinese, and people of South Asian descent. These seekers would spend additional time, even days, in prayer and supplication for a divine touch.[21]

In 1907, at the request of C. P. Jones, Mason, D. J. Young, and J. A. Jeter, Mason went to the Azusa Street Revival to inquire into the new teaching on Spirit baptism.[22] Initially, Mason was concerned about what he saw upon his visit. However, on the second night of his visit he received Spirit baptism, and later recalled the event with keen specificity.[23] After this life changing experience, Mason stayed in Los Angeles to learn the doctrine taught by Seymour. After leaving Azusa, he did not go directly home, but visited Virginia where he preached the message of Pentecost and shared his testimony. He preached in churches and in the open air to crowds as large as 6,000, comprised of black and white supplicants who responded to his message of salvation, sanctification, and Spirit baptism. During this itinerant thrust, Mason even managed to

---

[21] Gastón Espinosa, *William J. Seymour and the Origins of Global Pentecostalism: A Biography and Documentary History* (Durham, NC: Duke University Press, 2014), 53–60; William J. Seymour, *The Azusa Street Papers: The Apostolic Faith Mission Newsletter, 1906–1908* (Scotts Valley, CA: CreateSpace Independent Publishing Platform, 2013), 7–29; Stanley M. Burgess and Gary B. McGee, *Dictionary of Pentecostal and Charismatic Movements* (Grand Rapids, MI: Zondervan, 1988), 778–81.

[22] Robert R. Owens, "Bishop Charles Harrison Mason: The Apostle of Reconciliation," in *With Signs Following*, 64.

[23] Calvin White, *The Rise to Respectability: Race, Religion, and the Church of God in Christ* (Fayetteville, AR: University of Arkansas Press, 2012), 34.

establish the C. H. Mason Memorial Church of God in Christ.[24] It is this pneumatological experience that represents the final stage in Mason's theological evolution— bringing together sanctification and power in a manner that produced spiritual and material deliverance. Mason's Azusa Street experience had a profound impact on his ministry and theology.

According to Weaver, Seymour encouraged Mason and his team to experience a spiritual metamorphosis through Spirit baptism, and that tongues are a sign that follows the experience. Like Seymour, who was the son of slaves, so was Mason. Both experienced slave religion and were products of the Baptist church. In addition, Seymour believed that spiritually transformed African Americans would be supernaturally empowered to love their enemies and overcome racism. Mason also believed that this power would enable his people to overcome both racism and classism. Theologically, while C. P. Jones and the Holiness Movement envisioned the baptism of the Spirit as a "second blessing," or a second work of grace, Seymour understood this experience as a third work of grace accompanied by *glossolalia* (i.e., speaking in tongues). What Seymour said publicly and in private counsel resonated with Mason. So impactful was the experience that Mason stayed at Azusa for five weeks to undoubtedly learn and absorb as much from Seymour and the revival as possible.[25]

The Quest for Social Resurrection

Mason's ministry began in 1893, after the optimistic Reconstruction (1867–1877) came to a grinding halt under the presidential administration of Rutherford B. Hayes. As a result, Southern revenge moved quickly to dismantle the political, economic, and social gains of former slaves and their progeny. The system of Jim Crow guaranteed that blacks would suffer persistently as a permanent underclass to be exploited and discarded. In this cultural milieu, slave religion offered Mason a framework through which to interpret the sweltering socio-economic violence perpetrated against his people without recourse. According to Raynard Smith, "In their desire to seek relief from their oppressive conditions, the slaves sought the comfort of their religion. Slave religion provided African Americans with the ability to interpret their world events from a liberationist perspective."[26]

Key to Mason's strategy for spiritual uplift was the practice of slave religion. Emerging out of slavery, black Baptists in Mississippi began without ordained clergy,

---

[24] Owens, "The Apostle of Reconciliation," 65–66.

[25] Weaver, "Mark the Perfect Man," 124–34.

[26] Raynard D. Smith, "Seeking the Just Society: Charles Harrison Mason's Quest for SocialEquality," in *With Signs Following*, 97–99.

formal structures, or educational programming. This situation was complicated by conflicting religious culture, polity, and organization. For Mason and others, the goal was the transformation of slave religion by eliminating practices deemed heathen by evangelicals.[27] In slave religion, the ring-shout captured the essence of the tradition. While there were various configurations, after the main service, the congregants would gather in a circle around several supplicants. Those who were encircled and those in the circle began clapping, singing, and praising God until the experience would heighten into a frenzy of praise, shouting, weeping, and laughing. The goal could be to convert supplicating sinners, while creating an atmosphere for an encounter with God.[28] The essence of the ring-shout was reconstituted through more powerful charismatic, New Testament forms. From the early days of the COGIC, Elton Weaver notes this phenomenon:

> Members who got physically sick but could not afford medical doctors were anointed with oil. Hands were placed on their bodies to heal them. Many who recovered testified that they had been healed by Mason's touch. He used unconventional techniques like positive speaking to counter negative thinking, protest prayers, prophecy, laying on of hands, blessed oils and handkerchiefs, spiritual singing, praise music, dancing and shouting, speaking in tongues, and other cultural expressions as therapeutic release mechanisms. . . . Blacks who attended his church felt safe from danger, expressed themselves freely, and were always told they were important. Mason's religions, techniques, and ideas of black progress and equality were a healing catharsis.[29]

In the throes of social death, the Exodus became the paradigmatic narrative for black existence. Existential continuity and solidarity with the Israelites provided an interpretive lens through which to see God as Liberator. While embracing the liberation motif in Scripture, Mason was convinced that social equality was the divine intent. To complement a tempered social activism, Mason called for patient humility in prayer as a strategy of active non-violent resistance. He was convinced that through supplication, God would gradually, but certainly, ameliorate the situation. In effect, this provided the downtrodden with hope, while modulating black activism and the inevitable retaliation of angry whites.[30] Mason's sentiments are well represented in a piece published in the *Truth*, a paper produced earlier on during Mason's affiliation and collaboration with C. P. Jones. The article was entitled, "A Message of Hope for the Black Man: How He May Get Thro [sic] This Awful Time." While temperate on social activism, Mason holds out

---

[27] Daniels, "The Cultural Renewal of Slave Religion," 59–60.
[28] Daniels, "The Cultural Renewal of Slave Religion," 85–89.
[29] Weaver, "Mark the Perfect Man," 142–43.
[30] Smith, "Seeking the Just Society," 99–101.

hope for divine intervention. At this juncture, despite the lived realities of his people, he maintained a remarkable confidence in God's ability and willingness to act on behalf of oppressed people as they persist in prayer:

> We must not tire in prayer. We must groan and bear, grin and endure, love our enemies, bless them that curse us, do good to them that hate us, make the best of everything and be all the while looking to God. . . . The colored people need to do this that [sic] now, neither ought there be delay. Nineveh did it. Are we better than they? . . . O if our leaders would humbly consider this! We could then change sentiment in America. God would do it.[31]

Since Mason was convinced from Scripture that everyone came from one blood and was therefore equal before God, he strove to embody this conviction. Despite Jim Crow, Mason routinely fellowshipped with white believers, and accepted invitations to preach in white churches. Not only were whites welcome to full participation in the COGIC, but they also held leadership roles and even had a conference of white churches within the denomination. Other white ministers were allowed to use the COGIC charter for ministry credentialing and savings on railroad travel. When a group of white clergy left to establish the Assemblies of God, Mason attended the meeting and blessed them, although he was not formally invited. Alas, the power of segregation was too formidable to resist. In the 1930s the conference of white churches was dissolved, as it was believed that the whites were attempting to start a separate denomination. So ended the vision of an inclusive community that had been initially birthed by William Seymour.[32]

Local Church Structure

At the local level, church polity was ordered like a family. The pastor modeled the role of a father, and the church mother, the role of a mother. The church mother operated as the church disciplinarian, teacher, and enforcer of COGIC standards of conduct. On the other hand, the church father or pastor legitimized the mother's instructions, by officially endorsing and reinforcing the teachings based on his pastoral authority. While the pastor and church mother were not normally married to each other, together they modeled gender relationships to a bedraggled people surrounded by instability from social, economic, and racial disparities.[33] Many church mothers were spiritual trailblazers who preached on street corners, conducted revivals, and laid the foundations for new church plants. At times, their spiritual authority and charismatic leadership

---

[31] Smith, "Seeking the Just Society," 100–101.

[32] Smith, "Seeking the Just Society," 104.

[33] Anthea Butler, *Women in the Church of God in Christ: Making a Sanctified World* (Chapel Hill, NC: The University of North Carolina Press, 2007), 49.

rivaled the authority of the male leadership in the church.[34] With church mothers as the primary enforcers of the sanctified life, Anthea Butler argues that in this context, COGIC women became the exemplars or models for the sanctified life.[35] As a result, the proliferation and expression of sanctification as the fundamental COGIC distinctive would not have been possible without the tireless, selfless, and oftentimes unheralded labors of both named and unnamed COGIC women.

Early Church Growth

As a result of being surveilled by the government during World War I under suspicion of subverting the war efforts, Mason gained publicity as his name was bandied about in major newspapers. In the 1920s and 1930s his popularity grew as COGIC adherents who migrated from the South established COGIC churches in major urban centers. During these challenging economic times, Mason and his churches ministered to the needs of the poor by not only preaching the gospel, but by clothing, feeding, and healing them.[36] Mason used his influence and holiness as a weapon of nonconformity to combat racial stereotypes and oppression. By the time of Mason's death in 1961, holiness as a way of life had effectively challenged the religious status quo and dominant culture to carve out a vibrant, lived religious tradition, as the COGIC touted one million members worldwide.[37] By reformulating and institutionalizing slave religion, Mason effectively radicalized and weaponized holiness as a lived religious form for higher spiritual, economic, and social development. Through the service, piety, morality, and modesty of COGIC women, sanctified living was effectively concretized as the religious distinctive of the movement.

Social Context

As unlikely as Mason and the COGIC story may be, understanding the brutal social milieu within which both emerged exposes the remarkable resilience and persistence of both the man and the movement buoyed by an exilic vitality. The end of Reconstruction in 1877 brought the end of black political and social progress. Southern Democrats regained control of government and implemented a brutal social order of submission and exploitation of black people. Sharecropping replaced slavery as the next iteration of systemic oppression and economic servitude.[38] Fearing the machinations of

---

[34] Butler, *Women in the Church of God in Christ*, 50–52.
[35] Butler, *Women in the Church of God in Christ*, 76.
[36] Weaver, "Mark the Perfect Man," 243–50.
[37] Weaver, "Mark the Perfect Man," 288.
[38] White, *The Rise of Respectability*, 12.

black holiness worshippers, whites reacted violently to all-night services like the ones promoted by Mason. Shootings and severe beatings were not unusual. Whites felt that their laborers were unable to adequately perform their duties after such events. In Holmes County, Mississippi, where Mason experienced much ministry success, blacks represented the majority, but were confined to farm and domestic work. From 1870 to 1897, in Holmes County, the illiteracy rate among blacks was dismal, ranging from 35 to 41 percent. At the same time, upwardly mobile blacks, striving for racial uplift, disdained the emotional displays by ignorant, uneducated religious fanatics, like Mason.[39] In fact, the famous Ida B. Wells railed against uneducated and unseemly ministers, advocating for an educated clergy poised to teach morals and values. Contra Wells, according to Mason, it was this Baptist preoccupation with education, social, and political empowerment that at the same time neglected the spiritual needs of the people.[40]

The confluence of these circumstances placed Mason's followers in the social, economic, political, and religious margins, helping to forge a distinctive exilic identity. However, for these people, Mason's ministry offered hope. Women could more readily participate in services with unrestrained emotive worship and testimonies of God's grace. Uneducated men could gain respectability as spiritual leaders, despite being dismissed by the outside world. Those in need of healthcare, but who had no means to secure it, were attracted to Mason's faith in God's power to heal, which according to a myriad of testimonials, produced both material and cathartic results.[41] Birthed in the Mississippi Delta, the COGIC was born in the crucible of lynch mobs, Klansman, and withering white oppression. At the end of the nineteenth century, thousands of blacks, men and women, had been lynched and burned. This helped to fuel the black migration to the North and West. Between 1910 and 1960, more than 4 million blacks fled the South in hopes of a better life.[42] During this same time, the COGIC grew nationally and missionally into many of the urban centers populated by blacks. As in the South, the COGIC catered to the poor, which was part of its missional strategy and genius to socially uplift through Christian holiness. Early in the movement, the church enjoyed a strong contingent of white members. Initially known for its multicultural appeal, over time, the pressures of social stratification, along with the rise of white-led

---

[39] White, *The Rise of Respectability*, 25–27.

[40] White, *The Rise of Respectability*, 22–23.

[41] White, *The Rise of Respectability*, 25–26.

[42] Ithiel C. Clemmons, *Bishop C. H. Mason and the Roots of the Church of God in Christ* (Largo, MD: Pneuma Life, 2012), 82–83.

Pentecostal denominations, such as the Assemblies of God and the Foursquare Church, resulted in whites leaving the COGIC to attend predominantly white fellowships.[43]

Church Culture

Unlike other denominations at the time, the COGIC created a revolutionary ministry model and church culture that effectively leveraged the gifts, talents, resources, and passion of women to grow and sustain the church. Women were not only instrumental, but influential in helping to plant, build, and sustain ministry. Furthermore, the COGIC resisted acquiescing to white religious practices and standards. According to Clemmons, the confluence of a number of factors contributed to the work of women being essential to the organization.[44] First, the holiness movement of which C. H. Mason had been a part featured women leading, preaching, and pastoring. This egalitarian spirit manifested at Azusa, carried over into the Pentecostal Movement, where both male and female leadership were common. Second, with the end of Reconstruction, blacks suffered intense economic exploitation with few paths for upward mobility. Recognizing education as the key to upward mobility, the black community focused on educating women. In turn, these women became catalysts for community activism and organizational support for the church. Third, during the women's suffrage movement, African American men were more likely to support women having the right to vote than were white men. While these historical factors were crucial, Mason's personal investment in female leadership was decisive.[45]

In slave tradition, there were two important principles that probably informed Mason's commitment to women in ministry: (1) the spiritual equality of women, which promoted the use of their spiritual gifts; and (2) the shared responsibility of men and women in community and the field. While slave women functioned authoritatively in spiritual and civil spaces, they were still subject to male leadership. Furthermore, this model appears to be an adaptation of West African society, in which women wielded power in certain domains and had political representation. For example, in the "dual-sex" system, a man functioned as the overall head, while a woman was responsible for overseeing the concerns of the women. In Mason's model, women could teach, but not hold the title of preacher or pastor. At the local level, the church mother was the head of women's ministry under pastoral oversight. This model was perpetuated at the jurisdictional and national levels. The term "mother" was used for the head of women's

---

[43] Clemmons, *Bishop C. H. Mason and the Roots of the Church of God in Christ*, 82–100.

[44] Clemmons, *Bishop C. H. Mason and the Roots of the Church of God in Christ*, 100–103.

[45] Adrienne M. Israel, "Mothers Roberson and Coffey Coffey—Pioneers of Women's Work: 1911–1964," in *Bishop C. H. Mason and the Roots of the Church of God in Christ*, ed. Ithiel C. Clemmons (Bakersfield, CA: Pneuma Life, 1996), 103–105.

ministry and faithful senior women who comprised the mothers board. When the pastor was absent, the church mother was in charge. By harnessing the power of women, maintaining slave worship, and the preeminence of prayer, Mason was able to effectively preserve and translate the spiritual power and essence of slave religion into a vibrant religious tradition.[46]

Social Engagement

As he traveled throughout the South, Mason would preach to diverse crowds. On many of these occasions, he used his pulpit to comment on racial injustice. Due to his renunciation of racism, Mason called for a national boycott of bus companies that offered poor treatment of black customers. In 1931, through his *Whole Truth* newsletter, he lauded the railroad for hiring blacks and providing better service to the black community. He encouraged his followers to support the railroads because in doing so, they were protecting thousands of jobs for African American workers.[47] Mason supported the National Council of Negro Women founded by the renowned Mary McLeod Bethune. Bethune's affiliation with Lillian Brooks Coffey, the second national head of the COGIC Women's Department, gave COGIC women greater influence and exposure.[48] Anthea Butler makes important connections between the social engagement of COGIC women in civic matters, and the overall shift of the tradition from a more interior focus on sanctification, to taking sanctification to the world. She notes that political and social realities of the 1940s and 1950s brought this shift. The work was couched in sanctified language to normalize the work. External alliances and relationships were pursued with the intent to transform the world through a sanctified lifestyle. This brought civic, social, and political capital to the movement, enabling expansion beyond its more parochial roots.[49]

As Mason's success grew in Memphis, Tennessee, so did his opposition. Progressive blacks strove to refine the black community to accommodate and win the approval of whites. Instead of refined liturgies and well-ordered services, Mason's services were critiqued as fanatical and chaotic, unleashing uncouth "holy rollers." Interpreting these events, progressive blacks saw Mason's services, which catered to uncultured poor folks, as an impediment to social progress. Furthermore, it was believed that Mason's otherworldly focus and message left him without a response to the pressing social issues of the day. Nevertheless, as oppressed people yearned for relief from their existence, the

---

[46] Israel, "Mothers Roberson and Coffey," 105–110.

[47] Smith, "Seeking the Just Society," 104–106.

[48] Clemmons, *Bishop C. H. Mason and the Roots of the Church of God in Christ*, 119–20.

[49] Butler, *Women in the Church of God in Christ*, 119–20.

COGIC provided a cathartic approach to faith that attracted many. Mason's spiritual demonstrations, including exorcising demons and interpreting unknown tongues, convinced other poor blacks, steeped in slave religion, that Mason exercised control over the spirit realm.[50]

During the Great Depression, challenging social and economic conditions created a space for the organization to grow, as poor blacks left their rural surroundings and migrated to Memphis. Soaring unemployment and squalid living conditions bred outbreaks of diseases such as typhoid. While progressives perceived Mason's message as ethereal, the poor flocked to Mason for the promise of divine healing. In fact, Mason's revivals during this period were known as "emergency rooms of the soul."[51] Testimonials of God's healing power were abundant. In addition to healing services, the church started to teach the poor about health and hygiene. As alcoholism and domestic problems exploded among both blacks and whites, the COGIC holiness stance prohibited its members from consuming alcohol, while providing support to men looking to abandon their families. Because of these priorities, COGIC members were sought out by employers for being a dependable labor pool. Mason garnered support among whites, as they perceived his message as a helpful social control for blacks.[52]

Mason's Vision of Holiness as Wholeness

For Mason, denying ungodliness and worldly lusts meant to live a "clean life."[53] Thus, clean living, while made possible by God's grace and not human effort, was the responsibility of the believer to pursue. This clean life included freedom from vices such as smoking, drugs, sexual immorality, and some alleviation of social oppression. As an adept folk theologian, Mason drew out implications relevant to the embodied reality of his own dispossessed people.

His is not a repudiation of culture *in toto*, but a much needed "higher development," informed by an exilic, *non-Evangelican* [54] vision of holiness, as he never

---

[50] White, *The Rise of Respectability*, 101–104.

[51] White, *The Rise of Respectability*, 105.

[52] White, *The Rise of Respectability*, 104–106.

[53] Daniels, "A More Excellent Way," 116.

[54] *Evangelican* (Evangelical faith + the priority of Americanism) is a term that I chose as it is readily confounded with the term *Evangelicals*, just as this belief system is often confused with true evangelical faith. *What is an Evangelical?* Following Mark Noll, evangelicalism is not a static construct, but a coalescing of movements, alliances, and influential individuals towards what has been discerned as "evangelical" trajectories or impulses stemming from the mid-eighteenth-century revivalism in Northern Europe and North America. According to historian David Bebbington, these include being born-again or a conversion experience, the ultimate authority of the Bible for faith and praxis, evangelism, activism, and the centrality of Christ's work on the cross. Yet, these alone have not yielded a cohesive, well-defined sect of Christians (Mark Noll, *The Scandal*

taught his followers to abandon culture or society. Instead, he taught that through Spirit baptism and holy pursuit, poor black folks could rise out of sin, poverty, relegation to the bottom of society, and lighten the scourge of racial injustice.[55] Sanctification was the key for black folks to progress and gain strength as a people. To live holy in the context of this Holiness-Pentecostal context meant to overcome the things that hindered moral and natural progress. It divinely enabled self-control and moderation over passions and destructive patterns of behavior. Holy Spirit-empowered living would not only bring moral and material success but self-empowerment and self-reliance that were not dependent upon societal uplift.[56]

In a message preached circa 1924, entitled, "God's Oath," Mason asserts the universality of sanctification and declared, "All are to be righteous." His religious affections are circumscribed by holiness and sanctification. He references Isaiah 60:21, which states, "Thy people also shall be all righteous: they shall inherit the land for ever, the branch of my planting, the work of my hands, that I may be glorified." In the context of Isaiah 60, the writer describes the future eschatological kingdom of God. During this time of enormous prosperity and spiritual transformation, those in Zion will all be holy and righteous. This will include all the nations of the world who have come to serve Yahweh. At this time, the promise to Abram, namely making him a great nation (Gen 12:2); the eternal bequeathing of the land to his descendants who will multiply as the dust of the earth (Gen 13:15–16); the multiplication of Abram's descendants like the stars of heaven (Gen 15:5); the innumerable multiplication of

---

of the Evangelical Mind [Grand Rapids, MI: Eerdmans Publishing, 1994], 8–9). A common, but controversial term used to describe this political phenomena is the term "Constantinianism." This term, popularized by the late ethicist and theologian, John H. Yoder, refers to the rise of the church under the Roman emperor, Constantine, during the fourth century. In short, under his reign, Christianity became the religion of the Roman Empire. As a result, the church enjoyed protections and privilege from the state, which resulted in its prophetic witness being compromised. In this new context, the church shared power with, and at the behest of, the empire, while offering no prophetic witness against the evils of empire (John H. Yoder, *The Christian Witness to the State* [Scottsdale, PA: Herald, 2002], 95–97). However, the implications and meaning of Constantine's reign relative to this phenomenon have recently been contested by some scholars (D. Stephen Long, "Yoderian Constantinianism?," in *Constantine Revisited: Leithart, Yoder, and the Constantinian Debate*, ed. John D. Roth [Eugene, OR: Pickwick Publications, 2013], 100–23). As a result, I redefine this phenomena as *Evangelicanism* to sidestep this debate and avoid unnecessary distraction from the task at hand. For Mason, progress and "higher development" were both spiritual and material. This included the heart lifted to God and outreach to fellow African Americans and other marginalized groups. Beyond the Wesleyan and Keswickian higher life teachings, this was not purely spiritual, but holistic progress—mind, body, soul, and spirit. Mason used his own commitment to spiritual growth as an exemplar of God's ability to overcome structural barriers of race and class. While a proponent of education and acquiring property, clean living was the bedrock for success in life (Daniels, "A More Excellent Way," 111–28).

[55] Smith, "Seeking the Just Society," 104–109.

[56] Frederick L Ware, "Charles Harrison Mason as Sign Reader and Interpreter," in *With Signs Following: The Life and Ministry of Charles Harrison Mason*, ed. Raynard Smith (St. Louis, MO: Chalice, 2015), 48–49.

Abram's descendants (Gen 16:10); and the multiplication of his descendants as the sand of the sea with victory over their enemies (Gen 22:17), will all be completely and ultimately fulfilled.[57] God's oath to Abraham, referenced in Luke 1:73–75, will culminate in the eschatological kingdom where righteousness dwells. This end time reality is defined by the ethical righteousness and justice demanded by Yahweh but historically sporadic and elusive to the nation of Israel (cf. Isa 48:1– 22; 59:1–21). In this passage, it is not just Israel, but the whole world that has embraced holiness and righteousness. Mason understands holiness as the path or highway to the fulfillment of God's oath to Abraham and God's redemptive purpose through Abraham.[58]

Therefore, holiness and righteousness are the prerequisites for the fulfillment of God's covenantal promises to Abraham. While this passage is eschatological, Mason effectively holds to a realized eschatology, where there is a clear "now and not yet" tension. As the saints await the eschaton, or the coming of the Lord, they enjoy a modicum of the blessing of Abraham, including peace, provision, power, healing, deliverance, and victory over natural and spiritual enemies. There is no strict promise/fulfillment hermeneutic established between the Old Testament and the New Testament. Mason's canonical approach envisions all of Scripture as the inspired, infallible word of God and creates continuity between the testaments. While affirming material blessings, Mason's sense of continuity emphasizes spiritual benefits, with both material and spiritual blessings being covenantal and conditional. In general, this promotes a cumulative effect where the New Testament revelation does not entirely supplant that of the Old Testament. The Old Testament themes regarding divine retribution upon the wicked, with material healing and prosperity for the righteous, are united with the spiritual blessings of the New Testament. This more capacious perspective makes ample room for both spiritual and material blessing and thereby provides a robust theological perspective suited for the situatedness and lived realities of Mason and his oppressed people. Scripture is not interpreted through some abstract philosophical lens, but in the context of their location and adopted in response to the complexity of their lived reality.[59]

In this same sermon, it is significant that out of all the superlatives applied to believers in 1 Peter 2:9, Mason focuses on "holy nation." In general, the focus of

---

[57] Gary Smith, *The New American Commentary: Isaiah 40–66* (Nashville, TN: Broadman & Holman, 2009), 627.

[58] This notion is captured in COGIC hymnody. An example is the congregation song entitled, "There's A Highway to Heaven." The chorus is insightful: "It's a highway to Heaven/None can walk up there but the pure in heart/It's a highway to heaven/I am walking up the King's highway." Clemmons, *Bishop C. H. Mason and the Roots of the Church of God in Christ*, 164.

[59] Amos Yong, *Spirit-Word-Community: Theological Hermeneutics in Trinitarian Perspective* (Eugene, OR: Wipf and Stock, 2006), 262–63.

holiness is to create a community in which the character of God as exemplified by the people of God overflows in love for neighbor and alien residents as themselves. By covenantal observance, Israel was to be a community sanctified by God's gracious righteousness. This was to enable their response to the divine call as a holy nation and as a kingdom of priests, set aside as agents of redemptive grace in the world.[60] In living out their calling, not only did Mason and the COGIC create a distinct community and way of being in the world that undermined the religious, social, and cultural power structures of the day, but as noted, they created an alternate reality. In this alternate universe, those who were marginalized in their natural location and vocation were welcomed and invited to hold power, position, and prestige in their spiritual location and vocation. In Zion, they thrived as bishops, pastors, church mothers, missionaries (i.e., leading women), teachers, ministers, deacons, brothers, and sisters in a world structured around the place where God's presence dwelt.[61] Indeed, despite the downward pull of daily life, living this type of life created a self-understanding maintained by the saints as a "peculiar people" (KJV), "a people for his own" (NET), "God's very own possession" (NLT), and "a people for his possession" (ESV).

COGIC Articles of Religion on Holiness as Wholeness

An example of the holistic dimensions of sanctification is demonstrated in the narrative of God's deliverance of the Hebrew boys in Daniel 3. This text was included in the article of religion on salvation because it demonstrates God's power and ability to deliver. "Salvation comes from God through Christ. He is our strong deliverance. Daniel 3:17: 'If it be so, our God whom we serve is able to deliver us from the burning fiery furnace, and he will deliver us out of thine hand, Oh, King. By grace are we saved through faith and that not of yourselves: it is the gift of God.' Eph 2:8. 'It comes to us

---

[60] Burgess and McGee, *Dictionary of Pentecostal and Charismatic Movements*, 430.

[61] In redemptive history, Zion develops as the dwelling place of God. Here, God is in the midst of his people. The Lord loved and chose Zion (Ps 78:68; 132:13) where his glorious presence rested (Ps 50:1, 2). His fire was in Zion, where he was enthroned (Ps 9:11; 99:1, 2) and ruled over the nations (Isa 24:23). Zion as the city of God is the object of all who thirst for the presence of God (Ps 42:1, 2; 63:1, 2). The Lord is the strength of Zion. Therefore, it will never fall (Ps 46:5). All who hate Zion will be put to shame (Ps 129:5) ("Zion, Daughter of," in *Baker Encyclopedia of the Bible*, eds. Walter A. Elwell and Barry J. Beitzel, 2 vols. [Grand Rapids, MI: Baker Book House, 1988], 2202–2204). For Mason and the COGIC, the Zion motif carried significant freight, and represented their affinity with the ancient people of God, and more importantly, being a dwelling place for the presence of God. An excerpt from an early COGIC publication concerning the annual convocation is instructive of their self-understanding: "'Blow the Trumpet in Zion, sanctify a fast, call a solemn assembly. To sanctify means to set apart for God—a fast to consecrate ourselves for the work He has given us to do, to humble ourselves before God, and to repent of all sin and disobedience in our lives'" (Butler, *Women in the Church of God in Christ*, 72).

through faith in God.'"⁶² According to Weaver, Mason indeed saw deliverance encompassing spiritual and social liberation. In this context, the marginalized could overcome both personal and social encumbrances. Mason even contended that his own experience of sanctification produced his religious transformation. This is true because the gospel not only removes corruption, but regenerates a person, making all things new. This regeneration impacts both the spiritual and social trajectory of a person. In fact, sanctification held the promise of transformation for both individuals and communities.⁶³ While salvation and sanctification may be theologically distinct, in the lived theology of the "sanctified church," sanctification is the goal of salvation. The terms are almost interchangeable.

It is noteworthy that deliverance is connected to Daniel 3:17. In the third chapter of Daniel, three young Hebrew exiles, under the threat of death, refuse to worship the graven image of Nebuchadnezzar, king of Babylon. While resisting the seduction of state induced idolatry, Shadrach, Meshach, and Abednego are exposed to the overwhelming power of the state via the king. They refuse to bow down and are cast into a blazing furnace that is stoked to be seven times hotter to express the king's anger at their perceived insolence. Not only does God miraculously deliver them from the fiery furnace, but they emerge completely unscathed, and are also promoted to positions of prominence in Babylon.

Most importantly, Yahweh is glorified. Laws are even changed to revere Yahweh as a unique and powerful god. In addition, both the king and the state are transformed as a result of Shadrach, Meshach, and Abednego's sanctification and commitment to Yahweh. Clearly, this passage holds promise for both spiritual and social transformation, as personal faithfulness in the face of persecution can lead to radical individual, communal, and political change through the power of God. Not only were the young men delivered from the "enemy" of death, but also experienced social uplift by being promoted to positions of prominence in Babylon. The exilic consciousness or being "in Babylon, but not of Babylon" created space for them to live and even serve in Babylon, while not succumbing to the pagan and godless practices of the king or the state. Furthermore, the concept of salvation is couched in the language of liberation or being made free, as stated below:

> Salvation comes when a man believes the truth of the Gospel. "Ye shall know the truth and the truth shall make you free." St. John 8:32 . . . "Because it is written, Be ye holy: for I am holy." 1ˢᵗ Peter 1:16. Salvation is deliverance from dangers and enemies. In its ordinary use, the word is used to denote deliverance from sin through faith in Christ by the Power of God. The Gospel of Jesus Christ through

---

⁶² Jones and Bryant, *Manual of the Church of God in Christ*, 7.
⁶³ Weaver, "Mark the Perfect Man," 60.

faith in the believer is salvation from sin, shame, and disgrace. Ex. 14:13; Luke 1:69.[64]

Salvation demands believing the truth of the gospel and imitating the holiness of God. Using the language of deliverance, salvation is deliverance from dangers, enemies, sin, shame, and disgrace through faith in Christ by the power of God. The biblical references in support of this position are also instructive. Exodus 14:13 states, "And Moses said unto the people, Fear ye not, stand still, and see the salvation of the LORD, which he will shew to you today: for the Egyptians whom ye have seen today, ye shall see them again no more forever." According to theologian James Evans, African Americans read the Bible with "new eyes" informed by their oppression and desire for liberation. He argues that

> The Exodus experience was an archetypal myth that, while drawn from Scripture, became the lens through which the Bible was read. . . . The Exodus account reflected in a striking way the experience of the slaves. It required no stretch of the imagination to see the trials of the Israelites as paralleling the trials of the slaves, Pharaoh and his army as oppressors, and Egyptland as the South.[65]

Following this train of thought, Raynard Smith contends that God as liberator emerged from the slaves' reading of Exodus. This hermeneutic influenced Mason as he recognized that just as divine intervention ended slavery, the same would be required to bring racial justice and equality after slavery.[66] Given this framework, for Mason and the COGIC, salvation expands beyond mere spiritual redemption and freedom from sin. It now includes social and political liberation and uplift. In Exodus 14:13, God will bring a permanent deliverance from every Pharaoh, the archetypal oppressor, and freedom from the associated shame and disgrace. In this context, oppression is inclusive of both material and spiritual encumbrances.

The last example comes from Luke 1:69, where the Scripture says, "And hath raised up an horn of salvation for us in the house of his servant David."[67] This messianic reference to Jesus as "an horn of salvation" metaphorically speaks of his saving power, as horns in Scripture represent power (Ps 75:4–5, 10; 148:14; 2 Sam 22:3). So, the motifs of God's salvific liberation and power are prominent themes in COGIC soteriology. The "new eyes" of Mason and the COGIC can see God's liberating power not just in Exodus, but wherever it is to be found in Scripture, while manifesting in the lives of believers.

---

[64] Jones and Bryant, *Manual of the Church of God in Christ*, 12.

[65] Smith, "Seeking the Just Society," 99–100.

[66] Smith, "Seeking the Just Society," 100.

[67] Smith, "Seeking the Just Society," 100.

Theological Summary

Through affiliations with men such as William Christian, C. P. Jones, and William J. Seymour, Mason cultivated a theological basis for racial equality, political and social uplift. While resisting cultural assimilation, COGIC leaders and members fought to improve the opportunities and promote racial and social uplift in their communities. COGIC scholar, Raynard Smith, contends that God as liberator emerged from the slaves' reading of Exodus. This hermeneutic influenced Mason and others as they recognized that just as divine intervention ended slavery, the same would be required to bring racial justice and equality after slavery.[68] Nevertheless, in this quest for economic, social, and political justice, the holiness ethic was never lost to the fierce urgency of self-preservation. To the contrary, holiness was the catalyst to upward mobility and dogged self-determination in worship and the world.

Furthermore, as demonstrated through the existential realities of this renewal movement, exilic existence is fraught with many challenges related to social marginality, including poverty. During the Great Migration, the COGIC focused expansion on the large, poor urban centers in the North and West, beyond the Jim Crow South. The movement reached a cross-section of people with the gospel. However, understanding that the socially sick, not the socially whole, were in need of a physician, evangelizing the poor and marginalized was strategic and fundamental to COGIC existence. Daniel Smith-Christopher argues that to be exilic is to be missional, as influence is not based on the wielding of worldly, even violent, power, but spiritual integrity.[69] He argues that Scripture has too often been misread to confine social marginality to spiritual matters. Instead, diasporic people present real material and social alternatives over against the dominant cultural mythologies and ideologies.[70] To this point, Cone's argument for liberation speaks of God's preference for the poor:

> If we take seriously the objective reality of divine liberation as a precondition for reconciliation, then it becomes clear that God's salvation is intended for the poor and the helpless, and it is identical with their liberation from oppression. That is why salvation is defined in political terms in the Old Testament and why the prophets take their stand on the side of the poor within the community of Israel. As we have demonstrated, throughout the biblical story, God stands with the weak and against the strong. Thus fellowship with God is made possible by God's righteous activity in the world to set right the conditions for reconciliation. God's setting right the conditions for divine-human fellowship is liberation, without

---

[68] Smith, "Seeking the Just Society," 100.

[69] Daniel L. Smith-Christopher, *A Biblical Theology of Exile* (Minneapolis, MN: Fortress, 2002), 200–201.

[70] Smith-Christopher, *A Biblical Theology of Exile*, 201.

which fellowship would be impossible. To speak of reconciliation apart from God's liberating activity is to ignore the divine basis of the divine-human fellowship.[71]

Consistent with what Cone advocates, Mason took his stance "with the weak and against the strong." This was not white against black, but with the powerless against the powerful. As has been discussed earlier, Mason gave voice, place, and space to the poor. His movement was built on poor people consigned to the social margins of society. According to Clemmons, "Mason always held in tension and balance the dynamic of holiness, spiritual encounter and spiritual empowerment, and prophetic Christian social consciousness."[72] Mason's prophetic witness was not confined to spiritual matters. He greatly helped to meet the spiritual, relational, and material needs of people. While feeding, healing, and clothing the poor, he affirmed the poor by telling them that God loved them but was against their oppressor. He instructed his hearers that God would use natural disaster to devour the rich.[73] By offering creative strategies for spiritual renewal and social equality, Mason's and the COGIC's impact and imprint upon black religious life in America are indelible. I submit that the COGIC posture of radicalizing holiness as the path to wholeness offers a rationale and a calculus that values both spiritual and embodied existence and is thereby worthy of consideration by the broader Christian tradition.

Considerations for the Broader Church

To this point, social location matters in the interpretive process and the creation of meaning, especially theological meaning. Consequently, the world, the word, and worship are experienced through a different set of lenses for those in exile and on the margins. Due to human creatureliness and fallenness, our knowledge is partial, perspectival, finite, and thus fallible, but not altogether skeptical. Although we are all located in bodies with features and frailties that shape our cognitive capabilities, culturally and linguistically, we are all located with ingrained narratives, culturally shaped values, and biases.[74] This understanding should not only encourage interpretive humility, but hopefully promote the active engagement of Afro-Pentecostal and other Christian diasporas and their exilic members as teachers of diasporic strategies for the church to survive and thrive. In the opinion of this author, critical to evangelical renewal is a level of humility that hears and recognizes that the oppressed and exilic communities have something important to say about their lived religious experience.

---

[71] James Cone, *God of the Oppressed*, rev. ed. (Maryknoll, NY: Orbis, 1997), 210.
[72] Clemmons, *Bishop C. H. Mason and the Roots of the Church of God in Christ*, 46.
[73] Weaver, "Mark the Perfect Man," 248–49.
[74] Amos Yong, *Spirit-Word-Community*, 175–84.

Finally, the COGIC has demonstrated through a Pentecostal Holiness theology and a vibrant lived religion that holistic salvation is inclusive of every dimension of human existence. The testimony of Scripture is that salvation brings the *shalom* of God to every aspect of our lived experience (John 10:10). This is inclusive of the spiritual, socio-economic, emotional, and relational aspects of life. As discussed, these aspects of existence were not excluded from Mason's or the COGIC's pursuit of Christian holiness in every dimension of life.

Ivan Hartsfield (ihartsfield@oru.edu) is the senior pastor at Thrive Christian Ministries (2thrivenow.org) and Adjunct Professor in the College of Theology and Ministry at Oral Roberts University, Tulsa Oklahoma, and Grand Canyon University, Phoenix, Arizona, USA.

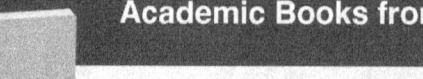

Managing Financial Sector Crisis

Do "Faith" and "Leave it to God" Matter?

Rebecca Attah, Christine Avortri, Emmanuel Appah, and Alexander Preko

Keywords *faith, leave it to God, financial sector clean-up customers, coping strategies, Ghana*

Abstract

The purpose of this study is twofold: first, to elucidate the understanding of two religious concepts related to the financial sector clean-up among bank customers; and second, to explore how these concepts have been employed as strategies to mitigate the impact of financial sector clean-up shocks in Ghana. This qualitative research is anchored in the theory of belief and meaning-making theory, utilizing purposive and snowball sampling methods, with twenty-eight in-depth interviews for data gathering. The findings of this study revealed that financial sector clean-up customers understood religious faith as "aggressive faith," "passive faith," and "offensive faith," which were found to be coping strategies. Additionally, the interviewees shared their thoughts about "leave it to God" as a concept referring to things that we, as human beings, have no control over or things beyond human imagination, such as death, destiny, and natural disasters. These findings could assist financial institutions, regulators, and customers facing financial crises in successfully using religious concepts as coping strategies during times of financial uncertainty. This study's objectives address evident research gaps in financial management literature. This study made the first attempt to combine two theories that proved useful and complementary in explaining the stress and coping mechanisms of financial sector clean-up customers from a developing country perspective, which has been overlooked in early studies.

Introduction

The influence of religious beliefs, practices, and disclosures on financial behavior, including savings, investment, and spending habits, has been well-documented. This study underscored the importance of community relations disclosures in evaluating corporate creditworthiness.[1] Furthermore, a study conducted revealed a positive correlation between religiosity and financial literacy.[2] Despite this, some scholars contend that integrating religious concepts into the analysis of financial behavior might lead to conflicts in financial decision-making.[3] Within management literature, researchers have established a positive relationship between religious beliefs and effective stress management.[4]

Recent bank collapses have occurred on a global scale, including notable institutions such as Silicon Valley Bank and Signature Bank in the US and Credit Suisse in Europe.[5] Although the banking crisis has had worldwide implications, our primary focus will be on the unique circumstances in Ghana. Our investigation will explore the ways individuals in Ghana employ religious concepts to manage stress stemming from bank collapses. By examining this phenomenon within the Ghanaian context, we aim to develop a more profound understanding of religion's role as a coping mechanism during periods of financial turmoil.

The purpose of this study is twofold: first, to elucidate the understanding of two religious concepts, "faith" and "leave it to God," related to the financial sector clean-up among bank customers; and second, to explore how these concepts have been employed as strategies to mitigate the impact of financial sector clean-up shocks. Initiated in 2017, Ghana's financial sector clean-up aimed to address pervasive issues such as corruption, inadequate governance, and mismanagement within the banking sector.[6] However, this study has highlighted that an unintended consequence of policy is non-stationarity, and policy is constantly attempting to achieve conditions that will result in this consequence.[7] This intervention inadvertently led to liquidity challenges for the

---

[1] Zied Ftiti, Maher Jeriji, Sourour Kammoun, Waël Louhichi, and Amel Zenaidi, "Corporate Social Responsibility Disclosure and Corporate Creditworthiness:Evidence from the UK," *International Journal of Finance & Economics*, 2022, https://onlinelibrary.wiley.com/doi/10.1002/ijfe.2733.

[2] Taqadus Bashir, Asba Arshad, Aleena Nazir, and Naghmana Afzal, "Financial Literacy and Influence of Psychosocial Factors," *European Scientific Journal* 9:28 (2013).

[3] Walid Mansour and Mouna Jlassi, "The Effect of Religion on Financial and Investing Decisions," in *Investor Behavior: The Psychology of Financial Planning and Investing*, eds. H. Kent Baker and Victor Ricciardi (Hoboken, NJ: Wiley, 2014), 135–51; Markus Mättö and Mervi Niskanen, "Religion, National Culture and Cross-Country Differences in the Use of Trade Credit: Evidence from European SMEs," *International Journal of Managerial Finance* 15:3 (2019), 350–70.

[4] Stephanie Graham, Susan Furr, Claudia Flowers, and Mary Thomas Burke, "Research and Theory: Religion and Spirituality in Coping with Stress," *Counseling and Values* 46:1 (2001), 2–13.

[5] Stephen G. Cecchetti and Kermit L. Schoenholtz, "Making Banking Safe," *SSRN*, 2023, https://papers.ssrn.com/sol3/papers.cfm?abstract_id=4513903.

[6] Bank of Ghana (BOG), *Bank of Ghana Financial Stability Report*, December 2019, https://www.bog.gov.gh/wp-content/uploads/2020/09/Financial-Stability-Review-Dec-2019.pdf.

[7] Muhammad Ali Nasir and Jamie Morgan, "Paradox of Stationarity? A Policy Target Dilemma for Policymakers," *The Quarterly Review of Economics and Finance* 87 (2020), 142–45.

remaining financial institutions. Consequently, loan demand persisted, withdrawals increased, and customer deposits declined.[8] In this study, we conceptualized "faith" and "leave it to God" as referring to the idea of trusting in a higher power to provide for financial needs and taking a passive approach to managing finances. Despite the importance attributed to the concepts of "faith" and "leave it to God" in the literature, much scholarly attention in exploring how these concepts work with financial sector clean-up customers in the financial sector of a developing country has been overlooked, creating a knowledge gap. Molen et al. examined how people cope with the stress of poverty and found faith to be the main coping strategy.[9] Additionally, some earlier studies discussed how people use the concept of "leave it to God" as a coping mechanism when faced with situations they cannot control.[10] Although these earlier studies have documented the relevance of the concepts, no study has qualitatively (1) explored the understanding of these two religious concepts among financial sector clean-up customers, and (2) assessed how "faith" was used as a coping strategy in the minds of the customers during the waiting time when they were hoping their money would be paid to them. This study adopted belief theory and meaning-making theory to investigate the financial sector clean-up customers' behavior. In the context of financial behavior literature, the theory of planned behavior suggests that beliefs and values can have a significant impact on attitudes toward money and financial decision-making.[11] Additionally, we employed the "meaning-making of coping" concept to elucidate the strategies Ghanaians implemented to manage stress while awaiting the release of their funds during the financial sector clean-up. This theory posits that when confronted with difficult or ambiguous circumstances, individuals may endeavor to comprehend their experiences by constructing narratives or belief systems that enable them to discover meaning and purpose in their lives.[12]

This study assumes that the customers rely on their religious faith as a coping strategy in making meaning while waiting for their savings to be repaid. Some

---

[8] Frederick Affum, "The Unintended Effects of Bank of Ghana's Clean-Up Exercise on Unaffected Financial Institutions: Evidence from Yilo Krobo Municipality, Ghana," *Asian Journal of Economics, Business and Accounting* 17:1 (2020), 1–12.

[9] Kirk Vander Molen, Kieran Fogarty, Michele McGrady, and Mary Lagerwey, "Religious Problem-Solving Styles and Self-Efficacy with Problem-Focused Coping in a Faith-Based Poverty Alleviation Programme," *Mental Health, Religion & Culture* 23:10 (2020), 888–901.

[10] F. Dancel, "Utang Na Loob [A Debt of Goodwill]: A Philosophical Analysis," in *Filipino Cultural Traits: Claro R. Ceniza Lectures,* ed. R. Gripaldo (Washington, DC: Council for Research in Values and Philosophy, 2005), 4–109.

[11] Icek Ajzen, "The Theory of Planned Behavior," *Organizational Behavior and Human Decision Drocesses* 50:2 (1991), 179–211.

[12] S. E. Park, W. H. Lee, and K. H. Oh, (2017), "The Prayer Experiences of Patients with End-stage Cancer," *The Korean Journal of Hospice and Palliative Care* 20:1 (2017), 26–36.

customers also make sense of the situation by leaving the "payment of their savings" to God to decide for them. Significantly, this study is valuable to various stakeholders, including policymakers, financial institutions, practitioners, and customers globally. Specifically, we have contributed to the extant literature in three ways. First, our study is among the few on the African continent that have attempted to extend the understanding of these religious concepts in the financial sector, with a focus on customers of financial institutions affected by the clean-up. This new insight will support the financial literacy agenda, which aids in educating individuals on how to earn, spend, save, borrow, and protect their money. Second, our findings have demonstrated the relevance of "faith" as a coping strategy during financial sector clean-ups. Third, we have made a contextual contribution by filling a knowledge gap through an investigation into the neglected field in the financial literature from the developing country perspective. The study is structured into three sections. Section one includes an introduction and literature review, while section two explains the methods used for the study. The last section deals with the discussion of results, conclusions, implications, and future research directions.

Literature Review

Contextual Background

The financial sector clean-up in Ghana was initiated by the Bank of Ghana in 2017, with the aim of improving the stability and reliability of the financial sector.[13] The clean-up was a comprehensive exercise aimed at addressing various issues affecting the sector, including the poor financial health of some banks, weak corporate governance practices, and inadequate risk management systems.[14] The Bank of Ghana took several measures to address these issues, such as revoking licenses of some banks, merging certain banks, and injecting capital into others. The financial sector clean-up was a significant event in the history of Ghana's financial sector, as it had far-reaching implications for the financial sector, customers, and the economy as a whole. On August 16, 2019, the Bank of Ghana successfully concluded the restructuring of banking, specialized deposit-taking (SDI), and non-bank financial institutions (NBFI) sectors, an initiative that commenced in August 2017. This restructuring involved revoking the licenses of nine universal banks, 347 microfinance companies (with 155 already non-operational), thirty-nine microcredit companies/money lenders (ten non-operational), fifteen savings and loans companies, eight finance house companies, and

---

[13] BOG, *Bank of Ghana Financial Stability Report*.
[14] BOG, *Bank of Ghana Financial Stability Report*.

two non-bank financial institutions that were no longer in operation.[15] The clean-up was expected to improve the stability and reliability of the financial sector, which would, in turn, boost the confidence of depositors and investors in the sector.[16] However, Affum's study revealed the following effects: deposits remained consistently low while withdrawals surged substantially.

This trend was attributed to widespread fears of financial losses and diminished confidence within the banking community. In contrast, lending activities persisted undisturbed. Customers previously associated with defunct financial institutions redirected their loan applications to those still operational. However, certain institutions faced difficulties in fulfilling loan requests due to liquidity constraints stemming from limited cash deposits.[17]

Theoretical Underpinning

The theory of beliefs and meaning-making theory are the two underlying theories deployed for this study within the financial sector clean-up literature in non-Western country contexts. First, the theory of beliefs was applied to explore insights into financial sector clean-up customers' beliefs in the Supreme Being for repayment of their locked-up monies. The second theory was useful to explain how customers made meaning out of the situation: locked-up monies during the financial sector clean-up exercises.

Theory of Belief

The theory of belief is considered a general framework for reasoning with unforeseen events or uncertainty.[18] Typically, beliefs are associated with cognition or the brain, representing how people make sense of something they are thinking about. For example, a person's brain might anticipate how things should relate to each other. Early scholars established a connection between beliefs and faith, as faith involves belief in a spiritual force. The doxastic theory holds that belief is a cognitive attitude that involves accepting a proposition as true.[19] For many around the world, religious belief centers

---

[15] BOG, *Notice of Revocation of Licences of Insolvent Savings and Loans Companies and Finance Houses, and Appointment of a Receiver*, https://www.bog.gov.gh/wp-content/uploads/2019/08/Revocation-of-Licenses-of-SDIs-16.8.19.pdf.

[16] BOG, *Bank of Ghana Financial Stability Report*.

[17] Affum, "The Unintended Effects of Bank Of Ghana's Clean-Up Exercise on Unaffected Financial Institutions."

[18] Robert J. Ackermann, *Belief and Knowledge* (London: Palgrave, 1972), 31–50.

[19] Francesco Berto and Mark Jago, *Impossible Worlds* (Oxford: Oxford University Press, 2019).

on an unseen realm that, though distinct, is intimately connected to the visible one.[20] To these believers, the ethereal world is an essential component of existence, not just an abstract contrast to the physical realm.[21] This theory suggests that beliefs are formed as a result of a combination of evidence, experience, and reasoning.

The theory of planned behavior (TPB) posits that human behavior is influenced by three key considerations: behavioral beliefs, which pertain to the anticipated consequences and experiences of the behavior; normative beliefs, which concern the expectations and behaviors deemed acceptable by significant others; and control beliefs, which relate to factors that might either aid or hinder the execution of the behavior.[22] For our analysis, we will delve deeper into the concept of behavioral belief, exploring its relationship with faith and expectations. Belief is primarily aimed at guiding action rather than declaring absolute truth.[23] Additionally, other scholars assert that the belief in God is the fundamental cornerstone of the Christian faith.[24] They articulate that to believe in God means to trust him, align with his purposes, commit oneself to him, and live aware of his omnipresence. To believers, the entire world is a testament to God's presence.[25] An individual's beliefs shape their perception and understanding of the world. In this study, the affected customers believed in the Supreme Being as a source of a repayment solution to their situation. This study assumes that faith begins with one's belief and trust in the Supreme Being, that God will help in finding solutions to the repayment of their locked-up funds. With this assertion, we used the theory of belief to explore individual customers' faith in retrieving their money from financial institutions. The importance of the theory to this study can be understood by expanding the frontiers of the theory within the domain of financial sector clean-up literature, a neglected but essential area in a developing country context.

---

[20] Stephen Ellis and Gerrie Ter Haar, *Worlds of Power: Religious Thought and Political Practice in Africa*, vol. 1 (New York: Oxford University Press, USA, 2004).

[21] Gerrie ter Haar, *Religion and Development: What's in Two Names*, Symposium on the 10th Anniversary of the Chair of Religion and Development, 11 June 2009 (The Hague: Institute of Social Studies, 2009).

[22] Icek Ajzen, "Behavioral Interventions Based on the Theory of Planned Behavior," 2006, https://people.umass.edu/aizen/pdf/tpb.intervention.pdf.

[23] Jonathan Leicester, "The Nature and Purpose of Belief," *The Journal of Mind and Behavior* 29:3 (2008), 217–37.

[24] Alvin Plantinga and Nicholas Wolterstorff, eds., *Faith and Rationality: Reason and Belief in God* (Notre Dame/London: University of Notre Dame Press, 1983).

[25] Plantinga and Wolterstorff, eds., *Faith and Rationality*.

Meaning-Making Theory

Alternatively, the role of religion as a meaning system in coping with adversity was investigated by Park.[26] Subsequently, the meaning-making theory was formulated, differentiating between global and situational meaning, as well as between "meaning-making efforts" and "meaning made."[27] The findings reveal that the connections between religion and adjustment fluctuate over time following a loss, with these associations being mediated by meaning-making coping strategies. Building upon this research, Davis et al. presented the theory of religious meaning-making and attachment within the context of disasters, underscoring the significance of religious meaning-making in managing adverse situations.[28] By utilizing these two theoretical frameworks, we examined the methods Ghanaians employed to navigate stress and maintain hope of recovering their deposits during the financial sector clean-up. In particular, we investigated the ways in which their beliefs, attitudes, and perceived control shaped their behavior, as well as how they leveraged religion and meaning-making approaches to address the challenges they encountered. Overall, this study embraces the assumption that customers of the financial institutions hold on to their religious faith as a coping strategy in making meaning and getting their savings paid back.

Faith

The concept of faith has been a topic of discussion for centuries and has been explored from various perspectives, including religious, psychological, and philosophical. Faith is often associated with hope, optimism, and resilience, as it provides a foundation for individuals to cope with life's challenges. The Bible verse, "Now faith is the substance of things hoped for, the evidence of things not seen" (Heb 11:1), is one of the most recognized definitions of faith. In this literature review, we will explore how faith influences coping strategies in different contexts.

---

[26] Crystal L. Park, "Religion as a Meaning-making Framework in Coping with Life Stress," *Journal of Social Issues* 61:4 (2005), 707–29.

[27] Crystal L. Park, "Making Sense of the Meaning Literature: An Integrative Review of Meaning Making and Its Effects on Adjustment to Stressful Life Events," *Psychological Bulletin* 136:2 (2010), 257.

[28] Edward B. Davis, Cynthia N. Kimball, Jamie D. Aten, Benjamin Andrews, Daryl R. Van Tongeren, Joshua N. Hook, Don E. Davis, Pehr Granqvist, and Crystal L. Park, "Religious Meaning Making and Attachment in a Disaster Context: A Longitudinal Qualitative Study of Flood Survivors," *The Journal of Positive Psychology* 14:5 (2019), 659–71.

Application of Faith as a Coping Tool for Stress Management

Fawns investigated the coping strategies of teachers in managing stress and found that faith-based practices such as prayer, meditation, and spiritual/mystical experiences, as well as beliefs, behaviors, feelings, and involvement in church communities, helped in coping with life challenges. The study revealed that teachers who regularly engaged in these practices had a more positive outlook on life, experienced less stress, and were better equipped to handle difficult situations.[29]

A study conducted by Molen et al. examined how people cope with the stress of poverty and engage with its causes and potential solutions.[30] The study found that individuals who collaborated with God were more likely to utilize problem-focused coping strategies compared to those who did not. Collaborating with God involves trusting in a higher power and seeking guidance through prayer and religious practices. The study showed that individuals who collaborated with God were more likely to act to address the root causes of their poverty and were less likely to experience feelings of helplessness and hopelessness. This suggests that the way in which individuals approach their relationship with a higher power can impact their ability to manage stress and work towards improving their situation.

Similarly, a study by Pargament and Hahn examines how individuals use their faith to cope with major life stressors, including financial stress.[31] The authors found that individuals who used positive religious coping strategies, such as prayer and seeking social support from their religious community, tended to have better financial well-being and outcomes. There has been extensive research on the concept of faith as a coping strategy when dealing with stressful events in the health sector compared to the financial sector. For example, Levine et al. studied breast cancer survivors and found the main themes as: (1) God as a comforting presence; (2) questioning faith; (3) anger at God; (4) spiritual transformation of self and attitude towards others/recognition of own mortality; (5) deepening of faith; (6) acceptance; and (7) prayer by self.[32] Other scholars who also found faith as a key coping strategy when dealing with the uncertainty of their illnesses are Roh et al., McCoy, Carrion et al., and Park et al.[33]

---

[29]Rebecca Lynn Fawns, "Teachers, Faith, and Coping: An investigation," 2006, https://scholarlycommons.pacific.edu/uop_etds/2595/.

[30] Molen, Fogarty, McGrady, and Lagerwey, "Religious Problem-solving Styles and Self-efficacy with Problem-focused Coping in a Faith-based Poverty Alleviation Programme," 888–901.

[31] Kenneth I. Pargament and June Hahn, "God and the Just World: Causal and Coping Attributions to God in Health Situations," *Journal for the Scientific Study of Religion* 25 (1986), 193–207.

[32] Ellen G. Levine, Grace Yoo, Caryn Aviv, Cheryl Ewing, and Alfred Au, "Ethnicity and Spirituality in Breast Cancer Survivors," *Journal of Cancer Survivorship* 1 (2007), 212–25.

[33] Soonhee Roh, Catherine E. Burnette, and Yeon-Shim Lee, "Prayer and Faith: Spiritual Coping among American Indian Women Cancer Survivors," *Health & Social Work* 43:3 (2018), 185–92; **Brenda G. McCoy**, *God Will Get Me Through: African American Women Coping with Breast Cancer and*

Similarly, Donkor and Sandall studied Ghanaian women with infertility problems and concluded that their Christian faith helped them in coping with the stigma of childlessness.[34]

Moreover, in a study by Bradshaw and Ellison, it was revealed that engagement in religious activities and maintaining a belief in an afterlife contributed to reducing the detrimental effects of financial hardship on both objective and subjective aspects of financial distress.[35] Conversely, meditation was identified as an effective strategy for mitigating the negative impacts specifically on objective financial hardship. Overall, these studies suggest that faith can be a valuable resource for individuals dealing with stress and major life challenges.

Leave It to God

The use of "leave it to God" as a coping mechanism for unmet expectations has been widely studied in the literature. According to Dancel, this coping mechanism relies on the belief that the outcome of events and situations is in the hands of a higher power, rather than under human control.[36] Religious coping has been described as a passive form of coping, a form of denial, a defense against anxiety, and the last resort for people in untenable situations.[37]

Pargament et al. conducted a study on the role of various religious coping efforts in dealing with negative events among a sample of 586 members of Christian churches.[38] The study found that beliefs in a just, benevolent God, the experience of God as a supportive partner in coping, involvement in religious rituals, and the search for support through religion were associated with more positive outcomes. Similarly, attributions to God's will appear to represent a benign, external, alternative explanation

---

Implications for Support Groups (Denton, TX: University of North Texas, 2005); Iraida V. Carrion, Malinee Neelamegam, Terri D. Lewinson, Keisha Polonio, and Crystal Bonano, "Words of Wisdom from Older Immigrant Latino/as with Cancer," *Humanities and Social Sciences Communications* 9:1 (2022), 1–7; SoonBok Esther Park, Won Hee Lee, and Kyong Hwan Oh, "The Prayer Experiences of Patients with End-stage Cancer," *The Korean Journal of Hospice and Palliative Care* 20:1 (2017), 26–36.

[34] Ernestina S. Donkor and Jane Sandall, "Coping Strategies of Women Seeking Infertility Treatment in Southern Ghana," *African Journal of Reproductive Health* 13:4 (2009), 81–93.

[35] Matt Bradshaw and Christopher G. Ellison, "Financial Hardship and Psychological Distress: Exploring the Buffering Effects of Religion," *Social Science & Medicine* 71:1 (2010), 196–204.

[36] Dancel, "Utang na loob: A Philosophical Analysis."

[37] Kenneth I. Pargament, "God Help Me: Advances in the Psychology of Religion and Coping," *Archive for the Psychology of Religion* 24:1 (2002), 48–63.

[38] Kenneth I. Pargament, David S. Ensing, Kathryn Falgout, Hannah Olsen, Barbara Reilly, Kimberly Van Haitsma, and Richard Warren, "God Help Me: (I): Religious Coping Efforts as Predictors of the Outcomes to Significant Negative Life Events," *American Journal of Community Psychology* 18 (1990), 793–824.

to chance attributions.[39] Wilt et al. conducted a study on religious coping and perceived divine intervention in relation to managing life challenges and promoting spiritual growth.[40] The study found that collaborative religious coping had the strongest positive relationship with spiritual growth and struggle resolution, followed by active religious surrender and passive religious deferral. Additionally, perceived divine intervention independently predicted spiritual growth and struggle resolution.

Other studies have explored the effectiveness of specific religious coping strategies, such as surrendering to God's will. Wong-McDonald and Gorsuch found that surrendering to God's will can be an effective coping strategy for managing stress and challenges and is associated with positive religious and spiritual outcomes.[41] Finally, a study on the Attachment to God Inventory (AGI) and Religious Coping Activities Scale (RCAS) found that individuals with secure and preoccupied attachment styles used more Christian activities and ideas in coping, while those with a fearful attachment style showed greater anger and doubt toward God.[42] Overall, the literature suggests that religious coping can be an effective way to manage stress and challenges, especially when combined with a collaborative approach and a belief in divine intervention. Different religious coping strategies may be more effective for different individuals depending on their attachment style and beliefs.

Research Methodology

To investigate the role of "faith" and "leave it to God" concepts in helping financial sector clean-up customers cope with the 2017–2019 financial crisis in Ghana, we employed a qualitative research approach with interpretative phenomenological design utilizing interview-based methods. This study focuses on the 2017–2019 financial sector clean-up period due to the significant number of bank collapses and the widespread loss of customers' savings. The clean-up aimed to restore stability and integrity within the Ghanaian financial sector. We used the interpretative phenomenological design to explore how customers of the financial cleanup made sense

---

[39] Kenneth I. Pargament and June Hahn, "God and the Just World: Causal and Coping Attributions to God in Health Situations," *Journal for the Scientific Study of Religion* 25 (1986), 193–207.

[40] Joshua A. Wilt, Nick Stauner, Valencia A. Harriott, Julie J. Exline, and Kenneth I. Pargament, "Partnering with God: Religious Coping and Perceptions of Divine Intervention Predict Spiritual Transformation in Response to Religious-Spiritual Struggle," *Psychology of Religion and Spirituality* 11:3 (2019), 278.

[41] Ana Wong-McDonald and Richard L. Gorsuch, "Surrender to God: An Additional Coping Style?," *Journal of Psychology and Theology* 28:2 (2000), 149–61.

[42] Laura B. Cooper, A. Jerry Bruce, Marsha J. Harman, and Marcus T. Boccaccini, "Differentiated Styles of Attachment to God and Varying Religious Coping Efforts," *Journal of Psychology and Theology* 37:2 (2009), 134–41.

of their personal and social worlds, anchored on their faith and their understanding of what the Supreme God can do to retrieve their monies.

Ghana presents a compelling case for examination in 2022 for several reasons. First, this study was conducted during a time of severe economic crisis in the country. For instance, the Ghanaian currency, the cedi, lost 57% of its value against the US dollar between January and October 2022,[43] resulting in a substantial increase in Ghana's debt from $7.5 billion in 2012 to $29.4 billion in October 2022.[44] Second, Ghana experienced high inflation (40.4%) in October 2022,[45] along with banking crises involving non-performing loans, government bond holder instability, treasury bill rates, and Ghana's domestic debt exchange program (haircut), among other issues. Collectively, these challenges created a financial crisis reminiscent of the 2017–2019 period within the Ghanaian financial sector. This context provided the impetus for our research team to conduct the current study.

Subsequently, we used purposive sampling, snowballing, and convenience sampling approaches with the aim of reaching out only to financial sector clean-up customers who were ready, willing, and available to take the interview. This working population was adopted due to the aim of this paper. Purposive sampling was used to scan for only those affected by the financial sector clean-up.

Snowball sampling was useful in referrals, where some interviewees recommended their friends or relatives who had similar experiences to be interviewed. In addition, convenience sampling was utilized in gathering data from interviewees who were willing and available for the interview. We interviewed twenty-eight participants, which is in line with the recommendation for a qualitative sample size using an in-depth interview approach.[46] Furthermore, we were guided by the rich (quality) and thick (quantitative) data collection strategy offered by Saunders and Lewis, keeping in mind the data saturation method to achieve the purpose of this study.[47] The data saturation method was to halt the interview when no new information was discovered in the data gathering. This justified the appropriateness of the sample size used in this study. To avoid recall bias in this study, we were guided by the work of Moreno-Serra et al., where the interview

---

[43] Ekwo Dontoh, "Ghana Gold Miners Ordered to Sell 20% of Refined Bullion to Central Bank," *Bloomberg.com*, November 25, 2022, https://www.bloomberg.com/news/articles/2022-11-25/gold-miners-ordered-to-sell-20-of-refined-bullion-to-ghana.

[44] "Ghana External Debt," *Census and Economic Information Center*, accessed April 8, 2023, https://www.ceicdata.com/en/indicator/ghana/external-debt.

[45] BOG, "Monetary Policy Committee Press Release," November 28, 2022, https://www.bog.gov.gh/wp-content/uploads/2022/11/MPC-Press-Release-November-2022-1.pdf.

[46] John W. Creswell and Cheryl N. Poth, *Qualitative Inquiry and Research Design: Choosing among Five Approaches* (Thousand Oaks, CA: Sage Publications, 2016).

[47] Mark Saunders and Philip Lewis, *Doing Research in Business and Management* (London: Pearson, 2017).

questions were carefully designed to reflect the financial sector clean-up incidents in 2017–2019.[48] We also welcomed the interviewees by first providing a short narrative of the clean-up incidents, which lasted for an average of three minutes, to warm-up the discussion (icebreaker) before the main questions were posed to the interviewees.

For this study, a comprehensive interview guide was developed in English, including probing questions that aimed to address the specific objectives of the research.

1. Which financial institution were you saving with before the financial sector clean-up? Do you have a particular financial institution that you will only save with now? Why?
2. How did you perceive the financial sector clean-up in your own ways?
3. What are the specific impacts of the clean-up on your saving habits?
4. How does the "faith" concept help you to cope with financial shock?
5. How does the "leave it to God" concept help you to cope with financial shock?
6. What will you look for when choosing a financial institution after the clean-up?

To ensure the quality of the interview guide, it was reviewed by four financial experts from industry and academia who provided feedback on "faith" and "leave it to God" related questions. The researchers carefully considered and incorporated the experts' suggestions before conducting the final interviews from November 2022 to January 2023. The experts suggested rephrasing of questions 2 and 4 for clarity as these questions were considered as leading and double-barreled questions. Each interview, which lasted between 45 to 60 minutes, followed a predetermined format.

Before participating, the interviewees were informed of the purpose of the study and completed a consent form. Confidentiality and anonymity were guaranteed to ensure ethical considerations were met. We adopted thematic analysis with the support of NVivo 12, using the "in vivo coding" method, which allows the researchers to use the actual words of the interviewees in the coding process. To achieve rigor in reliability, validity, and trustworthiness in the data analysis and reporting of findings, we followed the recommended steps offered by Nowell et al. in their study striving to meet the trustworthiness criteria.[49] First, we individually read and familiarized ourselves with the transcriptions (data). This allowed the researchers to make follow-up phone calls for clarity on some of the points made by the interviewees. Second, we generated twenty-four initial codes from the data, which allowed the researchers to understand what was happening in the data. Third, during the coding process, we identified and collated all

---

[48] Rodrigo Moreno-Serra, Misael Anaya-Montes, Sebastián León-Giraldo, and Oscar Bernal, "Addressing Recall Bias in (Post-) Conflict Data Collection and Analysis: Lessons from a Large-scale Health Survey in Colombia," *Conflict and Health* 16:1 (2022), 1–14.

[49] Lorelli S. Nowell, Jill M. Norris, Deborah E. White, and Nancy J. Moules, "Thematic Analysis: Striving to Meet the Trustworthiness Criteria," *International Journal of Qualitative Methods* 16:1 (2017), https://journals.sagepub.com/doi/full/10.1177/1609406917733847.

potential texts into three themes. Fourth, we reviewed the themes to find out whether there was coherence between the coded data extracted and the themes. Fifth, we defined and named the themes as "faith as coping strategies," "making meaning of leaving it to God," and "faith understanding" in the financial sector clean-up context. We also defined and named three sub-themes as "passive faith," "aggressive faith," and "offensive faith." Sixth, we presented concise, coherent, and logical findings of this study.

Findings

The data coding yielded mixed results. Some interviewees held a 50/50 belief that their money would be paid back, while others relied solely on their faith in a higher power or the intervention of a Supreme Being to receive their savings. In summary, the coding revealed coping strategies that emerged in relation to how the "faith" of the customers enabled them to cope with the situation.

Table 1: "Faith" as Coping Strategies

Coping Types (Themes)	Specific Coping Strategies
Theory of Beliefs	I know God's hand is on me.
	God will intervene on behalf.
Biblical saying (axiom) of intervention	Pray to God to have mercy upon us to get our money.
	God will restore all I lost.
	Prayer meetings every Thursday (collective prayers).
Aggressive Faith	Pray on my own to God (individual prayers). Morning prayers and kept asking Him for a favor. God will fight for me.
	I have handed everything to God.
Passive Faith	God knows what is good for us.
	God knows how we will survive.
	I request God's intervention.
Offensive Faith	I give a seed of sacrifice regularly on the altar.
	God was my only hope.
	I called on him day and night.
	God is in control of everything.
	Our pastor preached to encourage us.
	I know I am not alone; God is there for me.
	I was disappointed in my God for allowing this to happen to me.
Meaning making theory	"If I get it fine and if I don't fine."

(Leave it to God) Common saying (axiom) of relaxing the mind.	"I am still young, so life continues." "Life itself is full of breaks and things happened for a reason." "Nothing happens for nothing; it is good or bad."

"Leave it to God."

Based on the assumptions of the meaning-making theory, participants construed three varied understandings of the "leave it to God" concept. First, it can be used to understand things that we (human beings) have no control over or things beyond human imagination, such as death, destiny, and natural disasters. Second, some participants believed that in the field of business, there is no room for "leave it to God." The fact that they have given their money, they need to get it back through all means. Third, the concept can be applied depending on one's amount of money (savings); if it is a small amount of money, they can leave it to God.

> "My money with the bank was small, so I left it to God." (A Christian, Businessman, 24 years old)

> "[…] 'Life itself is full of breaks and things happen for a reason'. We live in this world without knowing what our God has for us." (A Christian and Businessman, 36 years old)

> "I will never save with any bank in my life. […] I lost a huge sum of money, and now I have decided to keep my money in my room or on my MoMo account (phone account with phone company)." (A Muslim Businesswoman, 39 years old)

"Meaning of Faith"

In this context, "faith" is understood as a deep-seated belief in a higher power, which provides individuals with the conviction that their efforts will be rewarded in the end. The interviewees expressed their faith in Supreme Beings and the actions they take to ensure the eventual return of their lost savings. Interestingly, it was evidenced that the interviewees made meaning from the financial crisis as "passive faith," "aggressive faith," and "offensive faith." This signifies that the theory on meaning making was really relevant in supporting the forms of faith discovered in the analysis. The extractions from the data are shown in the Table 1.

For the Christian businesswoman, faith is demonstrated through regular offerings and sacrifices made at church to strengthen her relationship with God. She believes that these actions will help her recover her lost money. Similarly, the Muslim trader has faith that Allah will restore what she has lost, even if it does not happen immediately.

In both cases, faith serves as a source of hope and perseverance for these individuals, guiding them through challenging times and motivating them to continue taking actions that they believe will eventually lead to the recovery of their savings.

Discussion of Results

The study seeks to explore the understanding of two religious concepts related to the financial sector clean-up of customers, which are anchored on the belief and meaning-making theories. In all, the findings substantiate that customers made meaning of the situation by having beliefs in a Supreme Being as coping strategies in getting their money paid to them. These findings on "faith" and "leave it to God" supported the meaning-making theory and belief theory, strengthening the argument that one's faith is about having the belief or feeling that something will happen one day. Empirically, it is evidenced in the study's findings that customers believed in their faith that the Supreme God would intervene or assist them in having their money paid. This is regarded as one of the contributions of this study to finance literature from a developing country perspective.

Evidently, the findings of our study showcased that the faith of the affected customers played a significant role in managing the shocks and trauma they experienced. For example, the preaching and support by their religious leaders during the time of crisis brought comfort to them. Furthermore, this study has made the first attempt to contribute to finance literature by extending faith as a coping strategy to manage crises in the financial sector and regrouping "faith" as a coping strategy into "aggressive," "passive," and "offensive faith" dimensions, which differentiate our findings from earlier studies by Levine et al., Roh et al., McCoy, Carrion et al., Park et al., and Donkor and Sandall, in faith-related subjects.[50] We operationalized aggressive faith as customers' active engagement in religious activities such as daily prayers to God, placing money on the altar, sacrifices, fasting, regular prayer meetings, and engaging the support of their religious leaders. According to literature, those who were involved in these aggressive religious activities found more meaning in their situation and overcame their stress faster.[51] "Passive Faith" is considered as customers who were more relaxed and trusted God as overseeing every situation. They, therefore, resorted to statements or

---

[50] Levine, Yoo, Aviv, Ewing, and Au, "Ethnicity and Spirituality in Breast Cancer Survivors," 212–25; Roh, Burnette, and Lee, "Prayer and Faith," 185–92; McCoy, *God Will Get Me Through*; Carrion, Neelamegam, Lewinson, Polonio, and Bonano, "Words of Wisdom from Older Immigrant Latino/as with Cancer," 1–7; Park, Lee, and Oh, "The Prayer Experiences of Patients with End-stage Cancer," 26–36; Donkor and Sandall, "Coping Strategies of Women Seeking Infertility Treatment in Southern Ghana."

[51] Fawns, "Teachers, Faith, and Coping"; Molen, Fogarty, McGrady, and Lagerwey, "Religious Problem-solving Styles and Self-efficacy with Problem-focused Coping in a Faith-based Poverty Alleviation Programme," 888–901.

words such as "God will fight for me; I have handed everything to God; Allah knows what is good for us; God knows how we will survive; God is in control of everything." "Offensive faith," also regarded as "blame-shifting" faith, is where customers were frustrated and disappointed in their Supreme God for allowing them to suffer from the financial institutions. They expressed their disappointment in this way: "I was disappointed in my God for allowing this to happen to me." Importantly, all these findings strengthen the faith literature.

In line with the findings associated with "leave it to God," this study explored the extent to which customers understood and adopted it as a coping strategy. "Leave it to God" was understood by customers in three formative ways. First, customers who believed that human beings have no control over uncertainty embraced the concept of "leave it to God" as a coping strategy, which gave them a sense of comfort and peace to overcome the shock within a short time. Second, it was understood that in the field of business, there is nothing like "leave it to God"; given that it is an institution that collected their money, they must do all that is requested to get it back. Third, the understanding of the concept also depended on the amount of money customers had in their accounts with the financial institution, influencing the use of "leave it to God" as a coping strategy. These revelations are important to current literature, as these varied understandings buttress the extant findings by Wong-McDonald et al. and Pargament et al., who also found that individuals who embraced the concept of "leave it to God" as a coping strategy in times of uncertainty often had a sense of comfort and peace to overcome the shock.[52] In addition, the meanings constructed by customers in relation to "leave it to God" supported the assumption of the meaning-making theory, which posits that recovering from a stressful event involves reducing the discrepancy between its appraised meaning and global beliefs and goals. This signifies that coping with stressful situations like financial crises, where customers can engage or embrace the "leave it to God" concept, helps to reduce their discrepancies.

Conclusion

In conclusion, the study has highlighted the role of faith and the concept of "leave it to God" as coping strategies for managing shock during the financial sector clean-up in Ghana. The findings suggest that faith can be a significant source of comfort, hope, and meaning-making for affected customers. However, the effectiveness of faith as a coping strategy depends on the individual's approach and operationalization of the two

---

[52] Wong-McDonald and Gorsuch, "Surrender to God," 149–61; Pargament, Ensing, Falgout, Olsen, Reilly, Van Haitsma, and Warren, "God Help Me," 793–824.

concepts (leave it to God, faith in God) in the context of their religious beliefs and practices.

Moreover, the study shows that the concept of "leave it to God" has varied meanings and implications for affected customers. While some find comfort in the idea of surrendering control to a higher power, others see it as incompatible with the pursuit of justice and restitution. The study also suggests that the amount of money individuals have at stake with the collapsed financial institutions can influence their coping strategies. Overall, this study sheds light on the complex interplay between two religious concepts (faith and leave it to God) as coping strategies and financial sector crises in Ghana, providing insights for further research and practical interventions. This study not only classified how people respond to and make meaning of faith, but also provided a comprehensive overview of religious practices and activities that demonstrate how they apply their faith during crises. We have also extended the financial literature by exploring varied understandings of the "leave it to God" concept in a financial context, from both global and emerging economy perspectives, which has been neglected in prior studies.

Implications

Theoretically, this study extends two psychological theories, belief and meaning-making theories, to understand how affected customers of collapsed financial institutions apply their faith and perceive the Supreme God as having authority over every occurrence. These theories imply that the level of meaning customers of financial institutions make of their faith and how they connect to God as a Supreme Being have a significant relationship to how easily they overcome shocks during financial sector crises. The practical implications of this study for stakeholders in the financial sector include the need to acknowledge the role of faith and "leaving it to God" in shaping customers' responses to crises. Financial institutions could collaborate with religious leaders to provide emotional and spiritual support to affected customers. Moreover, policymakers (Bank of Ghana and Ministry of Finance in particular) could consider incorporating religious and cultural dimensions into their crisis management strategies to address the diverse coping strategies of affected customers.

Limitations and Future Research Areas

This study has its own limitations, which call for further research in the future. First, only two religious concepts were considered for this study. There might be other religious concepts that could be used for coping strategies by customers of the affected financial institutions. Second, the themes identified, as well as the coding, should be tested quantitatively for a different perspective on coping strategies in the financial sector. Additionally, these themes should be tested in other sectors apart from the financial sector. This will ensure the relevance of the themes in other sectors and add to the literature. Third, future research should consider examining how the financial sector clean-up has affected the saving behaviors of customers.

Rebecca Attah (Rattah@oru.edu) is an Associate Professor in the College of Business, Oral Roberts University, Tulsa, Oklahoma, USA.

Christine Avortri (Christine.avortri@cibgh.org) is Head of Professional Education and Development, Chartered Institute of Bankers, Ghana.

Emmanuel Appah (e.appah@ewu.edu) is Assistant Professor of Finance, Edward Waters University, Jacksonville, Florida, USA.

Alexander Preko (alexander.preko@upsamail.edu.gh) is a faculty member in the Department of Marketing, University of Professional Studies, Accra, Ghana.

Pentecostalism and Current Development in West Africa

Reimagining the Pentecostal Landscape, Politics, and Vision

Fred Cudjoe Adadey
Barnabas Yisa

Keywords *African Pentecostals, progression, Pentecostal theology, development, politics, imaginary social space*

Abstract

A growing body of literature on African Pentecostals in sub-Saharan Africa is highlighted in this article, highlighting a more defined contribution of African Pentecostals to the development landscape. Until recently, the African Pentecostal development landscape recorded little visibility at the national level, on the assumption that their experience only highlights cultural and theological relevance. However, this emerging visibility has identified, as a conceptual category, an imaginary social space with practical ramification. Based on a critical analytical review of literature, this article examines the shift from traditional Pentecostal theology to a more focused attention on the social transformation created by a post-colonial discourse on development in Africa. We argue that there is an imaginary social space occupied by Pentecostal theology, providing it, not just a voice of influence as a social movement, but a reconstructive identity of power in development that also integrates into political spheres. The cases of the Redeemed Christian Church of God, Nigeria, and the Church of Pentecost, Ghana, exemplify this. Their social space has distinctive expressions that link a constructive integral aspect of Pentecostal theology to contribute to their social responsibility. This article suggests that such an understanding is better explained when considering African Pentecostal progression in this imaginary social space. We recommend that African Pentecostals and the development sector create awareness of this space through a dialogical approach.

Introduction

In recent years, Pentecostal social engagement in West Africa has led to many changes, especially in the community development landscape, accounting for the idea of secular transformation rather than the traditional Pentecostal theology of mission. An evaluation of the shift in theology from the first to the third response to Christianity to "set the captive free"[1] is crucial for understanding the contribution of African Pentecostals to community development. Despite the increasing literature on African Pentecostal development, the area of this "shift" remains insufficiently explained, suggesting a further analysis of this theological, social, and development landscape.

Terminologies such as "development," "African Pentecostals," and the "imaginary social space" employed here allowed us to make some inferences to understand them better. First, we adopt the term "African Pentecostals," often described as Africa's third response to Christianity, to identify their collective contribution, rather than their classification and categories.[2] By focusing on their progression and shift in theology, this article observes that they occupy a "space"[3] that highlights their contribution. Second, development is a broad, complex concept. To map its interaction, we borrowed from Richard Burgess' categories related to the intersecting landscape of politics, economics, human rights, and peacebuilding.[4] Finally, some scholars have identified this "space" as an "emerging development practice" of the African Pentecostal social movement in sub-Saharan Africa.[5] For instance, Johnson Kwabena Asamoah-Gyadu

---

[1] See J. Kwabena Asamoah-Gyadu, "Mission to 'Set the Captives Free': Healing, Deliverance, and Generational Curses in Ghanaian Pentecostalism," *International Review of Mission* 93 (2004), 370–371, 389–406, https://doi.org/10.1111/j.1758-6631.2004.tb00468.x. According to the author, the catchphrase to "set the captive free" is associated with the phenomenon of "healing deliverance" linked with Africa's new Pentecostal/Charismatic Movement and churches, serving as a restoration ministry that encompasses holistic pastoral care to their followers. At the heart of this movement is being freed to partake in the abundant provision of God through Christ. This also in a way de-identifies distinctly African Pentecostals with the emerging liberation theology that took shape in South America and elsewhere around 1968. Although it emerged under similar circumstances (poverty, hardship, deprivation) as the African Pentecostal movement, liberation theology focused more on the worsening social conditions created by dominant cultures. However, for the African Pentecostals, culture was crucial in their theological development. See also Kwame Bediako, "What is the Gospel?," *Transformation* 14:1 (1997), 1–4. Like Badiako mentioned, taking control of one's destiny (spiritual) within God's providence (material) for humankind was their ultimate eschatological call. Hence the infusion of African theological thought into Christianity that allows the gospel to be relevant in all areas of life for human flourishing, setting the captive free.

[2] J. Kwabena Asamoah-Gyadu, *African Charismatics: Current Developments within Independent Indigenous Pentecostalism in Ghana*, vol. 27 (Leiden: Brill, 2005), 14–23.

[3] A conceptual category we identify as imaginary social space with practical ramification.

[4] Richard Burgess, *Nigerian Pentecostalism and Development: Spirit, Power, and Transformation* (London: Routledge, 2020), ii.

[5] Although we considered increasing literature on these various spaces and emerging development practices, we confined ourselves to the works of Burgess (*Nigerian Pentecostalism and Development*),

perceived this space in the Ghanaian context as created by Africa's third response to Christianity based on contextual and cultural factors and its post-independence development challenges.[6] Other researchers agree with this contention by noting sociological, contextual, and theological aspects.[7] For instance, they explained that the introduction of neoliberal reforms, which led to the deterioration of the quality of life and an increased inequality gap in Nigeria, created this space. By leaning on these scholars, this article linked these thoughts and explored the definition of this "space" and likened it to an "imaginary social space." The rationale is that this imaginary social space with practical ramification sits within Africa's third response to Christianity with the realities of neoliberal reforms in context, giving room to African Pentecostalism to operate and experiment with its expression.

This study is divided into three sections. The first section introduces this imaginary social space by examining the African Pentecostal transition, vision, and social movement. Section two explains the post-independence and political landscape in this space, and with cases from the Church of Pentecost, Ghana, and the Redeemed Christian Church of God, Nigeria, it identifies the cause of the theological shift and the uniqueness of the imaginary social space. The last section concludes the article with a missiological implication, serving as an African Pentecostal contribution to occupying this imaginary social space and the need for dialogue.

The Imaginary Social Space

Scholars have yet to clarify whether Africa's third response to Christianity among Pentecostals in sub-Saharan Africa distinctively responds to its features in engaging social conditions across many countries. Although this expression appears inclusive of a development language in economic, socio-political, and cultural landscapes, its growth is fast becoming the expression of faith in sub-Saharan Africa.[8] While in some parts of West Africa, such as Ghana and Nigeria, this growing experience may be seen as

---

Asamoah-Gyadu (*African Charismatics*), and Afe Adogame ("African Christianities and the Politics of Development from Below," *HTS: Theological Studies* 72:4 [2016], 1–11) to enhance and define the imaginary social space.

[6] Asamoah-Gyadu, "*African Charismatics*," 38.

[7] See Burgess, *Nigerian Pentecostalism and Development*, 2–3; Adogame, "African Christianities and the Politics of Development from Below," 1–11.

[8] See Emma Tomalin, "Gender, Religion and Development," in *Handbook of Research on Development and Religion*, ed. Matthew Clarke (Cheltenham, UK: Edward Elgar Publishing, 2013), 453–70; J. Kwabena Asamoah-Gyadu, "Spirit and Empowerment: The African Initiated Church Movement and Development," in *African Initiated Christianity and the Decolonisation of Development* (London: Routledge, 2020), 33–50; Ogbu Kalu, *African Pentecostalism: An Introduction* (Oxford: Oxford University Press, 2008), 5–8.

contributing to "church growth,"[9] it has also unintentionally reintroduced theology into the development landscape. The reintroduction of theology into the development landscape seeks to create an identity for African Pentecostals. Thus, the revitalization of dual "epistemic theology"[10] of the coexistence of the physical and the spirit worlds defines what it means to set the captive free.

Richard Burgess' monograph provides a mapping of the "Pentecostal development" landscape that links failed neoliberal reforms and economic challenges in Nigeria to highlight the contribution of African Pentecostals in the imaginary social space.[11] Although Burgess focuses on Nigerian Pentecostals in studying this "emerging development practice," he extends the understanding of this development space, tracing it to the diaspora, particularly in Britain and the United States, to explain the relevance of its "contextual, sociological, and theological" factors.[12] The emphasis is that this new form of Christianity brings together effects of "democratisation and neoliberal economic reforms" away from the state into the public sphere to construct their identity.[13] This interfaces with Afe Adogame's view on "African social responsibility."[14]

For Adogame, this identity is partly due to much of the attention given to the Pentecostal theology of social responsibility, which explains the theology of mission in context.[15] This links Asamoah-Gyadu's approach to what it means to set the captive free.[16] Adogame's context focuses on Europe and Africa, where African Pentecostals function as religious support networks and "registered main charities" in partnership with some development sectors to influence their community.[17] Both Burgess and Adogame distinguished the essence of this theological identity within the competing imaginary social space.[18] Although both scholars examined this emerging development from their different socio-cultural contexts, they converged because of their similar struggles for identity, giving visibility to this development landscape. Similarly, in the

---

[9] Burgess, *Nigerian Pentecostalism and Development*, 34; Kalu, "African Pentecostalism," 4.

[10] Kalu, "African Pentecostalism," 4–5.

[11] Burgess, *Nigerian Pentecostalism and Development*, ii, thus, connecting the "intersecting spheres of politics, economics, health, education, human rights, and peacebuilding."

[12] Burgess, *Nigerian Pentecostalism and Development*, 2.

[13] Burgess, *Nigerian Pentecostalism and Development*, 3.

[14] Adogame, "African Christianities," 1–11. According to Adogame, such distinctive roles are visible because of the deteriorating government's conventional approaches, which could no longer be sustained.

[15] Afe Adogame, ed., *The Public Face of African New Religious Movements in Diaspora: Imagining the Religious "Other"* (London: Routledge, 2016), 7.

[16] Asamoah-Gyadu, "Mission to Set the Captive Free," 390.

[17] Adogame, "African Christianities," 4; Adogame, *The Public Face of African New Religious Movements in Diaspora*, 3.

[18] Burgess, *Nigerian Pentecostalism and Development*, 2–3; Adogame, "African Christianities" 4–5; Adogame, *The Public Face of African New Religious Movements in Diaspora*, 3–4.

development space, others refer to the Pentecostal Movement, linking with the African transition from colonial to postcolonial development, giving Pentecostals an inclusive outlook.[19] The assumption here is that this emerging development practice of African Pentecostals within the development space pays attention to theological and social factors to address moral ills and alleviate poverty in the local community.

Besides, Ogbu Kalu positions Pentecostals in context and discusses their progression, arguing that this new movement sought to find its identity and fill both the theological and social gaps within the African transition from colonial to a self-gratified identity.[20] This identity merges with the inclusive perceived secular roles. Allan Anderson also concludes, "Pentecostals do not always separate the spiritual from the physical, but integrate them in a holistic whole, leading to involvement in social issues and politics."[21] The confluence and continuing emphasis on this space and African Pentecostal theology suggests that the quest to refine a Pentecostal theology that takes root within the African context draws the developmental deficit and a political twist to it.

Several alternative observations by scholars indicate the influence of Africa's third response to social transformation and its impact in the West African context. Asamoah-Gyadu discussed the relevance of the response and its interface with the African Pentecostal transition, highlighting six thematic areas that identify the progression and idea of setting the captive free.[22] According to Dena Freeman and Olufunke Adeboye, although the circumstances that gave rise to the fall of neoliberal thinking and aided the rise of Pentecostalism into this landscape in Africa are distinctively different, they serve a similar struggle for theological identity.[23]

---

[19] Philip Ohlmann, Wilhelm Gräb, and Marie-Luise Frost, *African Initiated Christianity and the Decolonisation of Development: Sustainable Development in Pentecostal and Independent Churches* (London: Routledge, 2020), 16–17.

[20] Kalu, *African Pentecostalism*, 4–6.

[21] Allan H. Anderson, "Pentecostalism and Social, Political, and Economic Development," *Spiritus: ORU Journal of Theology* 5:1 (2020), 124.

[22] Asamoah-Gyadu, "Spirit and Empowerment," 34. According the author, the integration of charismatic renewal into expressions of Christianity brought a practical orientation towards salvation that created the theological space for rituals that accommodated real needs such as health, unemployment, marriage, and success in business; dynamic pneumatology in which the empowering presence of God was coveted not just for the manifestations of the gifts of the Spirit but also for various practical life concerns; the use of oral theology in liturgical expressions such as the use of locally composed choruses and the narrations of personal testimonies of salvation; and an innovative gender ideology in which space was created for women to exercise leadership based on their charismatic experiences rather than the stereotypes that excluded them from Christian leadership.

[23] See Dena Freeman, "Pentecostalism and Economic Development in Sub-Saharan Africa," in *The Routledge Handbook of Religions and Global Development* (London: Routledge, 2015), 2–4; and Olufunke Adeboye, "'A Starving Man Cannot Shout Halleluyah': African Pentecostal Churches and the Challenge of Promoting Sustainable Development," in *African Initiated Christianity and the Decolonisation of Development*, 115–20.

This third response gives visibility to a void we observed as the imaginary social space with practical ramification, highlighting a reconstructive Pentecostal theology. Other than one case of identity in this Pentecostal landscape, Asamoah-Gyadu's approach evidenced various contextual and cultural issues that support the theological space because of the post-independence development challenges in sub-Saharan Africa. For John Gichimu and Atinuke Abdulsalami, the task of extrapolating prayers, church services, sermons, rituals, and songs from more normative Christian conventions to a contextual form of African theology, engaging its diaspora community experience, could only be a response to an identity that satisfies theological and social needs.[24] As various scholars demonstrate, Pentecostals have transitioned over time into this imaginary social space, creating several platforms to evolve, contextualize, and extend their development practices. As such, the core argument is that the occupation of these multiple landscapes creates an imaginary social space yet with practical ramification within Africa's three responses to Christianity into which the African Pentecostals sought to fit, reconstructing an identity that is gradual and broad, and intentionally or unintentionally draws into the African political landscape.

African Pentecostal Vision and Pentecostal Transition

Many scholars may not easily connect the African Pentecostal vision with its social movements such as religious, cultural, and social capital.[25] The underlying assumption, as Gerrie ter Haar and Stephen Ellis mention, is that religion "seemed irrelevant to the processes they were analysing other than, perhaps, as an obstacle to modernisation."[26] This may be true, considering that African Pentecostals' experience has always assumed and highlighted cultural and theological relevance, giving its social responsibility little visibility at the national level of the development landscape. However, there are various movements that scholars accept as part of the traditional African Pentecostal theology of mission that covers its vision to set the captive free, encompassing the community's spiritual and social conditions. Crucial is the "prosperity gospel that makes material gain a spiritual virtue," and the Pentecostal civil responsibility that stretches into the political

---

[24] See John Njeru Gichimu, "Distinguished Church Leader Essay: Theology in African Initiated Churches—Reflections from an East African Perspective," in *African Initiated Christianity and the Decolonisation of Development*, 95–101; and Atinuke Abdulsalami, "Distinguished Church Leader Essay: Roles of Women in African Independent and Pentecostal Churches in Nigeria," in *African Initiated Christianity and the Decolonisation of Development*, 105–14.

[25] See Richard Burgess, "Pentecostals and Development in Nigeria and Zambia: Community Organizing as a Response to Poverty and Violence," *PentecoStudies* 14:2 (2015), 187–88.

[26] Gerrie ter Haar and Stephen Ellis, "The Role of Religion in Development: Towards a New Relationship between the European Union and Africa," *The European Journal of Development Research* 18:3 (2006), 352.

landscape.²⁷ How these movements are interrelated is often obscured, due to the lack of a clear "articulated theological foundation for social ministry" and the operational approaches they employ, giving them less visibility to their contributions.²⁸ We argue that this African Pentecostal transition holds a crucial "shared-value experience" for Pentecostals, whose vision is to be the voice of the disadvantaged.²⁹ As an actual course for African Pentecostals, this imaginary social space has thus optimized its vision and the reliability of the social movement within the increasing socioeconomic fragility of society.

Pentecostal progression has seen arguments of social movements linked to African Pentecostals and development. However, the non-reliability on external donors and distinctive features, such as cultural, social, and religious capital, set African Pentecostals as a point of departure from dependency. The rationale is demonstrated by David Korten's fourth-generation development paradigm as "relief and welfare," "community development," "sustainable system development," and "people centred," giving clear evidence of their perceived closeness to community organizing experience.³⁰

For instance, Asamoah-Gyadu believes that the surge in the social movement and progression of Ghanaian Pentecostals connected mediating factors such as religious and cultural "capital."³¹ Others contend that it has changed and shifted the community narratives and development dialogue as a point of departure from the neoliberal reforms in Nigeria, offering Pentecostals the voice of influence in the imaginary social space.³² However, the gap identified here is that although African Pentecostals have progressed

---

[27] Anderson, "Pentecostalism and Social, Political, and Economic Development," 123.

[28] Anderson, "Pentecostalism and Social, Political, and Economic Development," 128.

[29] Anderson, "Pentecostalism and Social, Political, and Economic Development," 124. As Allan Anderson notes, "There is an increasing awareness of the potential of Pentecostalism for a politically and socially relevant engagement, particularly because of its tendency to attract marginalised and working-class people."

[30] David C. Korten, *Getting to the 21st century: Voluntary Action and the Global Agenda* (West Hartford, CT: Kumarian Press, 1990), 3–10; Ignatius Swart, *The Churches and the Development Debate: Perspectives on a Fourth-generation Approach* (Stellenbosch: AFRICAN SUN MeDIA, 2006), 103, 148. Swart highlights this, drawing on the fourth-generational development paradigm as a "people-centred" approach, which he linked to the extension of responsibility and contended gradually changed the development landscape in Africa.

[31] J. Kwabena Asamoah-Gyadu, "Pentecostalism and the Transformation of the African Christian Landscape," in *Pentecostalism in Africa: Presence and Impact of Pneumatic Christianity in Postcolonial Societies*, ed. Martin Lindhardt (Leiden: Brill, 2015), 101.

[32] Burgess: "Pentecostals and Development." For further study see Burgess, *Nigerian Pentecostalism and Development*; Freeman, "Pentecostalism and Economic Development in Sub-Saharan Africa"; Asamoah-Gyadu, "Pentecostalism and the Transformation of the African Christian Landscape"; Paul Gifford, *Christianity, Development, and Modernity in Africa* (London: Hurst, 2015); Tomalin, "Gender"; Phillip Musoni, "African Pentecostalism and Sustainable Development: A Study on the Zimbabwe Assemblies of God Africa, Forward in Faith Church," *International Journal of Humanities and Social Science Invention* 2:10 (2013), 79; Barbara Bompani, "Religion and Development from Below: Independent Christianity in South Africa," *Journal of Religion in Africa* 40:3 (2010), 307–30.

into this space, there is little information on the cause of this shift in theology. Below, we attempt to identify the cause of the theological shift by drawing on the post-independence African Pentecostal and political landscapes. By identifying the cause of this shift, we hope to establish a case for the uniqueness of this imaginary social space.

African Pentecostals, Post-independence, and the Political Landscape

Some Pentecostal scholars recognized the 1940–1960s period as the first major wave of the Pentecostal Movement in West Africa.[33] The "Pentecostal movement was, to an extent, defined by its eschatology of premillennialism and expectation of the imminent rapture."[34] They limit their liturgical emphasis and hermeneutical stance on the theology of holiness for eschatological preparation.[35] By inference, this movement paid little attention to social development, as fundamentalists set their camp against modernism.[36] However, from the 1960–1970s, particularly in Nigeria and Ghana, the second wave of the movement expanded modestly in membership, with greater contextualization of Africanism and Pentecostal vision to set the captive free.[37]

The surge in Pentecostalism in the 1960s also witnessed a period of great expectation of post-independence euphoria on social and political development in the sub-region. Some leading political figures, for example, Kwame Nkrumah of Ghana (1909–1972),[38] rhetorically assured, "Seek ye first the political kingdom and all else shall be added unto you."[39] However, with the immediate post-independence political and social troubles in the 1960s, the expected socio-economic development in the sub-region was not realized.[40]

---

[33] Olufunke Adeboye, "'Arrowhead' of Nigerian Pentecostalism: The Redeemed Christian Church of God, 1952–2005," *Pneuma* 29:1 (2007), 26; Nimi Wariboko, *Nigerian Pentecostalism* (Rochester, NY: Boydell & Brewer, 2014), 1; Olufemi Vaughan, *Religion and the Making of Nigeria* (Durham, NC: Duke University Press, 2016), 139.

[34] Marius Nel, "Pentecostal Hermeneutical Considerations about Women in Ministry," *Studia Historiae Ecclesiasticae* 43:1 (2017), 2.

[35] Adeboye, "'Arrowhead' of Nigerian Pentecostalism," 36–37.

[36] Nel, "Pentecostal Hermeneutical Considerations about Women in Ministry," 6.

[37] Adeboye, "'Arrowhead' of Nigerian Pentecostalism," 28, 47; Anderson, "Pentecostalism and Social, Political, and Economic Development," 12.

[38] Rupe Simms, "'I am a Non-Denominational Christian and a Marxist Socialist': A Gramscian Analysis of the Convention People's Party and Kwame Nkrumah's Use of Religion," *Sociology of Religion* 64:4 (2003), 463.

[39] Samuel, K. Bonsu, "Seek Ye First the Political Kingdom," *Modern Ghana*, 2017, 1, https://www.modernghana.com/news/740576/seek-ye-first-the-political-kingdom.html.

[40] Vaughan, *Religion and the Making of Nigeria*, 140; Theodore Dalrymple, "Seek Ye First the Political Kingdom," *Law, and Liberty*, 2017, 1, https://lawliberty.org/seek-ye-first-the-political-kingdom/.

Rather than actualizing the dividends of political independence, the government could not fulfill its developmental responsibilities.[41] This created room for non-governmental and non-profit agencies, including faith-based organizations, to gradually venture into the imaginary social space for social responsibilities in West Africa. As promising, Pentecostals position themselves to meet society's needs. As Anderson argued, they appealed to underprivileged West African communities for membership.[42] This marks the beginning of the gradual Pentecostal incursion into areas of theological, social, and developmental landscape of responsibility in West Africa.

The third generation, emerging in the 1980s with mega-churches and prosperity gospels, has been playing a significant role in the socio-economic and political development of their societies.[43] With their mega-church philosophies, the Neo-Pentecostals tend to motivate "people to translate their salvation into practical everyday achievements in business, education, economics and family life."[44] Common to them in West Africa "is that God rewards faithful Christians with good health, financial success and material wealth, 'according to his glorious riches in Christ Jesus.'"[45] While this philosophy partly highlights the prosperity gospel, it does not sufficiently offer Pentecostals the theology of social responsibility for an incursion and shift in theology into the imaginary social space of development and political landscape. As such, we identify that this emerging Pentecostal visibility responded to theological, developmental, and social-political gaps for sociological, contextual, and cultural reasons to occupy this imaginary social space.

African Pentecostal Leadership and Upward Mobility

Here, we will examine how this imaginary social space with practical ramification interacts with the West African development narrative by considering the cases of the Redeemed Christian Church of God (RCCG), Nigeria, and the Church of Pentecost (CoP), Ghana, landscapes to understand the shift in theology. These cases connect the development, social, and theological landscapes, assuming their importance for four

---

[41] Adeboye, "'Arrowhead' of Nigerian Pentecostalism," 31, 43; Vaughan, *Religion and the Making of Nigeria*, 141–42.

[42] Anderson, "Pentecostalism and Social, Political, and Economic Development," 12. Anderson notes that Pentecostal churches "have a significant role to play in the social development of their members and their communities."

[43] Samuel Oluwatosin Okanlawon, "Churchpreneurship in the Nigerian Socio-economic Space with Particular Reference to the Redeemed Christian Church of God and Living Faith Church Worldwide," *International Journal of Religions and Traditions* 4:1 (2018), 33; Anderson, "Pentecostalism and Social, Political, and Economic Development," 6–11.

[44] Asamoah-Gyadu, *African Charismatics*, 1.

[45] Asamoah-Gyadu, *African Charismatics*, 2.

reasons: (1) they share some resemblance in the mode of social engagement; (2) their emergence around the 1950s coincide; (3) they suggest the cause of the shift; and (4) they have become arguably the most influential transnational networking Pentecostal movement in the history of Africa's third response to Christianity with a "missionary impulse."[46]

The Case of Ghana

In Ghana's case, this section attempts to draw on the CoP's experiences within this imaginary social space to situate Pentecostal leadership and upward mobility.

CoP and the Theological Space

The CoP is the largest Pentecostal denomination in Ghana, with a membership of about 9% of the population.[47] The shift in its traditional Pentecostal theology identified space for community development and social transformation in almost every district they occupy.

Prior to the leadership transfer between 1950–1982,[48] the CoP's core mandate was primarily the emphasis on the theology of holiness and Holy Ghost baptism, with no attention to social or political participation, like the RCCG theological thinking around the same time. However, the second-generation transformation, as a theological shift, occurred in a way that necessitated some usefulness. First, the leadership transfer is contextual and culturally relevant today because it witnessed a theological shift that engaged a biblical interpretation that "God is interested in the communities," addressing the local community's need. Second, it served as a point of departure from the "foreign outlook" in its context.[49] By inference, this oral culture exemplifies the vision that gives credence to the surge in the CoPs' emerging development practices, while simultaneously reinvigorating theology into the development space. Although the CoP's core receptor is "its oral cultural functions and social value," it does not entirely

---

[46] Burgess, "Pentecostals and Development," 1.

[47] Emmanuel Kwesi Anim, "An Evaluation of Pentecostal Churches as Agents of Sustainable Development in Africa," in *African Initiated Christianity and the Decolonisation of Development*, 195.

[48] For a good study of the history of the CoP, see Peter White, "Missional Branding: A Case Study of the Church of Pentecost," *HTS: Theological Studies* 75:4 (2019), 1–7; Opoku Onyinah, "Pentecostal Transformation in Africa: The Rise and Growth of the Church of Pentecost," *Pentecost Journal of Theology and Mission* 1:1 (2016), 12–35.

[49] Opoku Onyinah, "Distinguished Church Leader Essay: The Church of Pentecost and Its Role in Ghanaian Society," in *African Initiated Christianity and the Decolonisation of Development*, 184. According to Onyinah, "The church has become an Indigenous church, with a good blend of Christianity and African cultural features," such as "oral culture" filling the theological space created by its first-generational transformation.

underpin the shift.[50] Instead, oral culture as a logical system emphasised the importance of the contextual and theological relevance with practical ramification of the CoP in this imaginary social space. For the CoP, this is evident in their leadership landscape.[51]

We contend that although contextual culture played a crucial role and was intricately connected in highlighting the shift, it was not the trigger for the shift. Rather, we conclude that the core reason for the theological shift was leadership change, which impacted other areas. However, it is equally clear that the shift provided cultural recognition through effective identification, leading to various spaces. This gradual progression of expression has given visibility to the uniqueness of the imaginary social space for which the CoP has witnessed several transformations, covering social and development landscapes in the Ghanaian context and diaspora.

CoP and the Social Space

During Safo's leadership, the church grew.[52] The first social service established by Safo in 1982 was the Pentecost Social Service (PENTSOS).[53] Although PENTSOS and its responsibility were apolitical, it served the political situation symmetrically by helping address some socio-economic challenges, such as deprivation, education, and healthcare. Thus, according to the "records" of PENTSOS, it served its usefulness.[54]

On the international front, where African Pentecostals function as religious support networks and "registered main charities,"[55] the 2018 "State of the Church Address"[56] indicates the CoP's strong presence, spiritual capital, and self-funding social

---

[50] Onyinah, "Distinguished Church Leader Essay: The Church of Pentecost and Its Role in Ghanaian Society," 185.

[51] Prophet M. K. Yeboah 1988–98, Apostle Dr M. K. Ntumy 1998–2008, Apostle Prof. Opoku Onyinah 2008–18, and Apostle Eric Kwabena Nyamekye 2018.

[52] The first indigene to stir the CoP's affairs, the second generational transformation experienced tremendous social movement and responsibility as a result of the re-visioning of its outlook, imparting the church's missional landscape.

[53] Onyinah, "Distinguished Church Leader Essay: The Church of Pentecost and Its Role in Ghanaian Society," 189. PENTSOS's core mandate is to provide both the spiritual and physical needs of local communities.

[54] Onyinah, "Distinguished Church Leader Essay: The Church of Pentecost and Its Role in Ghanaian Society," 189. Onyinah notes that the church reported in the 2018 State of Church Address that by the end of December 2017, the church had eight health institutions—one hospital and seven clinics. The total outpatient department attendance at the church's eight health institutions in 2017 alone was 194,995. Altogether, a total of 17,682 admissions and 4,987 deliveries were recorded during 2017. The church currently runs eighty-four basic schools, three vocational schools, two senior high schools, and a university college and a magnificent convention center. The head office and the areas continue to sponsor needy student members at the tertiary level under the Pentecost Educational Scholarship Scheme.

[55] Adogame, *The Public Face of African New Religious Movements in Diaspora*, 3.

[56] Eric Nyamekye, *State of the Church Address*, May 8, 2019, thecophq.org/wp-content/uploads/2019/07/STATE-OF-THE-CHURCH-ADDRESS-2018.pdf. According to the CoP, diasporan figures are set at 53.9%, 18.4%, 9.6%, 3.2%, 2.9%, for the United States, the United Kingdom,

movement in the diaspora, presenting an understanding of decreasing Western theological influence. While these development praxes cannot be said for other Neo-Pentecostal movements in Ghana, they have all come under constructive criticism to pay taxes that offer accountability and prevent economic exploitation.

Some scholars suggest that building on this social cohesion and the managerial skills of the CoP could serve as a "Pentecostal model" in political governance if such an idea is propagated with ethical and social development policy.[57]

CoP and the Development Space

The significance of the CoP's development space that links Ghana's political landscape can best be summed up in its leadership approach to institutional management. The CoP's structure and governance are hierarchical with a "local-up" approach to leadership.[58] Although the leadership structure is hierarchical in appearance and management, it has a democratic outlook where, after every five years (per their constitution), leadership and administration are elected and given the mandate to lead.

In this respect, Ghana has seen significant contributions of some Pentecostal leadership to peacebuilding, political discourse, and religious tolerance in various forms. While this was not the case in the late 1970–1980s, with several military coups d'état that saw most churches in the trenches with no prophetic voice, their recent activities, such as peacebuilding and national government policy negotiations, have implications for the political landscape. While some scholars have highlighted the contribution of Pentecostal leaders in the development space,[59] others disagree in context.[60] Increasingly, there are notable "political positions and civil society organisations" CoP leaders occupy.[61]

Similarly, recent developments in Ghana note that Ghana's president appointed the immediate past chairperson of CoP, Opoku Onyinah, to chair the construction of "Ghana's National Cathedral."[62] Whether political or religious influence exists is an issue of contestation. In the spirit of peace, one could only submit that these

---

Germany, Canada, and Holland, respectively, marking territorial influence in social services and networking revenue generation.

[57] Anim, "An Evaluation of Pentecostal Churches as Agents of Sustainable Development in Africa," 195.

[58] See Opoku Onyinah, "The State of the Church Address," in *The Church of Pentecost: 43rd General Council Meetings* (Accra: Pentecost Press Ltd, 2018).

[59] Musoni, "African Pentecostalism and Sustainable Development," 79–80.

[60] See Gifford, *Christianity, Development, and Modernity in Africa*.

[61] Onyinah, "The State of the Church Address," 190. Such political and civil society positions include the Bank of Ghana, the Public Interest and Accountability Committee (PIAC), and significant state publications, making a case for the growing interest in inclusiveness in development.

[62] There are solid dissenting views in opposition equal to those for the national cathedral. Regardless, the chairperson has encouraged the progression of the cathedral.

appointments have served as a gradual upward mobility of Pentecostal leaders into prominent political spaces that rally support for inter-denominational tolerance and a balance in absolute political power and development. Although, as Anderson explains, African Pentecostal theology has also avoided any political involvement that could be a potential drawback for its evangelistic appeal,[63] some scholars hail this involvement as a democratic principle and gesture for inclusiveness rather than individualism.[64] We contend that the Pentecostal leadership's gradual mobility is crucial in this imaginary social space in Ghana, as it enables social cohesion against prevailing political conditions that descend into unnecessary deprivation and human suffering. In essence, the interplay between the shift and progression highlighted the significance of Africa's third response to Christianity, the challenges of post-independence, and the CoP's response, providing the imaginary social space visibility.

The Case of Nigeria

We take the RCCG not as representative, but to demonstrate the Pentecostal Movement's incursion into the imaginary social space in Nigeria.

RCCG and the Social and Development Space

The RCCG, with wider membership globally, has seen three generations of Pentecostal transformation.[65] Enoch Adejare, assuming Overseer's responsibility, immediately curved the church's renewed vision and reconstructive theological identity that propelled the church's social development space. Scholars often give credence to the liturgical transformation between 1981 and 1989 that saw the re-engineering of the church's operational framework, articulating its mission and vision.[66]

The three generational transformations coincide with the trajectory of Pentecostal theological shift from an exclusive mission focus to one of inclusive social responsibility and political participation, proffering the theological foundation that "Corporate Social

---

[63] Anderson, "Pentecostalism and Social, Political, and Economic Development," 123.

[64] Anim, "An Evaluation of Pentecostal Churches as Agents of Sustainable Development in Africa," 209.

[65] See Okanlawon, "Churchpreneurship in the Nigerian Socio-economic Space," 33. First, from 1952 to 1980, the church eschewed materialism but emphasized the theology of holiness and healing through fervent prayers. Second, the scenario changed in 1981 with Enoch Adejare Adeboye's appointment as the successor General Overseer (GO) of the RCCG.

[66] See, Adeboye, "'Arrowhead' of Nigerian Pentecostalism," 38; Vaughan, *Religion and the Making of Nigeria*, 187. Thus (1) "to make heaven and take as many people with us" (Redeemed Christian Church of God [RCCG], "Corporate Social Responsibility," 2021, https://www.rccg.org/rccg-csr), and (2) "to plant churches within five minutes walking distance in every city and town of developing countries and within five minutes driving distance in every city and town of developed countries." Third, from 1990 the RCCG's vision and mission in context entailed occupying the renewed theological and imaginary social space of service.

Responsibility"[67] (CSR) "has its root in Christianity and the church is meant to be an example for the world to follow and not the other way around."[68]

To fulfil its CSR, the RCCG identified eight sectors for its outreach and development projects: social, health, education, business, arts and culture, government, and sports.[69] In the education sector, RCCG has established forty-four (primary and secondary) schools, one university, and one college,[70] with scholarships to thousands of students nationwide.

Similarly, with fifty primary health centers, two modern hospitals, and one orphanage in the Redemption Camp, the RCCG connects national efforts against debilitating diseases, such as HIV/AIDS, COVID-19, cancer, and reproductive health care.[71] The RCCG's unprecedented social sector efforts further provide 223,100 free meals daily on average to people in need.[72] Similarly, in the business sector, the RCCG implements programs that create and support cooperative societies, youth empowerment and employment, vocational and skills education, and charity shops, accounting for over 96,000 beneficiaries.[73] Besides, with business networks nationwide, the RCCG's social activities in ending hunger and recognizing widespread misery and suffering has seen leadership launch full-scale welfare and humanitarian services, with rehabilitation as its core function. For instance, with a center in Lagos, the Christ Against Drug Abuse Ministry (CADAM) rehabilitates drug abuse victims and occultists in the campuses of higher institutions. In 2021, the RCCG reported that over 60.9 million people have benefited from its social responsibility programs. We agree that Adeboye's receptivity to novel ideas, within and outside the church, and the deployment of university graduates to high positions in the church structure, as well as female members' upward mobility, are fundamental to the RCCG's success, creating a niche for itself in the social space in Nigeria.[74]

---

[67] See RCCG, "Corporate Social Responsibility," n.p. Further, it served as a conscious avenue for Christians to make visible impact in various key areas of society. Where many view societal challenges and its scale all around the world we see an opportunity to take decisive effort to creating solutions as we work with people, communities, leaders, and governments worldwide.

[68] RCCG, "Corporate Social Responsibility," n.p.

[69] RCCG, "Corporate Social Responsibility," n.p.

[70] Adeboye, "'Arrowhead' of Nigerian Pentecostalism," 43; Okanlawon, "Churchpreneurship in the Nigerian Socio-economic Space," 34.

[71] Okanlawon, "Churchpreneurship in the Nigerian Socio-economic Space," 34.

[72] RCCG, "Corporate Social Responsibility," n.p.

[73] RCCG, "Corporate Social Responsibility," n.p.

[74] Adeboye, "'Arrowhead' of Nigerian Pentecostalism," 39; Okanlawon, "Churchpreneurship in the Nigerian Socio-economic Space," 34–35.

RCCG and Political Space

Nigerian Pentecostals' link to politics is often traced to the formation of the Pentecostal Fellowship of Nigeria (PFN).[75] Although the RCCG is a significant member of the PFN, it did not bring transformative and expansive advantages to the political landscape before the 1990s.[76]

Although initially the church leadership avoided direct partisan politics within the context of the reformed theology of service, they made it a duty for church members to pray for the unfolding political process in the country.[77] The policy of the RCCG in the initial stages of the fourth republic in 1999 was to encourage the general congregation to exercise their civic rights by voting during elections. However, the church did not mobilize electoral support for politically inclined members.[78] Instead, like the other Pentecostal churches under the PFN, in the fourth republic, the RCCG pursued a distinct political agenda suited to its mission and vision.[79] As democratic governance evolved, under its CSR, the RCCG defined its political and governance policy to "actively participate in public engagements with government bodies on how governance and policies could improve society."[80]

By inference, with a formal policy on political participation, the RCCG encourages its members to directly participate in partisan politics. As such, Yemi Osinbajo was elected in 2015 as the Vice President of the Federal Republic of Nigeria. RCCG leadership moved a step further in February 2022, transforming its program on politics to a full-fledged Office of Directorate of Politics and Governance, with similar offices at its zonal, area, and parish levels in Nigeria. The Directorate assists and mobilizes support for its members seeking elective political positions at all levels.[81] We conclude that RCCG neo-political participation is evidence of what Burgess inferred, as faith-based organizations "seek to empower their members to pursue political goals in the public sphere."[82] By implication, the RCCG is expanding its occupation of the imaginary social space in Nigeria's new political dispensation of democratic governance. Hence, considering the RCCG's developmental and political activities, it demonstrated the Pentecostal shift in vision from initial holiness to social responsibility and currently to the political arena.

---

[75] Vaughan, *Religion and the Making of Nigeria*, 151.
[76] Adeboye, "'Arrowhead' of Nigerian Pentecostalism," 54.
[77] Vaughan, *Religion and the Making of Nigeria*, 150.
[78] Adeboye, "'Arrowhead' of Nigerian Pentecostalism," 54.
[79] Vaughan, *Religion and the Making of Nigeria*, 151.
[80] RCCG, "Corporate Social Responsibility," n.p.
[81] RCCG, "Corporate Social Responsibility," n.p.
[82] Burgess, "Pentecostals and Development in Nigeria and Zambia," 178.

Missiological Implication for the Church

What lessons can the church learn from the thinking of secular development and the imaginary social space?

Missional Visibility

There are strong missiological and crucial reasons for the Pentecostals' emerging development practice in West Africa. One such is theology. Pentecostal belief in the involvement of God in everyday life, the power of the Holy Spirit, and the need for every believer to minister provides strong motivations for development. There is also the necessity to bring to bear the power of the Spirit on the shared value experience, converging both the spiritual and the required material blessing for society at large. The imaginary social space can serve as a starting point in identifying common grounds for dialogue between the development sector and the church as a mission agent.

Politics

As evidenced and demonstrated elsewhere in this article, African Pentecostals' indirect and/or direct involvement in social political development has given visibility to the thin line (middle ground) between the church's mission and the political landscape. This visibility (middle ground) is what we argue as the imaginary social space with practical ramification, providing African Pentecostals the intentional and/or unintentional experience and the emerging development practice. The church's aggressive and desperate development approach can serve as a model. Additionally, the awareness of this imaginary social space can allay the church's fear and suspicion of engaging in secular debate, harnessing these tools accordingly. In contemporary development, however, although the church's role in mission still assumes an apolitical position, its responsibilities most often stretch and align with the underlying "political development structures and goals," enabling development that cannot be overlooked, evidenced in their leadership mobility.[83]

As true to practice, this emerging development practice within the imaginary social space of the CoP and the RCCG meets most of these development goals. However, as

---

[83] See also the SDG Acceleration Toolkit of the United Nations Development Group (no longer available on the United Nations Sustainable Development Group website, originally at https://undg.org/2030-agenda/sdg-accelaration-toolkit/guidance/). For instance, in July 2014, the UN General Assembly Open Working Group proposed a document containing seventeen goals to be put forward for the General Assembly's approval in September 2015. This document sets the ground for the Sustainable Development Goals (SDGs) and the global development agenda to span from 2015–2030, to which most African nations have subscribed in order to access funding. These goals are already part of African Pentecostals' general vision and development scheme.

identified by Anderson, there are no "articulated theological foundations for social ministry" for Pentecostals that highlight their achievements at the national level.[84] We contend that the CoP's and the RCCG's roles in the development landscape are symmetrical to the political development areas of the sustainability development goals (SDG). Hence, it would warrant a dialogical approach for sustainable development of local communities, where the church is actively a model. The imaginary social space now constitutes a component of the entire Pentecostal mission in West Africa.

Conclusion

In this article, we have shown and drawn a trajectory of mission and vision of Pentecostals' shift from the traditional theology of mission to the theology of social transformation, conditional on Pentecostals moving into the imaginary social space and gradual extension into the partisan political landscape in West Africa. The shift we identified is triggered by a change in leadership in both cases, influencing the development landscape.

The failure of the governments to provide socio-economic development, increasing poverty and hopelessness, acute and rising unemployment, and governance failure combine to create an imaginary social space ready for non-governmental and faith-based organizations to provide alternative measures to set the captive free.

The critical recommendation in moving forward is that the church, especially the proliferated third-generation Pentecostals, creates awareness of this imaginary social space, which could serve as a mediating factor necessary for identity and as a contributing agent within the development sector that the church can no longer undermine in twenty-first-century West Africa.

Fred Cudjoe Adadey (adadeyf@roehampton.ac.uk) is research and community development coordinator at Prfinstitute.org, USA, and a PhD candidate (Theology and Religion) at the University of Roehampton, London.

Barnabas Yisa (yisaby@yahoo.com) is a consultant in communication and advocacy, currently providing support to Christian leaders and serving with Nupe Christian Fellowship International, Bida, Niger State, Nigeria.

---

[84] Anderson, "Pentecostalism and Social, Political, and Economic Development," 6.

A Joint Program of

Oral Roberts University, Tulsa, Oklahoma, U.S.A.   Yoido Full Gospel Church, Seoul, Korea.

This annual award is to recognize a significant contribution to the studies of global Spirit-empowered Christianity.

Nominated by institutions among Ph.D.-level dissertations officially completed in the previous year.

To be launched in 2025 among the 2024 dissertations.

For inquiries, contact wma@oru.edu

COVID-19 AND CHURCH ATTENDANCE BEHAVIOR TRENDS

EVIDENCE FROM GHANAIAN PENTECOSTAL-CHARISMATIC CHURCHES

JUSTICE A. ARTHUR
LYDIA ANDOH-QUAINOO

Keywords *consumer behavior, Pentecostalism, religious economies, COVID-19 pandemic, church attendance*

Abstract

The concept of religious economy views churches as corporate entities, pastors as marketers offering a range of products, and church members as consumers whose preferences shape the goods and services provided by ministers. Within this framework, church members react quickly to changing economic, social, and cultural conditions. The COVID-19 pandemic has not only had an economic impact, with job losses and financial struggles, but has also brought about social and cultural changes that have affected consumer behavior in many areas of life worldwide. For instance, during the pandemic, church gatherings were restricted or prohibited, socializing was replaced with social distancing, air travel was disrupted, and conferences were canceled, postponed, or moved to virtual platforms. These changes have led to significant shifts in consumer habits regarding church attendance in Ghana. This article draws on ethnographic data from two Pentecostal-Charismatic churches in Ghana to explore the various changes and trends in consumer behavior exhibited by members due to the COVID-19 pandemic. It argues that the pandemic has had a profound impact on church attendance behavior, as it has disrupted many aspects of life.

Introduction

The world faced the severe COVID-19 pandemic for a few years, which changed many aspects of everyday life. During the peak of the pandemic, numerous measures were implemented by national governments and international organizations such as the World Health Organization. These measures entailed the replacement of all forms of social gatherings with social distancing regulations, the grounding of all passenger flights as nations closed their air spaces to traffic, the cancellation or virtualization of conferences, and the enforcement of lockdown regulations that required people to stay at home. The pandemic has not only posed economic challenges to nations but has also brought about significant social changes.

In Ghana, the regulations were relaxed in August 2021 after the "third wave of infections." Nevertheless, some of the changes occasioned by the pandemic were so drastic that many facets of life had not returned to pre-COVID-19 levels, including church attendance. The lockdown measures in the West African nation included closing churches, chapels, and mosques. These closures changed many aspects of church life, including how COVID-19 has affected people's approach to church attendance. While African Christianity is diverse in its expressions, church attendance is an essential aspect of spiritual life that forms the basis of fellowship, worship, and discipleship in all its various forms. It is a fundamental practice that enables individuals to connect with their faith community, engage in meaningful worship, and grow in their spiritual journey. Whether it is attending regular services, participating in small group discussions, or joining in community events, attendance plays a crucial role in fostering a sense of belonging and deepening one's relationship with God.[1]

Some studies have suggested a link between church involvement (attendance and membership) and the spread of the COVID-19 pandemic.[2] One reason for establishing this connection is that church members engage in culturally specific practices to communicate with God, such as attending church services. In Africa, Christianity is not solely a matter of belief systems, but rather a way of life that involves adhering to prescribed social and cultural practices.[3] As such, attending church services is deemed essential for the spiritual development of church members.

This article aims to shed light on the impact of the COVID-19 pandemic on church attendance behavior in the Ghanaian Pentecostal-Charismatic context.[4] It seeks

---

[1] Rick Warren, *The Purpose Driven Church* (Michigan: Zondervan, 1995); John R. Bryson, Lauren Andres, and Andrew Davies, "COVID-19, Virtual Church Services and a New Temporary Geography of Home," *Journal of Economic and Human Geography* 111:3 (2020), 360–72.

[2] Paul Vermeer and Joris Kregting, "Religion and the Transmission of COVID-19 in the Netherlands," *Religions* 11 (2020), 2; Simon Dein, Kate Loewenthal, Christopher Alan Lewis, and Kenneth Pargament, "COVID-19, Mental Health and Religion: An Agenda for Future Research," *Mental Health, Religion & Culture* 23:1 (2020), 1–9; Sayed A. Quadri, "COVID-19 and Religious Congregations: Implications for Spread of Novel Pathogens," *International Journal of Infectious Diseases* 96 (2020), 219–21.

[3] Martin Riesebrodt, *The Promise of Salvation. A Theory of Religion* (Chicago: The University of Chicago Press, 2010); Christian Smith, *Religion: What It Is, How It Works, and Why It Matters* (Princeton: Princeton University Press, 2017).

[4] The churches described here belong to what Paul Gifford has referred to as "Ghana's New Christianity." For detailed reading see Paul Gifford, *Ghana's New Christianity: Pentecostalism in a Globalizing African Economy* (Bloomington and Indianapolis: Indian University Press, 2004); Marleen

to provide new perspectives to a growing body of literature on religion and pandemics.[5] The study examines changes in consumer behavior from the pre-pandemic period to August 2021, when the third wave in Ghana came to an end. The article is structured into four sections: a theoretical overview, the methodology employed, the findings and analysis, and the conclusion.

The Religious Market Model and Consumer Behavior

This article utilizes the religious market metaphor to elucidate the shifts and patterns in Pentecostal-Charismatic church attendance amidst the pandemic. The model views religious activity through an economic lens, positing that religious economies operate similarly to commercial economies, with a market and a set of organizations vying to cater to that market.[6] As with any commercial economy, the level of regulation plays a crucial role in the functioning of a religious economy. It is founded on the principle of religion operating within an unregulated market, where followers have the freedom to select where and how they worship.

Within this framework, religious organizations function as businesses, and their followers are viewed as customers who have the freedom to explore various religious offerings. Likewise, religious figures such as pastors are seen as producers, marketers, and entrepreneurs who respond to the challenges and possibilities of the religious marketplace.[7] The preferences of consumers play a significant role in shaping the goods and services offered by religious leaders. This freedom of choice directly influences the activities of religious producers as they strive to make their offerings appealing to potential customers. Given that consumers have a certain degree of autonomy, religious product producers must cater to their needs and preferences. The success of these

---

De Witte, "Business of the Spirit: Ghanaian Broadcast Media and the Commercial Exploitation of Pentecostalism," *Journal of African Media Studies* 3:2 (2011),189–204; J. Kwabena Asamoah-Gyadu, *African Charismatics: Current Developments within Indigenous Pentecostalism in Ghana* (Leiden: African Christian Press, 2005).

[5] Vincenzo Alfano, Salvatore Ercolano, and Gaetano Vecchione, "Religious Attendance and Covid-19: Evidence from Italian Regions," *CESifo Working Paper* 8596 (2020), 1–15; Vermeer and Kregting, "Religion and the Transmission of COVID-19 in the Netherlands," 1–12; Francesco Molteni et. al., "Searching for Comfort in Religion: Insecurity and Religious Behaviour during the COVID-19 Pandemic in Italy," *European Societies* (2020), 1–15, https://doi.org/10.1080/14616696.2020.1836383; Justice A. Arthur, "African Pentecostal Church Life in the Post-COVID-19 Era," *Missio Africanus Journal of African Missiology* 6:1 (2021), 1–19, https://missioafricanus.com/journal/.

[6] Roger Finke and Rodney Stark, "The Dynamics of Religious Economies," in *Handbook of the Sociology of Religion*, ed. Michelle Dillon (Cambridge: Cambridge University Press, 2003), 100; Rodney Stark and Roger Finke, *Acts of Faith: Explaining the Human Side of Religion* (Berkeley: University of California Press, 2000), 27–31.

[7] Shane Lee and Philip Luke Sinitiere, *Holy Mavericks* (New York: New York University Press, 2009).

producers in this market environment is determined by how effectively they package and market their commodities to resonate with the consumers' tastes.[8]

Moreover, consumers in this framework are highly responsive to economic, social, and cultural shifts. The COVID-19 pandemic, which began in late 2019, has caused significant financial strain on countries worldwide, resulting in job losses for many individuals. It has also led to social and cultural transformations that have impacted consumer behavior in various aspects of life, including attendance at religious services. Church members, as consumers, have adapted to these sociocultural changes brought about by the pandemic. Furthermore, the pandemic has influenced how pastors create and offer religious products and services, leading to a corresponding change in church attendance patterns.

Within the religious market framework, consumer behavior is influenced by external and internal factors such as the social environment, economic situation, and the customer's personality.[9] The social, economic, and personal changes that the COVID-19 pandemic has exacted have considerably changed how firms and consumers behave.[10] Both firms and consumers are adapting quickly to the frequent transitions that are taking place.[11] According to Mehta et al., during times of crisis, such as a pandemic outbreak, consumer behavior can be categorized into three approaches: economic, psychological, and sociological.[12] The economic approach is based on consumers' understanding of their basic needs within the micro economy. The psychological approach focuses on the connection between the consumer's psyche and behavior. Lastly, the sociological approach is based on how consumers react in different situations or how social events impact their behavior. As a result, consumer interests are constantly being challenged and traded in the market.[13] Consequently, during times of crisis, people's reactions to negative economic or social impacts can vary greatly, leading to the emergence of new consumer habits. For instance, Lenka Svajdova has noted that the COVID-19 pandemic has already affected consumer behavior in the retail industry, resulting in a decrease in consumer confidence but an increase in average spending and

---

[8] Lee and Sinitiere, *Holy Mavericks*, 150; Stark and Finke, *Acts of Faith*, 27.

[9] Katarina Valaskova, Katarina Kramarova, and Viera Bartosova, "Multi Criteria Models Used in Slovak Consumer Market for Business Decision Making," *Procedia Economics and Finance* 26 (2015), 174–82.

[10] Seema Mehta, Tanjul Saxena, and Neetu Purohit, "The New Consumer Behaviour Paradigm amid COVID-19: Permanent or Transient?," *Journal of Health Management* 22:2 (2020), 291–301.

[11] William Bridges, *Managing Transitions: Making the Most of Change*, 4th ed. (London: Nicholas Brealey Publishing, 2017).

[12] Mehta, Saxena, and Purohit, *The New Consumer Behaviour Paradigm amid COVID-19*, 291.

[13] Mehta, Saxena, and Purohit, *The New Consumer Behaviour Paradigm amid COVID-19*, 292; Valaskova, Kramarova, and Bartosova, *Multi Criteria Models Used in Slovak Consumer Market for Business Decision Making*, 174.

a decrease in purchase frequency.[14] Similarly, Flatters and Wilmot have emphasized the critical impact of the 2008 global recession on consumer behavior and trends.[15] Against this backdrop of changing consumer behavior during crisis periods, we became interested in investigating the trends in church attendance and behavior adjustments of Pentecostal-Charismatic Christians in Ghana.

While the metaphor of religious markets offers us a valuable, even self-evident, lens to consider church members as consumers within the religious landscape, it has some apparent limitations, too. Foremost, it is based on the rational choice theory, which prioritizes cognitive and calculable factors and cannot fully account for non-rational influences that also impact economic behavior.[16] Additionally, the use of the market metaphor in relation to Pentecostalism has, at times, created a negative portrayal of the movement as the "ideological agent" of American capitalism in the global south.[17] Due to these weaknesses, our use of the religious economy metaphor is not to suggest that church attendance behavior can be comprehensively explained only in economic terms, though it is a significantly helpful lens to explore the lived experiences of Pentecostal-Charismatic Christians in the African context.[18]

Methodology

The study employed a combination of traditional and cyber ethnographic methods to investigate church attendance at two of Ghana's leading Pentecostal-Charismatic churches: the Church of Pentecost (CoP)[19] and the International Central Gospel

---

[14] Lenka Svajdova, "Consumer Behaviour during Pandemic of COVID-19," *Journal of International Business Research and Marketing* 6:3 (2021), 34; Lydia Andoh-Quainoo, "Psychological Factors in Continuance Digital Media Behaviour: Smartphone, Internet and Social Media in Young Consumers," *Pentvars Business Journal* 13:1 (2021), 46–58; Ludvík Eger, Lenka Komárková, Dana Egerová, and Michal Mičík, "The Effect of COVID-19 on Consumer Shopping Behaviour: Generational Cohort Perspective," *Journal of Retailing and Consumer Services* 61 (2021), 1–11.

[15] Paul Flatters and Michael Willmott, "Understanding the Post-recession Consumer," *Harvard Business Review* 87:7–8 (2009), 64–72.

[16] Bernice Martin, "Pentecostal Conversion and the Limits of the Market Metaphor," *Exchange* 35:1 (2006), 64–65.

[17] Martin, "Pentecostal Conversion and the Limits of the Market Metaphor," 67.

[18] Asonzeh Ukah, *A New Paradigm of Pentecostal Power: A Study of the Redeemed Christian Church of God in Nigeria* (Trenton, NJ: Africa World, 2008).

[19] We selected two different strands of Pentecostal churches, being aware of the heterogenous nature of Pentecostal/Charismatic Christianity. The Church of Pentecost (CoP) is a classical Pentecostal church, part of the group of Pentecostal churches that evolved in Ghana because of the revivalist movement in the first two decades of the twentieth century. It has branch churches in all the districts of Ghana as well as international churches in Africa, Europe, North America, South America, Asia, and Australia.

Church (ICGC).[20] It involved extensive observation and participant observation, as well as in-depth interviews with pastors and church members who produce and consume religious goods. Due to COVID-19 protocols, cyber ethnography was employed when the physical environment was not conducive to traditional methods.

Integrating data from both types of ethnography is crucial because one of the fundamental aspects of ethnography is observing a group of people in their natural environment, including online spaces.[22] Cyber ethnography is particularly valuable in examining how online communities inform the study of physical communities, such as churches and their social interactions. This approach is especially relevant during the COVID-19 pandemic, as the internet has become a primary setting for many people's lived experiences. Additionally, cyber ethnography enables the identification of information-rich religious actors in digital spaces, which can then be followed up with traditional ethnography. Moreover, this method has proven useful in reaching adherents who may not be comfortable with face-to-face interviews due to the pandemic.

The traditional ethnographic study commenced in December 2020 and concluded on August 20, 2021. Additionally, structured interview guides were utilized to collect online data from June 6 to August 20, 2021. In both instances, the purposive sampling method was employed to select branch churches and respondents. This method was chosen to facilitate a comprehensive analysis of church attendance behavior among a homogeneous group of Pentecostal-Charismatic Christians.

The cyber ethnography participants were reached through Google Form links sent via email and social media platforms such as WhatsApp and Facebook Messenger. A total of fifty responses were gathered from both cyber sources and traditional ethnography. From these fifty respondents, twenty-five individuals were selected from each of the two Pentecostal-Charismatic churches, consisting of five clergy members and twenty church members. To ensure a balanced representation of consumer perspectives from both urban and rural areas, three city-based branches and three rural-based branches were chosen from both the CoP and the ICGC.

---

[20] The International Central Gospel Church (ICGC), founded by Mensa Otabil, is a Neo-Pentecostal church or what is usually referred to in Ghana as a Charismatic church. These churches began in the 1970s and 1980s through local initiatives. The ICGC could also be described as a megachurch with branches in many parts of Ghana and internationally in Africa, Europe, and North America.

Data Analysis and Results

This study sought to primarily investigate the various consumer behavioral patterns in relation to church attendance. It examines these trends under three different periods: the pre-COVID-19 era, the COVID-19 era, and the post-COVID-19-vaccine era.[21]

Pre-COVID-19 Church Attendance Behavior

To begin with, let us examine the church attendance rates in the pre-COVID-19 era in the CoP and the ICGC. The data indicates that attendance was not a major issue during this time, particularly on Sundays when churches recorded significant turnout. Some of the respondents opined that

> "We had about 80–100 people attending church regularly before COVID-19. These members came out of their own volition. I was attending church about 5–6 times a week" (Resp. 21 L).[22]

> "We were attending church regularly; I could attend church service thrice a week" (Resp. 6 M).

> "Church attendance was massive before the lockdown, and I could attend church at least twice a week" (Resp. 10 M).

Regarding church activities and church service experience in the pre-COVID-19 period, most churches were operating at peak levels. Adherents attested that they always had a fulfilling experience at church. They could interact freely with other members of the church community and participate in sacraments like communion. These are some of the responses:

> "We could interact freely and share fellowship and love. We had a wonderful experience with God through fruitful worship" (Resp. 22 M).

> "Our time in church was truly fulfilling, and we could engage in activities like praise and worship without looking over our shoulders" (Resp. 36 M).

> "There was a great sense of fellowship as there were no restrictions on time and activities like the Lord's Supper" (Resp. 21 L).

It could be inferred from the various responses that church attendance was a truly satisfying experience for many church members. Unfortunately, the global pandemic significantly changed church attendance behavior as churches resorted to a new norm of deploying virtual platforms to remain relevant and competitive in the religious

---

[21] The post-COVID-19-vaccine era is defined as the period between when mass vaccination began in Ghana to the end of the third wave—March 2 to August 10, 2021.

[22] "L" signifies leaders' voices while "M" indicates church members' voices.

market.²³ This also led to frequent disruptions and the absence of dynamic church activities, as consumers were primarily deprived of the emotional release prominent in Pentecostal-Charismatic church services in Ghana.

Church Attendance Behavior during COVID-19

COVID-19 affected church attendance behavior in several ways. Foremost, churches in Ghana were banned from physical meetings at the peak of the pandemic because of protocols implemented to prevent the spread of the disease. There was an unprecedented adaptation from church communities, including in places of worship, from pastors and their congregations. Many had to meet in smaller groups with social distancing protocols, while others resorted to virtual services, which were live-streamed or recorded, edited, and broadcasted as real-time experiences but also stored on digital platforms for open access. For some churches, the telemediated services were augmented with small group meetings. Evidence gathered from members indicates that in the era of COVID-19, people were very much interested in church activities. The digital platforms gave members who were in lockdown the opportunity to worship within the virtual community. Some respondents expressed the following views:

> "I always participated in organized online services" (Resp. 8 M).
>
> "I could attend church services during the lockdown through online and television services" (Resp. 43 M).
>
> "I was always willing to be in church, so I participated mostly in the online services" (Resp. 24 M).

While these responses give us an idea of church members' interest in church attendance during the lockdown period, it is difficult to establish the veracity of these assertions.

Disruption of Church Routine by the COVID-19 Protocols and Telemediated Services

Next, due to the vast interest in church services even during the lockdown period, respondents were asked if they were aware of the protocols instituted by the state to control the spread of the virus. This was to gauge their knowledge of and adherence to the established guidelines. The majority of respondents confirmed their familiarity with all the protocols, including regular handwashing, use of hand sanitizers, social distancing, wearing of facemasks, temperature checks, and avoiding physical contact

---

²³ Hazel O'Brien, "What Does the Rise of Digital Religion During COVID-19 Tell Us about Religion's Capacity to Adapt?," *Irish Journal of Sociology* 28:2 (2020), 242–46.

such as handshakes and hugs, common in Pentecostal-Charismatic contexts. While some churches in urban areas were able to implement all COVID-19 protocols and ensure strict adherence, some local churches in rural settings faced challenges in acquiring critical equipment like thermometer guns and commercial handwashing buckets, making it difficult to comply with the guidelines. More significantly, the COVID-19 protocols were seen as disrupting the regular routines of the church, to which it took many attendees a considerable amount of time to adapt. At the same time, some never got used to it.

> "The pandemic has reduced the liberty to dance, sing praises, and interact freely in church" (Resp. 4 L).

> "The Pentecostal style of worship and activities such as crusades, rallies, and evangelism have all been put on hold. Dancing, clapping, and jumping have all been replaced with sobriety" (Resp. 8 L).

> "For more than one year, we have never had any fundraiser in the church" (Resp. 36 L).

In addition, the implementation of protocols and subsequent adoption of telemediated worship services in churches raised concerns among consumers regarding the quality of their church experiences. Some members reported feeling disconnected due to issues with sound quality, while others expressed that their virtual worship experience did not compare to their in-person experience. This may be attributed to the lack of physical participation and interactions with fellow church members. Despite producers of religious goods and services adapting their strategies to meet consumer demands, it became apparent that many church members struggled to adjust to digital services. In fact, some respondents asserted that virtual church platforms compromised the quality of the worship experience. The following are sample responses:

> "It felt like church was boring and dull" (Resp. 1 M).

> "There was no sense of fellowship at all in online services though the word ministration [sermon] was powerful" (Resp. 16 M).

> "Although the word of God did not change [during the COVID-19], I felt apprehensive about the experiences in church that if this is the way the church will be, it will be very problematic going forward" (Resp. 47 L).

> "Church service was very challenging, and if you were not determined, you would not attend the services like you used to" (Resp. 6 M).

> "Generally, the church was not interactive" (Resp. 27 M).

> "Online service was not so inspiring. Something was lacking although I can't put my finger on what that is. It was simply not the same" (Resp. 29 L).

The findings reveal the specific needs and preferences of different members of the church community, which were not fully satisfied by the implementation of telemediated worship services during the pandemic. As a result, some members expressed a degree of discontentment. It also suggests that certain individuals require a sense of release and excitement as an integral part of their worship experience, a need previously met by traditional church services before the COVID-19 outbreak.

Loss of Fellowship

Despite the challenges posed by the shift to online services and small group meetings, some church members remain convinced that the Holy Spirit's presence was palpable. This is supported by various perspectives that suggest that as producers within the religious market, the church could only meet the demands of a segment of the consumers in a complex market altered by the pandemic:

> "The Holy Spirit was very much alive in our services during the COVID-19 period. However, the services were mostly limited to prayer meetings mainly. No musical instruments were deployed. Hence, church service differed from in-person fellowship" (Resp. 26 L).

> "Online service was good but not as enjoyable as in-person services. But the church leadership reacted quickly in transforming the worship style amid the pandemic" (Resp. 47 M).

> "The service experience was never the same, although the presence of God was felt, and the cell system provided a near pre-COVID-19 service experience. Word ministration [preaching] was also top-notch" (Resp. 16 L).

> "Members were not free to express themselves fully in dancing and worship. Many members yearned for the interactive aspects of fellowship" (Resp. 24 L).

These findings suggest that during the height of the pandemic, churches explored new ways of fostering fellowship, but not all individuals found online experiences to be fulfilling. While the platform for church services did not always meet market demands, members generally expressed satisfaction with the sermons delivered through online sources. However, some respondents noted that online church services lacked certain aspects that made Pentecostal-Charismatic church experiences truly fulfilling. Telemediated church services presented challenges for some consumers, particularly those who lacked computer skills or struggled to adapt to new ways of congregating as a church. Nevertheless, some responses indicated that certain church attendees enjoyed virtual services and found them to be more satisfying. Some even expressed appreciation for live-streamed or pre-recorded church services. Here are a few responses:

> "Digital service was fun for me. I was able to pay my tithes and enjoyed the preaching of God's word" (Resp. 6 M).

> "The virtual church gave me a new experience with the word of God. The word became so real to me than before" (Resp. 38 M).

Undoubtedly, one of the most significant obstacles faced by online services during this time was the increased demand for interpersonal connections. As per national guidelines, all forms of physical contact were prohibited in church settings, including hugging, handshakes, and close dancing, all of which are integral components of African Pentecostal-Charismatic congregational worship. Social distancing measures were implemented in lieu of physical interactions, leading to significant alterations in how members communicate. As a result, the pandemic and the accompanying protocols had a profound impact on fellowship within these communities.

> "We could not interact as we used to do. We could only respond to people's comments on church sessions. Physical counseling services with pastors could only be held online" (Resp. 15 L).

> "The virtual service allowed for participation, but members missed being together" (Resp. 24 L).

> "Close fellowship was missing" (Resp. 37 M).

Finally, there were some negative experiences during the lockdown, although people were in touch with the church through small groups and digital services. These were some responses of people's feelings:

> "I felt like a prisoner" (Resp. 24 M).

> "Very boring and sad" (Resp. 13 M)

> "I felt very disorganized and wished we could meet as a church" (Resp. 2 L).

> "I felt very devastated and frightened. I had never experienced such a situation before" (Resp. 16 M).

> "I felt very sad, especially when the aged were left out of online church services" (Resp. 28 L).

According to these findings, it appears that a significant number of Christians experienced negative emotions and feelings of sadness when they were unable to gather in person. If this situation had persisted, it is conceivable that a considerable number of Christians may have experienced depression. This underscores the importance of attending church services as a valuable resource for managing negative moods.

Deconstructing Traditional Notions of "Church" and Church Leadership

The COVID-19 pandemic prompted a reevaluation of some time-honored theological perspectives in African Pentecostalism, particularly regarding assumptions about the church and its leadership. One key area of discussion was the traditional understanding of the church. In the African Pentecostal context, the term "church" typically refers to physical buildings, institutions/organizations, or groups of Christians. However, the pandemic has raised important questions about what it truly means to be a church without a physical place of worship. It has challenged the notion of the church as an institution defined by buildings, budgets, and offices and has demonstrated that a church can exist beyond the confines of a physical structure. The rise of virtual communities has necessitated a deconstruction of the church as a physical community, as people can now come together in shared experiences and time, even if they are not physically present in a church building.

Also, amidst the COVID-19 pandemic, African Pentecostalism faced a significant challenge to its traditional understanding of church leadership. The outbreak of the virus prompted a reevaluation of the strict hierarchical structures that had been in place for years. It became evident that the presence of clergy was not always necessary for the thriving of churches, and this realization sparked a need for a new approach to church leadership. The following respondents affirm this notion:

> "It's been a period of reflection. COVID-19 is challenging some of our beliefs and doctrines. Women are administering the Lord's supper (communion) because the pastors can not be there because of the restrictions. Yet in our church, women can't be ordained as pastors" (Resp. 36 L).

> "The pastor can preach to us virtually, but in terms of the sacraments, he cannot be in every home. Someone has to do them in our homes, including single-parent homes, where many of them are led by women. Does God oppose these women from administering sacraments? I don't know. I think we have to come again on some of the teachings we have held so dear to" (Resp. 41 L).

The pandemic-induced closure of churches meant that in many homes, someone provided spiritual leadership and administered sacraments like communion to the family. In many instances, those who offered spiritual leadership were women, which will be a big challenge in some African Pentecostal churches such as the CoP. The reason is that many of these roles are reserved for ordained ministers who are strictly men. COVID-19, therefore, called for a rethink of some of the church's long-held theological views and practices, particularly with regard to gender roles in church leadership.

Post-COVID-19-Vaccine Church Attendance Behavior

Following the lifting of the ban on church meetings, congregations were advised to gather for a maximum of two hours while adhering to all safety protocols. Despite members resuming their regular routines at work, markets, and other social events, churches faced a longer road to recovery. The post-COVID-vaccine church experienced setbacks in areas such as low church attendance, loss of fellowship, welfare concerns, and reduced quality of service and activities.

Low Church Attendance Levels

Respondents were asked to describe the post-COVID-vaccine church behavior at the individual and organizational levels. At the individual level, three general responses were gathered from church members. Some revealed that their church attendance had not been affected by the COVID-19 pandemic. These are some of the responses:

"It has not affected my church attendance" (Resp 12 M).

"I attend church regularly online and in person. There is no problem at all" (Resp 40 L).

"As a serious believer, attending church services is so important you shouldn't allow anything to affect it. My church attendance has not been affected" (Resp. 47 L).

A second group believed that even though the COVID-19 pandemic severely disrupted their church attendance behavior, they had been able to bounce back to church. A third group admitted that the COVID-19 pandemic had affected their church attendance behavior. These are excerpts from the responses:

"Personally, I feel sluggish to attend church sometimes after the pandemic" (Resp. 10 M).

"Many Christians have become relaxed in church attendance and must be supported to attend church" (Resp. 29 L).

"Church attendance has been reduced by as much as 35%. For example, 100 people used to attend weekday services, now it is only 65 people who attend regularly" (Resp. 38 L).

"After the Covid, attendance has reduced by 10%" (Resp. 12 L).

"Generally, the number of people who attend church service has reduced to about 70%. 30% of members are often absent from church. The general attendance has decreased by 10–15%" (Resp. 20 L).

The data indicate that attendance at the chosen churches decreased by 10% to 40% even after the vaccination drive had commenced. On the other hand, some participants attributed the decline in church attendance to factors other than vaccination:

"Many Christians are not committed to the things of God. Those who are not too willing to attend church services now have the perfect opportunity to stay away from church" (Resp. 27 M).

"Some people are just hiding behind the covid effects" (Resp. 15 M).

"Some have generally become lazy or watch services on television to compensate for in-person church service" (Resp. 2 M).

Alternatively, the decline in church attendance may be attributed to a gradual adaptation of church members to the current circumstances, a temporary lapse in spiritual commitment following an extended period of pandemic-related isolation, a greater emphasis on family bonding due to the pandemic, or primarily financial concerns and COVID-19-related stress.

Financial Stress and Welfare Issues

One of the main reasons for decreased church attendance is the economic impact of the pandemic. This has a ripple effect on the microeconomy of individual church members, ultimately affecting the church's overall income. The respondents noted that a significant number of people have been laid off, lost their businesses, or have seen their businesses struggle due to the pandemic's impact on the national economy. As a result, many individuals have been unable to fulfill their tithing and offering obligations; some have even had difficulty affording transportation to church. Additionally, some have had to prioritize their families' basic needs over attending church and participating in related activities. Here are some responses:

"Some of my church members have lost their jobs, which has affected attendance and offerings" (Resp. 21 L).

"Money to even board public transport to church is difficult to come by for some of us" (Resp. 43 M).

"Some of us can't even feed our family, let alone pay tithes and offerings. Things are difficult" (Resp. 6 M).

Financial stress on individuals has impacted church income as the primary sources of funding for the two churches are tithes, offerings, and other donations from members. Accordingly, this has stalled evangelistic activities and capital-intensive church projects. For instance, some respondents shared the following views:

"For more than one year, we have never had any fundraising in the church" (Resp. 21 L).

"Special services like anointing and mid-week services have all been put on hold, so the church is also suffering a lack of funds (Resp. 14 L).

"Some activities like prayer and offerings are done at the cell group level, which limits what is coming in" (Resp. 9 L).

"We have put our church building on hold because income flows are seriously affected" (Resp. 44 L).

Moreover, churches have been affected financially by COVID-19, which has caused them to delay projects and address welfare concerns. As a result, church members have begun to question the welfare strategies of their respective churches, and the churches themselves are reconsidering their approach to welfare issues. These are the views of some respondents:

> "The church does not care about the members. It had no plan for some of us who desperately needed support during the lockdown" (Resp. 10 M).

> "We can't continue to give only for us to be abandoned at the time of our need" (Resp. 19 M).

> "The executive council should consider how welfare issues are addressed in the local [assemblies]. At one point, we were using our money to solve some of the problems. How long can this continue?" (Resp. 37 M).

COVID-19 Anxiety

Another significant factor contributing to the decline in church attendance during the pandemic is the concern of contracting the virus in group settings. The interlocutors emphasized that anxiety over disease transmission, particularly among the elderly and those with underlying health conditions, is a crucial factor in the reduced attendance at church services. This fear was so intense that some individuals continue to avoid attending church even after receiving vaccination. The level of anxiety was particularly high among senior citizens and the elderly. The following feedback from respondents affirms this factor:

> "Some people are afraid of contracting the COVID-19 disease, especially those with underlying health conditions" (Resp. 3 L).

> "Some people have become too hygiene conscious because they fear COVID-19" (Resp. 7 M).

> "Some members are still afraid of contracting COVID-19 in church" (Resp. 21 L).

While certain church members may harbor a general fear of pandemics, others hold a distinct apprehension. They maintain a belief that life is fragile and fleeting, and that death could come at any moment. This outlook has instilled a desire to live right with God.

> "The pandemic has instilled fear in me towards the things of God. Hence, my desire to attend church has increased, although I attend only online services" (Resp. 8 M).

> "The pandemic has shown that death is so close to us. It has also made me more willing to attend church services" (Resp. 20 M).

"People are very conscious of the disease, so it creates fear, anxiety, and insecurity" (Resp. 26 M).

Quality of Experience at Church

Pentecostal-Charismatic liturgy places great emphasis on the experience. However, due to the ongoing pandemic, numerous restrictions and regulations were implemented, forcing churches to adopt alternative strategies to maintain the quality of their services. These regulations impacted activities such as all-night prayer meetings, as churches were required to operate within a two-hour service period and adhere to social distancing guidelines for seating arrangements. These arrangements engendered time consciousness, often making churches rush through their liturgy. One respondent observed: "Church activities are conducted in a rush. It has affected singing and dancing such that people are not able to feel free and dance anymore" (Resp. 47 M). These activities mentioned by the respondent are significant in Pentecostal-Charismatic church worship experiences. It generates a sense of emotional and spiritual release among church attendees.

During the period when the vaccination had just begun in Ghana, the church experience was affected. Although some church members viewed the changes brought about by COVID-19 negatively, others believed that these changes enhanced their connection with God. Some respondents recounted their stories as follows:

> "The pandemic has reduced the liberty to dance, sing praises, and interact freely in the church, but it opens the opportunity for us to do things differently" (Resp. 4 M).

> "As soon as church resumed, people who had greatly missed congregational worship were so joyous. They avowed that worship was awesome as the presence of God was manifested greatly. Post-COVID-19 fellowship levels are generally low. The restrictions have also taken away full satisfaction. Many people, however, believe that half of a loaf is better than none" (Resp. 21 L).

> "Church is not as lively as it used to be before the COVID-19—everything has changed now" (Resp. 35 M).

> "The Pentecostal activities such as crusades, rallies, and evangelism have all been put on hold. Also dancing, clapping, and jumping have all been replaced with sobriety" (Resp. 8 L).

Generally, the church has been impacted in various ways due to the pandemic and its protocols. These include reduced church attendance, financial stress experienced by both individuals and the church as a whole, increased anxiety related to COVID-19, and a decline in the quality of church services.

Conclusion

Based on preceding discussions, it could be inferred that prior to the COVID-19 pandemic, church attendance was generally satisfying for both members and clergy in the two churches. However, the pandemic disrupted in-person meetings and church routines, leading to the introduction of telemediated services and a loss of fellowship due to the sustained adoption of virtual services. This shift in consumer behavior forced churches to reconsider traditional theologies and practices, including finding new ways to be a church, recognizing gender dynamics in church leadership, and adapting liturgies to remain competitive and relevant. Unfortunately, the post-COVID-19-vaccine period was marked by low attendance, financial and welfare issues, COVID-19 anxiety, and a decline in the quality of church services.

Justice A. Arthur (jaarthur@pentvars.edu.gh) is the Director of Postgraduate Studies and Research at Pentecost University in Accra, Ghana.

Lydia Andoh-Quainoo (landoh-quainoo@pentvars.edu.gh) is a lecturer in the Faculty of Business Administration at Pentecost University in Accra, Ghana.

BAYLOR UNIVERSITY PRESS

Joy L. Vaughan

Phenomenal Phenomena

Biblical and Multicultural Accounts of Spirits and Exorcism

$69.99 $48.99 Hardcover | 275 pages | 6 x 9
ISBN 978-1-4813-1836-5

"An excellent compendium of scholarship and an interdisciplinary study of spirit possession in the Gospels and Acts."

—**DANIEL K. DARKO,** *Dean for Global Engagement and Professor of Biblical Studies, Taylor University*

The Holy Spirit and Higher Education
Renewing the Christian University
Amos Yong and Dale M. Coulter
Paperback | $49.99 $34.99 | 320 pages | 7 x 10
ISBN 978-1-4813-1814-3

The Holy Spirit before Christianity
John R. Levison
Hardcover | $44.99 $31.49 | 272 pages | 6 x 9
ISBN 978-1-4813-1003-1

A Profound Ignorance
Modern Pneumatology and Its Anti-modern Redemption
Ephraim Radner
Hardcover | $54.99 $38.49 | 463 pages | 6 x 9
ISBN 978-1-4813-1079-6

Receive a 30% discount and free shipping (US addresses)
Use code 17AARSBL23 until 12/31/23 at
www.baylorpress.com | 1.800.848.6224

REVIEWS

Pentecostal Orthodoxy: Toward an Ecumenism of the Spirit. By Emilio Alvarez. Downers Grove, IL: InterVarsity Press, 2022. xiv + 174 pp.

Emilio Alvarez, associate provost at Asbury Theological Seminary and archbishop of the Union of Charismatic Orthodox Churches, provides an academic yet intimately personal and pastoral work in *Pentecostal Orthodoxy*. As a scholar-practitioner within the movement he is describing, he credibly articulates Pentecostal orthodoxy as a movement within Pentecostalism that attempts to recover the Great Tradition of the church and blends the three historic streams of the church (sacramental/liturgical, evangelical, and Pentecostal/Charismatic). This blending or "amalgamation" is not designed to exclude or assert superiority over other traditions but to create an "ecumenism of the Spirit" (142). The "ecumenism of the Spirit" that is portrayed gives "segments of Pentecostalism" the "opportunity to recover the Great Tradition" (11). This recovery of the Great Tradition precipitates the first aim of the work, to show the shift of some North American Pentecostals from their fundamentalist roots to a more historic Christian faith (5). The second aim of the work is to show how this recovery of orthodoxy is not at odds with Pentecostalism (5). Finally, the work outlines "the theological and historical qualifications" for Pentecostal orthodoxy, noting in particular the contributions of Afro-Latino Pentecostals to this movement (5).

After a laudatory foreword from John Behr, Alvarez introduces his aims, relevant terms with their definitions, and the organization of the work. Chapter one outlines several historical movements within paleo-orthodoxy seeking to recover and blend the three historic streams of the church, covering evangelical orthodoxy, the convergence worship movement, the ancient-future movement, and Pentecostal orthodoxy in detail. Chapter two posits that Pentecostalism is not antithetical to orthodoxy by showing the continuity between Pentecostal orthodoxy and the Great Tradition, Christian monastic traditions, and Christian mystical traditions.

Chapter three proposes that Pentecostals need not abandon their tradition because of their theological retrieval of the Great Tradition (77). Alvarez then provides his journey of recovering the Great Tradition for himself and three other individuals' stories, showing that he is not alone in his experience. Chapter four develops the case for a Pentecostal orthodoxy more by focusing on Afro-Latino Pentecostals doing this work and the pitfalls of the "politicization" and misuse of and ignorance concerning clerical garb, ranks, apostolic succession, and authority. In chapter five, Alvarez problematizes spiritual ecumenism and its focus on human action and prayer, proposing instead an "ecumenism of the Spirit," which provides the opportunity for "creating amalgamated ecclesial communities" (142). Finally, Alvarez finishes chapter five by proposing how Pentecostal dialogues with Catholics, Orthodox, and others could be strengthened by adopting Pentecostal orthodoxy.

Alvarez mostly meets his three aims. First, Alvarez fulfills the aim of showing the shift of some North American Pentecostals from fundamentalist evangelicalism to a more historically grounded faith via the recovery of the Great Tradition. This is done especially well in chapter one's outline of various paleo-orthodox movements and chapter two's linkage of Pentecostal orthodoxy with monasticism and mysticism. Second, Pentecostalism is shown not to be at odds with recovering the Great Tradition. This is shown through the traditioning of Pentecostal orthodoxy within the monastic and mystical Christian traditions (45). However, it is even more poignantly demonstrated via the personal stories provided in chapter three. Third, the work attempts to outline the theological and historical qualifications of Pentecostal orthodoxy and admirably shows the contributions of Afro-Latino Pentecostals to the movement. Alvarez does provide extensive quotations from the early church, which provide a theological base for his understanding of the church's "classic consensual teaching" (21–22). Some fascinating historical moorings for Pentecostal orthodoxy are also included, including William Seymour's surprising use of liturgical ordination rites and an episcopal polity (104). However, the brevity of the work inhibits the expansive theological and historical work that could be done to cover the movement more fully. Alvarez is to be commended for highlighting the presence and importance of Afro-Latino Pentecostals in their recovery of the Great Tradition and for recognizing the white-normative bias of many that can be seen within the scholarship as well as noted from Alvarez's personal observation (101, 115).

Pentecostal Orthodoxy will prove useful for scholars in the fields of Pentecostalism, liturgical studies, ecumenical studies, and those studying doctrinal development. This work provides the first major exploration of the Pentecostal orthodoxy movement. More can be done to express the theological and historical underpinnings of Pentecostal orthodoxy. For instance, Alvarez emphasizes orthopathy in regard to Pentecostal orthodoxy, but the blend of orthopathy, orthodoxy, and orthopraxy can be observed within Pentecostalism and would be fruitfully commented on in further work. This work can be done within each stream of the historic church, but especially within Pentecostalism. In ecumenical studies, some of the hypothetical questions and possibilities that Alvarez posits in his final chapter could provide fruitful material for theological and historical exploration. For the pastor, this work provides the nascence of steps forward, particularly through the inclusion of personal stories, to retrieve the Great Tradition while remaining authentic to one's tradition.

S. Slade Hogan (slade111s@oru.edu) is a PhD student in Contextual Theology at Oral Roberts University, Tulsa, Oklahoma, USA, and Pastor of the Community Church of Milton, Milton, New Hampshire, USA.

Tongues of Fire: A Systematic Theology of the Christian Faith. By Frank Macchia. Eugene: OR: Cascade Books, 2023. 478 pp.

Historically, Pentecostalism has displayed a reluctance to formulate comprehensive systematic theological proposals. This reluctance forces Pentecostals to borrow from the theological methodologies and linguistic underpinnings of Protestant and Evangelical traditions in the construction of their theological systems. Often conflicting with the ethos of Pentecostalism, these adopted theological systems are incapable of capturing the ethos of the Pentecostal tradition. *Tongues of Fire: A Systematic Theology of the Christian Faith* by Frank Macchia attempts to remedy these incompatibilities by utilizing traditional theological categories to construct a comprehensive systematic theology centered upon Pentecost, the primary theological symbol of Pentecostal theology. Macchia's work challenges Protestant and Evangelical traditions to explore Pentecostal sensibilities within traditional theological structures, by prioritizing the theological narrative of Pentecost as central to the construction of its systematic theology. Engaging the traditional loci of Christian theology from the vantage point of Pentecost, Macchia provides a voice for Pentecostal scholarship within traditional pursuits of systematic theology, without relinquishing the spirituality that shapes the theological expression of Pentecostal spirituality.

Tongues of Fire begins with a section devoted to the task of theology. The pneumatological influence of Pentecost is immediately felt by the assertion that the tongues of Pentecost are an essential facet in theological development. Macchia asserts that the tongues of Pentecost declare the wonders of God, making Pentecost an inherently theological event in which God reveals himself as a God who creates, redeems, and indwells. Building upon God's self-revelation through the Pentecost narrative, Macchia promotes theology as a constructive discipline that focuses on doctrinal development, from the sacred text of Scripture to the systematic categories of theological product that have developed throughout the history of the church. Such a theological proposal is rooted in the salvific narrative of Scripture and is historically situated in the finite and socially conditioned language of the church's witness.

Pursuing dogmatics through the lens of Pentecost affords Macchia the opportunity to construct a systematic theology in which christology and pneumatology are mutually informative. Macchia argues that the incarnation and atonement of the Divine Son prevailed as the orthodox position of the Christian faith at the expense of the Spirit. Christology in the West has tended to reduce the Spirit to the utilitarian purpose of bearing witness to Christ in the world. To avoid this tendency, Macchia argues for a Spirit-Christology, which views Christ's incarnation, life, death, and resurrection as leading to Christ's outpouring of the Spirit at Pentecost.

Appropriately, Macchia engages three theological giants as dialogue partners to represent the broad classifications of modern Protestant theology. Friedrich Schleiermacher represents the liberal stream, with an emphasis on the enlightenment of human consciousness. Karl Barth represents the neo-orthodox stream, which reflects a shift away from the soul's journey with God towards the self-revelation of God through his Son Jesus Christ as the authoritative revelation of the Christian faith. Paul Tillich represents the correlation stream, which was an intentional attempt to mediate the tensions between Schleiermacher's emphasis on experience and Barth's emphasis on the proclaimed Word of God. Macchia's willingness to employ these three theological titans as interlocutors provides an opportunity for the dialectic encounter between the Pentecostal narrative and the traditional theological methods that are to come.

Having laid the foundation on which the narrative of Pentecost can interface with traditional theological systems, Macchia begins the heavy lifting of integrating the Pentecost narrative with the categories commonly utilized within the Protestant tradition. Using Pentecost, Macchia expands the epistemological horizons of the traditional categories of theology beyond propositional statements to encompass both the affective and embodied sensibilities of Pentecostal theology. This endeavor has the potential to aid in strengthening the cause of Pentecost in the Western world by providing opportunities to integrate traditional theological systems with the sensibilities found within Pentecostal spirituality. With Pentecost at the center, Macchia's theological proposal can appeal to traditional Protestant theological systems without disregarding or abandoning the basic structures of those systems.

This undertaking by Macchia is not an easy task. The distinct epistemological and ontological views of Pentecostalism are difficult to integrate with Evangelical and Protestant theological systems. Many of Macchia's colleagues, such as (but not limited to) Daniel Castelo and Ken Archer, argue that Pentecostal spirituality is incompatible with Protestant and Evangelical modes of theology. Nonetheless, Macchia presses forward with his attempt to use Pentecost as the filter for traditional theological categories. Adopting Pentecost as the primarily theological symbol to construct systematic theology, Macchia provides the scaffolding that Pentecostals can engage with traditional theological systems of theology without compromising the integrity of the theological narrative that undergirds the production of Pentecostal theology.

Macchia's work serves to demonstrate the capability of Pentecostalism to incorporate itself into traditional Protestant theological structures. Macchia leaves little doubt that traditional Protestant theological development would benefit by assimilating the Pentecostal narrative into its theological systems. In a time when the growth of Pentecostalism significantly dwarfs that of Protestant and Evangelical traditions, Macchia's work should be received as an opportunity for a reassessment of the theological systems employed by Protestant and Evangelical traditions through the theological narrative of Pentecost. *Tongues of Fire*'s masterful incorporation of the Pentecostal narrative into traditional Protestant and Evangelical theological systems serves to display the constructive role Pentecostal scholarship can have in shaping and reforming Evangelical and Protestant theology.

Michael Young (mdyoung@seu.edu) currently serves as an adjunct professor at Pacific Rim University in Honolulu, Hawaii, USA.

A Pneumatology of Race in the Gospel of John: An Ethnocritical Study. By Rodolfo Estrada Galvan, III. Eugene, OR: Pickwick, 2019. 362 pp.

Rodolfo Galvan Estrada, III, is a New Testament scholar who currently serves at Vanguard University. His academic credentials include a PhD from Duke Divinity School. His expertise in New Testament and his experience as a Mexican-American provide the background for this ethnographic exploration in which he connects the work of the Spirit in the Gospel of John with a narrative of subversion in which the ethnic ideologies that could have affected the Johannine community are redefined in light of the Spirit's renewal.

The first part of the book establishes the different nuances of Johannine pneumatology and the ethnic issues surrounding the original audience. The author describes how the pneumatology of John's gospel differs from the Synoptics, unveiling perspectives that include an eschatological, polemical, and socio-scientific understanding. The main theme for Estrada is that the Spirit can be properly understood in the Fourth Gospel as the social context of the Johannine community (13). His thesis explores the implications of a pneumatic discourse that responds to "the ethnic ideologies of the Greco-Roman world" (23). To reach his objective, he employs the ethnocritical method to insert the ministry of the Spirit in a multiethnic reality that was present in the Greco-Roman world. Estrada's pneumatology of race starts with the history of the socio-cultural ideologies of the Greeks and Romans, and their implications to the relationship with the Jewish community.

Part two explores the central argument of the author in light of the Spirit's appearances in the discourses of Jesus. Estrada applies his thesis to instances in which Jesus interacts with people from different ethnic backgrounds and social statuses. For the author, the Spirit's role in Jesus' discourse has cultural implications for the Johannine communities. The author places the ethnocritical lens to conclude that the Spirit anoints Jesus to reach to all ethnicities, facilitates spiritual birth to non-Jews without the natural genealogies that created racial prejudice and superiority in Israel, calls for a unified corporate worship without mutual rejections, and warrants infilling for Jews and Greeks alike. In all of the chapters of this section, Estrada summarizes the pneumatological truths that would have deeply transformed the inter-ethnic relationships of the Johannine community. Within the overall argument of part two, there is a recurrent theme that emerges: the work of the Spirit throughout the narrative is both the ideal picture and the prophetic reality to heal the prejudices that could have affected members of the Johannine community.

Finally, in part three, the author explores the Spirit as paraclete in light of impending persecution for the disciples. The author grounds the Spirit-paraclete ministry in the

Farewell Discourses to walk with the disciples' in their impending persecution. Estrada posits that the world is understood as an ethnic group that will persecute the disciples and the ethnic Johannine community. His argument closes by interpreting the Johannine Pentecost as an event that moves the Johannine community into a hostile world to proclaim their faith as true children of God. For the author, the ethnic ideologies that were imported from the Greco-Roman world provided the context to see the Spirit as the source of a pneumatoethnic identity for the Johannine community. Such ministry was prescriptive because the Johannine community had a solution against racial inequality and reconciliation. The implications of this "pneumatic solution" (298) carries out perpetually as believers today must learn to live in unity in a world that could be as ethnically oppressive as the Greco-Roman society in the New Testament.

The strongest arguments of the author relate to the understanding of the cultural background of the Greco-Roman world to which the audience belonged. His thorough research of historical documents and commentaries demonstrates how the ethnic complexities of the original audience galvanized a distinct pneumatology. His ethnographic approach nuanced widely accepted theological truths in Johannine literature. Likewise, the author's approach presented theories that could solve problematic passage such as the flesh and Spirit discourse of John 6 (170) and the open-ended nature of the Johannine Pentecost (287).

The author also successfully handles a presumptive bias due to his ethnic identity. Despite proposing new, and occasionally ground-breaking, insights to Johannine scholarship, he is never off-tempo with other commentaries, nor does he impose an anachronistic lens to his study of the Fourth Gospel. He accomplishes this by exploring the layers of the multiethnic cultural context to cement his conclusion that it played a part in the pneumatology of the Johannine community. As the discussion moves to the Farewell Discourses, the author's assumption that multiple ethnic ideologies necessitated a pneumatology of unity slightly fades to accommodate more traditional pneumatological theories, albeit with a focus on ethnic identity language.

Rodolfo Estrada has provided a vital addition to New Testament studies—one that is apropos with the current times of ethnic and racial differences affecting society. The contributions of this volume could further the discipline of contextual hermeneutics and popularize similar ethnographic studies in other portions of biblical literature. It could also serve as a scholarly demonstration of contextual theology on the biblical text emerging from a member of the Latino Diaspora in the United States.

Harold Gutierrez (hgutier2@oru.edu) is a PhD student in Contextual Theology at Oral Roberts University, Tulsa, Oklahoma, USA. He currently serves as intercultural ministries director for the BC/Yukon District of PAOC and is an adjunct faculty member at Summit Pacific College in Abbotsford, British Columbia, Canada.

Oneness Pentecostalism: Race, Gender, and Culture. Edited by Lloyd D. Barba, Andrea S. Johnson, and Daniel Ramírez. University Park, PA: The Pennsylvania University Press, 2023. 282 pp.

About twenty years ago, I was teaching a course in systematic theology at an interdenominational evangelical seminary in Toronto. The institution served many theological communities, including the Pentecostal Assemblies of Canada (PAOC), a historic and Trinitarian leaning denomination. In the class, a PAOC student articulated a position that was very close to Oneness theology. The encounter suggested that the separation between Trinitarian and Oneness Pentecostalism was not as definitive a break as has been claimed. The PAOC has a historical origin different from the Assemblies of God, as David Reed ably argues. Howard Goss, a Oneness Pentecostal and cosigner of the dominion charter, remained with the PAOC even after it embraced a Trinitarian position. For eighteen years, Goss pastored the very church my forementioned student attended. Reed's historical reconstruction helps to make sense of this curious encounter.

The book is organized around the prominent themes of race and gender. Mexican Oneness Pentecostals were a significant cluster, the focus of chapters by Daniel Ramírez, Patricia Fortuny Loret de Molan, and Daniel Chiquete. Of particular interest was Ramírez's claim that the Assemblies of God origins narrative of Hot Springs (1914) and St. Louis (1916) needs to be relativized as a number of pre-1914 Mexicans were already practicing Jesus' name water baptism, such as Juan Navarro, Luis Lopez (1909), Francisco Llorente (1912), and Romana Valenzeula. Daniel Segraves' reconstruction of Andrew D. Urshan's theology is rooted in his Persian heritage, with Syrian and Nestorian Christian influences that provide much insight to be plumbed by theologians on both sides of the debate with implications for ecumenical dialogue. And there are excellent chapters by Rosa Sailes and Dara Colby Delgado on African American Oneness developments especially among women in which resistance to cultural racism provided an important lens for understanding the differences from other Oneness Christians.

Chapters by Sailes, Andrea Johnson, Delgado, and de Molan tackle the complex issue of gender in which Oneness Pentecostal women replicate the patriarchal attitudes and structures while also arguing how these women subvert expected norms as they fulfilled their religious calling. Geneva Brazier, an African American woman with a fundamentalist theology grounded in a strict Oneness and Holiness ethos, would subvert that ethos by decorating for Christmas and enjoying baseball and marbles, behaviors that violated Pentecostal Assemblies of the World (PAW) restrictions. Moreover, she was committed to social activism, civil rights, and justice in confronting the racism of her day. In a complementary manner, Delgado explores the gender politic in the PAW in which men adopted a passive-aggressive approach in its progressive patriarchalism. Black women were entrepreneurial, innovative, and agents of activism as they resisted patriarchal norms, even while PAW men worked to limit women's liberty to protect male authority. Johnson examines how women held some authority and as evangelists could perform marriages, funerals, baptisms, and communion but only in emergencies. The mission field offered more advantages as women were freer from gender challenges. Again, Oneness women challenged patriarchal norms while navigating within patriarchal structures. De Molan examines the norms and rules for women associated with the Luz del Munda Church, a Mexican church that combines Pentecostal theology and norms with regional Catholic culture. Women are denied access to the upper echelons of power and can only be in charge and work at the lower rung of the church hierarchy. However, de Molan adopts a Foucauldian analysis in that the deployment of power has both formal and informal arrangements, and Luz del Mundo women predominantly operate in informal settings. De Mola's transgenerational analysis finds a considerable range of diversity that makes gender relations and forms of power highly paradoxical.

These chapters triangulate with contemporary scholarship investigating women and power in global Pentecostal settings. With years of gaining improvements and rights for women in both the secular and religious spheres, and the purported egalitarian values brought by ecstatic rituals such as glossolalia, why are Pentecostal women not more represented in the upper echelons of leadership? The answer resides in the "gender paradox" in which Pentecostal women were willing to negotiate (intentionally or unintentionally), giving up formal authority to men who embraced holiness codes that supported the family and the well-being of the marriage. In other words, male conversion placed restrictions around alcohol consumption, smoking, gambling, and womanizing that brought men back into the family system. Pentecostal women desired these holiness regulations and in order to maintain this newfound comportment, they were willing to divest of their religious power and allow men positions of formal authority (e.g., see Elizabeth E. Brusco, *The Reformation of Machismo: Evangelical Conversion and Gender in Columbia* [Austin, TX: University of Texas Press, 1995]).

An implicit theme is the role of migration in the development of the complex tapestry of Oneness Pentecostalism. Ramírez and Reed point to migration of both sides of the US border, in which Mexicans took their newfound faith down to Mexico (either voluntarily or through forced expulsion), and Europeans across the northern border. Lloyd Barba explores migration of Okies from the midwest and southern states to California, bringing with them a more bombastic and confrontational form of Pentecostalism, thereby transforming the more conciliatory and cosmopolitan Oneness Pentecostals that already existed on the west coast. Sailes contends that the migration of

Robert and Geneva Brazier from Alabama to Chicago, in which Geneva eventually pastored Oneness churches and founded a family legacy passed on to her children and grandchildren in which community action, social justice, and civil rights were exemplified to address the plight of impoverished African Americans.

How should one theorize about these migrations within the US and across borders? Ramirez suggests that Mexican migration was socio-political as well as faithful Pentecostals following their religious calling. Barba demonstrates a south and midwest to west migration that was in part due to the droughts and economic turmoil of the mid-twentieth century. The northern border was more porous as people crossed back and forth with relative ease. What were the mechanisms that spurred migration and how did they fit in the broader global flows?

Oneness Pentecostalism is an impressive contribution to Pentecostal studies. Although Pentecostal scholarship has exploded, there has been scant research produced on Oneness Pentecostalism, as the editors rightly note. The editors and contributors are to be commended for organizing and implementing this interdisciplinary volume. An edited volume is as strong as its weakest chapter. *Oneness Pentecostalism* does not have any weak chapters, and this is its strength. The book exposes a sector of global Pentecostalism that has been under-researched and provides a richer picture of the complex maze of a twentieth-century religious movement.

N.B. A longer version of this review was presented in the Manchester Wesley Research Centre/ Pentecostal Theological Seminary panel at the American Academy of Religion in San Antonio, Texas, 2023.

Peter Althouse (palthouse@oru.edu) is Professor of Theology and Religion at Oral Roberts University, Tulsa, Oklahoma, USA.

Spiritus
ORU JOURNAL OF THEOLOGY

Volume 9, Number 2 (Fall 2024)

Spiritus: ORU Journal of Theology
Volume 9, Number 2 (Fall 2024)

ISSN: 2573-6345

ISBN:

Copyright © 2024 Oral Roberts University; published by ORU's College of Theology and Ministry and the Center for Spirit-empowered Research.

All rights reserved. To reproduce by any means any portion of this journal, one must first receive the formal consent of the publisher. To request such consent, write *Spiritus* Permissions – ORU COTM, 7777 S. Lewis Ave., Tulsa, OK 74171 USA. *Spiritus* hereby authorizes reproduction (of content not expressly declared not reproducible) for these non-commercial uses: personal, educational, and research, but prohibits re-publication without its formal consent.

Each issue is available at no cost for authorized uses at www.oru.edu/spiritus and may be purchased in print using the "Buy" button at this site.

Spiritus: ORU Journal of Theology is published semi-annually in Spring and Fall.

One-year subscriptions may be purchased at the following rates: US $50 within USA; US $65 to Canada and Mexico; approximately US $80 elsewhere (adjusted, as needed, to cover shipping costs).

Subscriptions begin upon (1) release of the next issue and (2) successful deposit by *Spiritus* of the correct subscription rate and receipt of complete shipping information: subscriber name, full postal address, subscriber email address, and telephone number (including international country code prefix). Subscribe at *Spiritus* Subscriptions. (Send subscription correspondence, including address changes, to the same.)

— ORU COTM, 7777 S. Lewis Ave., Tulsa, OK 74171 USA.

Spiritus: ORU Journal of Theology is indexed through the Digital Commons (https:// www.bepress.com/impact-analytics/) and in the ATLA Religion Database published by the American Theological Library Association, 5600 South Woodlawn Avenue, Chicago, IL 60637. *Spiritus* contents may be searched at www.oru.edu/spiritus and through any web search engine. (Because another "Spiritus" journal is published by The Johns Hopkins University Press, searches for contents from ORU's *Spiritus* may succeed better by using the full title and subtitle.)

Cover designer: ORU art alumnus Hye Ji Byun and Prof. Jiwon Kim.

Compositor: Daniel Isgrigg

ORU JOURNAL OF THEOLOGY

EDITOR

Jeffrey S. Lamp, Senior Professor, New Testament & Instructor, Environmental Science

ASSOCIATE EDITORS

Wonsuk Ma, Distinguished Professor of Global Christianity and Executive Director, Center for Spirit-empowered Research
Daniel D. Isgrigg, Associate Professor, College of Theology and Ministry

REVIEWS EDITOR

Robert D. McBain, Research Coordinator, Center for Spirit-empowered Research

EDITORIAL ADVISORY BOARD

Allan Anderson, University of Birmingham, UK
Candy Gunther Brown, Indiana University
Kwabena Asamoa-Gyuadu, Trinity Theological Seminary, Ghana

UNIVERSITY ADMINISTRATION

William M. Wilson, President
Kathaleen Reid-Martinez, Provost
Adrian E. Hinkle, Dean, College of Theology and Ministry

Spiritus: ORU *Journal of Theology* . . .

- Publishes studies from all disciplines pertaining to Spirit-empowered Christianity, from established and emerging scholars

- Emphasizes theological and cognate studies and works from and about Christianity in the Majority World

- Reviews pertinent scholarly works and some professional and popular works of merit

- Publishes scholarship to benefit especially Spirit-empowered Christian communities globally.

Find instructions for submitting articles and reviews for consideration at http://DigitalShowcase.ORU.edu/Spiritus/. This site receives all submissions leading to publishing decisions.

Views expressed in *Spiritus* are those of the contributors only.

Their publication in *Spiritus* does not express or imply endorsement by Oral Roberts University.

Correspondence (not related to submissions or subscriptions) is welcomed at <Spiritus@ORU.edu> or

Spiritus — ORU
Center for Spirit-empowered Research
7777 S. Lewis Ave.
Tulsa, OK 74171 USA.

CONTENTS

Editorial

Editorial: Most Likely You Go Your Way…
Jeffrey S. Lamp 147

Essays

PCCNA and USCCB Historic Exploratory Dialogue: From Mass to the Vatican then "Little Rome."
Harold D. Hunter 151

A Catholic Perspective on the New Relationship Between the Pentecostal Charismatic Churches of North America and the United States Conference of Catholic Bishops
Walter F. Kedjierski 157

Initiation Sacraments and Directions for Catholic-Pentecostal Dialogue: An Essay for the Exploratory USCCB/PCCNA Dialogue
Kimberly Hope Belcher 173

Initiation (Water Baptism) in North American Pentecostalism
Frederick L. Ware 187

Response to Frederick L. Ware
Kimberly Hope Belcher 201

Response to Kimberly Hope Belcher
Frederick L. Ware 205

Varieties of Healing: A Catholic Perspective
Andrew Prevot 207

Healing in the Pentecostal Tradition
David Han 229

Response to David Han's "Healing in the Pentecostal Tradition"
Andrew Prevot 245

A Pentecostal Appreciation of Andrew Prevot's "Varieties of Healing: A Catholic Perspective"
Harold D. Hunter 247

A Brief Consideration of the Sacrament of Marriage from a Catholic Perspective for Pentecostal Christians
Walter F. Kedjierski 253

Lex Orandi, Lex Serviendi: Roman Catholic Theology of Ordained Ministry in Select Texts from the Rites of Ordination
Leonardo J. Gajardo 273

Called: A Pentecostal Theology of Vocation
Martin W. Mittelstadt 295

Response to Martin Mittelstadt
Leonardo J. Gajardo 319

Response to Walter Kedjierski and Leonardo Gajardo
Martin W. Mittelstadt 323

Reviews

Pentecostal Prophets: Experience in Old Testament Perspective. By Stephen D. Barkley.
Wonsuk Ma 326

Phenomenal Phenomena: Biblical and Multicultural Accounts of Spirits and Exorcism. By Joy L. Vaughan.
Daniel D. Isgrigg 329

Christ Centered: The Evangelical Nature of Pentecostal Theology. By Robert Menzies.
Michael Young 332

Follow the Healer: Biblical Foundations for Healing Ministry. By Stephen Seamands.
Sam M. Barsoum 335

The Kaleidoscopic City: Hong Kong, Mission, and the Evolution of Global Pentecostalism. By Alex R. Mayfield.
Van Hnuai Kim 338

Soon and Very Soon: A Biblical and Theological Study of the Events Surrounding Jesus Christ's Second Coming. By David K. Hebert.
Cletus L. Hull, III 341

Editorial: Most Likely You Go Your Way...

Jeffrey S. Lamp, Editor

This issue of *Spiritus* is a special one indeed. Almost three years ago I received a message from Martin Mittelstadt of Evangel University concerning the dialogue underway between representatives of the Pentecostal and Charismatic Churches of North America (PCCNA) and the US Conference of Catholic Bishops (USCCB). This dialogue would take place over a three-year period (2021–2003), with papers and responses addressing three topics from the perspectives of Pentecostals and Roman Catholics. The participants expressed an interest in having the presentations from this dialogue published in journals representing both traditions. Professor Mittelstadt suggested that *Spiritus* be the repository of these studies on the Pentecostal side (the journal *Worship* will publish them on the Roman Catholic side), to which the editorial team gladly responded, Yes! The dialogue completed, Mittelstadt's team worked to compile the papers and send them my way for the editorial task of readying them for publication.

This was no small task! A total of fifteen separate offerings arrived in a combined document, along with author bios and photos. Disaggregating them into separate files and combining them with their respective bios and photos was the first step. But then came the task of reading them for the purpose of editing. What at first just seemed a daunting editorial task turned into a real delight. Before me was the fruit of a lengthy dialogue, a dialogue that was not only a gathering of learned scholars describing and responding to the positions of the two traditions on some potentially controversial topics—sacraments/ordinances of initiation, healing, and vocation—but also a time of refreshing and mutual edification. I could sense this in reading the submissions, so much so that I was often engrossed in soaking it all in and had to go back and do my job as editor.

As I noted, we have collected here fifteen pieces, consisting of three cycles of papers read and responses given by representatives of PCCNA and USCCB. Harold Hunter, International Pentecostal Holiness Church Ecumenical Officer, and Walter Kedjierski, Executive Director of the Secretariat for Ecumenical and Interreligious Affairs of the USCCB, launch this issue with general commentary on the proceedings of the dialogue from Pentecostal and Roman Catholic perspectives, respectively, providing historical context and personal reflections on the discussions. The first cycle of papers, presented in 2021 in Washington, DC, at a Catholic retreat center called the Washington Retreat House, addressed the topic of initiation, primarily baptism, in the two traditions. Frederick Ware of Howard University presented the quite varied positions of Pentecostals, drawing on personal testimony to do so, while Kimberly Belcher of the University of Notre Dame presented the Catholic position. The second cycle, presented in 2022 at Oral Roberts University (ORU) in Tulsa, Oklahoma, covered the topic of healing (appropriately enough). David Han of Pentecostal Theological Seminary and Andrew Prevot of Georgetown University provided illuminating discussions of how healing is perceived in the two traditions.[1] The final cycle of papers, covering the topic of vocation, was presented on the campus of the University of Notre Dame in Notre Dame, Indiana. This topic proved sufficiently complex as to require two papers from the Roman Catholic perspective. The concept of vocation in the Catholic Church is understood from two angles: the sacraments of marriage and Holy Orders. Walter Kedjierski presents an insightful look at marriage from the Catholic perspective, much of which may be unknown to many Pentecostals, while Leonardo Gajardo, a priest in the Roman Catholic Diocese of Gary, Indiana, presents a Catholic understanding of ordained ministry. Martin Mittelstadt of Evangel University presents what is essentially a view of what vocation should be from a Pentecostal perspective in light of its somewhat narrow focus on church ministries.

At the end of the day, this collection of papers and responses was not only informative (at least from my perspective), but also very encouraging. While it may have been the preconception of many of the dialogue participants that there was not too much common ground between these two traditions, what eventuated was a recognition by all that there was a great deal of common ground that encourages continued discussion and provides a foundation for engaging in those areas in which there is substantial disagreement. In a world wracked with division, it is refreshing to see a concerted effort to understand one another and find common ground for discourse.

And now, the answer to the question some of you may have regarding the title of this editorial. First, some background. I was pastor of Spiro First United Methodist Church in Spiro, Oklahoma, 1995–2000. In June of 2000, I gave my final sermon before moving to Tulsa to take a full-time faculty post at ORU. The title of that sermon was the title of this editorial. Kudos to those who recognize it as part of the title of an old Bob Dylan song. In the way it was the title of my farewell to Spiro, it is also my farewell to *Spiritus*. To my surprise, I have been editor for eight volume years. As with any undertaking, there have been times of exhilaration, mostly when an issue is actually published, and times of great stress, but in the final analysis, I am happy with what the

---

[1] David Han was not available to respond to the paper by Andrew Prevot. It then became the responsibility of co-chair Harold Hunter to write the Pentecostal response to Prevot's paper.

journal has been able to accomplish in this time. As of the Spring 2025 issue, Mark Roberts of ORU will serve as editor. There are so many to thank for what has taken place here. I thank all who have contributed articles and book reviews, both those that were published and those that were not. I thank Wonsuk Ma for bringing the journal back from a thirty-two-year hiatus and making it a part of the scholarly culture at ORU. Sally Shelton and Robert McBain served as book review editors during this time. And Daniel Isgrigg has served in the herculean role of managing editor, which entailed all of the processes that take the articles I give him to the actual published issues people can actually read. I cannot thank him enough. He has been an indispensable part of the effort to produce this journal. And a great thanks to the College of Theology and Ministry at ORU for its support of the journal.

So to complete the title of the song, "Most Likely You Go Your Way, and I'll Go Mine." I am not leaving ORU, nor is this a final goodbye to the journal. I have lived with it for too long to let it slip away from my life. I will be a supporter of its efforts, and maybe here and there try to get something published in it. Any journal that has had downloads to Antarctica must be doing something right. Perhaps that is my proudest moment as editor.

Jeffrey S. Lamp (jlamp@oru.edu) is Senior Professor of New Testament and Instructor of Environmental Science at Oral Roberts University, Tulsa, Oklahoma, USA.

PCCNA AND USCCB HISTORIC EXPLORATORY DIALOGUE

FROM MASS TO THE VATICAN THEN "LITTLE ROME"[1]

HAROLD D. HUNTER

Venerated Apostolic Faith Mission South Africa (AFM/SA) ecumenist David DuPlessis was the Pentecostal co-organizer of the oldest and most prestigious Pentecostal dialogue. Talks with the Vatican in Rome have passed fifty years. DuPlessis would be eclipsed by anti-apartheid crusader Frank Chikane and now the AFM is the first church from the Pentecostal World Fellowship (PWF) to join the World Council of Churches (WCC). Those present with the WCC Central Committee (June 2021) witnessed AFM President Henri Weideman make mention of DuPlessis as part of his acceptance speech.

DuPlessis set in motion a series of Pentecostal "Lone Ranger" ecumenists, although AFM would come to write their own story. These early ecumenists have impacted the academy but what about Pentecostal churches? Of course, it is a fair question about how many churches are listening when the dialogues are often removed from current issues faced by pastors.

Cheryl Bridges Johns published an article that showcased competing models of Pentecostal ecumenism. I was identified as someone who always got endorsements from the head of his/her church for a wide range of engagements involving NCC Faith and Order, WCC, Ecumenical Patriarchate, and various bilaterals.[2] Fast forward to the second decade of the twenty-first century and now official Pentecostal dialogues are processed through organizations like Pentecostal Churches of North America (PCCNA) and the PWF. When I put together talks with the Ecumenical Patriarchate—2010–2012—it was the first time that the PWF had endorsed any bilateral dialogue.

This monumental sea change along with the rise of ecumenical officers in North America like the late Church of God in Christ scholar Leonard Lovett, Cecil M. Robeck, David Cole, Frank Patrick, David Moore, and Harold D. Hunter, along with

---

[1] While a student at a Pentecostal college in Cleveland, Tennessee, I first attended Roman Catholic mass at age 19. My first visit to the Vatican was 1989 where I was able to greet Pope John Paul II. The first edition of the PCCNA-USCCB exploratory dialogue was hosted by the USCCB in Washington DC's "Little Rome."

[2] Cheryl Bridges Johns, "Remodeling Our Ecumenical House," in *Pentecostal Theology and Ecumenical Theology*, eds. Peter Hocken, Tony Richie, and Christopher Stephenson (Leiden: Brill, 2019), 146–47.

the Church of God (Cleveland, Tennessee) ecumenical commission led by David Han, deserve attention due to the evolution of the approval process for conciliar ecumenism, bilaterals, and multilaterals. Parts of that new reality will be reviewed as illustrated in the historic PCCNA-USCCB (United States Council of Catholic Bishops) exploratory dialogue so that upcoming Pentecostal ecumenists have a clear path. I will not, however, give details about the work I did together with Prince Guneratnam and others to organize the PWF CUC (Christian Unity Commission) five years earlier at the Pentecostal World Conference in Calgary, Canada.

Dialogue Participants, Oral Roberts University, 2022

In the early 1980s, I was a full-time faculty member at the Church of God seminary in Cleveland, Tennessee, now known as the Pentecostal Theological Seminary (PTS). Some months after my 1983 Society for Pentecostal Studies (SPS) program hosted by PTS, Jerry Sandidge came to Cleveland on behalf of David DuPlessis. Sandidge was looking for church headquarters that would designate official representatives for the ongoing talks with the Vatican. I positioned Church of God of Prophecy (CGP) to endorse this notion. However, I subsequently declined the invitation from the CGP headquarters because at the time I thought teaching at PTS might create unnecessary distractions and also thought sending a CGP bishop at first would be an advantage.

This is not the only time I gave up my seat to make room for minoritized voices. CGP had taught me to take the last seat. While there were unfortunate aspects of that move on my part, one positive thing was opening a relationship with Jack Radano who represented the Pontifical Council for Promoting Christian Unity (PCPCU) in talks with Pentecostals led by DuPlessis. Radano made possible a 1989 General Audience with Pope John Paul II where I greeted him in front of St. Peter's Basilica. I have also been with Pope Francis various times including a 2022 General Audience inside the Vatican and more importantly in 2021 with global faith leaders of all religions working toward COP26.

In 2015, I made a routine visit to the PCPCU at the Vatican in Rome. This was part of a trip that would continue on to Antalya, Turkey, for the WCRC-Pentecostal Dialogue. There are parts of one conversation at the Vatican that kept those exchanges safely lodged in my memory. I came away from that visit convinced that now was the time to work toward a dialogue in the USA between Roman Catholics and Pentecostals even though earlier attempts had failed. I had taken a similar trajectory with the Eastern Orthodox launching direct talks with the Ecumenical Patriarchate in Constantinople. When those talks went on hiatus then I launched an academic version in the USA linked to the annual AAR/SBL meetings.[3]

Once back in the USA, with the approval of International Pentecostal Holiness Church (IPHC) Presiding Bishop A. D. Beacham, Jr., I advocated for the prospect of a PCCNA-USCCB dialogue. As the IPHC Liaison to the Greater Christian Community all my ecumenical activities were subject to the approval of the IPHC Presiding Bishop. I then put the concept before the PCCNA Christian Unity Commission—that is the steering committee then the full commission—which was later taken up by the PCCNA executive committee.[4]

At the same time, Christian Churches Together (CCT) attracted many of those who would make decisions for both PCCNA and USCCB. IPHC is a charter member of CCT (USA) and is the only member of the PWF and PCCNA that is also a member of CCT. Open Bible Churches was a member of CCT when Jeff Farmer was president

---

[3] Harold D. Hunter, "An Emmaus Walk with Ancient Fathers and Mothers: From the Sawdust Trail to the Ecumenical Patriarchate," in *Leadership, Spirituality, and the Holy Spirit*, eds. Wonsuk Ma and Robert Menzies (Tulsa, OK: ORU Press, forthcoming 2024), volume honoring the 70th birthday of Younghoon Lee.

[4] Some may not realize that PCCNA was created during the so-called "Memphis Miracle" in 1994 when PFNA (Pentecostal Fellowship of North America) was dissolved. More information can be found in the PCCNA *Reconciliation* magazine that I created and co-edited with Mel Robeck. Relevant information can be found in Harold D. Hunter, "Attacking Systemic Racism for the Common Good: Excerpts from the History of the 'Racial Reconciliation Manifesto,'" in *The Politics of the Spirit: Pentecostal Reflections on Public Responsibility and the Common Good*, eds. Chris Green and Daniela Augustine (Lanham, MD: Seymour Press, 2023), 39–50. This article uses the "Racial Reconciliation Manifesto" to judge the racial dimension of that transition by drawing attention to PFNA blocking Pentecostals of color and Oneness Pentecostals from membership or even participation. After Howard Goss, United Pentecostal Church, came to a 1948 meeting toward forming PFNA, the group quickly adopted a National Association of Evangelicals statement in part to exclude Oneness Pentecostals. I then speculate on what might have happened had the Pentecostal Assemblies of the World (PAW) been a member of PFNA that would have included the legendary Bishop Brazier in Chicago.

of Open Bible Churches. Other PCCNA churches have declined invitations to join CCT. However, PCCNA approved an official observer for the 2023 CCT meeting in Savannah, Georgia.

The executive director of CCT for years was Carlos Malave who was faithful to attend annual PCCNA meetings and contribute to discussions with the CUC. The next leader to emerge in 2022 was Monica Schaap Pierce who joined the 2022 PCCNA CUC by Zoom and was present in-person for the 2023 PCCNA CUC in Albuquerque. Schappe Pierce also came to the 2022 IPHC General Conference in Jacksonville, Florida.

Another piece of the puzzle was Bro. Jeff Gross. During the 1983 SPS at the Church of God seminary in Cleveland, I wanted to invite someone from the NCCCUSA. However, the SPS executive committee did not endorse such a move. Further, I was not allowed to invite James Cone to be a keynote speaker. I was president of SPS in 1984 when we were hosted by Gordon-Conwell Theological Seminary outside Boston, Massachusetts. Brother Jeff came at the behest of William G. Rusch to invite Pentecostal scholars to participate in the NCCCUSA Faith and Order Commission.

I knew about Rusch because I had used his book on the Holy Spirit in my PTS class on pneumatology. I gave up part of the time allocated to me as SPS President for Bro. Jeff to extend this invitation. My memory is that among those who were first to respond to this invitation were Edith Blumhofer (Assemblies of God), Cheryl Bridges Johns (Church of God, Cleveland), Cecil M. Robeck (Assemblies of God), Jerry Sandidge (Assemblies of God), and Harold D. Hunter (Church of God of Prophecy).

Now called Faith and Order Tables, this body expanded my ecumenical network in the USA and beyond. I also played a minor role in getting Bro. Jeff elected as an SPS president. This echoed my earlier work in 1982 when at the SPS annual meeting, hosted by Fuller Theological Seminary, I helped get through a constitutional change that translated into Reformed scholar J. Rodman Williams and then Roman Catholic Charismatic scholar Peter Hocken following me as presidents of SPS.

During the February 2018 PCCNA conference in New Orleans, members of the PCCNA CUC steering committee met with a subcommittee of the PCCNA executive committee. According to then PCCNA president Jeff Farmer in an email to the PCCNA CUC steering committee, a motion was made and passed to advance this dialogue I had proposed. When discussing my proposal with the PCCNA CUC while in New Orleans, we were fortunate to include Monsignor Juan Usma Gomez from the Vatican in our deliberations.

It is also the case that all the USCCB ecumenical officers I have engaged acknowledged the impact Bro. Jeff Gros had on them. Brother Jeff had advocated for a USA dialogue with Pentecostals. By 2020, it would be announced that this exploratory dialogue was endorsed by both the PCCNA and USCCB.[5] The USCCB team is led by Rev. Dr. Walter F. Kedjierski, an ecumenical expert who has led with wisdom, compassion, and insight. We are most fortunate to have engaged the excellent USCCB team, a charisma to the church universal. The agreed themes were initiation, healing, and vocation/mission, which echoes Roman Catholic sacraments. Details about the three years may be found in press releases easily found by the web links in this footnote.[6] Our host each year has gone above and beyond to enable our ministry.

This historic dialogue provides an opportunity to review the emerging model of Pentecostal ecumenism linked to both PCCNA and PWF. The core member churches of PCCNA were identified as candidates for members of the Pentecostal team. I steadfastly campaigned for racial, gender, and faith tradition diversity. Note that each member of the Pentecostal team was endorsed by his or her church and received financial support.

Rev. Dr. Harold D. Hunter, International Pentecostal Holiness Church, chair.

Rev. Dr. Frederic Ware, Church of God in Christ, 2021–2023, paper read 2021.

Rev. Dr. David Han, Church of God (Cleveland, Tennessee) 2021–2023, paper read 2022.

Rev. Dr. Martin Mittelstadt, Assemblies of God, 2021–2023, paper read 2023.

Rev. Dr. Tammy Dunahoo, International Church of the Foursquare Gospel, 2021–2022.

Rev. Jennifer Thigpen, International Church of the Foursquare Gospel, 2023.

---

[5] Some will point to the lack of Oneness Pentecostals. I share that concern as the SPS executive committee member that took in Manuel Gaxiola-Gaxiola in 1982. Gaxiola was the first Oneness Pentecostal to join SPS and I was heavily criticized for receiving him at the time. However, beyond the Goss PFNA story mentioned earlier, one of the dramas at the 1994 launch of PCCNA was a request to include Oneness Pentecostals. A PAW minister came to the platform, where I and others were seated, to ask for such consideration, but that has never been realized. Since this dialogue is endorsed by the PCCNA then only member churches can be members of the team. However, during our September 2022 meeting at ORU, I accepted a Oneness Pentecostal as an observer who is a PhD student at ORU.

[6] Rev. Dr. Walter K. Kedjierski is executive director of the USCCB Secretariat for Ecumenical and Interreligious Affairs. Here is his personal reflection on how we started:
https://www.usccb.org/news/2021/celebrating-new-relationship-pccna-and-usccb. Press release for 2021: https://www.usccb.org/news/2021/pentecostalcharismatic-christians-and-roman-catholics-engage-exploratory-ecumenical. Press release for 2022:
https://www.usccb.org/news/2022/representatives-catholic-and-pentecostal-churches-meet-ecumenical-dialogue. Press release for 2023: https://www.usccb.org/news/2023/representatives-catholic-and-pentecostal-churches-meet-ecumenical-dialogue. PCCNA released identical reports under their own name like 2022 at https://pccna.org/documents/2022.09.23_USCCB.pdf. and 2023 at https://myemail.constantcontact.com/Representatives-from-Catholic-and-Pentecostal-Churches-Meet-for-Ecumenical-Dialogue.html?soid=1109615552491&aid=XBKb_B_X5tI.

Dialogue Participants, University of Notre Dame, 2023

Harold D. Hunter (hdhpctii@gmail.com) is the International Pentecostal Holiness Church Ecumenical Officer and an Adjunct Professor at ORU Graduate School of Theology, Tulsa, Oklahoma, USA.

A Catholic Perspective

on the New Relationship Between the Pentecostal Charismatic Churches of North American and the United States Conference of Catholic Bishops

WALTER F. KEDJIERSKI

Introduction

"My family has just gotten bigger." That was a closing sentiment of one of the Pentecostal participants after the first gathering of theologians representing the Pentecostal Charismatic Churches of North America (PCCNA) and the United States Conference of Catholic Bishops (USCCB). Although many associate ecumenical dialogues with their academic components, i.e., deeply delving into the distinctions and convergences in our respective understandings of the Christian tradition, successful dialogues also leave room for the active presence of the Holy Spirit to touch hearts. "There is no ecumenism worthy of the name," says the document on ecumenism from the Second Vatican Council, *Unitatis Redintegratio,* "without interior conversion" (i.e., a change of heart).[1] Hearts were surely touched during our interactions as the participants came to appreciate each other's unique journeys of faith as brothers and sisters in Christ, and I am most grateful for that gift.

The theme for the 2023 Society for Pentecostal Studies conference is "In Our Own Tongues: Amplifying Pentecostalism's Minoritized Voices," taken from the voices of those who heard Peter's inaugural Pentecost address described in Acts 2. The question participants have been called to consider is, "Why not reimagine and rethink our Pentecostal/Charismatic faith, theology and practice from the purview of the periphery?" I believe the Spirit who unites is actively at work in that question, and it is the same question that Pope Francis has called Catholics around the world also to consider in light of their own living of the Christian tradition. Pope Francis writes in his encyclical on human fraternity, *Fratelli Tutti:*

> Love also impels us towards universal communion. No one can mature or find fulfilment by withdrawing from others. By its very nature, love calls for growth in

---

[1] Decree on Ecumenism *Unitatis Redintegratio, Vatican Council II: Volume 1—The Conciliar and Post Conciliar Documents,* gen. ed. Austin Flannery, OP (Northport, NY: Costello Publishing Company, 1998), 7.

openness and the ability to accept others as part of a continuing adventure that makes every periphery converge in a greater sense of mutual belonging. As Jesus told us: "You are all brothers" (Mt 23:8).[2]

Pentecostals and Catholics have made a commitment to understand the perspectives of those we may have ignored in the past for the sake of "convergence into a greater sense of mutual belonging." The line of demarcation between Pentecostal and Catholic Christians in our pasts undoubtedly caused us to ignore each other. The new exchange between the PCCNA and the USCCB is another substantive step toward eschewing past refusals to speak with each other. It is a new commitment for Catholics and Pentecostals to reach across the aisle in recognition of the gifts of the Spirit they could offer each other. This motivation coincides with the wisdom of the increasingly popular movement in dialogue known as "receptive ecumenism,"[3] a model that highlights the exchange of gifts between communities as opposed to the differentiated consensus model that compares doctrines. I believe it is a method that could be particularly helpful in dialogue with Pentecostals who place such a strong emphasis on pneumatology and the gifts of the Spirit.

This Dialogue's Place among Many

Dialogue between Catholics and Pentecostals has been taking place for decades—in fact, the first ecumenical engagements Classical Pentecostals had were with Catholics beginning with dialogues organized between some Classical Pentecostal Churches and the Pontifical Council for Promoting Christian Unity in Rome in 1972. Eventually the net of Pentecostal ecumenical relationships would widen to include the World Alliance of Reformed Churches, the World Council of Churches, the Lutheran World Federation, and on the national level full Pentecostal membership in an organization known as "CCT USA"—Christian Churches Together. CCT is the only ecumenical conciliar organization in the United States in which both the US Conference of Catholic Bishops and Pentecostals enjoy full membership.[4] This is due in large part to

---

[2] Pope Francis, *Fratelli Tutti*, October 3, 2020, 95, https://www.vatican.va/content/francesco/en/encyclicals/documents/papa-francesco_20201003_enciclica-fratelli-tutti.html.

[3] A good introduction to the method of receptive ecumenism can be found in Paul Murray's article, "Introducing Receptive Ecumenism," in *The Ecumenist: A Journal of Theology, Culture and Society* 51:2 (Spring 2014), 1.

[4] This is such a unique reality that, despite it being a national development, it was acknowledged by an international dialogue between some Classical Pentecostal Churches and the Pontifical Council for Promoting Christian Unity in its document "On Becoming a Christian: Insights from Scripture and Patristic Writings with Some Contemporary Reflection" in ¶ 20. It is available at http://www.christianunity.va/content/unitacristiani/en/dialoghi/sezione-occidentale/pentecostali/dialogo/documenti-di-dialogo/testo-del-documento-in-inglese1.html.

the conscious effort by those who wrote CCT's by-laws to ensure that none of the members ever has to compromise any aspect of their identities. Although CCT is one context in which American Pentecostals and Catholics already engage with each other, this new dialogue is the first attempt for scholars representing the USCCB and the PCCNA to enter into bilateral theological dialogue. Such a dialogue will, as Pope Francis puts it, give us the time to develop a deeper sense of fraternity and thus space for listening to and understanding one another.

The American context is one that offers unique opportunities for growth in mutual enrichment, attributable to both the origins of the Pentecostal movement in the United States[5] and a physical distance from the neuralgic circumstances for Catholics related to the mass exodus of Catholics from the Catholic Church to Pentecostal congregations in Central and South America.[6] These factors, in addition to the development of the Christian Unity Commission of the Pentecostal Charismatic Churches of North America in 2015,[7] made this an auspicious time for Catholics and Pentecostals to create a national ecumenical dialogue here in the United States.

An Exchange of Gifts: Prayer, Sacraments, and Liturgy

The individual who undoubtedly did the most to build this new dialogue, Harold Hunter, actively pursued a national ecumenical dialogue between Pentecostal and Catholic scholars for years. The records in the Secretariat for Ecumenical and Interreligious Affairs of the USCCB include copies of correspondence from Dr. Hunter to my predecessors dating back to at least 2010. There are also notes that were prepared by my predecessors promoting the idea of establishing a more formal relationship with Pentecostals, yet I am unaware of the contexts in which they were used. Harold shared with me details about many collaborative efforts he engaged in with the late Brother Jeffrey Gros, someone I, like many Catholic ecumenists, consider to have been a mentor. During Brother Jeff's ecumenical outreach, which included the crossing of many former barriers, he had the opportunity to address the Society of Pentecostal Studies a number of times and even as president in 2012.[8] In that presentation Brother

---

[5] The Azusa Street Revival Movement in 1906 is acknowledged by the Pontifical Council for Promoting Christian Unity's document "The Bishop and Christian Unity: An Ecumenical Vademecum" as what is "usually considered" the beginning of the Pentecostal Movement (47).

[6] For example, it has been noted that in 2023 for the first time Pentecostals might outnumber Catholics in Brazil. https://yourbibleversedaily.com/2022/01/wall-street-journal-catholics-are-losing-ground-rapidly-in-brazil-what-else-is-new/.

[7] The history of the Christian Unity Commission is recounted in the PCCNA's website: https://pccna.org/commissions_unity.aspx.

[8] Brother Jeff gave the Presidential Address to the society in 2012: "It Seems Good to the Holy Spirit and to Us: The Ecclesial Vocation of the Pentecostal Scholar," *Pneuma* 34 (2012), 167–84.

Jeff acknowledged groundbreaking foundations to Catholics and Pentecostal dialogue here in the US. Harold began his work with the international Roman Catholic-Classical Pentecostal dialogue in 1983 and has not only published extensively on Pentecostalism and ecumenism but also offered personal testimony to the dialogue group about his appreciation for aspects of Catholic prayer and spirituality. All of this background brought Harold to most fittingly serve as the Pentecostal co-chair of the exchanges that would be inaugurated in September of 2021. I have found collaborating with him in the development of this dialogue to be a blessing and appreciate the many gifts he has brought to our table.

Harold and I first met at the CCT annual forum in Montgomery, Alabama, in the fall of 2019. It was during that interaction that he approached Bishop Joseph Bambera of Scranton, the chairman of the Bishops' Committee on Ecumenical and Interreligious Affairs of the USCCB, and me as his staff member, to inquire about starting a Catholic-Pentecostal national dialogue. Ironically, Bishop Bambera would soon after that meeting be assigned to serve on the international Pentecostal-Catholic dialogue sponsored by the Pontifical Council for Promoting Christian Unity. Unfortunately, it was not long after that interaction that the normal day-to-day lives of all in the world were interrupted by a global pandemic. Despite that challenge, we were determined to make this aspiration come to fruition in an actual dialogue between Catholic and Pentecostal theologians.

On a cool winter's day in 2020 I made my way to a hotel near Washington, DC, where Harold was lodging. Given he was in my area, we decided to take the risk of meeting in person, despite the ominous reminders of the pandemic, namely mask regulations, prohibitions of in-person work, and news stories about lives lost. Harold graciously bought me a cup of coffee to dispel the chill I had from the walk over, and we dreamed together of the moment when we might begin a national theological dialogue between Catholics and Pentecostals. Those dreams seemed to be such a hopeful contrast to the sadness that surrounded us. Nevertheless, we were both convinced that it was the right time to proceed.

During that meeting Harold suggested that we spend the dialogue discussing issues related to prayer, liturgy, and sacraments. In accord with the spirit of receptive ecumenism as an exchange of gifts, he expressed his opinion, much to my surprise, that there might be some aspects of Catholic practice that could be beneficial to Pentecostals. As you could imagine, this was an unexpected request, especially given obvious observations that have been made in the past about the divergences of practice between our communities on such issues. The international dialogue had already noted:

> It is true that in worship Catholics are more oriented toward liturgical rites while Pentecostals emphasize the charismatic dimension of the worshipping assembly . . .

Charismatic manifestations like *glossolalia* and sacramentally orientated devotions such as exposition of the Blessed Sacrament may seem opposed to some.[9]

Nevertheless, the both of us felt that the group would be up to the challenge. I suggested that we divide up the three years of meetings around the three traditional ways sacraments are grouped together in Catholic thought: Initiation, as experienced through Baptism, Confirmation, and Eucharist; Healing, as experienced through Confession of Sins and Anointing of the Sick; and finally, Service or Vocation, as expressed through Holy Orders and Marriage. While traditional, the *Catechism of the Catholic Church* does explain that there are other ways of grouping the sacraments that are just as acceptable. However, these three groupings highlight stages of life that I felt could be beneficial to this initial sharing between our communities of faith. The *Catechism* explains:

> Christ instituted the sacraments of the new law. There are seven: Baptism, Confirmation (or Chrismation), the Eucharist, Penance, the Anointing of the Sick, Holy Orders, and Matrimony. The seven sacraments touch all the stages and all the important moments of the Christian life, they give birth and increase, healing and mission to the Church's life of faith. There is thus a certain resemblance between the stages of natural life and the stages of the spiritual life. Following this analogy, the first chapter will expound the three sacraments of Christian initiation; the second, the sacraments of healing; and the third, the sacraments at the service of communion and the mission of the faithful. This order, while not the only one possible, does allow one to see that the sacraments form an organic whole in which each particular sacrament has its own vital place.[10]

Leaving the language very broad, by simply assigning the general topics of initiation, healing, and service, offered to the theologians enough latitude to be themselves and express how their communities of faith live and manifest these three aspects of growth in the Christian life. Other than a general sense that the dialogue would develop the topic of liturgy and sacraments, as well as the "specific" topic of each of the three years, the theologians from our respective groups were given no further instruction. With plenty of room for the working of the Holy Spirit and the creativity of the theologians that could stretch across the aisle into another set of pews, we were ready to prepare for the dialogue.

This initial dialogue consisted of three annual meetings and was provisional/exploratory in status. There were a number of reasons for this decision. First of all, this dialogue was our first interaction, and there needed to be an opportunity to learn about the viability and potential of success for such an encounter before making a longstanding commitment. Secondly, I needed to present the results of the interactions

---

[9] "On Becoming a Christian," ¶¶ 189 and 191.
[10] *Catechism of the Catholic Church,* ¶¶ 1210 and 1211.

to the USCCB's Bishops' Committee on Ecumenical and Interreligious Affairs so that they could discuss it and discern whether or not to formally endorse the dialogue. Finally, observations from the experiences of the provisional dialogue helped the bishops' committee to discern if the presence of a bishop as Catholic co-chair would be useful to the relationship. I would also note that at the USCCB there are mundane financial matters involved with the distinction between exploratory, as opposed to official, dialogues.

Developments at Dialogue Sessions

Although one of the first aspects of this exploratory dialogue to be developed between the PCCNA and the USCCB was the overall theological theme and the topics of the papers, in addition, we felt strongly that there also be an exchange of faith experiences, religious cultures, and piety. Each day we were together was enshrined in prayer, one group leading in the morning and the other in the evening. Those daily prayers were developed in accord with the diverse spiritual expressions found in our various communities of faith. We also shared all of our meals in common, which offered the opportunity for the theologians and participants to share their faith journeys with one another in an informal setting. These dialogues also gave to all of the participants an opportunity to learn about their faith communities through brief pilgrimages to places of particular significance for Pentecostals and Catholics in the United States. Many of those sights made a lasting impact upon the participants.

The first dialogue session was held in September of 2021 in Washington, DC. The theme was "initiation." It was most appropriate to begin our time together with a dialogue on the beginning of the life of faith for the Christian. Lodging and dialogue sessions were at the Washington Retreat House. That retreat house is of particular historical significance for the Catholic ecumenical movement because it was built in the early twentieth century by Mother Luana White. Along with Father Paul Wattson, she founded the Franciscan Friars and Sisters of the Atonement, which is a religious community that has as its main charism the unity of Christians. This was the community that began the "Octave for Christian Unity," which would eventually become the "Week of Prayer for Christian Unity." A member of the Franciscan Sisters of the Atonement, Sister Nancy Conboy, SA, offered a presentation on the history of her community's involvement with ecumenism to our group. We also spent a morning at the National Shrine of Pope St. John Paul II. In addition to his considerable outreach to the Jewish community, St. John Paul was a strong promoter of ecumenism, authoring the first and thus far only papal encyclical on ecumenism, *Ut Unum Sint*. Another place we were able to visit was the Franciscan Monastery of the Holy Land, which includes life-sized replicas of a number of important monuments and shrines in the Holy Land.

We were led on that tour by Fr. Jim Gardiner, SA, who is a Franciscan Friar of the Atonement that has made his own contribution to the ecumenical movement in the United States. Finally, we were led on a tour of the Basilica of the National Shrine of the Immaculate Conception by the director of pilgrimages, Monsignor Vito Buonanno. The basilica is in a particular way an architectural representation of Catholicism as it is experienced throughout the United States. These visits enabled the Pentecostal team to have a fuller picture of the lives and history of Catholics in the United States.

The Pentecostal team also led us on thought provoking pilgrimages as they hosted our dialogue in September of 2022 at Oral Roberts University in Tulsa, Oklahoma. The first place the dialogue visited in Tulsa was the Greenwood Museum followed by a Pentecostal prayer service at the John Hope Franklin Reconciliation Park. These visits were sobering reminders of the destruction of the prosperous "Black Wall Street" during the tragic Tulsa Race Massacre of 1921. The visits also reminded us of the distressing historical development that preceded the massacre with the forced displacement of the Native Americans from their lands. These stark historical realities coincided well with the theme of that second meeting: healing. None of the Catholics had ever visited Oral Roberts University before. The experience of being in an environment that is saturated in Pentecostalism gave greater depth to our understanding of Pentecostalism. We appreciated the opportunity to visit the Oral Roberts Prayer Tower and the university's deliberate efforts to provide an environment conducive to the building up of the students' prayer lives. It was particularly refreshing to have the opportunity to interact not only with representatives of the theology faculty at Oral Roberts, including Wonsuk Ma, whose work in Global Christian Studies is an invaluable contribution to the ecumenical movement, but also those involved with Oral Roberts University's commitment to creation care. We also found the experience of participating in chapel worship with the university's president, Dr. Billy Wilson, to be a particularly joyful moment and were honored to be welcomed so graciously by Dr. Wilson and the students present.

The last session of this first, exploratory round, met in September of 2023 at the University of Notre Dame in Indiana. The theme was "vocation/service" and ministry, and it was another special opportunity to learn about how our faith communities live out their belief in the Lord Jesus and his love for all people. During this session, Dr. Kimberly Belcher invited us to observe a course she teaches entitled "Holy Communion and Christian Disunity." We also had the pleasure of interacting with graduate students in theology at a dinner hosted by the university's Office of Mission Engagement and Church Affairs. Jerry Powers of the Catholic Peacebuilding Network spoke to us about the university's promotion of Catholic peacebuilding efforts throughout the world. The group also enjoyed an experience at the Digital Visualization Theatre, a planetarium on campus, during which we heard a presentation by Keith Davis on "What the Ancients

Knew about the Heavens and What Scientists Know." Kim mentioned how she brings her undergraduate students to the theatre when she discusses the creation narratives of Genesis. Once again, we were the recipients of tremendous hospitality at Notre Dame. All of these journeys helped to flesh out the necessary human and spiritual dimensions for a successful ecumenical dialogue.

Reflections on Theological Exchanges

The theological exchanges during the dialogue sessions were thought-provoking and exposed numerous unexpected areas of convergence between us. The presentations, once completed, will be made available for the public to read and reflect upon through both the journal of Oral Roberts University, *Spiritus*, and the Catholic journal *Worship*. Allow me to simply offer a few basic points on the Pentecostal presentations that are particularly interesting to Catholic sensibilities.

The first presentation on the topic of "initiation" was given by Rev. Dr. Frederick L. Ware (Church of God in Christ) of Howard Divinity School and it addressed primarily "water baptism." The first point he mentioned that is of particular interest for Catholics is that "Pentecostals are rediscovering sacramental theology and exploring its relevance and application to Christian faith and practice in Pentecostal churches."[11] Given the high emphasis on sacraments in the Catholic Church this "rediscovery" is most intriguing and could develop into an area in which Catholics and Pentecostals can fruitfully share their experiences with one another. This "rediscovery," I would boldly suggest, could be the work of the Spirit through Pentecostalism to heal the divisions between Christians. It is interesting to note that Ware confined his paper to water baptism with a sensitivity toward Catholic practice.

Ware indicated that Pentecostals do not practice confirmation because adults are baptized. Yet, interestingly for Catholics, confirmation (or chrismation in the East) is not only associated with initiation and a personal testimony to faith but also the bestowal of the gifts of the Holy Spirit necessary to live the Christian life, which links it to baptism. One could suggest that confirmation is not perceived as necessary to the Pentecostal precisely because of an already high emphasis on the Spirit's work in the lives of all believers. This leads me to think that while not formally sacramental in a Catholic sense, *perhaps every day is a day of "confirmation" for a Pentecostal?*

It was particularly interesting to be exposed to the denominational statements on water baptism by Dr. Ware's paper. A number of those statements highlighted the immersion in water and use of the Trinitarian formula found in Matthew 28. Ware indicated that in the past many denominations would encourage baptism in the name

---

[11] Frederick L. Ware, "Initiation (Water Baptism) in North American Pentecostalism," *Spiritus* 9:2 (2024), 187.

of the Lord Jesus alone but this has developed into a more common use of the formula found in Matthew 28 as a specific mandate of the Lord Jesus. This development indeed draws our communities closer together, given that for Catholics the proper form of baptism is always the use of water (regardless of the water being poured or the practice of immersion) and invocation of the Trinitarian formula.[12] The PCCNA membership being reserved to Trinitarian Christians is helpful since in Catholic theology belief in the Trinity occupies a prominent place in the "hierarchy of truths"—a notion that has been very helpful in our ecumenical dialogues.[13]

There are two important asides I would like to make with respect to the above observations. First, one crucial question Ware asked is, "How much variation can be accommodated without compromising the integrity of the baptismal event in Christian experience?"[14] One of the points that Ware made is that "If there is anything that may be called typical, it is the diversity of experiences, thoughts, and perspectives among Pentecostals."[15] This begs the question for Catholics that, although denominational statements promote water baptism with the Trinitarian formula, what is the usual practice? For Catholics, matter, i.e., pure water, and form, i.e., the Trinitarian formula, are necessary for the validity of the baptism. Variations in practice compromising matter and form are a concern for Catholics, not only with Pentecostals, but also mainline Protestants and even Catholic ministers who might apply an overextension of variation

---

[12] In the *Code of Canon Law*, it states "Baptism . . . is validly conferred only by washing with true water together with the required form of words" (c 849). The *Directory for the Application of Principles and Norms of Ecumenism* is even more explicit in this regard: "Baptism is conferred with water and with a formula which clearly indicates that Baptism is done in the name of the Father, Son, and Holy Spirit. . . . Baptism by immersion, or by pouring water, with the Trinitarian formula is, of itself, valid. Therefore, if the rituals, liturgical books or established customs of a church or ecclesial community prescribe either of these ways of Baptism, the Sacrament is to be considered valid unless there are serious reasons for doubting that the minister observed the regulations of his/her own community or church" (93, 95a). Notably, the Catholic Church recognizes the validity of baptisms from Christian communities that prefer the notion of ordinance to sacrament when done in accord with proper matter and form. A prime example of this for us in the US is the Common Agreement on Baptism reached between the US Conference of Catholic Bishops and Reformed churches that was issued on November 16, 2010.

[13] As it states in the Secretariat for Promoting Christian Unity's document "Reflections and Suggestions Concerning Ecumenical Dialogue" from August 15, 1970: "It will be borne in mind that 'in Catholic teaching there exists an order of hierarchy of truths, since they vary in their relationship to the foundation of the Christian faith. Neither in the life nor in the teaching of the whole Church is everything presented on the same level. Certainly all revealed truths demand the same acceptance of faith, but according to the greater or lesser proximity that they have to the basis of the revealed mystery, they are variously placed with regard to one another and have varying connections among themselves'" (4, b).

[14] Ware, "Initiation (Water Baptism) in North American Pentecostalism," 196.

[15] Ware, "Initiation (Water Baptism) in North American Pentecostalism," 188.

to the conferral of the sacrament.[16] The upcoming annual forum of CCT will actually seek to address these issues while also relating baptism to the call to work for justice.

The second aside relates to an important caution Dr. Ware makes, one I find to be less of a caution and more of a convergence. He states, "Clearly, and without question, these rituals have been instituted by Christ. After giving these rituals, is there yet freedom for God to act beyond prescribed liturgy? How does God use the ritual, but also transcend it?"[17] This is indeed a question Catholics have considered, and an opportunity to make clear that Catholics do not consider the sacraments as in any way capable of limiting the activity of God. The *Catechism of the Catholic Church* explains this important nuance carefully so as on the one hand not to denigrate a Catholic sense of the importance of baptism while at the same time preserving the sovereignty of God:

> The Church does not know of any means other than Baptism that assures entry into eternal beatitude; this is why she takes care not to neglect the mission she has received from the Lord to see that all who can be baptized are "reborn of water and the Spirit." *God has bound salvation to the sacrament of Baptism, but he himself is not bound by his sacraments* [emphasis is in the original].[18]

From this official teaching document of the Church Catholics can offer a resounding yes to Dr. Ware's question of there being freedom for God to act beyond

---

[16] The Episcopal Church USA continues to discern the use of inclusive language in its liturgy and should this impact the baptismal formula of "Father, Son, and Holy Spirit" this would, in the view of the Catholic Church, render such baptisms invalid. See Fr. Matthew S. C. Olver's commentary on changes in the Eucharistic Prayers in his article, "New Rites: Expansive, Inclusive or Stifling?," *Covenant*, November 18, 2018, https://covenant.livingchurch.org/2018/11/14/new-rites-expansive-inclusive-or-stifling/. There was a recent issue of a Catholic deacon using the wrong words of the baptismal formula and invalidly baptizing an infant who would later on become a priest. This mistake necessitated that he participate once again in ceremonies for his baptism, confirmation, and ordination. This was a particularly grave situation because as a result this young man functioned as a priest when he was not in fact validly ordained, rendering many of the sacraments he conferred invalid. For more information read Michael Stechschulte's article in, "A Priest Discovered His Baptism Was Invalid. Its Ripple Effects Bring Heartache and Confusion to the Entire Church Community," *America Magazine*, August 24, 2020, https://www.americamagazine.org/politics-society/2020/08/24/detroit-priest-invalid-baptism-canonical-consequences.

[17] Ware, "Initiation (Water Baptism) in North American Pentecostalism," 199.

[18] Paragraph 1257. This is a summarization of the thought of Peter Lombard (twelfth century) who wrote, "Almighty God can and does give grace to men in answer to their internal aspirations and prayers without the use of any external sign or ceremony. This will always be possible, because God, grace, and the soul are spiritual beings. God is not restricted to the use of material, visible symbols in dealing with men; the sacraments are not necessary in the sense that they could not have been dispensed with. But, if it is known that God has appointed external, visible ceremonies as the means by which certain graces are to be conferred on men, then in order to obtain those graces it will be necessary for men to make use of those Divinely appointed means. This truth theologians express by saying that the sacraments are necessary, not absolutely but only hypothetically, i.e., in the supposition that if we wish to obtain a certain supernatural end we must use the supernatural means appointed for obtaining that end." https://www.newadvent.org/cathen/13295a.htm#I.

prescribed liturgy. How that might take place lies in the realm of the mystery of God's grace.

Dr. David S. Han of Pentecostal Theological Seminary offered the Pentecostal paper for our second meeting that he entitled "Healing in the Pentecostal Tradition." He began by emphasizing how fundamental the ministry of healing is to the identity of Pentecostals: "The experience of divine healing is, however, just as significant as that of Spirit-baptism. Donald W. Dayton would even argue: '. . . even more characteristic of Pentecostalism than the doctrine of baptism of the Spirit is its celebration of miracles of divine healing as part of God's salvation and as evidence of the presence of divine power in the church.'"[19] It is interesting to note that despite the tremendous emphasis Pentecostals place on healing that the international dialogue did not pick up the topic of healing in a substantive way until relatively recently. During the first dialogue (1972–1976) it was noted that healing should be a topic of conversation among numerous others. In October of 1979 the dialogue met in Rome and the topic of healing was discussed alongside a consideration of the relationship between Scripture and Tradition. In subsequent documents and discussions, healing was acknowledged as one among many manifestations of the work of the Spirit but not given particular attention. However, during the last round of the international dialogue, Catholic and Pentecostal theologians devoted an entire session to the topic of healing at their 2013 meeting in Baltimore. The document produced by that round, "Do Not Quench the Spirit," dedicates a small section to healing and explicates the results of their discussions under three categories: healing in Scripture, healing in church history, and healing in the life of the church. It is apparent that more dialogue needs to be pursued in this area. Healing is not only an important part of Pentecostal life, but it has also been so in Catholic life, with the sacraments of Anointing of the Sick and Reconciliation as official public acts of the Church. The Catholic Charismatic Renewal also has a high emphasis on healing prayer. While some work has been done on Scripture and church history, a deeper appreciation and theological exploration of the phenomenological dimensions of healing, particularly as emphasized in Pentecostalism, would be helpful to Catholics and Pentecostals coming to understand each other better. Pope Francis in his letter for the World Day of Peace in 2021 urged all people to build a "culture of care." Given the recent pandemic and greater emphasis on promoting good health this would be an opportune time to discern how Catholics and Pentecostals together can bring the healing power of Christ to those around us.

There is another point made by Han that has the potential of being developed into a substantive dialogue. He notes: "Healing envisages a holistic restoration of human being. Practices of healing are constant reminders to affirm the truth that

---

[19] David S. Han, "Healing in the Pentecostal Tradition," *Spiritus* 9:2 (2024), 231.

human beings are only made whole when both their spiritual and bodily needs are brought to bear and met with nourishment."[20] This aspect of the healing ministry of the church emphasizes a Christian anthropology that understands the unity of the human person, body, mind, and spirit, in contradiction to contemporary trends that overemphasize materialism, reducing the human person to the bodily, and also Gnostic trends that denigrate the body and exalt the spiritual. Pope Francis has in a particular way pointed out the need to confront what he perceives to be an upsurge in Gnostic and Pelagian tendencies in today's world.[21] Ministers to the sick from both Pentecostal and Catholic churches understand that when an individual's body is in pain, it can impact the person's spiritual and emotional life, while when a person is spiritually or emotionally wounded, those wounds can manifest themselves in physical ways and even interfere with the healing processes of the body. This is surely a point of convergence that can assist in our mutual attempts to bring people closer to Christ during their times of need.

The final point of convergence I would highlight that is helpful to emphasize is that both Catholics and Pentecostals understand our rituals associated with healing as being consistent with and inspired by sacred Scripture. Han mentions: "Of a particular note, all of the official statements of classical Pentecostal denominations appeal to James 5:14–16. It is partly due to the fact that this is the only place where we are given a description of a specific procedure to follow."[22] When Catholic priests offer the

---

[20] Han, "Healing in the Pentecostal Tradition," 238.

[21] The Congregation for the Doctrine of the Faith issued a letter, *Placuit Deo*, to bishops about certain aspects of Christian salvation on February 22, 2018. It stated: "Pope Francis, in his ordinary magisterium, often has made reference to the two tendencies described above, that resemble certain aspects of two ancient heresies, Pelagianism and Gnosticism. A new form of Pelagianism is spreading in our days, one in which the individual, understood to be radically autonomous, presumes to save oneself, without recognizing that, at the deepest level of being, he or she derives from God and from others. According to this way of thinking, salvation depends on the strength of the individual or on purely human structures, which are incapable of welcoming the newness of the Spirit of God. On the other hand, a new form of Gnosticism puts forward a model of salvation that is merely interior, closed off in its own subjectivism. In this model, salvation consists in elevating oneself with the intellect beyond 'the flesh of Jesus towards the mysteries of the unknown divinity.'" It also stated: "The salvific sacramental economy is also opposed to trends that propose a merely interior salvation. Gnosticism, indeed, associates itself with a negative view of the created order, which is understood as a limitation on the absolute freedom of the human spirit. Consequently, salvation is understood as freedom from the body and from the concrete relationships in which a person lives. In as much as we are saved 'by means of offering the body of Jesus Christ' (Heb 10:10; cf. Col 1:22), true salvation, contrary to being a liberation from the body, also includes its sanctification (cf. Rom 12:1). The human body was shaped by God, who inscribed within it a language that invites the human person to recognize the gifts of the Creator and to live in communion with one's brothers and sisters. By his Incarnation and his paschal mystery, the Savior re-established and renewed this original language and communicated it in the economy of the sacraments. Thanks to the sacraments, Christians are able to live in fidelity to the flesh of Christ and, as a result, in fidelity to the concrete order of relationships that He gave us. This order of relationality requires, in a particular way, the care of all suffering humanity through the spiritual and corporal works of mercy" (14).

[22] Han, "Healing in the Pentecostal Tradition," 241.

sacrament of Anointing of the Sick, they read this same passage of Scripture. Although Catholics interpret the elders mentioned by James as having a responsibility reserved to a priest or bishop who has been officially ordained, precisely because this is an official act of the Church, both Catholics and Pentecostals engage in similar healing rituals. There is a laying on of hands and an anointing with oil. While the use of "anointed handkerchiefs" is not popular among Catholics, there are other practices of popular piety, like the use of water from the grotto at Lourdes, France, and the relics of saints, that are known to have similar impacts and meanings. Hence there is much in the way of convergence in regard to healing that should be explored.

Dr. Martin W. Mittelstadt of Evangel University offered the third Pentecostal paper entitled, "Called: A Pentecostal Theology of Vocation." It seemed to be particularly fitting to conclude our discussions with the notion of vocation since many of them eventually led to ways in which we could enrich each other's work of discipleship. The topic of a Pentecostal theology of vocation is one that has been of particular interest to Mittelstadt for a long time. He wrote: "For over twenty years, I have been teaching a required first-year course that includes an intense unit on vocation. With my department colleagues, we provide roughly fifteen sections of this course annually. I listen to the students' stories every day."[23] Due to these experiences, Mittelstadt was particularly reflective and insightful.

One of the most important points that Mittelstadt continually made in his paper was that a theology of vocation is deficient if it is only in reference to the clergy. He wrote,

> I believe the traditional narrative has led many Pentecostal believers toward church-related ministry because of minimalist theology of the call. Some of these folk, like me, have survived and thrived; others stumbled. Added to this, I have a concern for Pentecostal congregants who never receive the call to church-related ministry. Many struggle to understand why they receive no such call, and many more are left with little instruction and discipleship concerning their day-to-day vocations.[24]

This exclusive attention to the vocation of formalized ecclesial service was also a challenge in the Catholic Church. The *Baltimore Catehcism,* which was a text that was used to teach Catholic children in the United States about the faith before the 1960s, contained an illustration that on one side depicted a husband and wife with the caption, "good," while next to it was a picture of a priest and a nun with the caption, "better." Yet with the Second Vatican Council the Catholic Church recognized and emphasized the point that Mittelstadt is now making. It is referred to as the "universal call to

---

[23] Martin W. Mittelstadt, "Called: A Pentecostal Theology of Vocation," *Spiritus* 9:2 (2024), 297.
[24] Mittelstadt, "Called: A Pentecostal Theology of Vocation," 297.

holiness" and is described in the Dogmatic Constitution on the Church, *Lumen Gentium*, in this way:

> It is therefore quite clear that all Christians in any state or walk of life are called to the fullness of Christian life and to the perfection of love, and by this holiness a more human manner of life is fostered also in earthly society. In order to reach this perfection, the faithful should use the strength dealt out to them by Christ's gift, so that, following in his footsteps and conformed to his image, doing the will of God in everything, they may wholeheartedly devote themselves to the glory of God and to the service of their neighbor.[25]

Mittelstadt contends that there is a certain equality among faithful Christians, each following an individual calling from Christ. He even goes so far as to make this statement: "If the Spirit enlists everyone, patriarchy and hierarchy collapse."[26] As a Catholic my ears naturally perk up when I hear the word "hierarchy." However, I believe that the use of the term as Mittelstadt understands it, seemingly individuals who "lord their authority over others,"[27] would render this sentence correct for Catholics. Pope Francis has offered a distinct view of hierarchy that is a description of the authentic Catholic understanding of that term:

> Even when the function of ministerial priesthood is considered "hierarchical," it must be remembered that "it is totally ordered to the holiness of Christ's members." Its key and axis is not power understood as domination, but the power to administer the sacrament of the Eucharist; this is the origin of its authority, which is always service to God's people.[28]

Catholics understand that when their hierarchs are immersed in humble service as opposed to domination they are fulfilling the will of Christ. They would consider it a part of the diversity of callings that exist in the Church in keeping with the sentiments of 1 Corinthians 12:28. Mittelstadt emphasized this diversity as it exists in the Pentecostal tradition. He used imagery from the African American spiritual song tradition to make this point:

> Out of their spiritual songs, African-Americans gave rise to jazz, a genre that serves as a suitable metaphor for Pentecostal life in the Spirit. Pentecostal worship, liturgies, theologies, and—I suggest—vocations do not produce orchestral or symphonic performances; instead, Pentecostals celebrate oral and bodily spontaneity and improvisation. For this reason, *jazzolalia* serves as an imaginative

---

[25] *Vatican Council II: Volume 1—The Conciliar and Post Conciliar Documents*, ed. Austin Flannery, *Lumen Gentium*, the Dogmatic Constitution on the Church 39 (Northport, NY: Costello Publishing Company, 1988), 397.

[26] Mittelstadt, "Called: A Pentecostal Theology of Vocation," 301.

[27] Matt 20:25.

[28] Pope Francis, *Evangelii Gaudium*, The Joy of the Gospel, Apostolic Exhortation, 103. Available at www.vatican.va.

extension of first-century glossolalia. . . . If applied to vocation, the aphorism by Nigerian-American Pentecostal scholar Nimi Wariboko resonates well: "It-does-not-make-sense-but-it makes-spirit."[29]

Before one might jump to a conclusion that this is a far cry from Catholic perspectives on vocations, it would be wise to note well these sentiments of Pope Francis:

> Differing currents of thought in philosophy, theology and pastoral practice, if open to being reconciled by the Spirit in respect and love, can enable the Church to grow, since all of them help to express more clearly the immense riches of God's word. For those who long for a monolithic body of doctrine guarded by all and leaving no room for nuance, this might appear as undesirable and leading to confusion. But in fact such variety serves to bring out and develop different facets of the inexhaustible riches of the Gospel.[30]

The Catholic Church does accept a variety of paths and ways of thinking that lead to holiness. This is most clearly demonstrated by an examination of the collection of names of those canonized as saints by the Catholic Church. These are individuals who are held up as examples of living the Christian life with heroic virtue. They include people of all walks of life, men and women, young and old, hailing from highly diverse cultural and national backgrounds.

One point of divergence, which might be more of emphasis than practice, is the role of the community (to Catholics, the institutional Church) in the discernment of vocations. Given that the Catholic Church holds that its leaders have been given gifts of discernment (as in Matthew 16:18 Peter is acknowledged to have a wisdom about the identity of Jesus that comes from his heavenly Father), Catholics contend that the clergy have a special role in helping Christians to accept their vocations. Vocations are callings that come from God, and while there is a charismatic aspect of this particular individual being given a particular call by God, Catholics contend that this calling is only recognized as authentically from God through the discernment of the clergy. While Pentecostals do have seminary and congregational boards that discern when one is called to formalized Church ministry, this was not highly emphasized in the discussion.

Possibilities for the Future

This first exploratory dialogue between the PCCNA's and the USCCB's representatives concluded in September of 2023. By all accounts it was a success. All of the participants entered into the interaction with the greatest of respect and maturity. From the onset the theologians attempted to discern connections and convergences between our

---

[29] Mittelstadt, "Called: A Pentecostal Theology of Vocation," 303.
[30] Pope Francis, *Evangelii Gaudium*, 40.

practices and theology. The experience of praying together was particularly lifegiving. The USCCB's Bishops Committee on Ecumenical and Interreligious Affairs has been continually updated on the progress of this dialogue. In its October 2022 meeting the bishops unanimously agreed to send a member of the committee to the September 2023 session. The observations that Bishop Peter Smith, auxiliary bishop of the Archdiocese of Portland, Oregon, brought the bishops' committee to agree to elevate the status of the USCCB-PCCNA dialogue. We look forward to a future in dialogue together and an incorporation into the regular rhythm of the committee's ecumenical portfolio. Discernment will need to be made about the next topic to be developed. Another issue to consider is that the PCCNA is international in scope while the USCCB is confined to the United States. It might be appropriate at some point for the Catholics to consider including the Canadian Conference of Catholic Bishops in the dialogue. With widespread fluency in online platforms, it would be possible to be both financially responsible and have our theologians meet together with more frequency. Yet at the same time, given the mutual emphasis by Pentecostals and Catholics on the experiential, the importance of periodic in-person meetings cannot be overemphasized.

Conclusion: Reaching Out to the Periphery

I would like to conclude by returning to the theme for this conference, "Amplifying Minoritized Voices." When thinking about such voices my thoughts bring me to the theologians who graciously volunteered to participate in this first national dialogue between Pentecostals and Catholics. Harold and I were deliberate in seeking out a diverse group of participants. The theologians have included women and men, clergy and laity, as well as individuals with Asian, African American, Hispanic, and European backgrounds. We can celebrate together that there are "varieties of gifts but the same Spirit."[31] Should they maintain this mutual commitment to listening to all voices, especially those on the periphery, the US Conference of Catholic Bishops and the Pentecostal Churches of North America will surely come closer together

Walter F. Kedjierski (wkedjierski@drvc.org) is Executive Director of the Secretariat for Ecumenical and Interreligious Affairs for the US Conference of Catholic Bishops in Washington, DC.

---

[31] 1 Cor 12:4.

Initiation Sacraments and Directions for Catholic-Pentecostal Dialogue

An Essay for the Exploratory USCCB/PCCNA Dialogue

Kimberly Hope Belcher

Keywords *baptism, initiation, confirmation, Holy Communion, sacraments, Roman Catholic Church*

Abstract

This article surveys Roman Catholic understandings of initiation sacraments. It traces historical developments and current practices for the sacraments of baptism, confirmation, and Holy Communion. Throughout attention is paid to the areas where convergences and issues for further discussion between Roman Catholics and Pentecostals emerge.

Introduction

Our ancestors . . . were all baptized into Moses in the cloud and in the sea. They all ate the same spiritual food and drank the same spiritual drink; for they drank from the spiritual rock that accompanied them, and that rock was Christ. (1 Cor 10:1–4)

In the New Testament and other documentation from the early churches of the second and third centuries, there were a variety of different practices of initiation. In general, these communities' initiation included some of the following: the water bath known as baptism (that is, immersion), anointing with olive oil,[1] laying on of hands, and table fellowship.[2] Though these would later become separated into three different rites with different interpretations, in the pre-Nicene period, they were understood as one initiation into Christ and the church, bestowing on one the Holy Spirit and his gifts,

---

[1] Gabrielle Winkler and Sebastian Brock argue for the primacy of anointing in the earliest Syriac evidence, suggesting that some churches may have initiated using an anointing without any water bath. See, for example, G. Winkler, "The Original Meaning of the Pre-Baptismal Anointing and Its Implications," *Worship* 52 (1978), 24–45; Sebastian P. Brock, *The Holy Spirit in the Syrian Baptismal Tradition* (Piscataway, NJ: Gorgias Press, 2008).

[2] Nathan D. Mitchell, *Eucharist as Sacrament of Initiation: Forum Essay #2* (Chicago, IL: Liturgy Training Publications, 2007).

and leading one to a holy life. Unity in agapeic love was one primary mark of inclusion in the body of Christ, supported by a virtuous life, especially patience in suffering, and the charisms of prophecy, interpretation, and teaching (e.g. 1 Cor 13; 1 John 2). By the end of the fourth century, throughout the Christian world, most churches used rites[3] including preparatory teaching and exorcism, at least one anointing with oil, a water bath (immersion or submersion) accompanied by the Trinitarian name, hand laying, and participation in the Eucharist. We can call this general pattern the catechumenate.

In the contemporary Roman Catholic Church, there are also multiple initiatory practices. The best-known pattern is one inherited from the medieval "dissolution" of the fourth-century united rites, in which baptism, confirmation, and communion, which were received together in the catechumenate, are received years apart.[4] A child of at least one Catholic parent is often baptized in "infancy" (a technical term that means before the age of seven). In my experience it is common to have initiands from a few weeks old to toddlers of two years old, depending on the ethnic composition and socio-economic conditions of the parish community. Reconciliation and first communion are received at the age of seven or eight, and confirmation anywhere between age seven and late adolescence. In some Latino communities in the United States, it is not unusual to defer confirmation until one is preparing for marriage or to be a godparent for a new baptizand.

The other major pattern is a mid-century adaptation of the ancient catechumenate that has been adopted with slight differences by the Roman Catholic Church and many mainline Protestant churches. In this Rite of Christian Initiation for Adults, initiands age seven or older go through a period of spiritual and intellectual formation, culminating at the Easter Vigil with baptism, confirmation, and first communion. The Liturgical Movement that animated the mid-twentieth-century renewal of Catholic liturgy and spirituality was deeply inspired by the practice and reflection of the fourth- and fifth-century Christian churches. As a result, the adult initiation pattern, although it is less common, is more important for understanding contemporary Roman Catholic theological reflection on initiation.

Both of these patterns convey important truths about God's work of redemption. Sacraments for Catholics both represent and convey grace; as the medieval adage put it, they "effect what they signify." They do so not on their own magical power, but because it is God who communicates with us in the sacraments and uses them to accomplish our

---

[3] In this essay, I use "rite" to mean a whole, recognizable liturgy or part of a liturgy. In Catholic liturgical theology, neither "ritual" nor "rite" means something that is done without conscious intention or emotional impact; rather, Catholic liturgy is meant for "full, conscious and active participation" by each member (Vatican II, "Constitution on the Sacred Liturgy," ¶ 14). "Rite" does not exclude improvisation, but it does constrain it within certain boundaries.

[4] Nathan Mitchell, "Christian Initiation: Decline and Dismemberment," *Worship* 48:8 (October 1974), 458–79.

salvation. Thomas Aquinas uses the analogy of a hammer (sacrament) that is an instrument in the hand of a craftsman (God), whose will is reflected in the finished work.[5] He argues that the shorthand "sign of a sacred thing" (a common aphorism in medieval theology) is not adequate because every created thing is a sign of the creator (referencing Rom 1:20). Rather, "properly speaking a sacrament . . . is the sign of a sacred thing inasmuch as it is sanctifying human beings."[6] In particular, a sacrament points to Jesus Christ as the source of our holiness, as the one who makes us holy.[7] A sacrament, then, is a symbol of grace as well as a manifestation of God's work saving human beings.

The two contemporary processes of Roman Catholic initiation manifest different aspects of God's mysterious work of salvation. The process of initiation that begins with infant baptism and concludes in adolescence or early adulthood demonstrates our conviction that God adopts us because of a love that comes before any work we do.[8] It also shows that conversion is a lifelong call with many phases of development. It illuminates the familial intimacy of the Christian family, which was expressed in the early church with the kiss of peace. Adult initiation, on the other hand, highlights the importance of human cooperation in the process of salvation, the radical and ethical character of conversion, and the role of Jesus Christ's suffering, death, and resurrection. Both have themes of participation in the sonship of Jesus Christ, of being filled with the Holy Spirit, of being united with the church that is Christ's living body, of looking in hope towards the fulfillment of the promised kingdom in the age to come. For Catholics, both of these processes communicate something true about God's plan of salvation.

In this article, I will begin with baptism, which is the part of Christian initiation that Catholics most closely associate with our healing from sin and conversion to truth, as well as our conformity to Christ (Rom 12:2). It is the foundation of our spiritual life. Themes of Christ's death and resurrection, incorporation into the Body of Christ, and indwelling of the Holy Spirit are reflected in our rites of baptism. These theological

---

[5] Thomas Aquinas, *Summa Theologica*, IIIa, 64, articles 1–3.

[6] My translation. *Proprie dicatur sacramentum, secundum quod nunc de sacramentis loquimur, quod est signum rei sacrae inquantum est sanctificans homines.* Thomas Aquinas, *Summa Theologica*, IIIa, 60, 2, respondeo.

[7] He establishes this clarification by way of the observances in the Old Testament that can be considered sacraments: "Some things pertaining to the Old Testament signified the holiness of Christ considered as holy in Himself. Others signified His holiness considered as the cause of our holiness; thus the sacrifice of the Paschal Lamb signified Christ's Sacrifice whereby we are made holy: and such like are properly styled sacraments of the Old Law." Thomas Aquinas, *Summa Theologica*, IIIa, 60, 2, rep. obj. 2; translation by the Fathers of the English Dominican Province, 1920.

[8] Infant initiation grounds Catholic approaches to pastoral care for and inclusion of people with profound intellectual disabilities or developmental delays: see Edward Foley, ed., *Developmental Disabilities and Sacramental Access New Paradigms for Sacramental Encounters* (Eugene, OR: Wipf and Stock, 2020). My treatment of infant participation in liturgy in *Efficacious Engagement* (Collegeville, MN: Liturgical Press, 2011) provides a model for participation for non-verbal persons of any age.

themes have been important for the mid-century liturgical and pastoral renewal of the Roman Catholic Church, and they have also been important in ecumenical dialogue, especially in the mutual recognition of baptism. Confirmation is very tightly connected to baptism, and especially emphasizes the ongoing role of the Holy Spirit in the believer's call to holiness. Roman Catholic theologies of confirmation have also been strongly influenced by the Charismatic Movement in the United States. Then I will turn to Holy Communion as a sacrament of initiation, and the grounds for ecumenical discussion in this group surrounding that sacrament. I speak throughout as a Roman Catholic; nonetheless, I know that many of my points are held by most or all Christians. My language "Roman Catholics believe" reflects my position on this dialogue, not necessarily any distinctiveness about my points. The work is invitational, not excluding Pentecostal or Charismatic Christians, or indeed of any of our other ecumenical dialogue partners.

Baptism

The rite of baptism includes (1) the reading and preaching of scripture, (2) prayers for the new initiate, (3) blessing of the baptismal water, (4) an anointing with the oil of catechumens (blessed olive oil), (5) a question and answer profession of faith, (6) baptism with water by either infusion (pouring) or immersion, (7) clothing with a white garment, and (8) lighting a baptismal candle from the Paschal Candle; (9) child baptism also includes an anointing with chrism called "chrismation," while adult initiation includes a different anointing with chrism called "confirmation."

Catholic sacramental theology recognizes that both human beings and God act as agents in the sacraments. On the human side, the acts of baptism express, even for infants, a personal conviction about the lordship of Jesus Christ and a commitment to a Christian life. The best analogy for the agency and personal commitment of infant baptism is probably language and cultural identity. The child is baptized into and on behalf of the faith of the church, becoming part of a linguistic and cultural world of meaning that forms her or his identity for a lifetime. In a contemporary pluralistic environment, however, nourishing the Christian identity of those children (or adults!) baptized as Catholics by non-practicing or semi-practicing parents is an ever-present pastoral problem that occupies a lot of our ministerial energy.[9]

On the divine side, Catholics do not believe that baptism itself gives grace, nor that the human minister can give grace, but rather that God acts (according to the revelation

---

[9] See *Perspectives on Koinonia: Report from the Third Quinquennium of the Dialogue between the Pontifical Council for Promoting Christian Unity of the Roman Catholic Church and Some Classical Pentecostal Churches and Leaders (1985–1989)* (Pontifical Council for Promoting Christian Unity, 1989), §§43–44, 48.

made by Jesus, and out of love for human beings) within and through the scriptural reading and symbolic action of the sacraments to bless God's people with grace. This is appropriate to human beings, since human beings are symbolic and linguistic creatures, whose relationships, including the relationship with God, depend on communication. In this respect, human beings are created in the image of the Triune God whose very nature is one of communication, mutuality, and love, and especially reflect the person of the Word of God, who is the image of the Father, who returns a filial love for the Father's begetting, and who is the firstborn of creation (Col 1) and our model (Phil 2).

Paschal Mystery

Paul, in Romans 6, describes each Christian's baptism as a participation in Christ's death and resurrection: "We were therefore buried with him through baptism into death in order that, just as Christ was raised from the dead through the glory of the Father, we too may live a new life."[10] The mysterious way that God has united Christians with Jesus, so that we are joined to his saving work, is what we mean by the phrase Paschal Mystery. All the meanings of Christian baptism— or rather, of Christian initiation—are grounded in this one.

Adult baptism takes place at the Easter Vigil, late at night on the eve of Easter, where the history of the first covenant, from creation to Exile, is read and sung, culminating in this passage about baptism in Romans 6 and the account of Christ's resurrection. The Paschal Candle, which is used to bless the baptismal font and light the baptismal candle, is a sign of Christ, light of the world. The paschal character of baptism is also reinforced by the sign of the cross, which we trace on the foreheads of children and on the senses, hands, and feet of catechumens. When Catholics make the sign of the cross, either with or without holy water, they recall their baptism. The act of anointing, likewise, is an imitation of Jesus the Anointed One, who was anointed as a preparation for his burial (Mark 14). Most of all, immersion into the baptismal water shows the "dying to Christ." For this reason, immersion is preferred for Catholic baptism; however, infusion (that is, pouring water over the head) is also an acceptable form of baptism. Baptism is thus, for Catholics, about bearing in our bodies the cross of Christ and hoping for resurrection.

Baptism's association with the Paschal Mystery is also, historically, the origin of the liturgical or church year, which associates particular days of the year with events or aspects of the revelation of God's good news. In the early church, baptism at Easter or Pentecost gradually gave rise to the development of the major cycle of the church year: Lent, Holy Week, Triduum (Holy Thursday, Good Friday, Holy Saturday), Easter season, and Pentecost. Baptism at Christmas or Epiphany may also have been

---

[10] Roman Catholics in the United States use the New American Bible for liturgical readings, but in this article I have used the New International Version (NIV).

responsible for the development of an Advent/Christmas cycle. Early church homilies suggest, additionally, that Lent, Easter, and Pentecost were privileged moments of repentance and renewal for those who were already baptized, in solidarity with those undergoing Christian initiation. This baptismal character for the church year has been reestablished in the contemporary liturgical movement.

Although Roman Catholic churches in the United States generally use the same liturgical books and thus the same basic words and actions, there is significant variance in liturgical style and cultural performance. Charismatic Catholic, Latino Catholic, and Black Catholic churches celebrate the liturgical year in ways that reflect characteristic features of the Azusa Street movement. These variances are unfortunately not always obvious from published literature, but there are a few exceptions. Mary McGann, for instance, describes the pre-Lent revival at Our Lady of Lourdes in San Francisco, which features charismatic preaching, laying on of hands, an altar call, body postures and dance, and reference to the work of the Spirit.[11] Initiatory practices and eucharistic worship also might include some charismatic elements, which might provide a provocative opening for further convergences in the understanding of baptism.

Incorporation into Christ's Body

Participation in the Paschal Mystery, while deeply personal, is not individualistic. Rather, Catholics strongly emphasize that part of God's plan for human salvation is the gathering together of a priestly people from all the ends of the earth, who give thanks and praise to the Father through the Son in the Holy Spirit, who tell the Good News, and who work to bring the world closer to God's will ("on earth as it is in heaven"). Baptism, for Catholics, is powerfully associated with incorporation into this living community, the Body of Christ (1 Cor 12), such that we consider anyone who has been baptized in water in the name of Father, Son, and Holy Spirit to be a Christian and a member of Christ's church.[12] At the same time, we have theologies explaining "baptism by blood" (for martyrs) and "baptism by desire" (for those who desire baptism but do not receive it) that recognizes that some have been and continue to be incorporated into Christ's body without having received the rite of water baptism. God's bestowal of grace is not bound to the sacrament, even if we are assured that grace is bestowed in the sacrament. Adults preparing for baptism are also considered Christians eligible for Christian burial even if they die before the rite of baptism.

---

[11] Mary E. McGann, *A Precious Fountain: Music in the Worship of an African American Catholic Community*, Virgil Michel Series (Collegeville, MN: Liturgical Press, 2004).

[12] Pontifical Council for Promoting Christian Unity, "Directory for the Application of Principles and Norms on Ecumenism" (Libreria Editrice Vaticana, 1993), ¶ 99.

Incorporation into the church is expressed in the rite by the role of godparents or sponsors (on which the role of Christian parents in infant baptism is based) who are guides to those who are being baptized, by the Litany of Saints, which asks our departed brothers and sisters in Christ to join us in prayer for those being baptized, and by the kiss of peace and the Lord's prayer that follow baptism. The unity of the church, for Catholics, is most fully manifest in sacramental communion, which is most easily seen in the united celebration of baptism, confirmation, and communion in adult baptism. At the same time, children in the Catholic Church do not generally receive holy communion until after the age of seven. This practice developed in the second millennium, whereas the age for first holy communion was lowered from early adolescence to around seven at the beginning of the twentieth century and there has been study of infant communion (still the general practice in the East). The practice of Pentecostal churches that permit children who are members of the church to receive communion would be an interesting topic for further conversation on the interrelated questions of paedobaptism, membership in the church, and faith.

Indwelling of the Holy Spirit

Baptism is also closely associated for Catholics with the indwelling of the Holy Spirit. The incorporation into the body of Christ is accomplished by the Holy Spirit, but the Spirit is even more particularly associated with the cleansing of sins and the ongoing call to holiness. By the Holy Spirit, who is especially represented by water, oil, and fire, Christians are washed from both the guilt of the sins they have committed and from the residual sinfulness that is part of our experience of human nature after the Fall.[13] They are called to a life of holiness that will require continued conversion over the course of a lifetime. Holiness demands the exercise of the human will, but Christians are not abandoned to exercise that will alone. Rather, Christian people choose the good and follow Christ by cooperating with the Holy Spirit who dwells within as the grace of God. Although serious sin can compromise this active cooperation with the Holy Spirit, repentance restores the indwelling established in baptism.

Pre-baptismal anointing (with the oil of catechumens) and the prayer over catechumens preparing for baptism during Lent are exorcistic as well as preparatory, meaning they loosen any hold evil spirits have on those preparing for baptism and also weaken the habitual character of human sin itself. The pre-baptismal anointing asks God to "set him (her) free from original sin, make him (her) a temple of your glory, and send your Holy Spirit to dwell with him (her)."[14] The water "touches the body and cleanses the heart," as

---

[13] That is, "original sin."

[14] This text is from the rite of baptism for one child.

Augustine put it,[15] representing as well as effecting the interior cleansing from sin. The baptismal garment and the candle represent the ongoing work of the Holy Spirit in the soul, conforming her or him more and more to Jesus Christ. Both prayers refer to the call to continuing conversion grounded in baptism and to the eschatological end of baptism:

> My sisters and brothers, you have become a new creation and have clothed yourselves in Christ. Receive this baptismal garment and bring it unstained to the judgment seat of our Lord Jesus Christ, so that you may have everlasting life. . . .

Then the priest says to the newly baptized:

> You have been enlightened by Christ. Walk always as children of the light and keep the flame of faith alive in your hearts. When the Lord comes, may you go out to meet him with all the saints in the heavenly kingdom.[16]

The indwelling of the Holy Spirit, or grace, is primarily associated with the virtues and the spiritual practices of prayer, which are quite varied (often associated with particular religious orders). Catholics recognize the validity of the charismata of the New Testament but tend to think of them as rare (among, for instance, founders of those same religious orders).

Baptism in Ecumenical Dialogue

The mutual recognition of baptism is a fundamental aspect of Roman Catholic bilateral and multilateral ecumenical work. Recognizing the validity of one another's baptismal practices implies, for Catholics, acknowledging that however divided we are from one another, we are members of the single body of Christ and oriented toward the one heavenly kingdom to which he invites us. The final report of the international Pentecostal-Catholic dialogue of 1972–1976 includes several paragraphs of ecumenical reflection upon the differences in Pentecostal/Charismatic and Roman Catholic initiation. I excerpt them in full here since there are several issues that are identified for further dialogue. The reports of the most recent rounds of that dialogue (1998–2006 and 2011–2015), "On Becoming a Christian: Insights from Scripture and the Patristic Writings with Some Contemporary Reflections" and "'Do Not Quench the Spirit': Charisms in the Life and Mission of the Church," would also be a good resource for our review. These latter are not officially promulgated documents; they are study documents.

> 18. The Holy Spirit, being the agent of regeneration, is given in Christian initiation, not as a commodity but as he who unifies us with Christ and the Father in a personal relationship. Being a Christian includes the reception of grace through the Holy Spirit

---

[15] Augustine, *Tractates on the Gospel of John*, 80.3; trans. John Gibb, Nicene and Post-Nicene Fathers, vol. 7, ed. Philip Schaff (Buffalo, NY: Christian Literature Publishing Company, 1888).

[16] These versions of the texts are from the Easter Vigil initiation of adults.

for one's own sanctification as well as gifts to be ministered to others. In some manner all ministry is a demonstration of the power of the Spirit. It was not agreed whether there is a further imparting of the Spirit with a view to charismatic ministry, or whether baptism in the Holy Spirit is, rather, a kind of release of a certain aspect of the Spirit already given. An inconclusive discussion occurred on the question as to how many impartings of the Spirit there were. Within classical Pentecostalism some hold that through regeneration the Holy Spirit comes *into* us, and that later in the baptism in the Spirit the Spirit comes *upon* us and begins to flow from us. Finally, charisms are not personal achievements but are sovereign manifestations of the Holy Spirit.

19. Baptism involves a passing over from the kingdom of darkness to Christ's kingdom of light, and always includes a communal dimension of being baptized into the one Body of Christ. The implications of this concord were not developed.

20. In regard to baptism, the New Testament reflects the missionary situation of the apostolic generation of the Church and does not clearly indicate what may have happened in the second and following generation of believers.

21. In that missionary situation Christian initiation involved a constellation normally including proclamation of the Gospel, faith repentance, baptism in water, the receiving of the Spirit. There was disagreement as to the relationship of these items, and the order in which they may or should occur. In both the Pentecostal and Roman Catholic tradition laying on of hands may be used to express the giving of the Spirit. Immersion is the ideal form which most aptly expresses the significance of baptism. Some, however, regard immersion as essential, others do not.

22. In discussing infant baptism, certain convergences were noted:

a) Sacraments are in no sense magical and are *effective only in relationship to faith.*

23. *b)* God's gift precedes and makes possible human receiving. Even though there was disagreement on the application of this principle, there was accord on the assertion that God's grace operates in advance of our conscious awareness.

24. *c)* Where paedobaptism is not practiced and the children of believing parents are presented and dedicated to God, the children are thus brought into the care of the Christian community and enjoy the special protection of the Lord.

25. *d)* Where paedobaptism is practiced it is fully meaningful only in the context of the faith of the parents and the community. The parents must undertake to nurture the child in the Christian life, in the expectation that, when he or she grows up, the child will personally live and affirm faith in Christ.

26. Representatives of the charismatic movement in the historic churches expressed different views on baptism. Some agreed substantially with the Roman Catholic, others with the classical Pentecostal view.

27. Attention was drawn to the pastoral problem of persons baptized in infancy seeking a new experience of baptism by immersion later in life. It was stated that in a few traditions rites have been devised, involving immersion in water in order to afford such an experience. The Roman Catholics felt there were already

sufficient opportunities within the existing liturgy for reaffirming one's baptism. Rebaptism in the strict sense of the word is unacceptable to all. Those participants who reject paedobaptism, however, explained that they do not consider as rebaptism the baptism of a believing adult who has received infant baptism. This serious ecumenical problem requires future study.[17]

Confirmation

The historical development of sacramental confirmation is complicated and scholarly knowledge is still incomplete.[18] It certainly originated in the fourth-century post-baptismal rites in Rome, which included the presiding bishop anointing the candidate on the head with chrism, laying hands on the head, and praying for the sevenfold gifts of the Holy Spirit. Bishops were scarce in the rest of Europe, where presbyters (priests) increasingly did the whole rite of initiation, but over the medieval period, many Roman practices, including this one, were adopted all over the Latin West. One adaptation to episcopal scarcity was to have the presbyter perform the whole rite of baptism, including an anointing with chrism on the crown of the head, then give Holy Communion. When the bishop next passed through town, the parents of the baptized child were to take him or her to the bishop, who "confirmed" the baptism (though exactly what he did to do this is not always clear in our documentation). As late as the thirteenth century, liturgical laws were passed stating that this had to be done *before* age one, or age five, or age seven, etc. The age seems to have grown later and later to accommodate parents who chose not to or could not get a confirmation done.

Theological reflection on this now separated anointing and/or hand laying rite, meanwhile, developed several themes that might be interesting for this group. On one hand, it was closely associated with baptism: both were understood to convey the Holy Spirit. On the other, the separation of it from baptism proper (especially as infant baptism became more common) led theologians and bishops to speculate on its distinct purpose. This had several variants, among them: baptism is to birth as confirmation is to maturity; baptism bestows the Holy Spirit and confirmation strengthens its gifts for the work of preaching or evangelization; baptism reflects Christ's baptism (or his Passion) and confirmation his sending of the Holy Spirit at Pentecost.

---

[17] "Final Report of the Dialogue Between the Secretariat for Promoting Christian Unity of the Roman Catholic Church and Leaders of Some Pentecostal Churches and Participants in the Charismatic Movement Within Protestant and Anglican Church (1972–1976)," http://www.christianunity.va/content/unitacristiani/en/dialoghi/sezione-occidentale/pentecostali/dialogo/documenti-di-dialogo/testo-in-inglese3.html.

[18] For this discussion of the history of confirmation and its attendant theologies, see especially Maxwell E. Johnson, *The Rites of Christian Initiation: Their Evolution and Interpretation*, 2nd ed. (Collegeville, MN: Liturgical Press, 2007), 247–57.

Theologies of confirmation were still very unsettled at Trent, which had little to say on the subject, and historical studies done in the modern period only complicated the theological questions more. The mid-twentieth-century renewal revised the rite thoroughly, as the Constitution on the Sacred Liturgy decreed: "The rite of confirmation is to be revised and the intimate connection which this sacrament has with the whole of Christian initiation is to be more clearly set forth; for this reason it is fitting for candidates to renew their baptismal promises just before they are confirmed."[19] In addition, the renewed rite of confirmation doubled down on the rite's association with the Holy Spirit,[20] for example, by choosing an Eastern formula into the new prayer for anointing: "N., be sealed with the Gift of the Holy Spirit" over the traditional, Western Trinitarian formula. This makes the anointing more closely related to the prayer recited during the hand laying before it:

> All-powerful God, Father of our Lord Jesus Christ, By water and the Holy Spirit You freed your sons and daughters from sin And gave them new life. Send your Holy Spirit upon them to be their helper and guide. Give them the spirit of wisdom and understanding, The spirit of right judgment and courage, The spirit of knowledge and reverence. Fill them with the spirit of wonder and awe in your presence.[21]

Since Vatican II, this sacrament has taken on a number of different theological interpretations and pastoral purposes; it has been memorably labeled "a sacrament in search of a theology."[22]

Modern confirmation, then, poses a unique set of challenges for Catholic scholars, ministers, and ecumenists.[23] For many Catholic parishes, it serves as a rite of adolescent maturity, in which children baptized as infants have the opportunity at a particular age to

---

[19] Vatican II, "Constitution on the Sacred Liturgy," ¶ 71.

[20] Timothy R. Gabrielli, *Confirmation: How a Sacrament of God's Grace Became All about Us* (Collegeville, MN: Liturgical Press, 2013), 28–29.

[21] "The Signs and the Rite of Confirmation," https://www.vatican.va/content/catechism/en/part_two/section_two/chapter_one/article_2/ii_the_signs_and_the_rite_of_confirmation.html#:~:text=In%20the%20Latin%20rite%2C%20the,Churches%2C%20after%20a%20prayer%20of, ¶ 1299.

[22] Quoted without a specific source in William J. Bausch, *A New Look at the Sacraments* (New London, CT: Twenty-Third Publications, 1983), 92.

[23] For instance, ecumenically, the validity of confirmation in the first-generation Protestant communions (i.e. Lutheran and Reformed traditions) is uncertain: "In the present state of our relations with the ecclesial Communities of the Reformation of the 16th century, we have not yet reached agreement about the significance or sacramental nature or even of the administration of the sacrament of Confirmation. Therefore, under present circumstances, persons entering into full communion with the Catholic Church from one of these Communities are to receive the sacrament of Confirmation according to the doctrine and rite of the Catholic Church before being admitted to Eucharistic communion." Pontifical Council for Promoting Christian Unity, "Directory for the Application of Principles and Norms on Ecumenism" (Libreria Editrice Vaticana, 1993), ¶ 101.

affirm their baptismal vows. This purpose seems to fit an American need for a religious rite of passage, but it is at odds with confirmation's early history. Some dioceses have made an effort to reclaim the earlier sequence baptism, confirmation, communion, by celebrating confirmation just before first communion in the same year. At the same time, the combination of the sacrament's association with the Holy Spirit, with Pentecost, with the act of laying on of hands, and with strengthening or maturity led to adoption of a "baptism of the Holy Spirit" theology for confirmation, drawn directly or indirectly from the Pentecostal/Charismatic movements. At first members of the charismatic Catholic movement "strove to keep baptism in the Holy Spirit distinct from the sacraments of initiation in order to bolster, rather than obstruct or supplant the official sacramental life of the church."[24] Later, however, some theologians and pastoral ministers argued that baptism in the Spirit is the ideal consequence of confirmation or that baptism in the Spirit is a revival of the effects of confirmation. This theology of confirmation remains controversial, but in weaker terms, the association of confirmation with the Holy Spirit, with growth in spiritual maturity, and with strengthening in the spiritual gifts shows a broad influence of the Pentecostal tradition.[25]

Communion as a Sacrament of Initiation

Roman Catholic practice and teaching on the Eucharist or Holy Communion is a massive topic, but here I only want to briefly gesture towards the significance of this sacrament in Christian initiation. Nathan D. Mitchell has persuasively argued for the primacy of table practice in Jesus' own patterns of hospitality and discipleship.[26] Although it is not the beginning of initiation in the usual pattern, Communion continues to be the motive and the measure of the disciple's ongoing transformation and conversion. Even though it is not the end of the contemporary Catholic infant-to-adolescent initiation, it is the consummation of the Paschal Mystery, the foretaste of the heavenly kingdom, and the most complete earthly image of the unity of the Body of Christ. This should not be simplified into a picture of first Holy Communion as an initiation rite; rather, Holy Communion is an at-least-weekly renewal and integration of Christian initiation.

Communion is also the rite of Christian initiation that points most clearly towards the renewal of the created order. The consequences of Christ's incarnation, death, and resurrection are not restricted to human life and social behavior. The early church saw the Eucharist as the revelation of the new creation, when human and non-

---

[24] Gabrielli, *Confirmation*, 33.

[25] Gabrielli, *Confirmation*, 34–36.

[26] Mitchell, *Eucharist as Sacrament of Initiation*.

human creatures glorify and enrich one another. Creation was made to be nourishment for human creatures, as both the creation narratives in Genesis and the Psalms testify. In response, human creatures were to receive, to steward, to give thanks, and to share that creation. As a part of initiation, whether immediately after adult baptism and confirmation or some years after infant baptism, Holy Communion demonstrates that those who are Christians receive the good gifts of the world from God, recognize and thank God for them, and offer them "for the life of the world."[27]

Conclusion

Worship is always enacted in a tension between acts that are done once and those that are done repeatedly, between what is generally the case and exceptional cases. I have tried to attend to both ends of this spectrum in this brief treatment of Roman Catholic initiation today, with illuminating highlights from history. Roman Catholic theologies of initiation, taken as a whole, reflect a tradition where the effects of God's saving love are not always empirically evident right away (or perhaps in earthly life). There is a substantive amount of apophatic uncertainty in Catholic approaches to initiation. For instance, we recognize that not all who are baptized may be saved, and that some who are not baptized will be saved, but there is a certain hesitance to speculate about particular cases, to set up rules for what are exceptional situations. At the same time, the spirituality of Christian life and evidence of Christian holiness is always taken as stemming from the grace of sacramental initiation, even if it occurs significantly after initiation, as a growth or renewal or revival of the sacramental grace. The Catholic understanding of baptism, "sacramental revival," and continual conversion might be a productive source of further conversation about water baptism and baptism in the Holy Spirit. The deep mystery of God's salvation extended to human beings, and the limits of our very human understanding, should guide us to a better appreciation of one another's practices and theologies.

Kimberly Hope Belcher (Kimberly.H.Belcher.4@nd.edu) is Associate Professor of Theology (Liturgical Studies) at the University of Notre Dame, Notre Dame, Indiana, USA.

---

[27] This quotation from John 6 has been given an indelible liturgical interpretation by Alexander Schmemann in *For the Life of the World: Sacraments and Orthodoxy* (Yonkers, NY: St Vladimir's Seminary Press, 1973).

Academic Books from ORU PRESS

The Remaining Task of the Great Commission
&
The Spirit-Empowered Movement

Wonsuk Ma and **Opoku Onyinah**
Rebekah Bled, Associate Editor

GOOD NEWS TO THE POOR
SPIRIT-EMPOWERED RESPONSES TO POVERTY

Wonsuk Ma and **Opoku Onyinah**
Rebekah Bled, Associate Editor

HUMAN SEXUALITY
& the Holy Spirit

SPIRIT-EMPOWERED PERSPECTIVES

Wonsuk Ma and **Kathaleen Reid-Martinez**
Annamarie Hamilton, Associate Editor

PROCLAIMING CHRIST
In the Power of the Holy Spirit

OPPORTUNITIES & CHALLENGES

Wonsuk Ma and **Emmanuel Anim**
Rebekah Bled, Associate Editor

Buy through ORU.edu/ORUPress

Initiation (Water Baptism) in North American Pentecostalism

FREDERICK L. WARE

Keywords *baptism, initiation, Pentecostalism, sacramental theology*

Abstract

As Pentecostal theology grows in appreciation of sacramental theology, this Catholic-Pentecostal dialogue represents an immense opportunity for Pentecostals. Previous iterations of dialogue identified infant baptism and believer's baptism as topics of interest. Through a series of questions, this article identifies several challenges to baptism of both kinds. The complexity of issues is explored through contrasting Pentecostal experiences of water baptism and Pentecostal denominational and constructive theological interpretations of water baptism.

Introduction

Of the three sacraments of initiation, baptism and Eucharist are practiced in Pentecostal churches. Confirmation is not practiced because believers, not infants, are customarily baptized. In Pentecostal churches, baptism is called "water baptism" and Eucharist is called "Lord's Supper" or "Holy Communion." Each is regarded as an "ordinance," not a sacrament. In this article, I focus on water baptism.[1]

There is much to be learned on both sides of the dialogue. Pentecostals are rediscovering sacramental theology and exploring its relevance and application to Christian faith and practice in Pentecostal churches. Pentecostals' high emphasis on Spirit baptism naturally raises several questions about its relation to water baptism. Issues about grace, divine presence, spiritual experience and growth, and belonging to Christ and the church in regard to the Eucharist are similarly raised in water baptism. Catholic canon law, with limited exceptions, places the Eucharist outside of the bounds of fruitful dialogue, at least in this exploratory conversation.[2] My intuition is that our

---

[1] In past dialogues, the topics of infant baptism and believer's baptism seem to elicit the greatest interest and passion. See Killian McDonnell, "Five Defining Issues: The International Pentecostal-Roman Catholic Dialogue," *Pneuma: The Journal for the Society for Pentecostal Studies* 17:2 (Fall 1995), 177–78.

[2] *The Code of Canon Law*, 844, 908. According to canon law, since Pentecostal congregations and denominations are among Protestant churches that have no valid Eucharist, Catholics cannot receive the

Catholic dialogue partners may be interested in having a conversation about Pentecostal notions of the Holy Spirit's work in the ongoing reaffirmation of baptism, if indeed this act is primarily initiation and not repeatable.[3]

This article has four parts. In part 1, I share a personal recollection of my water baptism. This personal experience is by no means typical. It does, however, represent my engagement with the subject matter of this dialogue and accentuate the Pentecostal emphasis on testimony, the narration of one's life within Christ and the church. My recollection provides contrast to the varied experiences of other Pentecostals. If there is anything that may be called typical, it is the diversity of experiences, thoughts, and perspectives among Pentecostals.

In part 2, I review a few Pentecostal denominational statements on baptism. This section accentuates diversity, identifying the broad parameters but reoccurring themes of Pentecostal belief and practice. This section is significant, not because these statements represent unanimity. Within any Christian community, there are different interpretations. These statements are significant because of the relative uniformity accomplished through the polity structures of these denominations to present their beliefs to external audiences.

In part 3, I survey Pentecostal constructive theologies. Here, I examine the constructive work of Pentecostal theologians, past and contemporary, on water baptism. The recent rise of interest in sacramental theology appears to be predated, by several decades, by early Pentecostal leaders' observance of sacraments within the parent denominations from which they came.

In the final part, I conclude with reflections on the challenges and opportunities in future ecumenical dialogue on initiation through the rite of baptism.

Personal Recollections of Water Baptism

My Experience of Baptism

I was baptized at 13 years of age, about two months before my 14th birthday. It was a Sunday evening. The exact date, recorded on my baptismal certificate, is August 31, 1975. Several persons were baptized on that same day. These baptisms came at the end

---

Eucharist in these churches. Furthermore, by not being in full communion with the Catholic Church, Pentecostals cannot receive the Eucharist through the administration of Catholic priests. Given this deep divide separating Pentecostals and Catholics, an exploratory dialogue should begin with discussion on less controversial matters.

[3] As reported in *For a Synodal Church: Communion, Participation, and Mission*, the 2021–2024 Catholic Synod in North America has trended toward an emphasis on baptism, that is, on the dignity it accords and responsibility it entails for every believer as well as the communion with Christ and one another to which it invites every believer.
https://www.usccb.org/resources/North%20American%20Final%20Document%20-%20English.pdf.

of two, close to three weeks of the "All Saints Revival," daily worship services open to all Christians in the tri-state area.[4] However, most of the attendees were from Pentecostal churches. I do not recall the total number of baptismal candidates. I do remember the candidates being from all ages, some younger than me, but most were older. Days prior to the baptizing, persons were provided instructions on appropriate dress. The men's dressing room, monitored by the deacons, and women's dressing rooms, monitored by the deaconesses, were at opposite ends of the church facility. The baptismal pool was located in the church sanctuary behind the choir stand. The pastor conducted the worship and offered words to mark the start of the baptismal service. The candidates entered the pool one-by-one. There were deacons helping the candidates to enter and exit the pool. Already standing in the pool were two ordained ministers, one positioned on the left and the other positioned on the right. The water was mild temperature and came about chest-high. The persons seated in the sanctuary sang and, with every candidate, offered praise with clapping and shouts of "Thank you, Jesus" and "Hallelujah." I remember, when my turn came to enter the pool, the nervousness left me. I felt a sense of calm when I heard the words pronounced: "I baptize you in the name of the Father, and of the Son, and of the Holy Ghost." I gave myself to the care of the ministers who lowered me into the water. When I came up, I sensed "something" had happened to me and that from that moment, I would not be the same. I did not express the same emotion I saw in the other candidates. Some candidates came out of the water shouting with exuberant praise: "Hallelujah," "Thank you, Jesus," "Glory to God." My intuition, in words that I was not capable of expressing as a child of that age, was that I had reached a great milestone in my life and the beginning of a new phase in my Christian experience.

A Contrasting Experience of Water Baptism

My experience is by no means typical for all Pentecostals. For example, Steve Studebaker describes a very different type of experience and likewise acknowledges that his experience is not ordinary. Studebaker says:

> Nestled amid mountains and alpine forests, the cool waters of Medicine Lake in Northern California are where I was baptized. At the time and in the recall of memory, the natural beauty of the surroundings infused the experience with a mystical quality that my Pentecostal theology of water baptism does not. For three years, my family attended a Pentecostal church with a broken baptismal. During the period we were a part of that church, no effort was made to fix the baptismal,

---

[4] This area includes the regions of southwest Tennessee, eastern Arkansas, and northwest Mississippi.

no one seems to have missed the use of the baptismal, and to my knowledge no one in the church was baptized there or anywhere else.[5]

Infant Dedication and Programs of Formation

Many experiences led up to my moment of baptism. As an infant (newborn), I was presented to God by my parents in front of a large company of witnesses. They "dedicated" me to God in the sight of the congregation. I grew up within this congregation, which became an extension of family. I was nurtured in the Christian faith by the whole people of God. This nurture included prayer at home and at church services, Sunday school, and youth programs that were educational, recreational, and spiritual.

As far back as I can remember, I never felt alienated from God. I grew into discernment of God's presence with me and in the community. The gatherings for worship were attended with signs of God's presence. I heard adults speak of their spiritual experiences. I heard persons testify to divine healing from disease and sickness. Some of them spoke of lying at the point of death. By the prayer of the "saints," they were raised from their bed of affliction.[6] They spoke of how their lives were spared from great tragedy. They shared experiences of how God miraculously met their financial and physical needs. I heard the testimonies of persons who had been delivered from sin described as "troubled living," "broken homes," addiction to drugs and alcohol, and "hard life" on the streets and in back alleys. These testimonies were stories of radical transformation.

As a child these incidences about which persons spoke were not a part of my life experience, but I was told that if I believed on Jesus Christ, he would save me. I was told that Christ not only saves from sin but keeps persons from sin. This was my decision to come to Christ, believing that he would keep me from sin, and in his doing so, save me. I was growing into an awareness of the freedom given to me as a human being that in my decisions, the future of my life could turn for good or evil. I resolved to make a decision, the choice of Jesus Christ as my Savior and Lord, for the turn to good. It seemed like a natural step in my growth to embrace the faith to which I had been exposed from my infancy.

My baptism represented the success of the church's programs of formation for children. There were some children who grew up as I did in the church with all of the benefits of nurturing parents, guardians, and church members, and still at adulthood,

---

[5] Steve Studebaker, "Baptism among Pentecostals," in *Baptism: Historical, Theological, and Pastoral Perspectives*, eds. Gordon L. Heath and James D. Dvorak (Eugene, OR: Pickwick Publications, 2011), 201.

[6] Here, the term "saints" refers to church members who live righteously, aspiring to codes of moral and ethical conduct regarded as imperatives of Christian faith.

they did not come to accept the faith. As a child under the care of parents and grandparents who are members of the church, I was allowed, after my dedication, to receive the Lord's Supper.[7]

In my Pentecostal church, the Church of God in Christ, infant dedication functions as an alternative practice to infant baptism.[8] In most Pentecostal churches, baptism is *credobaptism* (believer baptism), not *pedobaptism* (infant baptism).[9] Among the scriptural references cited for justification for dedication is the passage from Luke 2, the story of Mary and Joseph's presentation of the infant Jesus for dedication at the temple (vv. 21–24, 39–40). Pentecostals dedicate their newborn children in public worship services that involve a high degree of ceremony and attract extended family and friends to witness this public confession of parents or guardians presenting the child to God and their solemn oath to rear that child in the Christian faith.[10] Children who have been dedicated are allowed to partake in the Lord's Supper. The International Pentecostal Holiness Church's permit of the practice of infant baptism is not an aberration. Pentecostals are in essential agreement regarding the inclusion and formation of newborns and children in the community of faith.

Denominational Statements on Water Baptism

Established in 1994, the Pentecostal and Charismatic Churches of North America (PCCNA) is an interdenominational fellowship of Pentecostal and Charismatic churches and denominations in the United States. The PCCNA is successor to the Pentecostal Fellowship of North America (PFNA), which was founded in 1948. The more than forty members of PCCNA are mostly denominations and churches, but include ministries, variously defined, and educational institutions. A commonality among the PCCNA members is their affirmation of the Trinity, in contrast to the

---

[7] Children who have been dedicated are included in the membership of the church. Most pastors interpret this to mean that children are allowed to receive the Lord's Supper. See "Children and Church Membership," *Official Manual of the Church of God in Christ* (Memphis, TN: Board of Publication of the Church of God in Christ, 1973), 84–85.

[8] "Baptism and Incorporation into the Body of Christ, the Church: Lutheran-Mennonite-Roman Catholic Trilateral Conversations 2012–2017," *The Mennonite Quarterly Review* 95 (January 2021), 76–77.

[9] In Andrew Ray Williams' "Water Baptism in Pentecostal Perspective: A Bibliographical Evaluation," *Spiritus: ORU Journal of Theology* 4:1 (spring 2019), 78, 82, he shows there is dissenting opinion on believer's baptism. Whereas Stanley Horton, William Menzies, and Michael Dusing argue that only believer's baptism is valid and consequently condemn the practice of infant dedication as an acceptable practice, Simon Tan claims there is very little difference between infant dedication and infant baptism and therefore recommends infant baptism as the better practice.

[10] "Service for the Dedication of Children," *Official Manual of the Church of God in Christ*, 227–31.

Oneness organizations that subscribe to a modalist theism. Because Oneness groups are not a part of the PCCNA, I will omit discussion of their beliefs about baptism.[11]

In the section that follows, I review a sampling of official denominational statements on baptism and the relation of these views of baptism to the Lord's Supper. This selection of statements is influenced by the present composition of the Pentecostal team in our dialogue. The statements are from the denominations with which the Pentecostal team members have affiliation and/or membership.

Assemblies of God

In the Assemblies of God's *Statement of Fundamentals of Truths*, it states, "The ordinance of baptism by immersion is commanded by the Scriptures. All who repent and believe on Christ as Savior and Lord are to be baptized. Thus, they declare to the world that they have died with Christ and that they also have been raised with Him to walk in newness of life."[12] The scriptural references are Matthew 28:19; Mark 16:16; Acts 10:47, 48; and Romans 6:4.

Church of God (Cleveland, Tennessee)

The Church of God *Declaration of Faith* states that belief, "In water baptism by immersion, and all who repent should be baptized in the name of the Father, and of the Son, and of the Holy Ghost," for which this doctrinal commitment is supported by scriptural references to Matthew 28:19; Mark 1:9, 10; John 3:22; and Acts 8:36, 38.[13]

Church of God in Christ

The doctrines of the Church of God in Christ states:

> We believe that Water Baptism is necessary as instructed by Christ in John 3:5, "Unless man be born again of water and of the spirit." However, we do not believe that water baptism alone is a means of salvation, but is an outward demonstration that one has already had a conversion experience and has accepted Christ as his

---

[11] Oneness Pentecostals share in common the nomenclature of ordinance and preference of baptism by immersion. Oneness Pentecostals diverge on the formula for baptism, insisting that the proper administration of the rite must be "in Jesus' name" (Acts 2:28). They also locate baptism as the second part of a tripartite experience of salvation, involving repentance, water baptism (in Jesus' name), and Spirit baptism.

[12] Assemblies of God, "Statement of Fundamental Truths," #6 Ordinances of the Church, https://ag.org/beliefs/statement-of-fundamental-truths#6.

[13] The brevity of these Church of God statements reflects its stance against "abuses and extravagance of ecclesiastical ritualism," as expressed in its self-definition in "The Church of God is . . . ," http://199.191.59.139/beliefs/church-of-god-is/. Statement on Water Baptism: http://199.191.59.139/beliefs/declaration-of-faith/. Scriptural support of doctrine on water baptism: http://199.191.59.139/beliefs/doctrinal-commitments/.

personal Savior. As Pentecostals, we practice immersion in preference to "sprinkling," because immersion corresponds more closely to the death, burial, and resurrection of our Lord (Col 2:12). It also symbolizes regeneration and purification more than any other mode. Therefore, we practice immersion as our mode of Baptism. We believe that we should use the Baptismal Formula given us by Christ for all "…in the name of the Father, and of the Son, and of the Holy Ghost" (Matt 28:19).[14]

International Church of the Foursquare Gospel

The Declaration of Faith, originally compiled by Aimee Semple McPherson, the founder, states:

> We believe that water baptism in the name of the Father and of the Son and of the Holy Ghost, according to the command of our Lord, is a blessed outward sign of an inward work; a beautiful and solemn emblem reminding us that even as our Lord died upon the cross of Calvary, so we reckon ourselves now dead indeed unto sin, and the old nature nailed to the tree with Him; and that even as he was taken down from the tree and buried, so we are buried with Him by baptism unto death: that like as Christ was raised up from the dead by the glory of the Father, even so we should walk in newness of life.[15] (The noted scriptural references are Matthew 28:19, 20; Acts 2:37, 38, 41, 22:16; Galatians 3:27, 28; Romans 6:4, Colossians 2:12; and 1 Peter 3:20, 21.)

International Pentecostal Holiness Church (IPHC)

The *International Pentecostal Holiness Church Manual* states:

> Baptism is intended only for those who have professed faith in the Lord Jesus Christ. It is a God-given illustration of each Christian's identification with Christ in His death, burial, and resurrection. Obedience to this ordinance demonstrates the believer's public confession of this fact to others.
>
> 1. All who unite with any local church on profession of faith in Christ should further confess Christ by receiving water baptism, preferably by immersion, as early as possible.
>
> 2. Baptism shall be administered according to the divine command of our blessed Lord, "In the name of the Father, and of the Son, and of the Holy Ghost [Spirit]."[16]

---

[14] Church of God in Christ, Inc.,"What We Believe," https://www.cogic.org/about-company/what-we-believe/.

[15] https://foursquaremissionspress.org/wp-content/uploads/2016/01/445_Declaration_of_Faith.pdf.

[16] *International Pentecostal Holiness Church Manual, 2017–2021* (Oklahoma City, OK: International Pentecostal Holiness Church, 2018), 61. https://iphc.org/wp-content/uploads/2018/06/IPHC-Manual-2017-2021-English.pdf.

Reoccurring Themes on Baptism and Its Relation to The Lord's Supper

Across these statements, there are five recurring themes. The first theme, which is most obvious, is the nomenclature of "ordinance." As ordinance, emphasis is placed on the institution and commandment (instruction) of Christ to which the appropriate response is obedience by all Christians. The second theme is faith. The rite is thought to require faith on the part of the participant and his/her declaration (testimony) of the same in public confession. Baptism is thus an outward demonstration of the participant's believer's baptism, although the IPHC allows infant baptism. A third theme is that of symbolic meaning. Baptism is regarded as a sign, emblem, or illustration (God-given) of death and burial and rising to new life. The fourth theme is on the mode by which baptism is supposed to occur. The mode is immersion, explicitly stated or implied as the proper (or preferred) mode, with IPHC allowing for variance in modes. The fifth theme is Trinity. The formula by which baptism is administered is "In the name of the Father, and of the Son, and of the Holy Spirit."

As with baptism, the Lord's Supper follows the same nomenclature of an ordinance, emphasizing obedience to the command of Christ, of which all Christians are advised to partake only upon self-examination. The Lord's Supper is likewise regarded as sign, symbol, commemoration, and reminder of Christ's death by crucifixion (for cleansing/salvation from sin) and promise of Christ's return (second coming). The theme of symbolism is emphasized for the bread and wine (fruit of the vine), representing Christ's body and blood. Pentecostals believe that Christ is present, but the brief statements do not make clear how Christ is present beyond the meaning of "spiritually" present.

Significance of Denominational Statements

Why examine the denominational statements? They are a gauge of where these denominations are in the development of consensus. These denominational statements are the product of the social processes and polity systems operative within these denominations and churches. In any organization, there is probability of different perspectives, possibly dissenting views to the statements that are produced through the denominational systems and processes. The statements are not representative of every single person's mind, but they do provide an indication of the consensus forged within these organizations. The statements are fluid in that organizations can revisit, modify as they grow, and learn for new situations that require reexamination of interpretations of Christian faith.

Pentecostal Constructive Theologies of Water Baptism

Denominational statements can be differentiated from what I call "constructive theological interpretations." The constructive theological interpretations are representative of individual thinking. And yet this individual thinking is significant to show how persons within these denominations and churches are on the cutting edge, leading their organizations into deeper reflection on the statements that they have produced. Sometimes the constructive theological interpretations reaffirm these denominational statements. Sometimes the constructive interpretations raise important questions, and point out conflicts and inconsistencies. Sometimes these constructive interpretations nuance and expound upon themes that are otherwise quite vague in these statements. At other times, the theological interpretations represent groundbreaking insights to drive and move forward the theological understanding and ministerial practice of the denominations and churches. Most notable now in Pentecostal history is a warming of Pentecostal theologians to sacramental theology.

Early Pentecostal Thinkers

In Kim Alexander's study of early Pentecostal theology, a careful study of denominational publications, she concludes that there are common emphases among these early Pentecostal thinkers.[17] According to Alexander, all early PFNA-type Pentecostals regard water baptism as an ordinance. Attention and concern about water baptism only arose by virtue of the introduction of what is referred to as "Finished Work" soteriology.[18] The common practice of Pentecostals was simply to focus on Christ and approximate the teachings and practices of the primitive church and evangelize the world with the proclamation of the gospel.

Alexander notes that Acts 2:38 became the paradigmatic formula with this introduction of Finished Work soteriology. She goes on to say that adherence to the Trinity dogma existed prior to this doctrinal controversy and this firm commitment to the Trinitarian conception of God persisted over time. The mode of baptism was by immersion, although not exclusively, as shown in the history of the International Pentecostal Holiness Church. To Alexander's analysis, James Hogsten notes that prior to the rise of Finished Work soteriology, various Pentecostal groups practiced baptism in Jesus' name, motivated by their Christocentric focus and quest to approximate practices

---

[17] Kimberly Ervin Alexander, "Matters of Conscience, Matters of Unity: Trinity and Water Baptism in Early Pentecostal Theology," *Journal of Pentecostal Theology* 17 (2008), 69.

[18] In Finished Work Soteriology, the Pentecostal three-stage experience of conversion, sanctification, and Spirit baptism is collapsed into two stages. This nuanced stage, stage one, is that of repentance where sanctification happens within conversion, and the believer subsequently grows in grace to reach the second stage of baptism in the Holy Spirit.

of the primitive church, but eventually gravitated toward the Matthean text (28:19) because of its suggestion that the commandment and formula for baptizing is attributed to Jesus.[19]

Recent Pentecostal Constructive Statements

In Frank Macchia's *Baptized in the Spirit: A Global Pentecostal Theology* (2006), he describes water baptism as an "eschatological gift," given as an ordinance and sign. As ordinance, water baptism is "obedient response to God's gracious self-giving."[20] Macchia cites Matthew 3:11, with parallels in Luke and Mark, where the prophet John says, "I indeed baptize you with water unto repentance: but he that cometh after me is mightier than I, whose shoes I am not worthy to bear: he shall baptize you with the Holy Ghost, and with fire." As sign, John's water rite points to and is fulfilled in Spirit baptism, which represents the transformed believers' empowerment for service and ministry. Macchia goes on to suggest that Spirit baptism fulfills conversion witnessed in water baptism. "Jesus' reception of the Spirit and his baptism is paradigmatic of the connection between baptism and the reception of the Spirit among Christians."[21] Water baptism functions as the fulfillment of the believer's act of repentance and faith.[22] For illustration of how this process of fulfillment works, Macchia uses an analogy of the wedding ceremony to explain the relationship between Spirit baptism and water baptism. "The wedding ceremony confirms and fulfills a commitment between two hearts joined together in love."[23] The ritual of water baptism confirms the relationship between the believer in God; it is not the relationship, only a sign of it.[24] Macchia admits that his interpretation of water baptism and Spirit baptism makes, if not impossible, very difficult the justification of infant baptism.[25] Spirit baptism is what brought the church into existence, and it will take no less for believers to realize new life in Christ by the same baptism.[26]

In Amos Yong's *Renewing Christian Theology: Systematics for a Global Christianity* (2014), a textbook in systematic theology from a Pentecostal perspective, he devotes a full chapter on "Ordinances and Sacraments." As with any systematic theologian, a

---

[19] James Douglas Hogsten, "The Monadic Formula of Water Baptism: A Quest for Primitivism via a Christocentric and Restorationist Impulse," *Journal of Pentecostal Theology* 17 (2008), 70–95.

[20] Frank D. Macchia, *Baptized in the Spirit: A Global Pentecostal Theology* (Grand Rapids, MI: Zondervan Academic, 2006), 65.

[21] Macchia, *Baptized in the Spirit*, 70.

[22] Macchia, *Baptized in the Spirit*, 66.

[23] Macchia, *Baptized in the Spirit*, 227.

[24] Studebaker, "Baptism among Pentecostals," 215.

[25] Macchia, *Baptized in the Spirit*, 227.

[26] Macchia, *Baptized in the Spirit*, 177.

major goal is to present the Christian faith in a comprehensive manner. Yong is comfortable using the words "ordinance" and "sacrament," considering that each is a sign of the presence of the Spirit and of the coming reign of God.[27] Each is pointing to something important in the lives of Christians.

Yong's preference is actually for the word "practice." Baptism and the Lord's Supper are practices, symbolic and efficacious, for encountering God in Christ through the Holy Spirit. These practices reposition and resituate persons within a new relationship that is the body of Christ and the fellowship of the Spirit. Yong goes on to note that Jesus' own baptism in water is paradigmatic.

Like Macchia, Yong regards baptism as an eschatological gift and focuses on the prophet John's relation of his practice of baptizing to the coming of Christ. The Spirit descended on Jesus at baptism. Yong says, "Jesus' own Spirit-baptized life is the reality into which his believers are invited through their own baptism in, with, and by the Holy Spirit."[28] Believer's baptism by water is identification with Christ, in his life, death, and resurrection, and solidarity with a fellowship of the community of faith that affirms God's ongoing work of salvation by the Holy Spirit.

A fair characterization of Pentecostal theology is that it is "developing." Two studies make this evident. First, Andrew Ray Williams reviews recent Pentecostal theological work on water baptism. He draws two conclusions. Though Pentecostals taking a descriptive approach have understood water baptism to be mainly symbolic, they have "[noted] a rich sacramentalism embedded in Pentecostal spirituality . . . that is (incoherently) assigned to certain spaces (altar) and not others (table, baptismal)."[29] Those Pentecostals taking a constructive approach to interpretation have likewise intuited a sacramentality on Pentecostal spirituality, either seeking to understand its rooting in the Wesleyan/Holiness tradition or examining it for application to reflections (special insight) on the Lord's Supper and baptism.[30] Second, Daniel Tomberlin suggests that future work of Pentecostal theology must address four areas: (1) the distinction but relation between infant baptism and believer's baptism; (2) the relation of water baptism to Spirit baptism; (3) the work of the Spirit in liturgy but the Spirit's freedom to transcend it; and (4) and the question of how water baptism is reaffirmed.[31]

---

[27] Amos Yong, *Renewing Christian Theology: Systematics for a Global Christianity* (Waco, TX: Baylor University Press, 2014), 130. Retrieved from https://1lib.us/book/11061533/f6686d/ on September 12, 2021.

[28] Yong, *Renewing Christian Theology*, 126.

[29] Williams, "Water Baptism in Pentecostal Perspective," 90.

[30] Williams, "Water Baptism in Pentecostal Perspective," 90.

[31] Daniel Tomberlin, "Believers' Baptism in the Pentecostal Tradition," *The Ecumenical Review* 67:3 (October 2015), 430–34.

Concluding Reflections on Challenges and Opportunities

I end this article with a set of introductory questions. This set of questions is not an exhaustive list and, by no means, a complete catalog of the issues. However, this set of questions represents what I discern as opportunities for further exploration of what our dialogue partners may contribute toward an understanding of these very important rituals in our church communities.

1. *How can the terms "sacrament" and "ordinance" be reconciled and integrated into a coherent perspective?*

This question deals with nomenclature. Be it named "sacrament" or "ordinance," the ritual is instituted by Christ and practiced by the church. Do the terms refer to a difference of kind or difference of degree or emphasis? If we are dealing with the same reality, how do we reconcile the terminologies and thus harmonize and synthesize the perspectives that emerge from separate nomenclature to promote greater understanding of Christian experience?

2. *How much variation can be accommodated without compromising the integrity of the baptismal event in Christian experience?*

This question deals with formula, mode, and administration. Admittedly there is great diversity in Christianity. This diversity is an occasion for celebration, the wonder of how God brings us into this one body of Christ. With diversity comes the challenging work of building relationships that lead to koinonia, harmony, cooperation, and fairness in a common life. Uniformity in rites does not necessarily mean conformity, but rather a regularity in practice and language that stabilizes the identity of the church as God's sign to the world of God's salvation and coming reign. If consistency in language and practice is desirable, then what does this uniformity look like?

3. *How do facilities and the frequency in administration affect baptism?*

This question deals with facilities for and the frequency of baptism. Pentecostals are known for their spontaneity, innovation, and creativity. Pentecostals transform mundane places into sanctuaries of worship. It is not uncommon in the Church of God in Christ for congregations to spring forth from what is called the "storefront" or "house church," buildings originally designed for commercial or residential use but now renovated to become sacred space. These newly created sacred spaces often lack the architectural structure for liturgical worship, although they function very well as places to gather the faithful. I found Studebaker's story of the church facility without an operational baptistery not a little interesting! In such cases, infrastructure impacts the frequency of baptism and the means by which it is administered. It should also be noted that the above denominational statements do not stipulate when water baptism should be scheduled. Weekly, monthly, annually, or upon need? The IPHC does state that the Lord's Supper should be administered at least once each quarter (every three months).[32] Should not water baptism also occur with a frequency paralleling the entry of new persons to the Christian community?

4. *How is baptism reaffirmed in the life and experience of the Christian?*

This question deals with the reaffirmation of baptism. The faith that characterizes the church's belief held individually and celebrated corporately is to be lived out. How do the rituals, whether they be called sacraments or ordinances, strengthen the faith of believers? In addition to the administration of baptism and the Lord's Supper, what programs of formation, for children and adults, does the church develop that promotes conviction, discipleship, moral living, and active participation? The issue underlying this question is how sacramental theology relates to practical theology, and vice versa.

5. *How do our presuppositions about human personhood affect (a) access to the rite of baptism and (b) communal practices of inclusion and belonging?*

In other words, how may baptism be interpreted and administered in a manner that accounts for the broad range of diversity in human experience such that differently-abled persons are fully included and belong in the church? If the model of the person is the rational, abled-bodied adult, not only infants but also other humans who are differently-abled are excluded from participation in the primary ritual for entry into the church. For example, persons with intellectual disabilities (i.e., conditions that limit cognitive functioning and skills) cannot confess faith in a way that conforms to the supposed model of intellectual ability. For reasons of health and safety, some persons cannot experience baptism by immersion because of severe illness, physical injuries, or musculoskeletal disorders. As with baptism, beliefs concerning salvation (i.e., teachings about who can and cannot be saved) may be influenced by our presuppositions about human personhood.

6. *How do we discern God's freedom to act beyond prescribed liturgy?*

The final question deals with the topics of liturgy and divine freedom. Clearly, and without question, these rituals have been instituted by Christ. After giving these rituals, is there yet freedom for God to act beyond prescribed liturgy? How does God use the ritual, but also transcend it? Would not an omnipotent God be capable of acting, with consistency, in a way we heretofore have not imagined?

---

[32] *International Pentecostal Holiness Church Manual*, 62.

It may be that the above questions are without definitive answers. The questions may be philosophical in nature. That is, they interrogate the language of Christian faith and practice of initiation into a fundamentally mystic communion.

Frederick L. Ware (flware@howard.edu) is Professor of Theology and Associate Dean for Academic Affairs at Howard University School of Divinity, Washington, DC. He is an Elder (ordained minister) in the Church of God in Christ.

Response to Frederick L. Ware

Kimberly Hope Belcher

Frederick Ware's essay on Pentecostal water baptism suggests that profound gaps in historical and official approaches to worship and doctrine can be bridged by the way the water is experienced, by both Pentecostals and Catholics, as a significant moment in the Christian's walk with God. Ware begins by highlighting the variance and spiritual depth of Pentecostal experiences of the water. From there, he guides readers through the official documents that ground and interpret that experience, into dialogue with individual Pentecostal theologians reflecting on that experience. In our dialogue, this trajectory was an important reminder to Catholics engaged in dialogue with Pentecostals to foreground reflection on the lived experience of baptism and its variety across Catholic contexts. In fact, Catholic sacramental theology springs from reflection on spiritual experience in the sacraments and on its limits. If we contextualize Catholic sacramental theology in its pastoral and spiritual context, we might be able to develop a differentiated consensus about Catholic sacramental theologies and Pentecostal ordinance theologies of water baptism.[1] This would be a significant step in ecumenical dialogue.

Recent ecumenical developments have often relied on the method of receptive ecumenism, in which each Christian community foregrounds those aspects of their partners' theology and practice that seem especially redolent of our shared experience with Christ. Rather than focusing on what we can demand of our ecumenical partners, we focus on what we can receive from them. Instead of concentrating on the minimum possible agreement necessary on contested issues, we seek out those aspects of our partners' lives of faith on which we recognize the stamp of Christ. Ware argues that Pentecostal theology is "developing" and describes an eagerness for ongoing learning, which suggests the fruitfulness of this approach.

In Ware's synthesis of recurring themes of baptism found in representative denominational statements, we find two aspects ("symbolic meaning" and "Trinity") that

---

[1] A differentiated consensus is an ecumenical document that articulates continuing differences in teaching on a topic as emphases within the context of a more significant agreement. For a full-length treatment, see Jakob Karl Rinderknecht, *Mapping the Differentiated Consensus of the Joint Declaration* (Cham, Switzerland: Springer International Publishing AG, 2016), who notes that the differentiated consensus of the JDDJ is possible only because Lutheran and Catholic claims about theological anthropology that have been taken to be contradictory are both "managing the same eschatological tension in Christian life" (39). Similarly, I have argued that both "sacraments of faith" and *ex opere operato* claims are attending to the mysterious cooperation between God and the human person in Kimberly Hope Belcher, "Ex Opere Operato and Sacraments of Faith: A Trinitarian Proposal," *Worship* 90:3 (2016), 225–45.

are already matters of consensus between Catholics and these Pentecostal statements. I agree with Ware that our understanding of faith in the context of baptism needs further discussion. Future dialogue rounds might explore this, as well as the related question of whether "sacrament" and "ordinance" are reconcilable ideas, especially in the context of an emerging "warming" of Pentecostal theologians to sacramental theology.

On the Catholic side, I am optimistic about cultivating a shared understanding of "sacrament" and "ordinance" that might end in a differentiated consensus. The apparent contradiction between sacrament models and ordinance models arose because theologians in the late Middle Ages were interested in what *distinguishes* sacraments from other forms of Christian worship, rather than what ties them together. While both sacraments and other kinds of prayer were communication with God, only in sacraments was God's activity for human beings considered to be secure (*ex opere operato*). Theologies of sacrament focused on the conditions necessary to be sure of God's grace, and to understand the complexity of pastoral situations in which God's grace was not evident.

Ahead of the Reformation, it was clear that the role of baptism in an individual's life of faith, as for Christians today, could not be summed up in a simple definition. Baptism and the other sacraments were a kind of scaffolding that supported the Christian's entire life with God, and the way that they bestowed grace in a Christian's life was every bit as powerful, nebulous, and complex as Ware's testimony. In contemporary Catholic theology, a closer connection between sacraments and extra-sacramental grace has developed, which might ground a comparison of Catholic and Pentecostal ritual and spiritual life.

Though the Catholic theology of sacrament is sophisticated, its purpose is to honor the "something" that Ware felt in the baptismal font: "I had reached a great milestone in my life and the beginning of a new phase in my Christian experience." In the middle of the twentieth century, Roman Catholic theologians, influenced by historical study and ecumenical conversations with both Orthodox and Protestants, grounded the idea of sacrament in the nature of Jesus, the primordial or Ur-sacrament. Thinking about Jesus as the ground clarifies that sacraments participate in Christ's mediation, and thus they are two-way communication. Just as Jesus is both divine and human, the sacraments include both the divine gift of grace and the human act of worship.[2] The divine gift is not caused by the sacrament as worship, but is, as Edward Schillebeeckx puts it, "by the power of Christ and God," which is promised in the sacraments.[3] This focus on Christ as the source of the sacraments relativizes questions about exactly how many sacraments are recognized in the various churches.

---

[2] Edward Schillebeeckx, *Christ the Sacrament of Encounter with God* (London: Sheed and Ward, 1963).

[3] Schillebeeckx, *Christ the Sacrament of the Encounter with God*, 85.

In dialogue with Protestants, contemporary Catholic liturgical theology identifies every liturgy as having these two elements: downward grace from God (sometimes referred to as the katabatic dimension) and upward worship by humans (the anabatic dimension). Any theology of sacrament must balance the tension between these elements, and the consequent difficulty of explaining under what circumstances the "something" of a sacrament will rise to conscious Christian experience. With Ware, this framework resonates with Frank Macchia's understanding of water baptism as an "eschatological gift," which also contains a tension between what has already been received and what is to come.

One of the most important motivations for this theological change comes from the experience of worship. The focus on divine grace was initially meant to pastorally help Christians who worried about whether they had really been baptized, but in the end it led to minimal liturgical experiences and indifference to whether they had an emotional and spiritual impact on Christians. In contrast, emphasizing the response to God, worship, as an essential part of sacrament means attending to its human dimensions. For Pentecostals, too, perhaps reflection on the significance of water baptism and its links to ongoing discipleship might be fruitful. In our dialogue, such conversation arose, along with reflection on the levels of participation available to young children and those with disabilities.

The emphasis on the human act of worship means that contemporary Roman Catholics are prepared to acknowledge the ordinance dimension of baptism and the Lord's Supper and to receive gratefully reflections on the experience of worship. In the experience of Ware himself, and of other Pentecostals, in how these are reflected in denominational statements, and in the reflections of contemporary Pentecostal theologians, there is an opportunity to discuss the possibility of a shared agreement on the divine action in water baptism, which Catholics understand as sacramental.

Ware provides some starting points for the particulars of a differentiated consensus on sacraments and ordinances. Aimee Semple McPherson's *Declaration of Faith* has language adapted from Romans 6 that could be interpreted sacramentally ("a blessed outward sign of an inward work . . . even as he was taken down from the tree and buried, so we are buried with Him by baptism unto death"). Amos Yong's consideration for the word "sacrament" and his understanding that baptism and the Lord's Supper are "practices, symbolic and efficacious, for encountering God in Christ through the Holy Spirit" likewise gives a strong foundation for dialogue. Finally, the work of Andrew Ray Williams on the "rich sacramentalism" accorded to certain liturgical spaces might also provoke thought in future dialogues. On the Roman Catholic side, it is critical that members of the dialogue be willing to think about pastoral purposes, the Christological and pneumatological foundations, and the practical implications of definitions of "sacrament," past and present. Like all Christian dialogues, this one will clarify for us what the Holy Spirit is saying to the churches.

New from Regnum Books

The Korean Healing Movement

The author is to be congratulated for this important, well-written, and ground-breaking study of three prominent healers in Korean Christianity. This is essential reading for understanding the Korean healing movement.
Dr Allan H Anderson, University of Birmingham

The Korean Healing Movement investigates three historic healing evangelists in Korea, representing different confessional traditions in various periods. This fine research will provide a model for other similar inquiries, particularly from the global South.
Dr Wonsuk Ma, Executive Director of Center for Spirit-Empowered Research, Distinguished Professor of Global Christianity

Jun Kim maintains that the healing movement is a key component of Korean Christianity historically. This is contextual theology at its absolute best, not only for Pentecostals, but for all those interested in the prominent themes emerging from Christianity outside the West.
Dr Frank D Macchia, Professor of Systematic Theology, Vanguard University

This is a well-researched book, supported by a wide bibliography. It is coherent, readable, interesting, clear, succinct and analytical. Not only is this book valuable and fascinating, it also provides a first-class template for similar examinations of key healers in other countries.
Dr Keith Warrington, Academic Dean, The New International University, Director of Word and Spirit, and Reader in Pentecostal Studies
Regents Theological College

Jun Kim is a Korean Pentecostal scholar and currently serves as the Academic Dean at Asia Pacific Theological Seminary and Vice-president of the Asia Pentecostal Society. Since 2004, he and his wife, Jane C. Kim, have been missionaries in the Philippines.

Order this and other Regnum titles from:

www.regnumbooks.net
Also available on Amazon

2024 | 240pp pb | ISBN: 978-1-917059-06-0

Response to Kimberly Hope Belcher

Frederick L. Ware

In Kimberly Belcher's succinct overview of the rites of initiation in the Roman Catholic Church, she not only accentuates the uniqueness of Catholic perspectives and practices but also emphasizes the deep mystery of God's salvation that requires, on the part of both Catholics and Pentecostals, humility at the limits of human understanding and respectful consideration of what various Christian traditions bring to the appreciation of these rites. I too affirm divine mystery. However, we arrive at this destination from two different paths.

My essay is characteristically Pentecostal in style, that is, with the use of testimony for reflection on rites of initiation. This method seems appropriate given the broad diversity among Pentecostals, not to mention the limited liturgical resources of a distinct Pentecostal nature. In addition to a large corpus of theological texts, Belcher notes that Catholics have liturgical books for conducting rites but enjoy some measure of improvisation in performance depending on the ethnicity and cultural tradition of the Catholic Christians gathering for worship. Without a prescribed liturgy, Pentecostal administration of rites (i.e. baptism and the Lord's Supper) is much more improvisational, even spontaneous regarding the timing of the ritual. While baptism can be administered at any time during the year for Catholics, Belcher says it is usually scheduled for the Easter Vigil. More often than not, Pentecostals do not strictly follow the liturgical calendar. In contrast, testimony is a consistent practice that reliably reports how ritual is experienced and perceived in Pentecostal churches.

Belcher subtly asks the question of whether Pentecostals' practice of child dedication is adequate for centering baptism in the life of the church. As Belcher describes the interrelation of infant baptism and adult baptism, the ritual of baptism is administered across the human life cycle, that is, at various ages, from infancy, through childhood, and into adulthood. Whereas infant baptism demonstrates God's love in our adoption before we do anything, adult baptism demonstrates human cooperation in God's plan of salvation. In combination, they show that conversion is a lifelong process. Though my narrative discloses my coming to faith and growing in faith over the course of my life, at least in the early years of my formation, Pentecostals tend to regard conversion as a crisis moment. In Pentecostal churches, the administration of baptism occurs shortly after the resolution of crisis, when a person is said to be converted or "saved." Still, it is possible for Pentecostals to describe their faith development and spiritual formation as a process unfolding over time if child dedication functioned, for them, like infant baptism to incorporate and nurture them in the church. The question remains regarding the centrality of baptism as the fundamental rite to signify initiation and belonging.

Belcher is unaware of, at least she does not discuss, Pentecostals' affirmation of the symbolism of baptism avowed by Catholics. Adhering to a theology of memorialism regarding the Lord's Supper, Pentecostals are keen on the symbolic meanings of baptism. They can affirm baptism as a sign of grace and tool that God acts graciously in and through. Pentecostals do not make baptism a requirement for salvation. Even Catholics, as Belcher points out, acknowledge that some persons may be saved even if they do not receive baptism.

A promising future lies ahead for Catholics and Pentecostals. Rebaptism, in the strict sense of the term and practice, is unacceptable to Catholics and most Protestant churches. The Catholic Synodal movement emphasizes our common baptism. The mutual recognition of baptism, a place where Catholics are already and where Pentecostals hopefully will come, is essential for multilateral ecumenical dialogue and cooperation.

Varieties of Healing

A Catholic Perspective

Andrew Prevot

Keywords *Catholic, sacrament, healthcare, charismatic, miracles, reconciliation, anointing, ecumenism*

Abstract

This article contributes to Catholic-Pentecostal ecumenical dialogue by offering a particular Catholic perspective on the shared Christian belief in Christ is the Healer. More specifically, it distinguishes several ways in which humans are called to participate in the healing work of Christ. It considers Catholic approaches to sacramental, charismatic, miraculous, biomedical, psychotherapeutic, social, and ecological healing. It reflects on the historical background, contemporary significance, and interconnections of these diverse areas of healing, while distinguishing such a holistic understanding of healing from the narrower concept of a cure. Acknowledging the problem of unhealed sufferers, it argues against blaming such persons for any alleged lack of faith on their part. It also cautions against false promises of a quick spiritual fix to complex bodily, social, and environmental problems.

Introduction

The created world is rich in the blessings of God, but it is also a place of deep wounds and sorrows. Things break. They fall apart. Our bodies succumb to illnesses and injuries. There are kinds of physical and mental suffering that last a lifetime or even generations: chronic diseases, traumatic losses, experiences of oppression. Many hearts are troubled by difficult emotions such as shame, anger, fear, and despair. Many minds struggle to feel whole and safe. Many wills are divided against themselves, torn between the call to holiness and the temptation to sin. In close connection with such corporeal, psychological, and moral maladies, which take place in the individual, there are fractures and toxicities that occur in larger social and ecological domains. Everything is related. A hurt in one place radiates in many directions. Individually and collectively, the world is crying out for healing.

Because the hurts are multiple, complex, and interwoven, so too are the needed remedies. Even so, many Christian churches and theological traditions hold that these remedies are united in the healing work of Christ. The New Testament reveals manifold ways that God provides healing through the Spirit-led ministry and redemptive actions of Jesus. As the incarnation of divine wisdom and compassion, Jesus responds to the needs of our bodies, souls, and communities and, indeed, the entire created order. Healing in a comprehensive sense is nothing other than salvation (Latin: *salus*). It is an overcoming of the destructive forces of evil, sin, suffering, and death. That Christ is the Healer is a central Christian teaching. The question for Christians is how to understand and participate in this great mystery.

The Gospels tell many stories of miraculous healings. Consider, for example, Mark's account of Jesus' healing of a hemorrhaging woman:

> Now there was a woman who had been suffering from a flow of blood for twelve years. She had endured much under many physicians and had spent all that she had, and she was no better but rather grew worse. She had heard about Jesus and came up behind him in the crowd and touched his cloak, for she said, "If I but touch his cloak, I will be made well." Immediately her flow of blood stopped, and she felt in her body that she was healed of her disease. Immediately aware that power had gone forth from him, Jesus turned about in the crowd and said, "Who touched my cloak?" And his disciples said to him, "You see the crowd pressing in on you; how can you say, 'Who touched me?'" He looked all around to see who had done it. But the woman, knowing what had happened to her, came in fear and trembling, fell down before him, and told him the whole truth. He said to her, "Daughter, your faith has made you well; go in peace, and be healed of your disease."[1]

Many who suffer from chronic health conditions and other types of long-lasting hurt in their lives can relate to the first part of this woman's story. For years they seek help from professionals and other trusted sources, they exhaust all their financial and emotional resources, and they find that their situation is still deteriorating. The next part of the story seems like a fantasy that is not likely to take place in the real world. This suffering person touches the garment of a wonderworker who is passing through town and is instantly cured. Jesus' healing power is so overabundant in him that it saturates even his garment and flows out to anyone who makes the slightest contact with it. The desperate in our world long for this kind of immediately restorative encounter, but it happens so rarely as to seem virtually inaccessible. One cannot count on it, and doing so may nurture unrealistic hopes that will soon be dashed.[2]

Identifying the reason for such healing with one's faith (as Jesus does in this story) can be dangerous for contemporary readers, insofar as it suggests that if such a miracle does not occur, it is one's own fault. Unhealed sufferers would not only be without a cure; they would be at least implicitly accused of lacking faith—adding insult to injury.

---

[1] Mark 5:25–34. All biblical quotations in this essay are from the New Revised Standard Version.

[2] Marleen Eijkholt, "Medicine's Collision with False Hope: The False Hope Harms (FHH) Argument," *Bioethics* 34:7 (2020), 703–11.

What first appears as a very consoling Gospel story could do more harm than good if it is not interpreted with care. I mention this concern because Christians and others who associate religious belief with the prospect of healing must face the reality that such connections are not always straightforward. The challenge of unhealed suffering raises difficult questions about the presence and choices of God (i.e., the problem of theodicy) and about the sinful ways some human beings manipulate others by promoting unreliable, quick-fix solutions, which they may even shroud in religious garb (i.e., the problem of charlatanism or "quackery").[3]

Nevertheless, I believe there are good ways to interpret the revealed mystery of Christ the Healer, including interpretations that make room for the ongoing possibility of miraculous and faith-based healings among other kinds of healing. In this essay, I offer a Catholic perspective on the varieties of healing that come directly or indirectly through Christ and that touch different dimensions of our wounded existence. With the word "indirectly," I mean to indicate that human beings are called to use their natural talents, acquired skills, and supernatural gifts (i.e., charisms and other graces) to participate in Christ's healing work, whether as clergy, faith healers, physicians, therapists, social activists, parents, educators, legislators, or whatever they may be.

I find it helpful to distinguish the following modalities of healing: sacramental, charismatic, miraculous, biomedical, psychotherapeutic, social, and ecological. However, I also recognize that the lines between them are porous and that this is not a comprehensive list. Any given experience of suffering might benefit from many of these modalities working in concert. Moreover, each of them addresses multiple levels of humanity's corporeal, spiritual, and relational nature, not just one alone.

Like other scholars, I distinguish the idea of *cure*, understood as a complete resolution of a health problem, from the more open-ended idea of *healing*, which may be interpreted in diverse ways and involve features such as emotional comfort, social inclusion, personal empowerment, holistic care, spiritual wellbeing, and lengthy processes of change and growth. This distinction between cure and healing does not map onto the distinction between the secular and the religious. Secular practices of healing, whether biomedical or otherwise, in many cases (e.g., late-stage cancer, Alzheimer's, schizophrenia, and many more) do not have cures to offer and so must rely on a larger notion of healing. Conversely, religious practices of healing sometimes result in miraculous cures, which cannot be explained by current scientific understanding.

I call what follows "a," not "the," Catholic perspective, because although I strive to be at least somewhat representative, my account of the varieties of healing inevitably reflects my historical context and my particular ways of receiving the doctrines,

---

[3] James Harvey Young, *American Health Quackery: Collected Essays by James Harvey Young* (Princeton, NJ: Princeton, 1992).

practices, experiences, and theological insights of the Catholic Church. My hope is that by clarifying a Catholic way of understanding and participating in the healing work of Christ, I can, if only in small ways, enrich the conversation between Catholic and Pentecostal Christians and increase our opportunities for mutual understanding and learning. Such dialogue may itself be a form of healing.[4]

Sacramental Healing

The Catholic Church recognizes seven sacraments. In different ways, all seven mediate the healing work of Christ.[5] The Eucharist symbolizes and enacts this healing work in a particular way. Before receiving communion, the assembly prays with the words of the centurion, "Lord, I am not worthy that you should enter under my roof, but only say the word and my soul shall be healed."[6] However, the healing effect of the Eucharist is not limited to souls. The sacrament is material.[7] It brings comfort to bodies through all five senses of taste, touch, smell, sound, and sight. It knits together communities of faith and strengthens them for greater social action, especially for the poor.[8]

Although all seven sacraments have healing properties in one sense or another, the Catholic Church designates two of them as "sacraments of healing," namely Anointing of the Sick and Penance or Reconciliation. The *Catechism* states,

> The Lord Jesus Christ, physician of our souls and bodies, who forgave the sins of the paralytic and restored him to bodily health (cf. Mk 2:1–12), has willed that his Church continue, in the power of the Holy Spirit, his work of healing and salvation, even among her own members. This is the purpose of the two sacraments of healing: the sacrament of Penance and the sacrament of Anointing of the Sick.[9]

In addition to highlighting the healing ministry of Jesus, the *Catechism* points to other biblical warrants for these sacraments. The classic text for the Anointing of the Sick is

---

[4] Karen R. J. Murphy, *Pentecostals and Roman Catholics on Becoming a Christian: Spirit-Baptism, Faith, Conversion, Experience, and Discipleship in Ecumenical Perspective* (Leiden: Brill, 2018), 10.

[5] Michael Marsch, *Healing through the Sacraments*, trans. Linda M. Maloney (Collegeville, MN: Liturgical, 1989).

[6] This prayer draws from Luke 7:6–7.

[7] Kimberly Hope Belcher, *Efficacious Engagement: Sacramental Participation in the Trinitarian Mystery* (Collegeville, MN: Liturgical, 2011), 27–30.

[8] John Hampsch, CMF, *The Healing Power of the Eucharist* (Ann Arbor, MI: Servant, 1999); *Catechism of the Catholic Church* (New York: Doubleday, 1995), 1391–1397; and Enrique Dussel, "The Bread of the Eucharistic Celebration as a Sign of Justice in the Community," in *Beyond Philosophy: Ethics, History, Marxism, and Liberation Theology*, ed. Eduardo Mendieta (Lanham, MD: Rowman & Littlefield, 2003), 41–52.

[9] *Catechism*, 1421.

from James: "Are any among you sick? They should call for the elders of the church and have them pray over them, anointing them with oil in the name of the Lord. The prayer of faith will save the sick, and the Lord will raise them up, and anyone who has committed sins will be forgiven."[10] For evidence of the apostolic authority to grant absolution in the sacrament of Penance or Reconciliation, Catholics turn to Jesus' saying in Matthew: "I will give you the keys of the kingdom of heaven, and whatever you bind on earth will be bound in heaven, and whatever you loose on earth will be loosed in heaven."[11]

Although these are important biblical reference points, to understand these sacraments well it is necessary to study their historical development after the time of the New Testament and to consider how they are being experienced and practiced today. The Anointing of the Sick underwent a significant shift in the Carolingian period (eighth–ninth centuries CE). Early Christian practices of praying, blessing with consecrated oil, and laying on of hands for the purposes of bodily and spiritual healing were transformed into an end-of-life ritual meant to prepare the soul for a happy afterlife. By the thirteenth century, scholastic theologians debated the nuances of this "extreme unction" but agreed that a final cleansing from sin was its effect.[12]

Throughout the Middle Ages, such extreme unction was often accompanied by a final act of contrition and a priestly absolution of sins. However, the sacrament of Penance or Reconciliation did not begin as a blessing meant only for one's final moments. In fact, its origins lie in a much more arduous process known as "canonical penance," whose purpose was not to ready one for death but rather to restore one to full (Eucharistic) communion. This was a practice that evolved in the first six centuries of the church. After confessing serious sins to a priest or bishop (sins such as apostasy or adultery), one would receive instructions about how to fast, pray, and discipline oneself for months or even years. After this gradual process, resembling the initiatory path of the catechumenate, one would eventually be welcomed back into the church during the Triduum. Because this process could only be done once, it was increasingly deferred until the end of one's life. Beginning as early as the sixth century CE, Celtic monks developed the sacrament in a new direction by hearing private confessions of both serious and minor (i.e., venial) sins as many times as one liked and by offering absolution before one performed the required acts of penance. These innovations, which were formally adopted by the Fourth Lateran Council in 1215, made the

---

[10] Jas 5:14–15 and *Catechism*, 1510.

[11] Matt 16:19 and *Catechism*, 1444.

[12] Charles W. Gusmer, *And You Visited Me: Sacramental Ministry to the Sick and Dying* (New York: Pueblo, 1984), 21–32; and Bruce T. Morrill, *Divine Worship and Human Healing: Liturgical Theology at the Margins of Life and Death* (Collegeville, MN: Liturgical, 2009), 142–44.

sacrament more accessible to ordinary Christians, by which I mean not only mortal sinners or people at death's door. Yet they also brought new challenges such as a detachment from communal worship, a transactional view of grace (wherein, for example, X number of prayers makes up for Y amount of sin), and a temptation toward scrupulosity.[13]

Since the Second Vatican Council, Catholic sacramental practice has been in a period of renewal, and the sacraments of healing are no exception. The "General Introduction" to *Pastoral Care of the Sick: Rites of Anointing and Viaticum* (1983) clarifies that the Anointing of the Sick should not be reserved for those who are immediately dying but should be given to any of "the faithful whose health is seriously impaired by sickness or old age." A note indicates that the Latin word translated as "seriously"— *periculose*—strikes a careful balance between restricting the sacrament to the dying and bestowing it indiscriminately on anyone with minor health issues (e.g., a common cold or regular aches and pains). This document emphasizes that the purpose of the sacrament is not merely the remission of sins before death but a reception of the healing work of Christ given through the Holy Spirit acting in the church. It acknowledges that a cure of the body's illness can be part of the grace imparted by this sacrament—that is, "if it will be beneficial to the sick person's salvation." However, the main effects to be expected are an inner strength to remain steadfast in faith, resist evil, and alleviate anxiety.[14]

Bruce Morrill describes these effects in relational terms, arguing that the sacrament responds to sick persons' "desire to know something of God's love and presence and [their] own value and purpose in relation to others and the world around [them]."[15] David Power contends similarly that the main effect of the sacrament is to overcome the various levels of alienation that one experiences in the midst of illness: "from one's own body, from friends and associates, from the doings of society, and from God."[16] Although the sacrament affirms the dignity of the suffering person as an irreplaceable individual, it does not occur in isolation but rather in the company of loved ones and in connection with the whole church. One rite is designed for use in a

---

[13] Peter E. Fink, SJ, "History of the Sacrament of Reconciliation," in *Alternative Futures for Worship*, vol. 4, ed. Peter E. Fink, SJ (Collegeville, MN: Liturgical, 1987), 73–89, at 79–82; and John T. McNeill and Helena M. Gamer, eds. *Medieval Handbooks of Penance* (New York: Columbia, 1990), 25–30.

[14] *Pastoral Care of the Sick: Introduction and Pastoral Notes* (Washington, DC: United States Conference of Catholic Bishops, 1983), nos. 1–8; and John C. Kasza, *Understanding Sacramental Healing: Anointing and Viaticum* (Chicago: Hillenbrand, 2007), 75–106.

[15] Morrill, *Divine Worship and Human Healing*, 161.

[16] David N. Power, "The Sacrament of Anointing: Open Questions," in *The Pastoral Care of the Sick*, eds. Mary Collins and David N. Power (London: SCM, 1991), 95–107, at 103.

relatively private setting such as a home or hospital room, but there are also specific rites for celebrating the sacrament in a large congregation (such as at a pilgrimage site) and in the context of a Mass. The sacrament should be one part of a fuller communal relationship with the sick person. There should be pastoral visits from church ministers (whether ordained or lay), including the distribution of holy communion; loving support from family and friends; and attention from healthcare professionals. The sacrament is not a substitute for these other means of healing but an effective sign of Christ's healing work within and through them.[17] Care for the dying remains part of the Church's sacramental practice, but instead of "extreme unction" the dying person is given Viaticum—that is, the Eucharist, with particular prayers and readings suited for such a weighty, end-of-life circumstance.[18]

Penance, now often called Reconciliation, has similarly benefited from post-conciliar efforts at liturgical renewal. In addition to private confession, there is now a rite for communal reconciliation and a combined form that involves a public liturgy of the Word, a time for individuals to visit a priest one-on-one, and a closing communal prayer of thanksgiving.[19] John Baldovin notes that, although participation in this sacrament has declined, this drop-off may reflect a positive awareness of God's mercy and a shifting understanding of sin, which may largely be good things. Nevertheless, he encourages Catholics to avail themselves of this sacrament in order to combat self-deception, develop a habit of self-examination, and appreciate the grace of God in their lives.[20] Other scholars such as Robert Schreiter and Denis Woods argue that this sacrament could be adapted to respond to social sin and intergroup conflict.[21]

---

[17] *Pastoral Care of the Sick: Introduction*, nos. 4, 51, 108, and 131; and Mary Collins, "The Roman Ritual: Pastoral Care and Anointing of the Sick," in *The Pastoral Care of the Sick*, eds. Mary Collins and David N. Power (London: SCM, 1991), 3–18.

[18] *Pastoral Care of the Sick: Introduction*, nos. 175–88; and Morrill, *Divine Worship and Human Healing*, 184–92.

[19] Fink, "History of the Sacrament," 84–85; and *Rite of Penance* (Washington, DC: United States Conference of Catholic Bishops, 2010).

[20] John F. Baldovin, SJ, "Why Go to Confession?," in *Catholic Sacraments: A Rich Source of Blessings*, eds. John F. Baldovin, SJ, and David Farina Turnbloom (Mahwah, NJ: Paulist, 2015), 99–102. See also Bruce T. Morrill, "Confessing Sin, Proclaiming Reconciliation in Contemporary U.S. Catholic Liturgy," *Liturgy* 34:1 (2019), 30–38.

[21] Robert J. Schreiter, "The Catholic Social Imaginary and Peacebuilding: Ritual, Sacrament, and Spirituality," in *Peacebuilding: Catholic Theology, Ethics, and Praxis*, eds. Robert J. Schreiter, R. Scott Appleby, and Gerard F. Powers (Maryknoll, NY: Orbis, 2010), 221–39, at 229–30; and Denis J. Woods, "Reconciliation of Groups," in *Alternative Futures for Worship*, vol. 4, ed. Peter E. Fink, SJ (Collegeville, MN: Liturgical, 1987), 33–42.

Charismatic Healing

Along with the sacraments of healing, Catholic teaching recognizes other ways to participate in the healing work of Christ, including practices called "sacramentals," such as blessings and exorcisms.[22] It also affirms the presence of "charisms," defined as "graces of the Holy Spirit which directly or indirectly benefit the Church, ordered as they are to her building up, to the good of men, and to the needs of the world."[23] Among these, the *Catechism* acknowledges "special charisms of healing" and cites 1 Corinthians 12:9 in support of this claim.[24]

For the past half century or more, there has been a vibrant charismatic movement in the Catholic Church, sometimes known as the Catholic Charismatic Renewal (CCR), encompassing millions of Catholics worldwide. Since Pentecost 2019, its global networks have been assisted by the Vatican-initiated service called Catholic Charismatic Renewal International Service (CHARIS). Although the CCR may have originated in the United States—specifically at a retreat at Duquesne University in 1967 at which Patti Gallagher Mansfield and other Catholics received trances, glossolalia, and Spirit baptism—it is also possible that it emerged concurrently in various contexts under the influence of Pentecostal Christian missionaries and, indeed, the free workings of the Holy Spirit.[25] The CCR has become a major feature of Catholicism in Africa, Latin America, and their diasporas. To some degree, its appeal in these contexts may be related to similarities between charismatic Christian experiences of the Holy Spirit and ecstatic styles of prayer, spirit possession, and faith healing indigenous to Africa and the Americas.[26] These connections may not be surprising given the Black religious background of William J. Seymour's Azusa Street revival.[27] In the global South, inculturated forms of Catholicism often have charismatic features.

---

[22] *Catechism*, 1671–1673.

[23] *Catechism*, 799.

[24] *Catechism*, 1508.

[25] Susan A. Maurer, *The Spirit of Enthusiasm: A History of the Catholic Charismatic Renewal* (Lanham, MD: University Press of America, 2010), 27–31.

[26] Isidore Iwejuo Nkwocha, CSSp., *Charismatic Renewal and Pentecostalism: The Renewal of the Nigerian Catholic Church* (Eugene, OR: Wipf and Stock, 2021), 181–217; Laurien Nyiribakwe, SJ, *Faith-Healing Ministry in Africa: A Catholic Bio-Social Ethics* (Chisinau, Moldova: Generis, 2021); Hosffman Ospino, "The Catholic Charismatic Renewal in the Hispanic Parish," in *The Holy Spirit: Setting the World on Fire*, eds. Richard Lennan and Nancy Pineda-Madrid (Mahwah, NJ: Paulist, 2017), 141–51; and Stan Chu Ilo, ed., *Pentecostalism, Catholicism, and the Spirit in the World* (Eugene, OR: Wipf and Stock, 2019).

[27] Iain MacRobert, "The Black Roots of Pentecostalism," in *African American Religious Thought: An Anthology*, eds. Cornel West and Eddie S. Glaude, Jr. (Louisville, KY: Westminster John Knox, 2003), 616–28.

The Second Vatican Council encouraged a renewed attention to spiritual gifts and a fruitful interaction with diverse cultures. *Presbyterorum ordinis* states, "While trying the spirits to see if they be of God, priests should uncover with a sense of faith, acknowledge with joy and foster with diligence the various humble and exalted charisms of the laity." *Gaudium et spes* adds that "the ability to express Christ's message in its own way is developed in each nation, and at the same time there is fostered a living exchange between the Church and the diverse cultures of people."[28] Regarding both charisms and cultures, the response from recent Catholic popes and bishops has been supportive, though they have emphasized a need for careful discernment, a maintenance of traditional teachings and structures of authority, and a guiding norm of Christian love and justice for the poor.[29]

On charismatic healing, a committee of US bishops has offered the following words of precaution: "First, even to suggest that failure to secure healing is due to the afflicted person's sinfulness or lack of faith is theologically untenable. Second, nonsacramental anointings sometimes employed in healing services should be very carefully distinguished from the Sacrament of the Anointing of the Sick." With these provisos in place, this committee of bishops affirms that charismatic healing can be a genuine gift of the Holy Spirit and "a sign that the kingdom of God is present."[30]

Like the sacraments of healing, charismatic gifts of healing are meant neither to replace appropriate medical care nor to guarantee an immediate cure. Although some full recoveries have been reported, they often result from more than spiritual interventions alone. Consider, for example, Susan Maurer's discussion of healing practices in the inaugural days of the CCR:

> Members of the group also came to believe that they had received the gift of healing. Mansfield describes how, upon hearing that her dormitory housemother had been hospitalized with phlebitis, she became convinced that the woman would be healed if Patti went to the hospital, laid hands on her, and prayed for her. After some initial hesitation, Patti did indeed go to the hospital the next day, where she took the woman's right hand and then traced a cross on the woman's forehead. Patti was astounded, when, a few days later, she saw the housemother back at

---

[28] *Presbyterorum ordinis: Decree on the Ministry and Life of Priests*, 7 December 1964, www.vatican.va, 9; and *Gaudium et spes: Pastoral Constitution on the Church in the Modern World*, 7 December 1965, www.vatican.va, 44.

[29] Committee for Pastoral Research and Practice, *Statement on Catholic Charismatic Renewal* (Washington, DC: United States Catholic Conference, 1975); Bishops' Liaison Committee with the Catholic Charismatic Renewal, *Pastoral Statement on the Catholic Charismatic Renewal* (Washington, DC: United States Catholic Conference, 1984); Maurer, *Spirit of Enthusiasm*, 36–43; Cardinal Léon Joseph Suenens and Dom Hélder Câmara, *Charismatic Renewal and Social Action: A Dialogue* (Ann Arbor, MI: Servant, 1979); and Austen Ivereigh, "Pope Francis Calls Upon the Catholic Charismatic Community to Work for Justice," *America: The Jesuit Review*, 30 May 2020.

[30] Bishops' Liaison Committee, *Pastoral Statement*, nos. 27–28.

school, and she attributed the woman's quick healing to the prayers that she had added to the woman's hospital treatment.[31]

In this example, we see that the healing actions (praying and laying on of hands) are analogous to those in the Anointing of the Sick. We also see that these means are not regarded as an alternative to hospitalization but as a help to it. Thomas Csordas observes that most Catholic charismatic healers and supplicants value the work of physicians and clinicians. They are "likely to pray that the results of conventional medical tests will be negative, that the adverse side effects of their medicine will be muted, that an upcoming surgical procedure will have a positive outcome, or that a person who is terminally afflicted will die peacefully."[32]

Positive outcomes of faith healing have been recognized by some medical researchers who do not presuppose the existence of God. For example, Howard Fields emphasizes the mind-body connection and argues that subjective feelings of God's nearness, the love of a religious community, and comforting bodily contact (e.g., laying on of hands) can promote a state of mind that has discernible benefits on material health indicators such as stress levels, inflammation, immune response, and cardiovascular function.[33] Although some researchers who aspire to test the effectiveness of faith healing take great pains to distinguish it from such placebo effects, because they want to know whether a purely supernatural process is at work, Anne Harrington suggests that the natural and supernatural perhaps cannot be so neatly separated. It may be that the healing power of Christ takes advantage of our close mind-body connections and relational constitution.[34] Sarah Coakley recommends St. Thomas Aquinas's theory of secondary causation as a helpful model for explaining how both divine and creaturely mechanisms of healing can be operative simultaneously.[35]

Miraculous Healing

A forthright Catholic perspective on healing must recognize the many instances in which sacramental and charismatic graces do not cure the afflicted and resist the temptation either to blame God or the believer for such disheartening results. Despite

---

[31] Maurer, *Spirit of Enthusiasm*, 31.

[32] Thomas J. Csordas, *The Sacred Self: A Cultural Phenomenology of Charismatic Healing* (Berkeley: University of California, 1994), 34.

[33] Howard L. Fields, "Meaning in the Neural Investigation of Pain," in *Spiritual Healing: Science, Meaning, and Discernment*, ed. Sarah Coakley (Grand Rapids, MI: Eerdmans, 2020), 95–96.

[34] Anne Harrington, "Prayer and Placebo in Scientific Research," in *Spiritual Healing: Science, Meaning, and Discernment*, ed. Sarah Coakley (Grand Rapids, MI: Eerdmans, 2020), 129.

[35] Sarah Coakley, "Introduction: Spiritual Healing, Science, and Meaning," in *Spiritual Healing: Science, Meaning, and Discernment*, ed. Sarah Coakley (Grand Rapids, MI: Eerdmans, 2020), 21.

our best medical and spiritual efforts, suffering often continues and increases, and there may be nothing anyone can do to halt its advance. Death comes for us all, and our hopes ultimately have to turn to the promises of eternity. Nevertheless, believing that miracles are possible in this life and that they do sometimes happen is a legitimate and widespread Catholic practice, and no Catholic account of healing would be complete without it. Although miracles may occur because of sacramental or charismatic activity, these are not the only channels through which God's wonders flow.

The veneration of Mary and the saints is a distinctive feature of Catholic popular piety and an area of the Catholic tradition in which the miraculous has figured prominently. Evidence of miracles has been used to determine whether Marian apparitions are authentic and whether a deceased person of exemplary moral character ought to be celebrated as a saint.[36] Many Catholics pray to Mary and to saints such as St. Jude (who is the patron saint of hopeless causes) and St. Margaret of Castello (who is the patron saint of disabled persons) to seek healing for themselves or their families. They visit shrines; say special prayers, including multiday novenas; use tangible objects such as holy cards, holy oil, medals, rosaries, and candles; and ask for intercessions. In some cases, they find that their prayers are answered, whether by inexplicable cures or by the discovery of helpful medical resources.[37]

Mexican and Mexican American Catholics have a particularly strong devotion to the caramel-colored figure of Mary known as Our Lady of Guadalupe. She appeared to an indigenous man named Juan Diego in December 1531; left a miraculous image of herself on his *tilma* (or cloak), which now hangs in the Basilica in Mexico City; and brought healing to Juan Diego's uncle and to countless pilgrims who visited the church that was built on the site of her apparition. Some Latino/a theologians interpret this event as a sacred blending of Spanish Catholic and Nahuatl religious cultures that, even today, helps to heal the wounds of Spanish imperial conquest and genocide.[38]

Such devotions can pose challenges to Christian ecumenical dialogue insofar as they show that Catholics do not offer their positive religious attention exclusively to

---

[36] Emma Anderson, "Healing and Ecclesial Response in Nineteenth-Century Catholic France," in *Spiritual Healing: Science, Meaning, and Discernment*, ed. Sarah Coakley (Grand Rapids, MI: Eerdmans, 2020), 40–58.

[37] Robert A. Orsi, *Thank You, St. Jude: Women's Devotion to the Patron Saint of Hopeless Causes* (New Haven, CT: Yale, 1996), 167–77; and Robert A. Orsi, "The Cult of the Saints and the Reimagination of the Space and Time of Sickness in Twentieth-Century American Catholicism," in *Religion and Healing in America*, eds. Linda L. Barnes and Susan S. Sered (New York: Oxford, 2005), 29–47.

[38] Lisa Sousa, Stafford Poole, CM, and James Lockhart, eds., *The Story of Guadalupe: Luis Laso de la Vega's* Huei tlamahuiçoltica *of 1649* (Stanford, CA: Stanford, 1998); Timothy Matovina, "Theologies of Guadalupe: From the Spanish Colonial Era to Pope John Paul II," *Theological Studies* 70 (2009), 61–91; and Jeanette Rodriguez, *Our Lady of Guadalupe: Faith and Empowerment among Mexican-American Women* (Austin: University of Texas, 1994).

Christ or, for that matter, the Holy Spirit. While acknowledging this challenge, I want to emphasize that it is precisely the extraordinary intimacy that Mary and the saints enjoy with Jesus and his Spirit that draws orthodox Catholics to them. Mary is Jesus' mother who suffered with him and now participates in his glory; the saints are faithful, Spirit-filled followers of his way of life who remind the church that true Christian holiness is possible and that it occurs in a rich variety of styles and contexts. Grace comes from the triune God through the missions of the Son and the Spirit but is mediated in history through loving relationships among the living and with the dead—relationships in which there is a sharing of sorrows, desires, and gifts. The *Catechism* helpfully distinguishes between *adoration* and *veneration*, arguing that adoration must be reserved exclusively for God. Veneration, by contrast, can be given to persons, images, or things that help us grow in relationship with God.[39]

Since the late sixteenth century, the process of becoming a Catholic saint has required two types of evidence, one to prove a life of exceptional virtue, the other to demonstrate a pattern of miracles (mostly miraculous healings) that can be attributed to this holy person's intercession. Although the first type of evidence is receiving increasing emphasis in recent years, the history of the second type reveals a fascinating synergy between Catholic beliefs in medical science and in the possibility of supernatural intervention. This synergy offers a particular window into the classic Catholic integration of *fides et ratio* (faith and reason).

Jacalyn Duffin's study of the Vatican records of processes of canonization over the last several centuries details the painstaking efforts that have been made to count as miracles only those healings and other salutary happenings that cannot be explained by the science of the day. As modern science advanced, so too did the rigor of the tests applied in cases of canonization. Working as a hemotologist, Duffin herself was asked to evaluate a set of bone marrow samples as part of a blind review process. She was only later informed that this evaluation was for a deliberation about whether to declare someone a saint. Her surprise led her to investigate the records of other such cases. This work led her to write a book on the subject and to gain a deeper appreciation for the truly unexplainable. When asked if she, a scientist and historian, believes in miracles, she now says, "Yes, I do."[40]

Biomedical Healing

According to the introductory chapter of *Incarnate Grace*, a recent publication of the Catholic Health Association of the United States, Catholic hospitals and healthcare

---

[39] *Catechism*, 2132; see also 2673–78 on Marian prayer and 2683 on praying with saints.

[40] Jacalyn Duffin, *Medical Miracles: Doctors, Saints, and Healing in the Modern World* (New York: Oxford, 2009), 3, 11–35, 183.

facilities treat as many as one-sixth of patients in this country (nearly five million a year) and employ approximately three quarters of a million workers including doctors, nurses, technicians, and other staff. They serve poor communities in rural and urban areas. They offer care for human life from its prenatal beginnings through its last hours. Although Catholic stances on controversial bioethical questions related to contraception, abortion, and euthanasia put Catholic healthcare at the center of divisive political battles and have an outsized impact on public perceptions, these wedge issues do not exhaust the meaning of Catholic healthcare. Between the mysterious processes of birth and death, there is the full span of a person's life, which is sacred and precious without exception. Catholic healthcare is about using medical treatments and holistic patient care to incarnate God's love for persons throughout their life stages, events, and situations.[41]

Neil Ormerod expresses the purpose of Catholic healthcare well when he writes, "Catholic health organizations are called on to reflect the mission of the church, to be the presence of Christ to a suffering person." He goes on to say, "What this means is that each and every moment in health care, no matter how dark or difficult, has the potential to be a moment of grace—counselling grieving parents; passing on the bad news of test results; performing an emergency surgery; or washing bedpans."[42] Striking in Ormerod's description of being Christ for others and mediating God's grace to them is that many of his examples do not involve a medical cure. Rather, they illustrate types of care that take place when no such cure was possible and a patient died, when prospects do not look good, or when someone requires assistance to take care of regular bodily functions. In biomedical contexts, healing means more than a quick fix. It means being with others in their need, serving them with humility, and finding ways to let them know they are loved and valued as persons.

In addition to examining the moral principles involved in particular medical procedures and choices, Catholic bioethicists—informed by Catholic social teaching—study the political, economic, and cultural structures and institutions that affect health outcomes.[43] They confront persistent inequalities in healthcare on both a local and global scale. They analyze challenges such as inadequate public funding for medicines,

---

[41] Therese M. Lysaught, "Introduction: Incarnating Caritas," in *Incarnate Grace: Perspectives on the Ministry of Catholic Health Care*, ed. Charles E. Bouchard (St. Louis: Catholic Health Association of the United States, 2017), 3–18, at 3, 5, 13, and 17; and Cardinal Joseph L. Bernadin, "The Consistent Ethic of Life: The Challenge and the Witness of Catholic Health Care," in *The Seamless Garment: Writings on the Consistent Ethic of Life*, ed. Thomas A. Nairn (Maryknoll, NY: Orbis, 2008), 109–116. For teachings on contraception, abortion, and euthanasia, see *Catechism*, 2370, 2270, and 2276.

[42] Neil Ormerod, "Health Care and the Response of the Triune God," in *Incarnate Grace: Perspectives on the Ministry of Catholic Health Care*, ed. Charles E. Bouchard (St. Louis: Catholic Health Association of the United States, 2017), 23, 31.

[43] Lisa Sowle Cahill, *Theological Bioethics: Participation, Justice, and Change* (Washington, DC: Georgetown, 2005).

treatment, and infrastructure; patterns of distribution that favor people of greater economic and racial privilege; and environmental problems such as pollution and water scarcity.[44] Paul Farmer (the co-founder of Partners in Health) and the Catholic ethicist Andrea Vicini articulate some helpful guidelines for a more equitable practice of global public health:

> How do we address such inequalities in health globally? First, we need to be aware that injustice is pervasive. Second, we must avoid desperation or complacent resignation; awareness of unacceptable disparities should animate social engagement to address and eliminate them. Third, it is necessary to make a preferential option for those who bear the brunt of these inequities.[45]

This perspective is very close to the views expressed by Pope Francis in recent encyclicals and public addresses.[46] Healthcare is not just an individual matter between doctor and patient. It is a social good that is only achievable through cooperation and solidarity.

It is easy to take for granted the existence of Catholic hospitals and health systems, but each one had to be constructed from the ground up, often at great sacrifice. Much of the credit for these achievements must go to Catholic organizations of women religious. Living vows of poverty, chastity, and obedience, many consecrated women have devoted themselves to the bodily and spiritual care of suffering people. Throughout the nineteenth and twentieth centuries, they raised funds to build hospitals and orphanages; they brought medical facilities to places where none existed before; and they gave special attention to the underserved: poor people, immigrants, and racially marginalized groups such as Blacks and Native Americans.[47]

Popular narratives about a modern divide between religion and science neglect the ways that religious institutions have facilitated access to modern medicine. Moreover, they overlook the significant contributions that Catholics such as Gregor Mendel, Louis Pasteur, and Jérôme Lejeune have made to medical science, specifically to the study of genetics, microbiology, and disabilities such as Down Syndrome.[48] Although the healing work of Christ is not limited to those biomedical practices that can be devised with the

---

[44] Philip J. Landrigan and Andrea Vicini, SJ, eds., *Ethical Challenges in Global Public Health: Climate Change, Pollution, and the Health of the Poor* (Eugene, OR: Pickwick, 2021).

[45] Paul Farmer and Andrea Vicini, SJ, "An Ethical Agenda for Global Public Health," in *Ethical Challenges in Global Public Health: Climate Change, Pollution, and the Health of the Poor*, eds. Philip J. Landrigan and Andrea Vicini, SJ (Eugene, OR: Pickwick, 2021), 193.

[46] Pope Francis, *Fratelli tutti: Encyclical Letter on Fraternity and Social Friendship* (3 October 2020), www.vatican.va, nos. 35 and 109; and Hannah Brockhaus, "Pope Francis: Lack of Basic Health Care Access Is a 'Social Virus,'" *Catholic News Agency*, 28 August 2022.

[47] Suzy Farren, *A Call to Care: The Women Who Built Catholic Healthcare in America* (St. Louis: The Catholic Health Association of the United States, 1996).

[48] Filip Mazurczak, "Ten Catholic Scientists," *The Catholic World Report*, 21 July 2022.

use of natural reason, these are apertures through which the image of the divine *Logos* can be seen in human history. Health-related research continues today at the Pontifical Academy of the Sciences and at Catholic universities throughout the world.

Psychotherapeutic Healing

The Catholic tradition has long recognized that it is not only bodies but souls that cry out for healing. Although emotions, desires, memories, perceptions, choices, and other phenomena associated with the soul are deeply shaped by what happens to and within the body, biomedical interventions, such as those provided by psychiatry, are not the only helpful means of addressing maladies of the soul. Sacramental anointing, charismatic faith healing, and even praying for a miracle may be beneficial avenues to pursue in some cases of mental distress, and one should not underestimate the positive effects that changes to one's social and natural environment can have on psychological health.[49] Nevertheless, psychotherapeutic healing is a distinct modality of care warranting specific attention. This is a growth area for Catholic reflection and practice.

For much of its history, Catholic spirituality has attributed the soul's suffering to the harmful effects of sin and vice and the struggles to overcome them. From St. Augustine to St. Teresa of Avila, there is a rich tradition of Catholic introspection, which seeks to give comfort and happiness to the soul by helping it detach from worldly values of pride, lust, wealth, and honor and conform to the will of God that is revealed in Christ's humility and self-giving love. Augustine, Teresa, and many other saintly guides in this tradition understand that the journey of spiritual transformation may be painful, but this is the pain of healing not destruction, and it is infinitely preferable to the bottomless misery of estrangement from God. What they ultimately seek and find on this path is the joy of being renewed in the likeness of Christ and the bliss of being wedded to him as one's Bridegroom.[50]

Although even secular authors have discovered genuine psychological insights in the classic sources of Catholic spirituality,[51] the modern field of psychology, with its various clinical and therapeutic methods, proceeds on a different set of assumptions. Its basic picture of the interior human drama does not focus on a conflict between sin and grace but rather on a bundle of diagnosable conditions, described in the Diagnostic and

---

[49] Kasza, *Understanding Sacramental Healing*, 153–59; Csordas, *Sacred Self*, 33; Duffin, *Medical Miracles*, 96–99; and Phillis Isabella Sheppard, *Self, Culture, and Others in Womanist Practical Theology* (New York: Palgrave, 2011).

[50] Augustine of Hippo, *Confessions*, trans. Henry Chadwick (New York: Oxford, 2008); and Teresa of Avila, *The Interior Castle*, trans. Kieran Kavanaugh, OCD and Otilio Rodriguez, OCD (Mahwah, NJ: Paulist, 1979).

[51] Julia Kristeva, *Teresa, My Love: An Imagined Life of the Saint of Avila*, trans. Lorna Scott Fox (New York: Columbia, 2015).

Statistical Manual of Mental Disorders (DSM), that may benefit from therapist-facilitated practices of communication, self-narration, behavior modification, and in some cases medication.

In 1953, Pope Pius XII gave an address to the Fifth International Congress of Psychotherapy and Clinical Psychology, in which he revealed a characteristic ambivalence in the Catholic response to this field. On the one hand, insofar as psychotherapy is a branch of science that seeks to help people, he applauded it as a proper use of reason. On the other hand, pushing back against the paradigm shift that it represented, he was clear that the woes of the human soul cannot be addressed without overcoming sin and entering into relationship with God.[52]

In recent years, there have been more robust engagements with mental illness and mental health from Catholic theologians, ethicists, and clinicians. Instead of feeling bound to choose between traditional spirituality and modern therapy, scholars now attempt to reconcile and integrate the two.[53] They respond in holistic, interdisciplinary ways to the psychological suffering of people living with trauma, depression, and suicidal ideation.[54] They avoid ascribing all psychological troubles to sin or vice and instead recognize that there may be biological, social, and personal factors at play that do not imply any deficiency of moral character. They emphasize the tender mercy of God who draws near to those in pain and brings comfort.

A particularly difficult area of needed healing in the Catholic Church stems from the crisis of clergy-perpetrated child sexual abuse (CPCSA) and sinful efforts on the part of clergy and laity to conceal, deny, or minimize this problem. Jennifer Beste gives an overview of psychological literature on the uniquely severe type of wounding that is caused by CPCSA. Although sexual abuse of children is always extremely damaging, when clergy do it, it has extra weight. Because priests act *in persona Christi* in the context of the Eucharist and take on a paternal role within the local Catholic community, children who are sexually abused by a priest can feel like they have been violated by God and by their father simultaneously. The long-lasting effects of CPCSA include disassociation, flashbacks, hyperarousal, self-blame, anxiety, depression, chronic

---

[52] Pope Pius XII, "On Psychotherapy and Religion," 1953, www.papalencyclicals.net/pius12/p12psyre.htm.

[53] Joann Wolski Conn, *Spirituality and Personal Maturity* (Lanham, MD: University Press of America, 1994).

[54] Elizabeth L. Antus, "'The Silence of the Dead': Remembering Suicide Victims and Reimagining the Communion of Saints," *Theological Studies* 81:2 (2020), 394–413; Jessica Coblentz, *Dust in the Blood: A Theology of Life with Depression* (Collegeville, MN: Liturgical, 2022); Lynn Bridgers, "Resurrected Life: Roman Catholic Resources in Posttraumatic Pastoral Care," *International Journal of Practical Theology* 15 (2011), 38–56; and Aaron Kheriaty, *The Catholic Guide to Depression: How the Saints, the Sacraments, and Psychiatry Can Help You Break Its Grip and Find Happiness Again* (Manchester, NH: Sophia Institute, 2012).

physical pain, impaired cognitive function, difficulty forming trusting relationships, and loss of positive connection with the church and God.[55]

Beste argues that part of the healing process for the Church must be a willingness to seek a "deep empathetic understanding of the embodied, psychological, and spiritual harm of clergy sexual abuse."[56] To do this, Catholics must listen to victims and survivors, learn from their journeys of therapeutic discovery and healing, and draw on the work of psychologists who study this type of post-traumatic stress. Only then can their solidarity have the emotional weight and focus that is required. At the same time, Beste emphasizes that this solidarity must also find expression in concrete actions and reforms that prevent further CPCSA. To heal and safeguard the embodied souls of all people, including children, it is necessary to confront the injustices that are embedded in the social structures of this fallen world, including injustices that have taken root in certain parts of the Catholic Church.

Social Healing

The healing work of Christ is inseparable from the work of justice. The revelation of the saving God through Jesus' ministry of healing is not only meant to touch the lives of individuals. It is meant to spark transformations in communities and whole societies and to bring them closer to the reign of God. The meaning of this reign is encapsulated in the words from Isaiah that Jesus attributes to himself: "The Spirit of the Lord is upon me, because he has anointed me to bring good news to the poor. He has sent me to proclaim release to the captives and recovery of sight to the blind, to set free those who are oppressed, to proclaim the year of the Lord's favor" (Luke 4:18–19). The messianic anointing of the Spirit that Jesus bears is made manifest through his liberation of the impoverished, the incarcerated, and the oppressed, as well as through his healing of a physical ailment (blindness). These modes of deliverance are not set apart from each other but rather united in his single mission and identity as the Christ.

It is important to acknowledge that some persons with disabilities such as blindness (whether partial or full and whether from childhood or adulthood) do not want to be "cured" or fixed. Instead, they want to be loved and accepted in their embodied and cultural differences. They want an end to the social stigmas that frame them as inferior simply because they do not meet the ableist norms of society. They want everyone to recognize that living with various kinds of limitation is an important part of what it means to be human, that we all depend on one another, and that our institutions and infrastructure should foster greater inclusivity and respect. This

---

[55] Jennifer Beste, "Envisioning a Just Response to the Catholic Clergy Sexual Abuse Crisis," *Theological Studies* 82:1 (2021), 35–38.

[56] Beste, "Envisioning a Just Response," 41.

perspective does not necessarily imply a refusal of Gospel healing narratives, but it does encourage Christians to read them with a "disability hermeneutic" that emphasizes personhood, agency, and social healing and that overcomes oppressive theological associations of disability with sin and defect.[57]

In addition to resisting ableism, the Catholic Church must work to free itself from other "isms"—social sins such as imperialism, racism, and sexism—that mark this world's distance from the reign of God and wound people not just as individuals but as groups. It must do this work in order to remain an effective sign of Christ's healing presence in history. In the fifteenth century, the Catholic countries of Spain and Portugal, with blessings from the pope,[58] persecuted Jews and Muslims for lacking "pure blood"; conquered Native peoples of the Americas, subjecting them to slavery, rape, and deadly diseases under the pretext of evangelization; and inaugurated the transatlantic slave trade (the commercial sale of African persons as chattel). How is healing possible from such historical horrors?

Developments in Catholic teaching on Judaism and Islam that promote interreligious understanding, Pope Francis's recent "Penitential Pilgrimage" to Canada in which he acknowledged crimes against indigenous nations (including abuse at residential schools), and promises from the Society of Jesus to raise one hundred million dollars in reparations for African American descendants of enslaved people are signs pointing in the right direction.[59] However, the level of expenditure directed toward social healing—measured in terms of financial investment, collective action, and physical and spiritual commitment—needs not only to match but to exceed the accumulated sins of the last five centuries or more if the Catholic Church is really going to meet the challenges that lie before it.

The work that remains to be done cannot be finished overnight. There will not be an immediate cure to social sin. Although the moral demands of crucified peoples

---

[57] D. A. Caeton, "Blindness," in *Keywords for Disability Studies*, eds. Rachel Adams, Benjamin Reiss, and David Serlin (New York: NYU, 2015), 35–37; Bethany McKinney Fox, *Disability and the Way of Jesus: Holistic Healing in the Gospels and the Church* (Downers Grove, IL: InterVarsity, 2019); Mary Jo Iozzio, "Solidarity: Restoring Communion with Those Who Are Disabled," *Journal of Religion, Disability & Health* 15:2 (2011), 139–52; and Amos Yong, *The Bible, Disability, and the Church: A New Vision of the People of God* (Grand Rapids, MI: Eerdmans, 2011).

[58] Pope Alexander VI, *Inter caetera: Division of the Undiscovered World between Spain and Portugal*, Papal Bull, 1453, https://www.papalencyclicals.net/alex06/alex06inter.htm.

[59] *Nostra aetate: Declaration on the Relation of the Church to Non-Christian Religions*, 28 October 1965, www.vatican.va; Kevin P. Considine, "Pope Francis' Apology to Indigenous Canadians Opened Door to Reconciliation," *National Catholic Reporter*, 2 August 2022; and Carol Zimmerman, "Jesuits Pledge $100 Million in Reparations to Descendants of Enslaved People," *National Catholic Reporter*, 17 March 2021.

cannot wait,[60] the building up of a new human community characterized by comprehensive justice, repentance, and forgiveness will take time. In this regard, Robert Schreiter argues that "social healing has to take into account the lingering, toxic presence of the past in society; it must diagnose and mobilize the energies of the present; and it must sketch out a vision for the future."[61]

M. Shawn Copeland interprets the Eucharist as an effective symbol of such social healing. She affirms the Catholic teaching, formulated by St. Augustine in Sermon 272, that communicants who receive the Eucharistic real presence under the outward signs of bread and wine become what they already are: the body of Christ. She explains, "As *his body*, we embrace with love and hope those who, in their bodies, are despised and marginalized, even as we embrace with love and forgiveness those whose sins spawn the conditions for the suffering and oppression of others."[62] Although the sacrament symbolizes and enacts Christ's double embrace—namely, of victims in need of justice and victimizers in need of conversion—its work is not complete until those who receive, and *are*, Christ's body take up an authentic praxis of discipleship in the world. She calls this work "Eucharistic solidarity."

There is one kind of social healing that must be sought between the oppressed and the oppressor. For such reconciliation to constitute a genuine (not superficial or counterfeit) peace, it must be grounded in the liberation of the oppressed from their unjust situation.[63] For example, there can be no true accord between the enslaved and the enslaver until slavery is abolished, efforts are made to atone for the grievous harms done, and all are able to greet one another as equal human beings. Pharaoh must yield, and the captives must be set free. There is another kind of social healing that must be sought between antagonists that are of similar moral standing—that is, cases in which no side is obviously more righteous or mistreated than the other and where what is needed is an end to rivalrous factions (as St. Paul reminds the Corinthian church). As a more recent example, consider the competing ethnic nationalisms that, in the 1990s, brought unspeakable violence to the Balkans.[64] Conflicts as small as interpersonal spats and as large as wars may call for the former (liberationist) or the latter (conflict-

---

[60] Martin Luther King, Jr., "Letter from Birmingham City Jail," in *A Testament of Hope: The Essential Writings and Speeches of Martin Luther King, Jr.*, ed. James Melvin Washington (San Francisco: Harper Collins, 1986), 289–302.

[61] Schreiter, "A Practical Theology of Healing, Forgiveness, and Reconciliation," in *Peacebuilding: Catholic Theology, Ethics, and Praxis*, eds. Robert J. Schreiter, R. Scott Appleby, and Gerard F. Powers (Maryknoll, NY: Orbis, 2010), 377.

[62] M. Shawn Copeland, *Enfleshing Freedom: Body, Race, and Being* (Minneapolis: Fortress, 2010), 127.

[63] James H. Cone, *God of the Oppressed* (New York: Seabury, 1975), 226–46.

[64] Michael K. Duffey, *Sowing Justice, Reaping Peace: Case Studies of Racial, Religious, and Ethnic Healing Around the World* (Franklin, WI: Sheed & Ward, 2001), 94–103.

resolution) type of social healing and, in many cases, both. Ernesto Valiente's account of the oppression, civil war, and reconciliation processes in El Salvador exemplifies such a combined case.[65] Catholic peacebuilding employs and interweaves both models by prioritizing the perspective of the victims and by seeking a healing that embraces all.[66]

Ecological Healing

As I bring this Catholic reflection on the varieties of healing to a close, I want to highlight that we live at a time when there is a need for healing not only of human bodies, souls, and societies but also of humanity's relationship with other species and the earth. Pope Francis's papacy and particularly his encyclical *Laudato si'*, which was given on the feast of Pentecost in 2015, have developed the Catholic Church's understanding of Christ's healing work with respect to the whole of creation and the present ecological crisis.[67]

One dimension of this crisis is the harm caused to non-human animal and plant life. The pope addresses this under a section called "Loss of Biodiversity." He laments, "Each year sees the disappearance of thousands of plant and animal species which we will never know, which our children will never see, because they have been lost forever. The great majority become extinct for reasons related to human activity."[68] Although such losses may negatively affect human beings by diminishing our supplies of food, medicine, and other resources, Pope Francis is adamant that we should not view other created things merely as instruments for our use but as possessing inherent dignity and value. To some degree, ecological healing means sustaining the conditions under which non-human life can flourish and give glory to God in its own right.

However, *Laudato si'* is not just a document about environmentalism. It is a plea for environmental justice. It expresses a concern for the wellbeing of the natural world that is at the same time a concern for the lives of other human beings, especially the poor and excluded. According to Pope Francis, ecological healing and the various aspects of human healing necessarily go together. He contends that "environmental impact assessment . . . should be linked to . . . possible effects on people's physical and mental health."[69] He is especially attentive to health problems that are caused by

---

[65] O. Ernesto Valiente, *Liberation through Reconciliation: Jon Sobrino's Christological Spirituality* (New York: Fordham, 2016).

[66] Schreiter, "Practical Theology of Healing," 371–72.

[67] Vincent J. Miller, ed., *The Theological and Ecological Vision of Laudato Si': Everything Is Connected* (New York: Bloomsbury, 2017); and Daniel P. Castillo, *An Ecological Theology of Liberation: Salvation and Political Ecology* (Maryknoll, NY: Orbis, 2019).

[68] Pope Francis, *Laudato si': On Care for Our Common Home*, 24 May 2015, www.vatican.va, no. 33.

[69] Pope Francis, *Laudato si'*, no. 183.

polluted skies, water ways, and urban centers and by droughts and diseases that are connected to the warming of the planet.[70] He also warns that the changing climate will bring disproportionately high amounts of suffering and political instability to the poorest regions of the world and aggravate already egregious levels of social inequality.[71] More generally, he insists that "we cannot presume to heal our relationship with nature and the environment without healing all fundamental human relationships."[72] Ecological healing depends on all aspects of human healing and, at the same time, is necessary for them.

Pope Francis ends his encyclical with two prayers.[73] The first one, which is addressed to "All-powerful God," includes the lines, "Bring healing to our lives, / that we may protect the world and not prey on it, / that we may sow beauty, not pollution and destruction." Although he believes we need to take responsibility for our actions, he places his greatest hope in the healing power of God—a power that enables us to care for the world and bring forth beauty from it. The pope's second prayer begins as a hymn of praise to the triune God. It is offered "with" all of creation, much like St. Francis of Assisi's "Canticle of Brother Sun." After acknowledging that "the poor and the earth are crying out," the prayer asks, "O Lord, seize us with your power and light, / help us to protect all life, / to prepare for a better future, / for the coming of your Kingdom / of justice, peace, love and beauty." Although the term "healing" is not mentioned in this prayer, the words that the pontiff chooses vividly depict what healing in a comprehensive sense involves: the safeguarding of life and a future shaped by the coming of God's reign.

Conclusion: That All May Be Well

In this essay, I have outlined a Catholic perspective on sacramental, charismatic, miraculous, biomedical, psychotherapeutic, social, and ecological healing, while observing some connections between them. I have drawn on Catholic magisterial teachings, historical figures, and constructive theological and ethical projects to formulate what, I hope, is a useful survey of various ways that Catholics strive to understand and participate in the healing work of Christ. Going beyond the narrow notion of a cure, healing takes on many different meanings and forms in Catholic tradition and practice.

However, such a flexible and capacious sense of healing does not imply that cures never happen—whether thanks to science, grace, or both—or that desiring a cure is

---

[70] Pope Francis, *Laudato si'*, nos. 20, 28–29.
[71] Pope Francis, *Laudato si'*, nos. 25, 48–52.
[72] Pope Francis, *Laudato si'*, no. 119.
[73] Pope Francis, *Laudato si'*, no. 246.

necessarily something naïve or misguided to do. In the midst of serious unhealed suffering, it makes sense that many people would want—like the bleeding woman in Mark's gospel—to reach out to touch Christ's cloak and find their bodies, souls, societies, and entire worlds revived. If we can help make such desires a reality, through ministry, medicine, activism, or prayer, then we ought to do so. We ought to become what we already are: Christ's body, or at the very least his garment—an imperfect membrane through which some contact with him might occur.

To heal and be healed in all the ways that are required of us as followers of Jesus, it seems we must develop a mature awareness of our gifts and vulnerabilities, while maintaining a childlike trust that indeed nothing is impossible for God. This is the sort of trust that the blessed Julian of Norwich displays when she welcomes Christ's reassuring yet counterintuitive words: "alle shalle be wele, and alle shalle be wele, and alle maner of thinge shalle be wel."[74] In the midst of seemingly inescapable suffering, violence, and death, this message may appear naïve or even insensitive. Yet to believe in Christ the Healer—in the bold and unapologetic ways that Catholic and Pentecostal traditions do—is to embrace something like this incredible notion. It is to proceed with the conviction that holistic healing is possible and already actual in our world, even if we cannot always see it, and even if there is still much required of us, as persons and communities, to bring it to light. The healing work of Christ has been given, and it is ours to receive and put into practice.

Andrew Prevot (andrew.prevot@georgetown.edu) is Professor of Theology and Religious Studies at Georgetown University, Washington, DC, USA.

---

[74] Julian of Norwich, *A Revelation of Love*, in *The Writings of Julian of Norwich*, eds. Nicholas Watson and Jacquelin Jenkins (Turnhout, Belgium: Brepols, 2006), Thirteenth Revelation, Twenty-Seventh Chapter.

Healing in the Pentecostal Tradition

David Han

Keywords *divine healing, atonement for sin and sickness, holiness and wholeness, Full Gospel, "promise and fulfillment," Word of Faith Movement, anointing with oil, laying on of hands*

Abstract

This essay provides a historical and theological overview of the Pentecostal experience of divine healing. The essay argues that, for Pentecostals, the experience of divine healing carries a paramount significance to the "heart" of their spirituality and theology. Like the experience of Spirit-baptism and speaking in tongues, Pentecostals experience healing as a foretaste of God's eschatological reign. The essay traces the development of healing practices among early and modern Pentecostals historically and theologically. Pentecostal practices of divine healing emerged out of various healing movements rooted in the earlier Holiness traditions, but they were later firmly developed into a doctrinal understanding associating healing with the atonement work of Jesus Christ. For Pentecostals, this move coincided with their promotion of the so-called "Full Gospel." For Pentecostals, healing is a vivid manifestation of the "holistic" nature of God's salvation wherein the atoning work of Jesus Christ not only frees individuals from their spiritual bondage to sin and death but also assures them of its overcoming power to experience freedom from the bodily bondage of sickness and disease. Delving into a "holistic" view of the life in salvation, the essay further offers a sanctificationist reading of healing while observing the challenges and problems that the "Word of Faith" movement generated over the years. In conclusion, the essay accentuates a strong eschatological impulse embedded in various Pentecostal practices of divine healing.

Introduction

Pentecostals are often identified with the experience of Spirit-baptism and speaking in (unlearned) tongues as the outward manifestation to warrant such experience. This experience is so prominently associated with Pentecostals, it has been described as the "crown jewel" of Pentecostalism.[1] Paralleling in significance is, however, the Pentecostal experience of divine healing. Like the phenomena of speaking in tongues for Spirit-baptism, Pentecostals would also consider the practices of laying on hands, anointing with oil, and/or using anointed handkerchiefs to be the distinctive liturgical acts through which divine healing occurs.[2]

It is also evident for Pentecostals that the experience of divine healing generates crescendo effects on their eschatological faith that dialectically juxtaposes the "already" and the "not yet" dimensions of the salvation journey (i.e., *via salutis*).[3] The healing occurrences were/are not merely attesting to the "charismatic" presence of the Spirit here and now; rather, they represent the inbreaking of the future of God into present realities allowing all the participants to be enraptured into the ecstatic moment of foretasting the glory of the coming reign of God. The upshot of this is that healing assures and even emboldens their eschatological faith that, soon, Jesus Christ is coming again and will usher in the Kingdom of God.

Seminal works by Donald Dayton and Steven J. Land capture well how the experience of divine healing cultivates eschatological impulses in Pentecostal spirituality.[4] As both Dayton and Land articulate, this is clearly evidenced in the promotion of the "Full Gospel." In pursuing the Full Gospel, Pentecostals emphasized a wholehearted devotion to God and a passionate longing to be one with Christ, which are rooted in and entailed the believer's dynamic participation in the workings of the Spirit. For Pentecostals, salvation involves more than grasping, and giving assent to, an abstract concept, but that which generates real and tangible traces in and through their faith experiences. Healing, for Pentecostals, provided tangible expressions of God's salvation in and through the Spirit.[5] So decisively prominent were the healing occurrences for modern Pentecostals, Dayton notes, "even more characteristic of

---

[1] Drawing from the previous works from Donald Dayton and William Faupel, Frank Macchia argues for a broader reading on the Pentecostal experience of Spirit-baptism: "Spirit baptism for Pentecostals is the experience that brings to realization personally what the eschatological latter rain of the Spirit brings corporately to an era of time." *Baptized in the Spirit* (Grand Rapids: Zondervan, 2006), 40.

[2] Steven J. Land, "Pentecostal Spirituality: Living in the Spirit," in *Christian Spirituality: Post-Reformation to Modern*, eds. Louis Dupré and Don E. Saliers (New York: Crossroad, 1991), 484–85.

[3] It is important to note that, for Pentecostals, healing is a matter of salvation. That is, healing is essentially related to the work of God's salvation insofar as it demonstrates God's intervening power to restore and make whole the broken realities humanity faces in the present.

[4] Donald W. Dayton, *Theological Roots of Pentecostalism* (Grand Rapids: Francis Asbury Press, 1987); see also Land's "Pentecostal Spirituality: Living in the Spirit," and *Pentecostal Spirituality: A Passion for the Kingdom* (Cleveland, TN: CPT Press, 1993).

[5] Allan Anderson, "Pentecostal Approaches to Faith and Healing," *International Review of Mission*, 91 (2009), 523–24. Anderson interestingly notes the restorationist motif embedded in the Pentecostal practices of divine healing: "Pentecostals responded to what they experienced as a void left by rationalistic Western forms of Christianity which had unwittingly initiated what was tantamount to the destruction of ancient spiritual values" (532).

Pentecostalism than the doctrine of the baptism of the Spirit is its celebration of miracles of divine healing as part of God's salvation and as evidence of the presence of divine power in the church."[6]

Tracing historically, Pentecostal practices of divine healing were largely influenced by the North American Holiness movements. As A. B. Simpson notes, the Holiness tradition generally identified divine healing as one of its "four great pillars in the temple of truth."[7] Some would trace further to the Wesleyan renewal movements of the eighteenth century and other Pietistic movements.[8] Although these threads of influence from prior movements are significant to note, and they are indeed woven into the fabric of modern Pentecostalism, it should also be noted that Pentecostals would distinctively characterize themselves as the "Latter Rain" movement with a strong restorationist motif. Identifying themselves closely with New Testament spirituality, Pentecostals readily embraced all of the powerful manifestations of the Spirit recorded in it and considered them to be readily available for now. As noted, for Pentecostals, the demonstratable experiences of the Spirit provided tangible glimpses of the future hope that is even now breaking into the suffering conditions of the present. Believing in and anticipating the divine intervention to heal represent more than a temporal restoration of the person's body; it demonstrates the gospel's redemptive power to make the person whole again. Each and every occurrence of divine healing manifests the truth that the Kingdom of God is already here, having been inaugurated in Christ's first advent, and is even now making its presence known in this broken world. Therefore, for Pentecostals, healing is closely intertwined with salvation and the journey it takes. Divine healing is a demonstratable benefit of the gospel's redemptive power as it concurrently forecasts the coming Kingdom.

This writing offers a broad Pentecostal reading on healing and Pentecostal practices associated with it. We will begin by reviewing how Pentecostals articulate healing in their ecclesial statements in which healing is closely identified with the atonement work of Christ. We will further investigate how Pentecostal doctrines and practices of healing represent the outgrowth of an intertwined past with the Holiness movement. We will also point out some distinctive ways that Pentecostals develop their

---

[6] Dayton, *Theological Roots of Pentecostalism*, 115.

[7] Frederic H. Senfit, "Introduction," in the 1925 edition of A. B. Simpson's writing, *The Fourfold Gospel* (Harrisburg, PA: Christian Alliance Publications, 1925), 4.

[8] Dayton's work, *Theological Roots of Pentecostalism*, is particularly helpful in this regard. See also Kimberly Ervin Alexander, "Three Hundred Years of Holiness and Healing," *The Asbury Theological Journal* 58:2 (2019), 57–77, as well as her monograph titled, *Pentecostal Healing: Models in Theology and Practice*, Journal of Pentecostal Theology Supplement Series (Blandford Forum, UK: Deo Publishing, 2006). Tracking in a similar vein, Land makes a broader claim about the crucial convergence between the Wesleyan tradition and Pentecostalism: "The Wesleyan tradition is vital for the present understanding and the future development of the [Pentecostal] movement" ("Pentecostal Spirituality: Living in the Spirit," 480).

own understanding of healing and healing practices. As we shall observe, for Pentecostals, healing has been deeply embedded in their salvation grammars and spiritual (ecclesial) practices. In the process, Pentecostals had to confront some notable challenges, such as the oppositional stance over the use of medicine or medical professionals among the early Pentecostals and the rise of the "Word of Faith" movements. Finally, we will examine how the eschatological tension of living "between the times" (i.e., between "the already" and the "not yet" dimensions of the Kingdom of God) informs the foundational understanding of Pentecostal healing and its practices.[9] We will further reflect on the Pentecostal practices of laying on of hands, anointing with oil, and using anointed handkerchiefs, as well as the significance of gathering at the altar while a worshipping community pray and tarry together in the Spirit.

Divine Healing and the Atonement

Modern Pentecostalism represents multifarious and complex histories and theological roots. When it comes to expressing doctrinal commitment to the practices of divine healing, however, Pentecostals show a remarkable unity in affirming the doctrine and its practices, while tracing its scriptural and theological foundation to the atonement work of Jesus Christ. To begin with, the Church of God (Cleveland, TN) in its Declaration of Faith succinctly states: "[we believe] divine healing is provided for all in the atonement."[10] The Statement of Fundamental Truths for the Assemblies of God similarly affirms the practices of divine healing and also relate them to the salvific work of Christ's atonement: "[D]ivine healing is an integral part of the gospel. Deliverance from sickness is provided in the atonement, and is the privilege of all believers."[11] The statement cites Isaiah 53:4–5, Matthew 8:16–17, and James 5:14–16 as the supporting scriptural references. The official statement from the International Pentecostal Holiness Church shows almost no variation: "we believe in divine healing as in atonement (Isaiah 53:4, 5; Matthew 8:16, 17; Mark 16:14-18; James 5:14-16; Exodus 15:26)."[12] As a whole, the scriptures referenced in these statements clearly accentuate the atonement motif for healing. They also highlight spiritual and ecclesial practices such as confessing sins, praying fervently with faith, laying on of hands, and anointing with oil on the sick.

---

[9] Steven J. Land, "A Passion for the Kingdom: Revisioning Pentecostal Spirituality," *Journal of Pentecostal Theology* 1 (1992), 19–46. Characterizing Pentecostal spirituality as being essentially "apocalyptic," Land states that their eschatological passion was "the unifying center of the [Pentecostal] movement" (41).

[10] "Church of God (Cleveland, TN) Declaration of Faith," accessed 30 November 2023, https://churchofgod.org/beliefs/declaration-of-faith/.

[11] "Assemblies of God Fundamental Truths," accessed 30 November 2023, https://ag.org/Beliefs/Statement-of-Fundamental-Truths#12.

[12] "International Pentecostal Holiness Church Articles of Faith," accessed 30 November 2023, https://iphc.org/beliefs/.

The United Pentecostal Church follows a similar theological trajectory in their ecclesial statement: "God has made Himself known through the ages by miraculous healings and has made special provisions in the age of grace to heal all who will come to Him in faith and obedience. Divine healing was purchased for us by the blood of Jesus Christ, especially by His stripes."[13] The reference to "faith" and "obedience" in the statement accentuates the co-operant nature of grace by which believers are invited to "participate" in the healing miracles of God. The *Declaration of Faith* by the Foursquare Church also traces healing Christologically (i.e., "the power of the Lord Jesus Christ"), while also connecting it explicitly to the believer's "active faith" and "obedience":

> we believe that divine healing is the power of the Lord Jesus Christ "to heal the sick and the afflicted in answer to believing prayer," that He who is the same yesterday, today and forever has never changed but is "still an all-sufficient help in the time of trouble," able to meet the needs of, and quicken the body into newness of life, as well as the soul and spirit in answer to the "faith of them" who ever pray with submission to His divine and sovereign will.[14]

The statement is also supported by the oft-cited scriptures: Matthew 8:17; 9:5; Mark 16:17–18; Acts 4:29–30; and James 5:14–16. The largest classical Pentecostal denomination in North America, i.e., the Church of God in Christ, also affirms the practices of divine healing, although their statement relates healing more closely to the "commandment" and "teaching" of Jesus:

> The Church of God in Christ believes in and practices Divine Healing. It is a commandment of Jesus to the Apostles (St. Mark 16:18). Jesus affirms his teaching on healing by explaining to His disciples, who were to be Apostles, that healing the afflicted is by faith (St. Luke 9:40–41). Therefore, we believe that healing by faith in God has scriptural support and ordained authority. St. James' writing in his epistle encourage Elders to pray for the sick, lay hands upon them and to anoint them with oil, and that prayers with faith shall heal the sick and the Lord shall raise them up. Healing is still practiced widely and frequently in the Church of God in Christ, and testimonies of healing in our Church testify to this fact.[15]

It is interesting to note that their statement makes explicit reference to the distinctive ecclesial practices such as laying hands on the sick and using the oil from the altar to anoint them. This is in keeping with what was scripturally commanded in the

---

[13] Terry Cross, "The Doctrine of Divine Healing," in *Transforming Power: Dimensions of the Gospel*, ed. Yung-Chul Han (Cleveland, TN: Pathway Press, 2001), 180.

[14] "Foursquare Church Declaration of Faith," accessed 30 November 2023, https://foursquaremissionspress.org/wp-content/uploads/2016/01/445_Declaration_of_Faith.pdf

[15] "What We Believe" (The Church of God in Christ), accessed 30 November 2023, https://www.cogic.org/about-us/what-we-believe/. It is interesting to note that the common scriptural text noted in all of these official statements is Jas 5:14–16. We will discuss this text closely in the later section of the article.

epistle of James. When one overlays these official statements by classical Pentecostals, what emerges is a strong, and shared, understanding that healing is intricately woven with the atonement work of Christ and the power of salvation it generates in the present workings of the Spirit. Furthermore, juxtaposing healing with "active faith" and "obedience," as well as Christ's "commandment" and "teaching," Pentecostals tend to accentuate the co-operant nature of grace by which believers are enabled to participate in the working out of salvation.

The Intertwined Pasts: Holiness and the Pentecostals on Healing

Donald W. Dayton's work, *Theological Roots of Pentecostalism*, traces how the Pentecostal doctrines and practices of divine healing represent the confluence of the Wesleyan renewal movement, the Pietistic emphasis on effectual prayer and faith, and the broad network of "faith healing" movements among the nineteenth-century Holiness leaders in North America.[16] Drawing on the "faith principles" of George Müller, Dayton notes, Charles Cullis published *Faith Cures* in 1879, which initiated the development of the doctrine of faith healing. Cullis took James 5:14–15 in particular as the key text to support a believer's need to seek earnest and effectual prayer for the healing of the body.[17] Following the trajectory set by Cullis, W. E. Boardman would eventually make the theological connection between divine healing and the forgiveness of sins. For Boardman, Jesus who bore our sins and pardoned us from them was/is the Great Physician who heals: "The new light that then opened upon my soul was marvelous . . . one of the things that came to me with great force and sweetness was the office work of our gracious Lord as the Healer."[18] Correlating the restoration of souls with the healing of the body was further carried out by *Triumphs of Faith*, the magazine that Carrie Judd Montgomery published. Citing Matthew 4:23, wherein Jesus not only preaches the gospel of the Kingdom but also heals the sick, she concluded: "Those who went to Jesus could not have thought of asking Him to restore their souls, and leave their bodies full of disease. . . . Why should they, why should we—when Christ is able and willing to give us both?"[19]

As the Holiness doctrines of divine healing began to spread, it would take another turn to arrive at the Pentecostal teaching that "healing is provided in the atonement." It coincided with the promotion of a Full Gospel by the Holiness leaders like A. B.

---

[16] Given the limited scope of this article, the study will selectively highlight only a few significant Holiness leaders and their contributions to the development of the doctrines of divine healing.

[17] Dayton, *Theological Roots of Pentecostalism*, 123–24. See also Alexander, "Three Hundred Years of Holiness and Healing," 65.

[18] Dayton, *Theological Roots of Pentecostalism*, 124. See also Cross, "The Doctrine of Divine Healing," 181.

[19] Carrie Judd, *The Power of Faith* (Buffalo, NY: Carrie F. Judd, 1880), 65.

Simpson who included divine healing in the "four distinctive motifs" of the Holiness tradition: salvation, healing, holiness, and the second coming of Jesus Christ.[20] Simpson reasoned: "If sickness be the result of the Fall, it must be included in the atonement of Christ which reaches 'as far as the curse is found.'"[21] For Simpson, the atonement of Christ effectively reversed the effects of the curse of sin and provided the foundation for a holistic recovery for human beings—the restoration of both one's soul and her/his body. The push to preach the Full Gospel meant then claiming the full benefits that Christ's atonement provides, which cannot be envisaged without the inclusion of bodily healing.[22]

Perhaps, one of the clearest expressions in this trajectory is found in R. Kelso Carter's *The Atonement for Sin and Sickness; or a Full Salvation for Soul and Body*. Alexander cites Carter who states: "sickness is a trace of man's inherited depravity and is from the devil. The vicarious atonement of Christ is explicitly for all depravity, including sickness."[23] The correlation between sin and sickness was also clearly evident in the writings of Asa Mahan. Mahan appealed to Matthew 8:16–17 and stated: "If the fact that Jesus bore our sins in His own body on the tree, is a valid reason why we should trust Him now to pardon our sins, the fact that 'He bare our sicknesses' is an equally valid reason why we should now trust Him to heal our diseases."[24]

Around the turn of the twentieth century when modern Pentecostalism had emerged, the doctrine and practices of divine healing were already widely accepted. The holiness rhetoric and impulse were already deeply embedded in the doctrinal understanding and the ecclesial practices of divine healing. The inaugural issue of the Azusa Street paper, *The Apostolic Faith*, thus included an explicit doctrinal statement expressing a firm commitment to divine healing with sermons on healing in the atonement.[25] Since the inception of their movement, therefore, Pentecostals understood and practiced divine healing as God's redemptive remedy to the full range of effects sin had caused and considered this divine remedy to be less than complete if the healing of the body is not in view.

Correlating healing with the atonement work of Jesus Christ, Pentecostals tended to support a dynamic view of Christ's atonement such as the *Christus Victor* theory by Gustaf

---

[20] Cross, "The Doctrine of Divine Healing," 180–81.

[21] A. B. Simpson, *The Gospel of Healing*, rev. ed. (New York: Christian Alliance Publishing, 1915), 34.

[22] Anderson, "Pentecostal Approaches to Faith and Healing," 524–25.

[23] Alexander, "Three Hundred Years of Holiness and Healing," 61. See R. Kelso Carter, *The Atonement for Sin and Sickness; or a Full Salvation for Soul and Body* (Boston: Willard Tract Repository, 1884).

[24] Asa Mahan, "Faith-Healing," *Earnest Christian* 48 (September 1884), 76.

[25] Alexander, "Three Hundred Years of Holiness and Healing," 65–66.

Aulén.[26] Their belief and practices of divine healing would then stand firmly on the foundation that Christ is the "victor" over sin and sickness. A believer should have a confidence in the God who heals and, therefore, participate in the demonstration of God's healing power through a prayer of active faith. This does not mean that Pentecostals are triumphalist. Pentecostals are always cautious to acknowledge that "the triumphal procession has not yet been marched . . . we have the victory over death, but we still bury our loved ones."[27] Instead of being triumphalist, Pentecostals understand divine healing in terms of the "spirit-body correspondence" wherein the salvation of Christ is envisaged to be holistic, delivering us from both the spiritual and the bodily bondage.[28]

Pentecostal Healing: A Sanctificationist Reading

Like the preceding Holiness movements, Pentecostals also promoted the Full Gospel with some variations around the doctrines of sanctification and Spirit-baptism. Some Pentecostals held a "fourfold" gospel motif in which the Pentecostal experience of Spirit-baptism replaced the Holiness emphasis on sanctification. For these Pentecostals, sanctification was viewed as a gradual movement in the life of salvation, not a post-conversion crisis experience. On the other hand, Pentecostals with a strong Wesleyan leaning held the "fivefold" gospel motif. The Pentecostal experience of Spirit-baptism was added to the "four distinctive gospel motifs" of the Holiness tradition. Like the Holiness movements, their understanding of the Full Gospel included sanctification; however, they understood sanctification to be characteristically both a gradual movement and an instantaneous work (i.e., "crisis experience") of God's salvific grace.[29] The Full Gospel then entailed a seamless progression in the salvation journey that coalesced a believer's salvific initiation (i.e., conversion experience) with the ongoing, post-conversion workings of the Spirit—sanctification, Spirit-baptism, healing, and the eschatological longing for the soon-coming of Jesus Christ. Regardless of the differences

---

[26] See (David) Sang-Ehil Han, "Weaving the Courage of God and Human Suffering: Reorienting the Atonement Tradition," in *Passover, Pentecost and Parousia: Studies in Celebration of the Life and Ministry of R. Hollis Gause*, eds. John Christopher Thomas, Rickie D. Moore, and Steven J. Land (Blandford Forum, UK: Deo Publishing, 2010), 171–90.

[27] Cross, "The Doctrine of Divine Healing," 191.

[28] Land, "Pentecostal Spirituality: Living in the Spirit," 484.

[29] Much of the distinction between the proponents of the fourfold and the fivefold gospel motifs had to do with whether the experience of sanctification can be instantaneously experienced. The proponents of the fivefold gospel motifs held the view of the "crisis and development" dialectic. That is, sanctification can be instantaneously experienced in the present life of a believer while effecting her/his ongoing development in the way of salvation. For the Wesleyan Pentecostals, sanctification as a post-conversion experience certainly represents the eradication of sin in the heart and life of a believer, but it also provides the infusion of a wholehearted love for/with God.

between the fourfold or the fivefold gospel proponents, it is important to note that the pursuit of holiness has been the overriding thread for all expressions of Pentecostalism.[30]

The upshot of all this is that the Pentecostal doctrine and practices of divine healing are intricately aligned with their grammars of salvation, especially the doctrine of sanctification. Insofar as sanctification represented the possibility of the eradication of sin in one's heart and life, healing became the visible sign of God's redeeming power to eliminate disease from the body.[31] This was particularly in keeping with the "two-fold" nature of salvation (i.e., justification and sanctification) that the Wesleyan soteriology emphasized.[32] As Vinson Synan notes, early Pentecostal leaders like Charles Parham correlated sanctification with divine healing: "Carrying the idea of sanctification tradition and perfection to its ultimate conclusion, he [Parham] taught that 'sanctifying power reached every part of our body, destroying the very root and tendency to disease.'"[33] Inasmuch as the promotion of the Full Gospel compelled Pentecostals to pursue a sanctified life, they were also led to anticipate and expect God's gracious intervention to make believers whole in and through the healing of their bodies.

Tracking the parallelism between sanctification and divine healing, Pentecostals with the Wesleyan leaning would draw from Wesley how he integrated the ideas of holiness and wholeness, advocating a therapeutic understanding of salvation. That is, Wesley often equated sin with "plague" or "diseases" and regarded human beings in need of a cure. Wesley was more focused on the effects of sin on human beings than the question of the origin of sin, and how grace enables us, believers, to participate in the divine work of salvation.[34] For Wesley, "we are pardoned in order to participate."[35]

Following this soteriological trajectory, Pentecostal doctrine and practices of divine healing unveil a few distinctive characteristics. First, Pentecostals understand the experience of healing in dialectical terms. While a believer can trust God to bring about healing at any moment, the individual is in no way removed from the present and

---

[30] See the unpublished presidential address of R. Hollis Gause at the Society for Pentecostal Studies (1970). While noting variegated roots and development among Pentecostals, Gause argues with clarity that all expressions of Pentecostalism in North America were birthed in the holiness milieu.

[31] Alexander, "Three Hundred Years of Holiness and Healing," 60. Alexander notes that the eradication of sin did not mean that a believer would be free from the *presence* of sin in this life although s/he can be freed from the *power* of sin instead of being perpetually struggling with it. Relatedly, healing provides the tangible evidence of the overcoming power of God's grace over the effects of sin, such as sickness and diseases. The co-operant nature of God's grace calls for a believer's ongoing participation in the enabling work of God's grace, both in the sanctifying work of God's grace and the healing miracles.

[32] Dayton, *Theological Roots of Pentecostalism*, 119.

[33] Vinson Synan, *The Holiness-Pentecostal Tradition: Charismatic Movements in the Twentieth Century* (Grand Rapids: Eerdmans, 1997), 192.

[34] Randy Maddox, *Responsible Grace: John Wesley's Practical Theology* (Nashville: Kingswood Books, 1994), 74.

[35] Maddox, *Responsible Grace*, 168.

future possibilities of suffering sickness. Although all instances of healing are temporary and, hence, provisional in nature, each and every instance of healing nevertheless provides a foretaste, and an assurance, of final healing at the eschaton.[36] Second, insofar as grace enables human participation in the work of salvation, Pentecostals actively participate in the prayer of faith and expect it to effect healing. In both instances, grace and human participation are understood to be dynamically intertwined with one another.[37] Third, juxtaposed with sanctification, healing envisages a holistic restoration. Practices of healing are constant reminders to affirm that human beings are only made whole when both their spiritual and bodily needs are brought to bear and met with nourishment.[38] Alexander thus cites Andrew Murray who stated: "In heaven, even our bodies will have their part in salvation. Salvation will not be complete for us until our bodies enjoy the full redemption of Christ. Shouldn't we believe in this work of

---

[36] The early Pentecostal literatures such as *The Church of God Evangel* share stories that describe the eventual death of believers as "dying in the faith" or being "victorious but in death." Sometimes, they were also critiqued for printing death notices as if they represent ineffectual prayers of faith. In response, the January issue (1920) of *The Church of God Evangel* includes a statement: "Our critics say we ought to give incidents of healing instead of notices of death. . . . It is like this: We are working to get people saved and ready for heaven, then when they have gone to heaven and our work has been thus far successful, where is there any reasonable objections for publishing it abroad. . . . No one objects to telling of one going to Europe, Africa or South America, then why object to telling of one who has gone to heaven" (*Church of God Evangel*, 11:5, 31 January 1920, 2).

[37] See the following testimony of a Pentecostal missionary on healing: "What seemed like an even greater act of divine intervention occurred . . . when my wife Olwen and I were travelling in Zambia towards Malawi with a van and trailer. A partial head-on collision with a large truck resulted in us both being at death's door. I lost a lot of blood from external injuries. A Catholic priest gave me the rite of extreme unction and a Polish nun stayed at my side in the small mission hospital, holding my hand, and imparting incredible strength. The Australian doctor said that it would be 'a miracle' if I were still alive the next morning. Lutheran nuns from Darmstadt came to assist the Catholics. We were flown to hospital in South Africa by air ambulance. I was released from hospital within two weeks. Olwen, however, went into a coma after two days, which was to last for seven weeks. People all over the world prayed. I believe that I had received divine assurances that Olwen would recover. One afternoon, after she had been comatose for four weeks, the German healing evangelist Reinhard Bonnke (who lived in South Africa at that time) came to pray for her and rebuke the 'spirit of death' that gripped her. She was in a deep coma with a 'decerebral' response to stimuli. The neurologist had pronounced his opinion that she would not recover from her vegetative state. The next day, the nurse reported that she had smiled, and three weeks later she was beginning to talk. Everyone, the neurologist included, admitted that this was an event that had exceeded all expectations. Although Olwen's injuries were extensive and she remained in hospital for six months, we are now the parents of two children, our oldest born eighteen months after the accident that changed our lives. That is another miracle and another story. I relate these stories because the issues that are discussed here have profoundly affected me and are taken very seriously. God used a Catholic priest, Catholic and Lutheran nuns, medical professionals, a German evangelist, and the prayers of many people to bring about our healing. I will not pretend that everything has been perfect thereafter. Olwen and I continue to suffer physical consequences from our injuries, but we know that we are still alive because of God's miraculous intervention and answer to prayers" (Anderson, "Pentecostal Approaches to Faith and Healing," 523–24).

[38] Anderson thus writes: "This holistic function, which does not separate the 'physical' from the 'spiritual', is restored in Pentecostalism, and people see it as a 'powerful' religion to meet human needs ("Pentecostal Approaches to Faith and Healing," 525).

redemption here below? Even here on earth, the health of our bodies is a fruit of the salvation which Jesus has acquired for us."[39]

Challenges in Pentecostal Practices of Healing

It is true that Pentecostal practices of divine healing have had some challenges. To note, the early Pentecostals considered the use of medicine or seeking help from medical professionals to be either unnecessary or a sign of lacking faith. A. J. Tomlinson, the founding presiding bishop of the Church of God (Cleveland, Tennessee), is known to have said: "There is no other way provided for the healing of the body except through Jesus Christ. To resort to other means and remedies is to transgress and disobey God."[40] To note further, F. J. Lee, who followed Tomlinson as presiding bishop, is also known to have characterized germs and flies as "allies to Satan" and even attributed some medical conditions such as rheumatism and swelling to demons. Tracing the stories of rebellious Israel in the wilderness, certain illnesses were also characterized as punishment for sin. Although the usefulness of medicines was not categorically dismissed, they were expected to be used only for those outside the church.[41] This extreme approach of denying or devaluing the use of medicine, as well as avoiding to seek the help of medical professionals, has been certainly toned down over the years. As a matter of fact, contemporary Pentecostals would count on the use of medicine and medical professionals as they pray for God's intervention to heal.

As Pentecostalism rapidly grew with the emergence of mass healing evangelists, another serious challenge arose with the spread of the "Word of Faith" movement. Notable representatives of the movement such as Kenneth Hagin, Kenneth Copeland, and Frederick Price trace their teaching to Galatians 3:13–14, arguing that believers are no longer bound by the curse of the Law. Hence, they concluded that "sickness and disease in the body of the believer is a reflection of how little of the word of faith that you have confessing over your own body."[42] Drawing largely from the writings of Essek W. Kenyon (1867–1948), a Baptist pastor who taught "the positive confession of the Word of God" and a "law of faith" working by predetermined divine principles, Hagin and others began to teach that any and all physical symptoms of sickness should come under the authority of the spiritual word of faith. With "positive confession" of, and "faith" in, the Word of God, believers should be able to live in divine health whatever circumstances or symptoms may be. For proponents of Word of Faith movements, the

---

[39] Alexander, "Three Hundred Years of Holiness and Healing," 61.

[40] A. J. Tomlinson, *The Last Great Conflict* (Cleveland, TN: White Wing, 1984; reprint of 1913 edition), 99.

[41] Alexander, "Three Hundred Years of Holiness and Healing," 67.

[42] Cross, "The Doctrine of Divine Healing," 194.

ground for healing was not a matter of dynamic engagement between God's enabling grace and human participation but, rather, exerting one's positive will to "name" and "claim" her/his desired outcome.[43] Against this kind of deviation on Pentecostal healing, Land rightly criticizes: "The crucially important gift, sign and ministry of healing, under the influence of an overly realized eschatology, showed symptoms of a much broader tendency toward human as opposed to divine sovereignty, technique as opposed to waiting upon the Lord, and inducement as opposed to gift."[44]

Eschatological Passions and Bodily Practices

Speaking out of the tradition, Pentecostal scholar John Christopher Thomas reminds us that various scriptural narratives on healing make clear that the curse of the present age is multifaceted and complex.[45] Certain instances of illness are attributed to God who may use it to teach, to punish, or to spread the gospel. At other times, illness is attributed to the evil spirits (Luke 13:10–17) or shown to be an attack by "sinister forces" (e.g., snake bite on Malta in Acts 28:1–6). It can also be attributed to natural causes or "infirmity" wherein sickness is spoken of in neutral terms. Reflecting through these scriptural narratives, Pentecostals would consider the occurrences of healing in the "promise and fulfillment" trajectory. This is closely aligned with how Pentecostals believe that the promise of the Spirit's outpouring in Joel 2:28 was fulfilled on the day of Pentecost in Acts 2. Again, the Spirit's outpouring in Acts 2 was only a "foretaste" of the coming Kingdom of God. As a foretaste, the experience of Spirit-baptism yields an eschatological longing for the day when God will be "all in all." The fulfillment of the promise in Acts 2 becomes yet another promise that awaits its ultimate fulfillment at the final consummation of all things.

Likewise, Pentecostals understand and practice divine healing with a profound sense of eschatological longing. It is true that healing instances provide the fulfillment of what was promised of the redeeming power of Christ's atonement here and now. They represent only a promissory assurance that God can and will bring about the ultimate healing at the end. Pressing toward claiming the Full Gospel, Pentecostals see divine healing as experiencing the foreshadowing of the trumpet sound expected at the return of Jesus Christ. Divine healing provides for the believers "perceptible" (i.e., "to see, smell, and taste") traces of eternity's wholeness. Allan Anderson is right to note that, for

---

[43] Cross, "The Doctrine of Divine Healing," 195–97. Critiquing the movement, Cross notes that, for these evangelists, healing was "as simple as *deciding to be well*" (197).

[44] Land, "Pentecostal Spirituality," 27.

[45] For a discussion on the full range of healing and deliverance from the New Testament perspective, see John Christopher Thomas, *The Devil, Disease and Deliverance: Origins of Illness in New Testament Thought* (Cleveland, TN: CPT Press, 2010).

Pentecostals, healing represents "a holistic salvation that encompassed all of life's problems . . . the realization of the coming of the kingdom of God."[46]

For Pentecostals, healing makes explicit the correlation between Christ's redemption (Passover) and Christ's reign (Parousia). The scriptures that are usually referenced to support the doctrine and the practices of divine healing underscore this point. Scriptures such as Isaiah 53:4–5 and Matthew 8:16–17 clearly affirm the claim that Christ's redemptive suffering is the foundation for the present possibilities of healing, whereas other scriptural references such as Mark 16:17–18 and James 5:14–16 attest to the manifestation of the Kingdom's presence that effects divine healing. In the latter texts, the disciples of Christ and the early Christians alike are encouraged to lay hands on the sick and anoint them with oil. Of a particular note, all of the official statements of classical Pentecostal denominations appeal to James 5:14–16. This is the only text where we are given a description of a specific procedure to follow. It should be also noted, however, that the text carries a strong reminder of Christ's eschatological reign. Prior to verses 14–16, James repeatedly reminds the readers that the coming of the Lord is near (see vv. 7–11) and that they are to be patient in the face of suffering and persecution. Thomas thus rightly asserts: "the role of elders as representatives of the community, and the significance of the anointing itself all suggest that to anoint 'in the name of the Lord' meant to act in conformity to the Lord's directives and on his behalf as eschatological agents."[47]

With a strong eschatological impulse interlaced with their healing practices, Pentecostals engage in bodily (and ritual) practices that they consider being mandated in the Scriptures. It is of critical importance to Pentecostals that these bodily practices often take place at the altar where the saints are expected to pray and tarry in the Spirit. When healing occurs, it is then not merely a private affair of the individuals affected but an occasion to rejoice by the entire community of faith that participated in prayer. Land correctly observes: "They are healed together, and they rejoice together . . . there has always been an emphasis on healing as part of the ongoing, ordinary liturgy of the local body."[48] In and through healing, the individuals affected and the congregation are conjoined in prayer to experience together the inbreaking of the coming reign of Christ.

Prayer for the sick by anointing with oil and laying on of hands has been central to the Pentecostal practice of healing. Laying on of hands and the anointing with oil, as instructed in James 5 and elsewhere in Scripture, are often practiced together, although, in the absence of oil, one may simply lay hands on the sick. The laying on of hands is a

---

[46] Anderson, "Pentecostal Approaches to Faith and Healing," 525.

[47] Thomas, *The Devil*, 17–18. Thomas makes a compelling case for the eschatological emphasis in the James text as he discusses in detail the use of the phrase, "in the name of Jesus," in both Jas 5 as well as in Mark 6:12–13 where Jesus sends the Twelve to preach conversion and lay hands on and heal, all owing to nearness of the Kingdom of God.

[48] Land, "Pentecostal Spirituality," 485.

visible sign by which the whole faith community is being identified with the sick, for whom the prayer of faith is being offered. Pentecostals understand that the use of oil is largely symbolic in nature since the power to heal does not originate in the oil itself. Though symbolic it may be, its significance cannot be ignored. For Pentecostals, the anointing with oil is associated with the inauguration of the Kingdom of God. By anointing the sick with oil, believers are invoking the inbreaking of the Kingdom's presence here and now. The early Pentecostals also considered the Spirit-filled believers themselves as another visible means to effect divine healing.[49] In other words, as they lay hands on, anoint the sick with oil, and offer a "prayer of faith," the physical touch of Spirit-filled believers carries with it the significance of a "sacramental ordinance." It is a visible means that is understood to be efficacious when it is observed in faithful obedience to the scriptural mandate by the sanctified church.

The anointed handkerchief was another means of grace by which the sick may be healed. Oil was often used to anoint handkerchiefs so that they could be sent to the sick. Sometimes, sick individuals would send a handkerchief to the church to be anointed and returned. This practice was common among Pentecostals from Azusa Street in Los Angeles to those in the Appalachian Mountains of Tennessee and North Carolina, as well as some other parts around the world. William J. Seymour, the founder of modern Pentecostalism, offered the following report from the Azusa Street revival:

> The Lord is graciously healing many sick bodies. People are healed at the Mission almost every day. Requests come in for prayer from all over. They are presented in the meeting and the Spirit witnesses in many cases that prayer is answered, and when we hear from them they are healed. Handkerchiefs are sent in to be blest, and are returned to the sick and they are healed in many cases. One day nine handkerchiefs were blest, another day sixteen.[50]

Providing an exegetical study of Acts 19:11–12, where Paul's handkerchiefs and aprons were used to heal the sick and to cast out evil spirits, Thomas thus asserts that "observations about the superstitious nature of such a practice and questions about whether or not Paul gave his approval to this action miss the point that for the reader

---

[49] It is interesting to observe that, as to the question of "who" can lay hands and anoint the sick with oil, A. J. Tomlinson (the first presiding bishop of the Church of God) responded: "We do not consider that men who are ordained as ministers are the only ones to pray, but anybody can pray. And often a few of the members pray for the sick and anoint them with oil and the sick are healed just as well as when the minsters pray" (Alexander, "Three Hundred Years of Holiness and Healing," 70).

[50] *The Apostolic Faith*, January 1907, 1. Alexander cites a similar story found in *The Evangel*: "We pray for the sick every day, but on Sunday about 12:30 we have special prayer and every Sunday we have from twenty to forty handkerchiefs to pray over besides quite a number of requests. When this time comes, we spread the handkerchiefs out on the altar and the saints gather around and the prayers are offered upon in the earnestness of our souls. We are often reminded of the experience of the apostles when the sick folks were brought in on couches and beds and placed in the streets with a hope that even a shadow of Peter might fall upon them" (Alexander, "Three Hundred Years of Holiness and Healing, 71).

these events indicate the powerful presence of God in Paul's ministry."[51] In their use of anointed handkerchiefs, Pentecostals are demonstrating a complete dependence and trust in the power and presence of God who can and will heal the sick through the prayer of Spirit-filled believers.

Conclusion

As we examined Pentecostal beliefs and practices on healing, there seem to emerge some significant and unifying features. First, for Pentecostals, healing is closely associated with their salvation narrative. Healing is a *redemptive experience* insofar as its provision is grounded in the atonement of Jesus Christ. Believing in, and practicing, healing miracles is to affirm that the redemptive power of God is operative in the lives of believers yielding tangible evidence to trace. Second, healing attests to the holistic nature of God's salvation. As a visible demonstration of God's grace, healing miracles evidence that the salvation of God brings a holistic restoration of both one's soul and body. Third, Pentecostal healing takes a sanctificationist approach in which the divine work of God's grace is co-operant in nature. Inasmuch as healing represents the inbreaking of God's grace onto the broken realities of human life, grace induces and enables believers to participate in the work of God through their active faith in prayer. It is likened to how sanctification, for Pentecostals, involves both the provision of God's grace as the foundation but also our co-operation with, and response to, the enabling power of God in the Spirit. Fourth, like the experience of Spirit-baptism, healing in the Pentecostal tradition is characteristically eschatological in nature. For Pentecostals, healing miracles vivify their eschatological vision of the coming Kingdom of God. Pentecostals understand that any and all healing instances are temporary and provisional in nature; however, when they occur, they point to the ultimate healing anticipated at the eschaton. Each instance of healing then generates a crescendo effect to the sounding of the last trumpet that would usher in the coming reign of God and his Kingdom.

David Han (dhan@ptseminary.edu) is the Vice-President for Academics and the Dean of the Faculty at Pentecostal Theological Seminary, Cleveland, Tennessee, USA. He holds the faculty rank of Professor of Theology and Ray H. Hughes, Sr., Professor of Evangelism.

---

[51] Thomas, *The Devil*, 276. See further Martin W. Mittelstadt, "Nothing to Sneeze At: Receiving Acts 19:11–12 in the Pentecostal Tradition," in *Reading St. Luke's Text and Theology: Pentecostal Voices: Essays in Honor of Roger Stronstad*, ed. Riku Tuppurainen (Eugene, OR: Pickwick, 2019), 73–83.

Response to David Han's "Healing in the Pentecostal Tradition"

Andrew Prevot

The second phase of the exploratory dialogue between the PCCNA and the USCCB that took place at Oral Roberts University in Tulsa, Oklahoma, helped me appreciate many similarities between Pentecostal and Catholic approaches to healing. Although differences remain, I now see that our two Christian faith communities are much closer in their understanding of this theme than I had previously recognized. These similarities include worship of Christ as Healer; affirmation of a close connection between salvation and healing; reference to biblical passages such as James 5; a holistic approach that encompasses soul and body; an anticipation of final eschatological healing; and a set of ritual practices involving prayer, laying on of hands, and anointing with sacred oil. These similarities demonstrate a common faith in a saving God who rescues us from sin, suffering, and death and invites our active participation and cooperation in the work of sanctification.

David Han's essay encapsulates all of these theological points, while highlighting some of the distinctive features of the Pentecostal tradition. He gives a great overview of the historical roots of this tradition in Holiness and Wesleyan movements and very helpfully clarifies how a once-stark opposition between spiritual and medical forms of healing, which was salient in some early sources, has been significantly softened over time. Han's emphasis on the centrality of healing to Pentecostal experience is quite striking. His contention that healing may even rival glossolalia and Spirit-baptism in its level of importance prompts me to wonder whether the Catholic Church has placed enough emphasis on this essential aspect of Christ's saving work.

Put more positively, I think Catholics could benefit from further dialogue with Pentecostals on this topic. Through such conversation and relationship, Catholics could learn to be more attentive to the promise of healing that is an integral part of the gospel. Although some Catholics, particularly in the Catholic Charismatic Renewal, have incorporated faith healing into their everyday religious practice, this is not standard for all Catholics. The two traditional Sacraments of Healing—namely Anointing of the Sick and Penance or Reconciliation (which offers healing from sin)—are a regular part of Catholic ministry. These sacraments powerfully mediate the healing grace of Christ to suffering people in the Catholic Church, using prayers, touch, and oil in ways that resemble Pentecostal practice to some degree. Nevertheless, my sense is that many Catholics would do well to learn more about the biblical origins, subsequent developments, and profound meanings of these sacraments and to take greater advantage of them in their daily lives. Further Catholic-Pentecostal dialogue could, in this way, spur Catholics to gain a deeper understanding of vital aspects of their own sacramental tradition, even while helping them grow in knowledge and love of their Pentecostal brothers and sisters.

One curiosity I have is whether Pentecostal Christians will find any value in the Catholic emphasis on *fides et ratio* (faith and reason). More specifically, I am interested in the way this principle suggests a fundamental compatibility between healing practices that are rooted in Christian belief and those that are grounded in scientifically-backed medical practice. While Catholics arguably could and should increase their appreciation of faith-based healing, they have been keen to prioritize reason in their healing efforts and to recognize it as a gift from God. Many Catholics have been leaders in the fields of bioethics, social ethics, public health, and medicine. They have developed major healthcare institutions that serve the needs of diversely religious and secular populations. They have not regarded this work as something in tension with their faith but rather as one concrete means of authentically practicing it. An open question for me is to what extent Pentecostal traditions share this sense of a deep synergy between faith and reason, particularly in the domain of healing. Although Han points out that earlier views presupposing a contradiction between the two are no longer dominant, I am intrigued to see what a positive Pentecostal articulation of the faith-reason connection might look like.

Finally, I would like to comment on the practice of blessing handkerchiefs and using them as a conduit of healing grace, particularly in cases where a more direct physical laying on of hands or anointing with oil is not possible. This practice reminds me of the way many Catholics venerate the relics of saints, including even items of clothing. Our two traditions share a belief that some mode of sanctifying human presence is communicable through non-human, tangible objects. We both intuit that things that have been blessed by a holy person, someone doing Christ's work in the world, are able to hold and transmit some measure of Christ's saving power. In neither tradition is faith merely an intellectual activity. It is a holistic experience that includes the body, the community, and the surrounding world. Faith is expressed not only in words but in rich material cultures. It is a way of perceiving the "sacramentality" of things, to use a Catholic word. Learning more about the material cultures of Pentecostalism has been one of the great gifts of this dialogue for me.

In closing, I want to thank David Han for his highly illuminating and engaging paper. It opens up many fruitful avenues for further conversation between Pentecostals and Catholics. Moreover, although I am certain this was not its main purpose, it also offers a helpful nudge to Catholics, who might otherwise neglect the parts of their own tradition that affirm the healing power of Christ. Are Catholics sufficiently mindful of the fact that healing is one of the core motifs of the gospel? Have they really opened themselves to receive such grace in their lives? These are good questions for Catholics to ponder.

A Pentecostal Appreciation of Andrew Prevot's "Varieties of Healing: A Catholic Perspective"

Harold D. Hunter[1]

It is a privilege to respond to a paper with impeccable scholarship by a scholar who marshals incredible resources to advance the conversation. Andrew Prevot designed a brilliant theological scheme tailored to the Roman Catholic-Pentecostal exploratory dialogue in the USA. The footnotes alone are worth the price of admission, in this case reading the entire paper and then investing hours in unpacking this treatise.

This masterpiece also reveals many convergences between our two traditions in terms of theological intent. Pentecostals start with Scripture, and despite restorationist impulses among some early Pentecostals, we read patristic mothers and fathers in original languages, albeit with differing hermeneutics.

It is also difficult for Pentecostals to recognize what they see with their eyes on Sundays, illustrating a sharp contrast between the two traditions. Yet after first reading Prevot's paper, I needed a moment of silence to soak in the presence of the living God.

What follows are Pentecostal historical theological reflections. Sadly, it will not be possible to cover all the categories utilized in Prevot's article, not even social justice. References to Pentecostals intend to refer to Pentecostal churches that are members of PCCNA. Except for the predominantly African American Church of God in Christ, the core group goes back to PFNA.[2] All these churches self-identify as being less than 150 years old.

Prevot's opening volley calls on liturgical language that when contextualized sounds very Pentecostal. Setting aside Pentecostal evolving definitions of the phrase "healing in the atonement," global Pentecostal scholars rightly affirm a *via media*. Prevot's appropriation of Neil Ormerod is a welcome invitation.

---

[1] David Han was not available to respond to the paper by Andrew Prevot. It then became the responsibility of co-chair Harold Hunter to write this article.

[2] See Harold D. Hunter, "Attacking Systemic Racism for the Common Good: Excerpts from the 'Racial Reconciliation Manifesto,'" in *The Politics of the Spirit: Pentecostal Reflections on Public Responsibility and the Common Good*, eds. Daniela Augustine and Chris Green (Lanham, MD: Seymour Press, 2023), 39–50. This article explains why Church of God in Christ was deliberately shunned by white PFNA leaders.

Observers must realize that emphasizing Pentecost far too easily accounts for almost a monolithic story about the triumph of the resurrection rather than the trial of the cross. Although twentieth-century Pentecostals sang for hours hymns about the cross that moved everyone to tears, such teaching was primarily left to the likes of J. H. King, who wrote *From Passover to Pentecost* in 1914.

Even traditional Pentecostals who eschew the notion of a fixed liturgy much less *ex opere operato* sacraments can see, with the aid of theological translation, the pastoral intent of sacraments like Penance or Reconciliation and Anointing of the Sick.

Consider the nexus of mediated grace illustrated in the Pentecostal practice of anointed handkerchiefs and Roman Catholic relics. Oral Roberts' famous healing campaigns started with the established Pentecostal practice of "healing lines," where he laid hands on the heads of those who sought physical healing. When Roberts moved to a weekly television broadcast, he would invite those watching to touch their television as a point of contact.

Marie Griffith provides insights about Pentecostals anointing handkerchiefs for the physical healings of those who were unwell, like the following.

> Q. This also inverts our understanding of Protestants as having no forms of mediated grace.
>
> A. Yes, that is exactly what these objects were. Like saints and prayer cards in the Catholic tradition, the handkerchiefs were a manifestation of mediated grace. You see that in the letters people send to the periodicals after they receive them. This is just a typical letter of gratitude: "I received the letter with the anointed handkerchief and wonderful blessings I received after I placed one to my body. I surely do feel so much better." Writers explain how they took this object, put it to the part of the body that had been ill, and felt the healing taking place in their body just from using the handkerchief. The handkerchiefs are most important, but there are other objects of mediated grace. People often used the periodicals themselves. We have a lot of accounts of people praying and putting copies of these denominational newspapers on some part of their body that was ill and feeling the healing take place.[3]

---

[3] Marie Griffith, "Material History of Religion Project: Prayer Cloths," https://www.materialreligion.org/journal/handkerchief.html. See also *Diary of AJ Tomlinson: 1901–1924*, compiled by Hector Ortiz and Adrian Varlack (Cleveland, TN: White Wing Publishing House, 2012), 235, 236, 237.

"We were deprived of having the Assembly on account of the Influenza epidemic that has been raging for more than two months. Thousands and thousands have died of the plague. Some of our people succombed [sic] but not many."

"We have had cases in our home for about six weeks. Only Iris and Milton have been down of our own family, but six or more friends that came in and took down [sic]. I have prayed for at their homes as high as thirty a day. Many handkerchiefs have been prayed over and anointed sent to the sick." (November 13, 1918)

Charismatic Healing

I first attended Mass at age 19 while a student at a Pentecostal college in Cleveland, Tennessee. Nineteen-year-old me (1968), living in a closed community, could never have conceived that I would read about charismatic healing from a premiere Roman Catholic scholar in my lifetime. However, since the 1980s, I have participated in various international bilaterals with traditions that have also changed their trajectory in this regard.

After sharing a healing story associated with Mansfield, Prevot goes on to note that most Catholic "charismatic healers" value the work of physicians and clinicians. The International Church of the Foursquare Gospel's legendary Angelus Temple still has canes and crutches in its museum. Unfortunately, the debate among some early Pentecostals led to divisions of communities. One example is the 1921 creation of the Congregational Holiness Church break from the Pentecostal Holiness Church due, in part, to the question over the use of physicians and medications.

Miraculous Healing

Pentecostals who venerate twentieth-century founders are in no position to disparage the elevated place of Mary present among Eastern Orthodox and Roman Catholics. Pentecostal scholars affirm not only the virgin birth but also honor Mary as Theotokos.[4]

Pentecostals have been so anti-Roman Catholic as to allow slander from the pulpit fed by dispensational eschatologies that many fail to preach about what is right before their eyes in Scripture. Pentecostals must embrace Mary rather than tearing out pages from their Bibles that teach us about her. Pentecostals who have worn as a badge of honor being called "people of the book," wearing out multiple Bibles from frequent readings, must not simply erase what the biblical text says about Mary.

Some may scoff at stories of uncircumspect practices among Pentecostals related to testimonies of miraculous healing along with current Pentecostal leaders who would ignore them. However, these stories often illustrate a primitive faith in unusual circumstances that deserve not to be ridiculed due to cultural sensitivities. That is to say, the unusual means not unique in their circumstances were employed to enable their faith. In fairness to both traditions, the official positions of the churches and PCCNA

... "A few more students entered the Bible School. One of them, Mrs. Bennie Terrill, was taken sick about a week ago and only lived about four days. She died in our home." (December 27, 1918)

[4] Lisa P. Stephenson, "Truly Our Sister?: Pentecostal Readings of Mary," in *Receiving Scripture in the Pentecostal Tradition: A Reception History*, eds. Daniel D. Isgrigg, Martin W. Mittelstadt, and Rick Wadholm, Jr. (Cleveland, TN: CPT Press, 2021), 112–24. While Stephenson affirms Mary as a "Pentecostal sister," she notes the resistance of an average Pentecostal to any notion that Mary is responsible for the divinity of Jesus.

leaders do not support extreme deviations from the norm. It is worth noting that some of the criticism leveled at these cultural idiosyncrasies rivals what would have been associated with Roman Catholic relics.

Consider how a typical Pentecostal responds when they get to the sarcophagus under the high altar inside St. Peter's Basilica at the Vatican in Rome. The tourist guide suggests those bones might be those of St. Peter. The irony is lost on those Pentecostals who loudly protest and often turn around and venerate places associated with their founders.

On the other hand, this spotlights the Pentecostal schism between tradition and Tradition. It is so keen for Oneness Pentecostals who missed the Enlightenment that they continue to view Trinitarian dogma as primarily a post-apostolic development. In the face of Nicaea 2025 commemorations where we are reminded about those who challenge Empire, this is not a question just for Pentecostals.[5]

Biomedical Healing

Given the youth of Pentecostal churches, it is difficult to fairly judge the question of biomedical healing. When I lived in Oklahoma City, Oklahoma, I most often went to Mercy Hospital. However, when Andrew Prevot read his paper, he did so on the Oral Roberts University campus in full view of Oral Roberts' City of Faith in Tulsa, Oklahoma. I have been a patient at City of Faith and always stop to look at the "healing hands" of faith and science that stand tall at the entrance to ORU.

Remember also the Azusa St. Mission in Los Angeles. During the heat of the Azusa Street Revival, the Upper Room in Los Angeles, led by Elmer Fisher, boasted an African American physician. Another sister location included Dr. Henry Keyes. One cannot tell the Azusa story without referencing the Pisgah Homes founded by Dr. Finis E. Yoakum. Yoakum imbibed the ascending Pentecostalism spirituality while using medical training for biomedical healing and social justice. The practice of revivalist Pentecostals at that time was to pray around the clock at the bed of a seriously ill person and remain in place regardless of the outcome.

In terms of the question of contraception, some may not know about the early Pentecostal teaching of "marriage purity." On the one hand, a Pentecostal presiding bishop can join Roman Catholic hierarchs leading the March for Life in Washington, DC. However, one of the first murders of a physician who did abortions was gunned

---

[5] See Harold D. Hunter, "Contrasting Pentecostal Models of Apostolicity: Embrace or Erase the Council of Nicaea," at "Towards Nicaea 2025: Exploring the Council's Ecumenical Significance Today," WCC Ecumenical Institute at Bossey, November 4–8, 2024. For more about Nicaea 2025, see https://www.oikoumene.org/events/nicaea-2025.

down by a Pentecostal. This tragic episode occurred while it was being said of white Pentecostals in the USA that they were not active in the political sphere.

Ecological Healing

To Prevot's question about faith and reason, it may help to look at the numbers of Pentecostal ecologists who have embraced faith and science along with the Pentecostal universities and conferences that bring this intersection to life. The implications for the health of humans in a day of climate refugees from the Global South are obvious. It should come as no surprise that the Pentecostal surge starting no later than the 1950s now goes around the world led by indigenous peoples from the Global South.

During the exploratory phase of the Roman Catholic-Pentecostal dialogue in the USA, both traditions drew attention to their commitment to climate justice, including the degree program in global environmental sustainability at ORU. An echo of this reality is that Kimberley Belcher and Harold Hunter are formally part of the ecumenical effort to foster an annual festival called Season of Creation that runs from September 1 to October 4.[6] A May 2025 conference in Assisi involving not only the Laudato Si' Movement but also various Vatican dicasteries nicely links the Season of Creation events with Nicaea 2025 projects.[7] Hunter created and chairs the Pentecostal World Fellowship (PWF) Creation Care Task Force and is partnering with the WCC for various ecumenical Nicaea 2025 events and publications.

Publications about and activism for ecological healing among Pentecostals are growing. The president of PCCNA is David Wells. Wells is also the general superintendent of the Pentecostal Assemblies of Canada (PAOC). PAOC has formally adopted a statement about ecology and their commitment to refugees including those ravaged by global warming. Wells and Hunter represented the PWF in the 2021 Faith and Science series that brought together global leaders of all religions. The group met with Pope Francis at the Vatican on October 4, 2021, and delivered our message to His Eminence Alok Sharma, President of COP26. The first member church of the PCCNA to adopt a formal statement about ecology was the Church of God in Christ, having accomplished this in 2013.[8]

---

[6] See https://seasonofcreation.org/. See Jeffrey S. Lamp, *Geoliturgy and Ecological Crisis: The Spiritual Practice of Caring for Creation* (Lanham, MD: Lexington Books, 2024).

[7] While the Roman Catholic Church did not officially co-sponsor the Season of Creation event in Assisi 2024, it participated through various Vatican observers (Dicastery for Divine Worship, but also other dicasteries) and with contributors to the systematic theology panels (Dicastery for Doctrine of the Faith and International Theological Commission), as well as various continental bishops' conferences.

[8] Harold D. Hunter, "Pentecostal Climate Justice: Ecological Activism Meets Restitution," in *Pentecostal Missiology & Environmental Degradation*, eds. Eugene Baron and Amos Yong (Carlisle, UK: Langham Global, 2025).

ORU

APPLY FOR THE FALL PROGRAM

PhD IN THEOLOGY

ORU's College of Theology & Ministry is excited to invite qualified applicants to be a part of the next Cohort. Renowned for its "globally positioned" orientation, this degree explores the contextual theologies of global Christianity and the phenomenal growth and emerging scholarship within the global Spirit-empowered movement. It aims to equip scholars and practitioners to engage, impact, and expand the Spirit-empowered ethos and faithfully serve the Kingdom of God.

Among the teaching faculty of world-renowned scholars in Pentecostal/Charismatic Studies are:

Dr. Wonksu Ma   Dr. Julie Ma   Dr. Eric Newberg   Dr. Peter Althouse

For more information contact: phdtheology@oru.edu or visit http://www.oru.edu/phd

A Brief Consideration of the Sacrament of Marriage

from a Catholic Perspective for Pentecostal Christians

Walter F. Kedjierski

Spiritus 9.2 (2024) 253–271
https://doi.org/10.31380/ 2573-6345.1371
© The Author(s) 2024

Keywords *marriage, ecumenical, Catholic-Pentecostal, sacrament, "covenantal marriage," ritual*

Abstract

In this article Kedjierski attempts to highlight areas of convergence between Pentecostal and Catholic understandings of the covenant of marriage while at the same time explicating the divergences of their respective theologies of marriage. He begins with a personal testimony as to why it is important, particularly for Pentecostals and other Christians, to understand why the ritual associated with marriage is important to Catholics. Then he proceeds to explain the Catholic view of marriage as a sacrament that could be intelligible to Pentecostal audiences, including the place of the Holy Spirit in the ritual and living out of marriage. Subsequent to this explanation Kedjierski explores three ways in which marriage is unique among the sacraments in the Catholic Church and then concludes with a consideration of three challenges to living out Christian marriage today that impact both Catholic and Pentecostal congregations.

Contextualization

This dialogue of representatives from the Pentecostal Charismatic Churches of North America and the US Conference of Catholic Bishops now concludes its reflections on ritual/liturgy/sacraments with a consideration of the final traditional grouping of sacraments in Catholic theology, the "Sacraments of Vocation or Service." This topic connotes an emphasis on Christian discipleship that has been a constant ancillary theme throughout all of our discussions. All of our conversations have included respectful efforts by both Catholics and Pentecostals to aid each other in our attempts to follow the Lord Jesus in our contemporary contexts. Hence it is fitting to conclude this round of dialogues with a consideration of the sacraments that, according to a Catholic perspective, confer the grace necessary for discipleship in the context of two vocations: the vocation to formalized and official church service as a member of the clergy, and the vocation to serve the Church and the world as husband and wife in the context of what Catholics refer to as the domestic church, the family.

While Martin Mittelstadt has chosen to consider this topic as a whole, representing the Pentecostal tradition, Leonardo Gajardo and I have divided up the Sacraments of Vocation/Service, with Leo taking on the Sacrament of Holy Orders, leaving me to offer these brief reflections on the Sacrament of Marriage in the life of the Catholic Church. Although I am an ordained priest who has promised to live in celibate chastity as a way to proclaim the kingdom of God, I write this article from the perspective of one who not only has witnessed numerous marriage liturgies in my over twenty years of priestly service, but has also grown up in a Catholic Christian family and witnessed, as a son, the living out of the Sacrament of Marriage by my parents. I look forward to the dialogue that will aid me in widening my perspectives and humbly hope for an openness from others to ways in which this article might enrich their own awareness of other points of view.

Introduction

Much ink has been spilled by Catholic theologians and canonists on the ethics and canonical dimensions of marriage and human sexuality. Given the synthetic nature of Catholic belief and practice it is not possible to ignore these essential elements of a Catholic understanding of marriage, yet the major emphasis of this article will be on the overall topic of our dialogue, our understanding of ritual and sacraments, as they relate to marriage. This topic will be developed through a) a personal testimony that will underscore the importance Catholics place on the use of what the Church deems to be valid rituals for marriage; b) a basic explanation of a Catholic understanding of marriage as a sacrament; c) a consideration of three aspects of the Sacrament of Marriage that make it unique from the other sacraments; and finally d) a brief exploration of contemporary challenges the Catholic Church faces in regard to current practices related to marriage. This topic will surely be the impetus for a lively exchange.

Personal Testimony

Pentecostals generally find great value in personal testimony and witness to the working of God in the lives of Christians. Hence, I wish to begin this article with an account of a personal experience that impacted members of my family and demonstrates why it is important for Pentecostals and Christians from other traditions to recognize the importance Catholics place on the proper matter and form of the Sacrament of Marriage. My mother's parents met while working at factories in Detroit during the Second World War, both of them motivated by the war effort to do their parts for the nation. My grandmother was an active member of the Church of Christ in Tennessee, a daily Bible reader ardently in favor of her strand of the Stone-Campbell movement's prohibition of the use of instrumental music in worship. My grandfather, on the other hand, was a Brooklyn-born son of Italian immigrants and a nominally practicing Catholic. Soon after, they fell in love and were married before a Justice of the Peace. My grandfather moved back to Brooklyn with my grandmother and a promise that he would help her to keep in touch and visit her family down in Tennessee and Kentucky. Regrettably, early in their marriage my grandfather almost lost his life, and his family members urged my grandmother to call a priest to his side to offer him the last sacraments. Yet upon learning that my grandparents were not married with the blessing of the Church the priest called upon quickly left their home without offering any prayers. My grandfather did recover from his injuries, and then he and my grandmother approached the Church to seek a blessing on their marriage. The Catholic marriage of my grandparents did not take place with the pomp and circumstance usually associated with Catholic rituals. Instead, a very simple, quiet ceremony was held, not in the church building, but in the rectory, the office and home of the parish priests.

This was the ordinary manner in which the Catholic Church treated ecumenical couples before the expansion of horizon[1] precipitated by the Second Vatican Council's documents on the Church *(Lumen Gentium)* and Ecumenism (*Unitatis Redintegratio*) that enabled Catholics to develop a far more positive view toward relations with Christians of other denominations. Joseph Champlin, one of the most well-known authors of materials for couples preparing for their weddings in the Catholic Church,[2] has noted the progression of the manner in which ecumenical couples preparing for Catholic marriage have been treated, at least here in the United States.

> The celebration of interreligious or mixed marriages, i.e., the wedding of a Catholic and one who is not a Catholic, has undergone significant modifications within the past half-century. For example, in the 1940s, the exchange of vows took place in the rectory or outside the church, in the 1950s, such weddings might be celebrated in the church, but outside the sanctuary; in the 1960s these moved inside the sanctuary; in the 1970s, they might include a previously prohibited nuptial Mass and blessing. This gradual change represents the church's attempt to

---

[1] Bernard Lonergan's *Method in Theology* (Toronto: University of Toronto Press for Lonergan Research Institute of Regis College, Toronto, 1971) explains the epistemological concept of "horizon" and offers an accurate description of what one could consider the shift in emphasis in the Catholic Church with the Second Vatican Council on other Christian traditions and in fact the nature of dialogue with the outside world in general: "A vertical exercise [of freedom] is the set of judgments and decisions by which we move from one horizon to another. Now there may be a sequence of such vertical exercises of freedom, and in each case the new horizon, though notably deeper and broader and richer, none the less is consonant with the old and a development out of its potentialities" (237).

[2] Champlin authored a book entitled *Together for Life* that laid out the Second Vatican Council's revision of the marriage liturgy and enabled the couples to choose options for Scripture readings and prayers. My parents used the earliest version of this book for their wedding in 1971 and it is still, in a form that has been updated numerous times, used frequently.

balance two pastoral concerns: the church wishes to encourage marital unions in which both share the same faith and religious practice, but it also wishes to show great solicitude for the many couples who enter interfaith marriages.[3]

When I consider this event from my family's history, my thoughts regularly turn to how my grandmother must have interpreted the way they were treated by clergy from the Catholic Church. In the context of her faith tradition there was nothing unusual nor immoral about being married before a civil official. The walking out of that priest during the family's hour of need must have been a perplexing and heart-wrenching experience for her. By the grace of God matters have changed, and I do not believe there are any couples today who would experience what my grandparents experienced so many decades ago. Nevertheless, undoubtedly there are still some individuals alive today who carry emotional wounds associated with similar experiences. While the likelihood of being treated similarly is practically impossible (I hope) today there is great value to other Christians coming to appreciate and understand the importance Catholics still place on couples entering into marriages that have the recognition of the Catholic Church, and in the cases of those who are baptized, sacramental marriages.

Marriage as a Sacrament?

Admittedly, there have been moments in the historic relations between Protestants and Catholics when the notion of marriage as a sacrament was highly polemical, spanning back to the origins of church divisions in the sixteenth century.[4] Some of these polemics may have been rooted in distinct understandings of what constitutes a sacrament[5] and, despite some real theological divergences that remain (which in some

---

[3] Joseph Champlin, "Marriage," in *The New Dictionary of Sacramental Worship* (Collegeville, MN: The Liturgical Press, 1990), 800.

[4] Martin Luther repudiated the idea of marriage as a sacrament in his *The Babylonian Captivity of the Church* (1520) and in his *Small Catechism* (1529) described marriage as worldly business that the Church should not govern nor order but could subsequently bless. Meanwhile the Council of Trent declared: "If anyone says that matrimony is not truly and properly one of the seven sacraments of the evangelical law, instituted by Christ the Lord, but has been devised by men in the Church and does not confer grace, let him be anathema" and "If anyone says that the Church cannot establish impediments dissolving marriage, or that she has erred in establishing them, let him be anathema" (Twenty-Fourth Session).

[5] While the *Catechism of the Council of Trent* defines a sacrament, in accord with the writings of St. Augustine, as "a sign of a sacred thing" (De. Civ. Dei, lib. x. c. 5), and St. Bernard of Clairvaux as "a visible sign of an invisible grace, instituted for our justification" (Serm. De Coen. Dom. C. 2) (Rockford, IL: Tan Publishers, 1982). One should note that these definitions from Trent have undergone significant development since the sixteenth century. Philip Melanchthon defined sacraments as "rites, which have the command of God and to which the promise of grace has been added" (*Apology of the Augsburg Confession*) and John Calvin defined a sacrament as "an earthly sign associated with a promise of God" (*Institutes of the Christian Religion*).

cases might be more related to ecclesiology than sacramental theology), these past 500 years have brought with them greater clarity and the exposure of some merely linguistic differences as opposed to distinctions of belief. The language of marriage as "covenant" or "covenantal relationship" to describe Christian marriage is now readily accepted by most Protestant and Catholic theologians.[6] Instead of revisiting the controversies of the past, this section is going to develop how official Catholic teaching (limiting itself to the West although Eastern Christian theology also recognizes marriage as a sacrament) came to understand and embrace the marriage of baptized men and women as one of the seven sacraments of the Catholic Church.

There are clear indications from as early as the dawn of the second century that Christians understood marriage to be holy and, in some way, raised up by Christ from its purely natural state.[7] Marriage was the last of the seven sacraments to be designated as such by the Catholic Church.[8] The first indication of its official recognition as a sacrament is from the Council of Verona in 1184, considerably late in the two-thousand-year history of the Church. Two particular issues proved challenging to the Church's officially embracing marriage as a sacrament. The first was the influence of

---

[6] Catholic theologian Michael Lawler highlights the Catholic Church's official acceptance of the language of covenant in reference to marriage in its document on the Church in the modern world (*Gaudium et Spes*) in his book *Secular Marriage—Christian Sacrament* (Mystic, CT: Twenty-Third Publications, 1992): "Marriage is described in that Constitution as a 'community of love' (n. 47), an 'intimate partnership of conjugal life and love'" (n. 48). The council's position could not be clearer. In the face of strident demands to downplay the conjugal love of the spouses, it declared that love to be of the very essence of marriage. The intimate partnership of life and love is rooted in a "conjugal covenant of irrevocable personal consent" (n. 48). Again, when faced with demands to retain the juridical and Gasparian word *contract* as a precise way to speak of marriage, the council demurred, and chose instead the more biblical word *covenant.* This choice firmly locates marriage as a personal, rather than an exclusively legal, reality and brings it into line with the covenant relationship between Christ and his church. The interpersonal character of the marriage covenant is further underscored by the choice, again in the face of a chorus of demands to the contrary, of a way to characterize the formal object of the covenanting." Given the language of marriage as covenant is biblically rooted it is ubiquitous in Protestant scholarship. Protestant authors who have written on marriage as a covenant include Paul F. Palmer, "Christian Marriage: Contract or Covenant," *Theological Studies* 33:4 (1972), 639–65; Jack O. Balswick and Judith K. Balswick, *A Model for Marriage: Covenant, Grace, Empowerment and Intimacy* (Downers Grove: InterVarsity, 2006); Gary D. Chapman, *Covenant Marriage: Building Communication and Intimacy* (Nashville: Broadman & Holman, 2003); and the Episcopal *Book of Common Prayer* (New York: Seabury Press, 1979) states "Christian Marriage is a solemn and public covenant between a man and a woman in the presence of God" (422).

[7] "From the beginning the Fathers regarded marriage as a religious affair. St. Ignatius of Antioch (+ about 107) demands the cooperation of the Church in the contracting of marriage. 'It befits the bridegroom and the bride to enter the nuptial relationship with the approval of the bishop so that the marriage may be according to the Lord and not according to concupiscence' (Pl. 5, 2). Tertullian also attests that marriage was contracted before the Church: 'How shall I be able to describe the happiness of a marriage which the Church performs, the offering of the sacrifice ratifies, and the blessing seals, to which the angels assent, and which the Heavenly Father recognizes?'" (*Ad Uxoruem* II 9), taken from Dr. Ludwig Ott, *Fundamentals of Catholic Dogma* (Rockford, IL: Tan Publishers), 401.

[8] A. M. Roguet, *Christ Acts through the Sacraments* (Melbourne, Australia: Hassell Street Press, 2021), 126.

schools of thought that denigrated the material and flesh and the second was the question of whether or not Christian marriage actually involves a conferral of grace (which, to Catholics, is an essential quality of each of the seven sacraments).

Matthew Levering has acknowledged that a significant factor in the Church's discernment of the sacramentality of marriage "was the Church's reaction to the twelfth century spread of Catharist and Albigensian rejection of the goodness of marriage."[9] For those who reject the value of materiality, the goodness of an institution, which many times results in the co-creation of new, enfleshed life, is problematic. There were also strains of thought prior to the twelfth century that questioned the inherent goodness of marriage, such as St. Jerome's notion that marriage was established subsequent to the fall[10] and interpretations of 1 Corinthians 7 that taught Christian marriage is meant to be a kind of "concession" for those who are unable to control their concupiscence. Abstinence, therefore, was understood to be a more "spiritual," and hence, holier state.[11] Thus, inclusion of marriage among the sacraments of the Church emphasizes its divinely ordained goodness and combats Gnostic tendencies to reject the sacredness of the material. As David William Antonio has written, ". . . Matrimony is a way of cooperating in the love and work of God, the Creator. This theological concept has very important implications. It is a break with theology's earlier insistence on the tainting of marriage with sin."[12]

Peter Lombard (1096–1160) included marriage in his own account of the sacraments and defined it in this way: "the marital union [*coniunctio*] of a man and a woman, between legitimate persons, holding together an indivisible way of life."[13] In

---

[9] Matthew Levering, *Engaging the Doctrine of Marriage: Human Marriage as the Image and Sacrament of the Marriage of God and Creation* (Eugene, OR: Cascade Books, 2002), 200.

[10] St. Jerome would explain in his letter to Eustachia: "For you know that virginity is natural to man while marriage is a result of the fall, consider that marriage produces virgins, returning in the fruit what it has lost in the root" (Available at https://www.newadvent.org/fathers/3001022.htm). "Under the influence of Platonic spiritualism, St. Gregory of Nyssa (De opif. Hom. 17) declared the sexual differentiation of mankind, and the marriage which is founded on it, to be a consequence of sin, foreseen by God. St. Thomas rejected the teaching of St. Gregory (S. th. I 98, 2)." (Ludwig Ott, *Fundamentals of Catholic Dogma* [Rockford, IL: Tan Books and Publishers, 2013], 460).

[11] For example, "Tertullian does not understand 7:2 to be an approval of marriage but rather an indulgence. He argues the 'good' of marriage is undermined because it is preferable only in comparison to burning (7:9)." Meron Tekleberhan, "The Reception and Appropriation of 1 Corinthians 7:1–9 in Selected Ethiopic Texts," *Collectanea Christiana Orientalia* 12 (2015), 235. Contrast these negative views of marriage with the official Catholic teaching articulated by the *Catechism of the Catholic Church*: "Both the sacrament of Matrimony and virginity for the Kingdom of God come from the Lord himself. It is he who gives them meaning and grants them the grace which is indispensable for living them out in conformity with his will. Esteem of virginity for the sake of the kingdom and the Christian understanding of marriage are inseparable, and they reinforce each other" (1620).

[12] David William Antonio, *An Inculturation Model of the Catholic Marriage Ritual* (Collegeville, MN: The Liturgical Press, 2002), 8.

[13] Peter Lombard, "Treatise on Marriage," *Sentences,* Book IV.

the sixteenth century the *Catechism of the Council of Trent* would define the Sacrament of Marriage as "the conjugal union of man and woman, contracted between two qualified persons, which obliges them to live together throughout life."[14] Conspicuously, there is no mention of the conferral of grace in either of these definitions. This should lead one to ponder, why was there a struggle in the Church's history with understanding marriage as bearing Christ's grace to the couple and how was the ambiguity resolved?

An aspect of marriage that sets it apart from the other sacraments offers a reason why its grace has not always been at the forefront of the minds of theologians, which even led to some classifying marriage as a "lesser sacrament" than the rest.[15] This is the fact that marriage, unlike all of the other sacraments of the Church, is not a purely Christian phenomenon. Marriage existed before there were Christians and still exists in various forms in every human society. Theologian Bernard Häring once wrote, "I recognize marriage, then, first of all as a secular, earthly reality which Christians have in common with the inhabitants of our pluralistic world, even if we have not the same ideas about its origin and ultimate good."[16] Originally, the rituals Christians used to enter into marriage were officiated at by the civil authorities just like all other marriages of the time, and subsequently blessed by the clergy.[17] The Catholic Church has always recognized the legitimate rights of the state to regulate and register marriages due to their public, legal ramifications, such as the right to inherit property or access to health care information.[18] While acknowledging the secular dimensions of marriage, it would be incorrect to assume that Catholics believe that marriage was totally conceived and developed by human beings alone. *Gaudium et Spes* articulates this clearly:

> The intimate partnership of married life and love has been established by the Creator and qualified by His laws, and is rooted in the conjugal covenant of irrevocable personal consent. Hence by that human act whereby spouses mutually bestow and accept each other a relationship arises which by divine will and in the eyes of society too is a lasting one. For the good of the spouses and their offspring as well as of society, the existence of the sacred bond no longer depends on human

---

[14] *Catechism of the Council of Trent* (Rockford, IL: Tan Books and Publishers, 1982), 362.

[15] Philip L. Reynolds, *How Marriage Became a Sacrament* (Cambridge: Cambridge University Press, 2016), 8.

[16] Bernard Häring, *The Sacraments in a Secular Age: A Vision in Depth on Sacramentality and its Impact on the Moral Life* (Boston: St. Paul Publications, 1976), 185.

[17] As Häring observed, "Before the Council of Trent, the validity of a marriage between Christians was never made dependent on a certain canonical celebration. When the Church evangelized the ancient world, she did not change the customary form of marriage, but she was present with the light, the comfort and the pedagogy of the Gospel, and with her prayer and support" (*Sacraments in a Secular Age*, 198).

[18] "The state is entitled to regulate the purely civil legal consequences of the contract of marriage (right of name and state, marital rights of property, right of inheritance), and to settle disputes about these matters" (Ott, *Fundamentals of Catholic Dogma*, 469). Refer to the 1917 *Code of Canon Law* canon 1016.

decisions alone. For God Himself is the author of matrimony, endowed as it is with various benefits and purposes.[19]

The Creator authored marriage as a means whereby husband and wife are invited to live more fully in the image and likeness of their Creator: "In the design of the Creator, matrimony has always, in all time and all places, had this fundamental sacramental value of freeing the human person from isolation, from imprisonment in selfishness, and committing him or her to the main dynamic of history, which is the growth of love and discernment."[20]

How did the Catholic Church come to understand that through the Sacrament of Marriage Christ confers grace on the couple? Scripturally, Paul's letter to the Ephesians, chapter 5, has been claimed as a foundational text to understanding marriage as a sacrament, especially given Paul's use of the word μυστήριον, translated into the Latin *sacramentum*. While it is true that prelates like Cardinal Donald Wuerl have gone so far as to claim that St. Paul referred to marriage as a "sacrament,"[21] at the same time one should be cautious about assigning contemporary understandings of terms to ancient texts. Catholic theologians of the past many times emphasized the term "mystery" as referring to marriage itself, while Protestant theologians instead emphasized the term referring to the relationship of Christ with the church. Scripture scholar Margaret Y. MacDonald reminds us that such interpretations need not be mutually exclusive:

> There is some uncertainty as to what exactly constitutes the mystery here. Does it refer to marriage between man and woman, only to Christ and the church, or to both? The apparent lack of clarity may be due to the close association between the two in the author's own mind. Given the use of the marriage metaphor throughout 5:22–33, it seems best to assume that the term "mystery" encompasses both human marriage (seen as a reflection of divine reality) and the relationship between Christ and the church.[22]

Paul, more than likely influenced by the plethora of marital imagery in the Old Testament related to the Lord's relationship with Israel, believed that married Christian couples are called to symbolize and proclaim with their lives the relationship of Christ with the church. Undoubtedly, it would be impossible for human beings to fulfill this calling without an abundance of God's grace.[23] Jesus' prohibition of divorce in

---

[19] ¶ 48.

[20] Häring, *Sacraments in a Secular Age*, 188.

[21] Donald Wuerl, *The Marriage God Wants for You: Why the Sacrament Makes all the Difference* (Frederick, MD: Word Among Us Press, 2015), 39.

[22] Margaret Y. MacDonald, *Colossians/Ephesians,* Sacra Pagina Series (Collegeville, MN: The Liturgical Press, 2000), 331.

[23] Cardinal Ouellet offers this fine explanation: ". . . because the sacraments effect that of which they are made signs, one must believe that in this sacrament a grace is conferred on those marrying, and

Matthew 19:10 is another indication of the special grace necessary for Christian marriage:

> The alarmed protest of Jesus' disciples against his strict doctrine (Matt 19:10) shows that a special grace is needed for people to live out the truth of Christian marriage. This special grace, Jesus implies, will come to those who have married each other as Christians, that is, within the context of the inaugurated kingdom, the Church. Since people will need a special grace to live out marriage in the way that Jesus intends it to be, Christians who marry will receive this grace.[24]

How exactly does this grace work in the lives of the couples? The *Catechism of the Catholic Church* describes it in this way: "Christ dwells with them, gives them strength to take up their crosses and so follow him, to rise again after they have fallen, to forgive one another, to bear one another's burdens, to 'be subject to one another out of reverence for Christ,' and to love one another with supernatural, tender and fruitful love."[25]

The Catholic Church's marriage rituals have undergone numerous revisions throughout recent centuries amidst calls for the grace of the sacrament to be clearly signified and the duties of the spouses to be more emphasized.[26]

> In the judgment of the [Second Vatican] Council Fathers, the Roman Rite promulgated by Pope Paul V in 1614 and still in use before the council did not adequately express the grace of the sacrament and the obligation of the spouses in spite of the modifications introduced by Popes Benedict XIV (1752), Pius IX (1872), Leo XIII (1884), Pius XI (1925) and Pius XII (1952). It was considered too juridical in orientation since it viewed marriage primarily as a contract.[27]

One of the recent developments in theology that precipitated a more explicit connection to the conferral of grace in the ritual has been a greater emphasis on the importance of pneumatology in our understanding of the sacraments:

> . . . the rediscovery of the Holy Spirit in Western theology opens new perspectives for sacramental theology in general and the theology of marriage in particular. The concern to establish the divine institution of the sacrament in the explicit, historical will of Christ in fact resolves a forgetfulness of the Spirit that has

---

that by this grace they are included in the union of Christ and the Church, which is most especially necessary to them, that in this way, in fleshly and earthly things, they may purpose not to be disunited from Christ and the Church." See Marc Ouellet, *Mystery and Sacrament of Love: A Theology of Marriage and the Family for the New Evangelization* (Grand Rapids, MI: William B. Eerdmans Publishing Company, 2015), 50.

[24] Levering, *Engaging the Doctrine of Marriage*, 205.

[25] ¶ 1642.

[26] *Sacrosanctum Concilium*, "The Constitution on the Sacred Liturgy," *Documents of the Second Vatican Council*, 77.

[27] Antonio, *An Inculturation Model of the Catholic Marriage Ritual*, 1–2.

impoverished the theology of the sacraments in the West. The Holy Spirit's role is precisely that of confirming and universalizing the whole truth of Christ. This mission of the Spirit consists in causing the Church, Christ's body and bride, to co-exist as his "helpmate" in giving life to the world.[28]

Liturgically, at the nuptial Mass, which is the rite clearly preferred by the Church for Catholics to enter into the Sacrament of Marriage,[29] a triple epiclesis is invoked. The first and second, which occur at every Catholic Mass, are the invocation of the Holy Spirit over the gifts of bread and wine, that "they may become for us the Body and Blood of Christ," and another over the people, that by partaking of the gifts they might also be transformed into the Body of Christ, bringing his presence to the world. These are found in the Eucharistic prayers. The third epiclesis, which is particular to the nuptial Mass, is invoked over the husband and wife during the nuptial blessing. David William Antonio notes:

> In speaking of the modifications introduced in 1991 on the formulas of the nuptial blessing . . . [the] more significant change is the addition of an epiclesis, not only to underline the indispensable role of the Holy Spirit but also to transform this formula into a genuine epicletic prayer. This is intensified by the kneeling posture of the spouses and the extension of hands by the ordained presider over them.[30]

The epicletic elements of the nuptial blessing are expressed in the prayers of the rite in these ways:

> Look now with favor on these, your servants, joined together in Marriage, who ask to be strengthened by your blessing. Send down on them the grace of the Holy Spirit and pour your love into their hearts, that they may remain faithful in the Marriage covenant. May the grace of love and peace abide in your daughter (n), and let her always follow the example of those holy women whose praises are sung in the Scriptures. May her husband entrust his heart to her, so that, acknowledging her as his equal and his joint heir to the life of grace, he may show her due honor and cherish her always with the love that Christ has for his Church.[31]

> May your abundant blessing, Lord, come down upon this bride (n), and upon (n), her companion for life, and may the power of your Holy Spirit set their hearts aflame from on high, so that, living out together the gift of Matrimony, they may be known for the integrity of their conduct and be recognized as virtuous parents.[32]

---

[28] Ouellet, *Mystery and Sacrament of Love*, 27.

[29] *Sacrosanctum Concillium*, 78.

[30] Antonio, *An Inculturation Model of the Catholic Marriage Ritual*, 68.

[31] *Order of Celebrating Matrimony*, 73.

[32] *Order of Celebrating Matrimony*, 209

> Graciously stretch out your right hand over these your servants (N. and N.) we pray, and pour into their hearts the power of the Holy Spirit.[33]

It is also interesting to note that in the case of the ritual used in what is considered a non-sacramental marriage, the Holy Spirit is still invoked upon the couple: ". . . may the power of the Holy Spirit set their hearts aflame from on high . . . ."[34] Hence just because a marriage might not be considered "sacramental" does not mean Catholics believe that the Holy Spirit is necessarily absent from it. This brief survey into the challenges to the Catholic understanding of marriage highlights how through the centuries the Church has come to more clearly understand and express it as a sacrament.

The Essentials of the Sacrament of Marriage

Although the emphasis on the Holy Spirit just mentioned is a welcome addition to the rite that more clearly articulates how marriage is grace-filled, the decision to incorporate an epiclesis into the nuptial blessing was not devoid of some controversy. Liturgical theologian Adrian Nocent wrote about his concern that this incorporation of an epiclesis into the nuptial blessing might make it appear as if the nuptial blessing is an essential moment in the Rite of Marriage for the sake of its validity.[35] Such an idea would be a departure with Western Christianity's understanding of what to Roman Catholics is the essential matter and form of marriage. This begs the question, what to the Catholic mindset is essential for the Sacrament of Marriage?

The *Catechism of the Catholic Church* succinctly describes what is essential for the couple to enter into a marriage: "The Church holds the exchange of consent between the spouses to be the indispensable element that 'makes the marriage.' If consent is lacking there is no marriage."[36] While the blessing of a member of the clergy and the expression of the outpouring of grace by the Holy Spirit are cherished by Catholics, ordinarily sought out and not to be omitted in Catholic rites,[37] what is essential for a marriage to take place in the Roman Catholic Church is the expression of consent of the couple. Of course, this consent needs to be freely given. Any form of coercion would render the marriage invalid. Another important point for validity is that the individuals who contract marriage must be free to marry. The canonical basis for determining freedom to marry is outside of the scope of this article but could certainly be included in further discussion.

---

[33] *Order of Celebrating Matrimony*, 207.
[34] *Order of Celebrating Matrimony*, 139.
[35] Adrian Nocent, "La nouvelle edition du ritual du marriage," *Ecclesia Orans* 8 (1991), 330–34.
[36] ¶ 1626.
[37] *Order of Celebrating Matrimony*, 24, 34, 42.

Catholics understand that while some marriages are sacramental there are other marriages that are certainly legitimate unions yet not sacramental. What is it that Catholics understand makes marriage a sacrament? The *Code of Canon Law* specifies it:

> The matrimonial covenant, by which a man and a woman establish between themselves a partnership of the whole of life and which is ordered by its nature to the good of the spouses and the procreation and education of offspring, has been raised by Christ the Lord to the dignity of a sacrament between the baptized. For this reason, a valid matrimonial contract cannot exist between the baptized without it being by that fact a sacrament.[38]

Hence, when a man and a woman, as baptized Christians, choose to enter into the covenant of marriage, should they do so in a valid manner, Catholics understand their marriages to be a sacrament. "Since they have already been baptized, they already participate in Christ's filiation in the Spirit; but now they participate as a couple, as the union of man and woman, in the community of the Trinity, which is essentially one, fruitful and indissoluble."[39] A baptized person and an unbaptized person, or two unbaptized persons, can certainly enter into a legitimate marriage but given Catholics understand baptism to be the gateway to the other sacraments those marriages are not technically considered sacramental.[40]

Contemporary society espouses a multiplicity of views on forms of family life and definitions of marriage. In the above quotation Cardinal Ouellet makes note of the three Augustinian principles about marriage that have been maintained as a part of the Catholic Church's understanding of marriage for many centuries. Augustine's treatise, *On the Goods of Marriage,* describes three necessary elements: *proles, fides, and sacramentum*—procreation, fidelity, and the sacrament.[41] More contemporary language used by Catholics renders these terms as: openness to children, unity, and indissolubility. In the *Rite of Marriage,* before the bride and groom offer their consent, they are ceremonially asked if they agree to accept Augustine's three elements of the "good of marriage":

---

[38] Canon 1055.

[39] Ouellet, *Mystery and Sacrament of Love*, 63.

[40] Antonio also offers a good explanation of the importance of the baptismal identities of those entering into marriage: "By reason of baptism, the sacrament of faith, a man and a woman are once and for all brought into the covenant between Christ and the Church, so that their marital communion is assumed into Christ's own love and enriched by the power of his sacrifice. As a sacrament of initiation, baptism radically inserts us into the mystery of the covenant relationship between Christ and the Church. In marriage the couple acts out of the covenantal relationship already established in baptism. This is the so-called baptismal foundation of marriage. The reason why marriage is a sacrament is that it is the act of two persons who through baptism have already entered the paschal and covenantal relationship with Christ. The universal call to holiness is given concrete expression in marriage" (*An Inculturation Model of the Catholic Marriage Ritual*, 9–10).

[41] Augustine, *De bon. coni.* 28.32.

N. and N., have you come here to enter into Marriage without coercion, freely and wholeheartedly? [unity – the couple is freely choosing to unite]

Are you prepared, as you follow the path of Marriage, to love and honor each other for as long as you both shall live? [indissolubility]

Are you prepared to accept children lovingly from God and to bring them up according to the law of Christ and his Church? [openness to children][42]

These questions, publicly asked by the officiant during the liturgy, would have already been asked privately when the bride and groom were given their mandatory prenuptial investigation to determine their freedom to marry. That moment of preparation is an opportunity not only to engage in a technical interview but is also a pastoral outreach to the couple, an attempt to aid its discernment of entering into such a serious, lifelong commitment. The questions manifest a Catholic view of the nature and purpose of marriage to all present and a public testimony of the couple's personal belief in the nature of Christian marriage.

Three Aspects of Marriage That Make It a Unique Sacrament

One of the ways in which one can come to better understand a Catholic view of marriage as a sacrament is to isolate those qualities that make marriage unique from the other six. While this is not an exhaustive list, and the Catholic theologians present might wish to bring up others in the conversation, this article will confine itself to three distinct aspects of marriage as a sacrament.

1. From the Secular to the Sacred

It was previously acknowledged that marriage stands out from the other sacraments in as far as it existed as a non-sacramental reality since the dawn of creation. How, therefore, did this pre-Christian reality take on a sacramental character? To begin with an image, directly across from St. Peter's Basilica in Rome one finds an Egyptian obelisk brought to Rome by the Emperor Caligula in AD 37. The obelisk is crowned with a metal cross that an old tradition says contains relics of the true cross of Christ. This method of taking realities and/or traditions outside of Christianity and "Christening" them was a regular part of early church life. Some scholars suggest that traditions such as the celebration of Christmas at the end of December may have had their roots in pagan festivals. The basilicas of ancient Rome like the Pantheon, which were formerly used to honor pagan gods and goddesses, were transformed into places of Christian worship. The sacraments have in and of themselves this principle of the ordinary being transformed for a far higher purpose. Water is consecrated and used in baptism and

---

[42] *Order of Celebrating Matrimony*, 60.

bread and wine in the Eucharist. Marriage falls in line with a civil union becoming something far more meaningful and sanctifying in light of Christ's presence in the lives of the couples.

One can discern how the Church came to recognize that Christ instituted the state of marriage as a sacrament, taking a former reality and transforming it into something renewed, through a brief survey of some of the Scripture texts of the New Testament related to marriage. A text that is frequently used at Catholic marriage liturgies describes the sign of the changing of water into wine by Jesus at the wedding feast of Cana.[43] Through the transformation of the water used for Jewish ceremonial washing into the festive wine, which could be understood as an allusion to the Eucharist as well as the festive rejoicing to be found in the kingdom of God, one could find an intimation to how Christ builds upon the Jewish roots of marriage to create a Christian institution. This brings to mind a related passage of Scripture when Jesus was challenged by the Scribes and Pharisees about the legality of divorce.[44] In this passage Jesus says: "Because of the hardness of your hearts Moses allowed you to divorce your wives, but from the beginning it was not so. I say to you, whoever divorces his wife (unless the marriage is unlawful) and marries another commits adultery." There has been a longstanding interpretation of this passage in the Catholic tradition related to Jesus returning marriage to what God originally designed marriage to be. Cardinal Ouellet explains:

> As a consequence of sin, the sacred institution of marriage was not always respected in the history of the Old Testament. From the time of the patriarchs and the spread of polygamy, Scripture records innumerable transgressions against the holiness of marriage (Gen. 16:1–4; Sam. 1:6; Deut. 21: 15–17). King David, though highly praised in the Bible, had his harem (2 Sam. 16: 20–22) as did Solomon (1 Kings 11:1–13).[45]

Catholic teaching contends that Jesus fully restored marriage to its original dignity and instituted it as a sacrament.[46] John Paul II described it in this way:

> The communion between God and his people finds its definitive fulfillment in Jesus Christ, the Bridegroom who loves and gives himself as the Savior of humanity, uniting it to himself as his body. He reveals the original truth of

---

[43] John 2:1–12.

[44] Matt 19:1–10.

[45] Ouellet, *Mystery and Sacrament of Love*, 34.

[46] Regarding the idea of Christ instituting the Sacrament of Marriage, Cardinal Ouellet makes this important point: "Vis-à-vis the scholastic tradition, contemporary theology understands the institution of the sacraments from a new angle. Christ is the author of the sacraments, but not because he specified in detail the matter and form of each sacrament. The institution of the particular sacraments appears today, rather, as fundamentally present in the birth of the Church from the paschal mystery" (Ouellet, *Mystery and Sacrament of Love*, 27).

marriage, the truth of the "beginning," and, freeing man from his hardness of heart, he makes man capable of realizing this truth in its entirety.[47]

Christian marriage becomes distinct from any other form of marriage, because the first relationship husband and wife enter into, through their baptisms, is their relationship to Christ. Subsequent to receiving the Sacrament of Marriage, they relate to Christ, not as individuals, but together as a couple united in him.

2. Marriage Can Become Sacramental without Use of the Marriage Ritual

Catholic marriage rites are used when at least one member of the couple is a baptized Catholic. As was previous mentioned, any validly contracted marriage between a baptized man and a baptized woman is considered by Catholics to be sacramental. In those instances when a baptized person and unbaptized person marry, or two unbaptized persons marry, the marriages they enter into are not considered sacramental. However, should the unbaptized persons choose Christ and become baptized, even without the use of a marriage ritual, their marriages instantaneously become sacramental. This is a very unique quality of the Sacrament of Marriage that demonstrates its connection to the Sacrament of Baptism.

3. Bride and Groom as Ministers of the Sacrament

Quite particular to the Sacrament of Marriage in Roman Catholic theology is the notion that the proper minister of the sacrament is not the clergy who officiate but the husband and wife. The officiant functions in the role of an official witness of the Church. One of the reasons for the Catholic Church becoming involved in regulating and recording marriages was to remedy the problems associated with widespread clandestine marriages before the Council of Trent, which led to individuals, particularly women, being deprived of rights to property and inheritance, and the legitimacy of children being questioned, due to no proof of the marriages taking place.[48] The liturgy is a public event[49] filled with witnesses. The responsibility of the officiant is, on behalf of the Church, to "receive the consent," in other words, to ensure that the couple freely and properly offers their consent to enter into what bride and groom understand to be a

---

[47] *Familiaris Consortio*, 13.

[48] More information on this can be found in Jutta Sperling's article "Marriage at the Time of the Council of Trent (1560–70): Clandestine Marriages, Kinship Prohibitions, and Dowry Exchange in European Comparison," *Journal of Early Modern History* 8:1–2 (2004), 67–108.

[49] Although there are certain rare circumstances in which Canon Law allows for the "secret celebration of marriage" there are still requirements for the recording of the marriage so that there is some type of proof that it was contracted.

Christian marriage. No one else has the right to give the bride's or groom's lives to anyone else; husband and wife must do so themselves. Given that the husband and wife are the ministers of the Sacrament of Marriage, the Catholic Church even permits them, under extreme circumstances (including the absolute impossibility of securing a member of the clergy or laity authorized by the bishop) to marry each other without an officiant, provided that at least two witnesses are present.[50] This is in major contrast with Eastern Christianity, which understands the minister of the Sacrament of Marriage to be an ordained priest.

These three points, marriage has been transformed by Christ into a sacrament, marriage can become sacramental without use of the marriage ritual, and the bride and groom are the ministers of the Sacrament of Marriage, make Holy Matrimony a unique sacrament in the life of the Catholic Church.

Challenges

As we conclude this consideration of the Sacrament of Marriage from a Catholic perspective, this article will present four contemporary challenges. Once again, this is not an exhaustive list, and our discussion could expose other areas that some might consider to be even more important challenges than the ones I will bring up to conclude this brief survey.

1. Helping Couples Understand Marriage Is Not Just a Day, It Is a Lifetime

Although one can clearly observe that the Rite of Marriage is sacred, most especially because it is conferred in a church setting, couples should recognize the entirety of their married lives as sacred. The Sacrament of Marriage is not only meant to be received, it is meant to be lived by both husband and wife. John Paul II described the importance of this contention well:

> . . . the gift of Jesus Christ is not exhausted in the actual celebration of the sacrament of marriage . . . just as husbands and wives receive from the sacrament the gift and responsibility of translating into daily living the sanctification bestowed on them, so the same sacrament confers on them the grace and moral obligation of transforming their whole lives into a "spiritual sacrifice."[51]

The faithfulness and fidelity of married couples signifies the faithfulness and fidelity of Christ to his bride, the Church. Marriage is a sacrament that is "lived into," one in which the couples continue to grow in holiness as they exchange self-sacrificial,

---

[50] Canon 1116.

[51] *Familiaris Consortio*, 56.

Christ-like love with each other. Husband and wife carry the graces of the sacrament with them every day of their married lives. Cardinal Ouellet points out how Pope Pius XI compared the grace of the Sacrament of Marriage, which remains with the couple throughout their married lives, to the Eucharist, which, according to Catholic belief, remains the Body and Blood of Christ well after the celebration of the liturgy:

> Bellarmine was cited in a key passage of *Casti Cannubii,* where Pope Pius XI compares the visible sacramental sign of marriage to the Sacrament of the Eucharist. In the Eucharist, the real presence continues under the sacred species, even after the celebration of Mass; similarly, the grace acquired during the wedding celebration continues under the species of the married life even after the celebration is over.[52]

This invocation of a relatedness to the Eucharist is a powerful reminder of the presence of God in the Sacrament of Marriage. Hence it is most appropriate that after the consent of two baptized Catholics in which they become husband and wife, the first action of the newly married couple is sharing at the table of the Lord in the Eucharist. The Eucharist is the food for their journey together as husband and wife as they live out the Sacrament of Marriage.

2. The "Baptized Unbeliever"

At times Pentecostals might find it perplexing that some Catholics lack fervor or knowledge of even the basics of the faith. A situation that poses a particular quandary for Catholic theology, what one might even call a theological oxymoron, is the "baptized unbeliever." There are Catholics who consider the faith as an element of their cultural identity as opposed to a phenomenon that is meant to offer direction to their whole lives. While many have different theories as to why this is such a widespread reality in Catholic circles there is none who can question this fact. These individuals who are baptized, and yet may not actively practice their faith or find meaning in it, unless they formally renounce their faith, have an obligation to be married in the Catholic Church (as was mentioned at the beginning of this article). At the same time, however, there is an important sacramental principle that it is essential to have faith in order to receive God's grace.[53] When the bride and groom approach the Church for

---

[52] *Familiaris Consortio,* 68.

[53] A good exploration of this issue was made by the International Theological Commission, "The Reciprocity Between Faith and the Sacraments in the Sacramental Economy," 3 March 2020, www.vatican.va. Pope Benedict XVI said: "Marriage is linked to faith, but not in a general way. Marriage, as a union of faithful and indissoluble love, is based upon the grace that comes from the triune God, who in Christ loved us with a faithful love, even to the Cross. Today we ought to grasp the full truth of this statement, in contrast to the painful reality of many marriages which, unhappily, end badly. There is a clear link between the crisis in faith and the crisis in marriage. And, as the Church has said and witnessed for a

marriage, if they are baptized, it is presumed that they have some type of faith. Unfortunately, it is sometimes due to social pressure that they choose to have their weddings in the Church. I am not suggesting that one should judge the faith of the couples, but there have been some who have been honest enough to openly admit this to their clergy. Perhaps it would be wise at some point to include in marriage preparation a greater emphasis on the central role of faith and one's relationship with Christ to Christian marriage. To assist with this, in addition to the usual marriage preparation, the priest or deacon might inquire about their views of the faith and its importance in their lives, as well as make greater efforts to evangelize those couples who find the gospel foreign to their experience.

3. "Lack of Due Discretion"

The third challenge I offer for our reflection is that at this point approximately 50 percent of Catholic marriages, in line with the rest of society, do not end with the death of one of the spouses. When those who seek to remarry in the Catholic Church appeal to church tribunals in order to secure an annulment, the vast majority of declarations of nullity are granted due to a "lack of due discretion" on the part of the groom, the bride, or at times both. This situation should cause the Catholic Church to pause and discern how to better educate couples on the rights, duties, and obligations of marriage. It may be that secular mentalities about marriage, especially questioning the possibility of making a life-long commitment, are so ubiquitous in our society that they are having an influence on couples preparing for marriage who may not even be conscious of this reality. Perhaps a greater emphasis on the theology of marriage, more time to discern with the couple the obligations they are about to undertake, and even a more vigorous insistence that couples delay their marriages until they demonstrate the necessary maturity to enter into marriage, could assist with this challenge. An effort has been made by the Dicastery of Laity, Family and Life to facilitate such an emphasis. In June 2022 it released a document entitled "Catechumenal Pathways for Married Life,"[54] which models marriage preparation after the process of Christian initiation. It suggests the use of three stages in the preparation of couples for marriage: evangelization and discipleship, accompaniment, and catechesis. While such practices might not be popular with couples preparing for marriage due to the commitment of their time

---

long time now, marriage is called to be not only an object but a subject of the new evangelization." "Holy Mass for the Opening of the Synod of Bishops and Proclamation of St. John of Avila and of St. Hildegard of Bingen as 'Doctors of the Church,'" 7 October 2012, https://www.vatican.va/content/benedict-xvi/en/homilies/2012/documents/hf_ben-xvi_hom_20121007_apertura-sinodo.html).

[54] Available at http://www.laityfamilylife.va/content/dam/laityfamilylife/amoris-laetitia/OrientamentiCatecumenatomatrimoniale/Catechumenal%20Pathways_ENG.pdf.

during an already busy moment of their lives it could save them a great deal of pain later.

4. Ecumenical and Interreligious Marriages

The final challenge for our reflection brings us back to the beginning of the article, the greater frequency of "mixed marriages"—marriages between Christians of different denominations or even between Christians and individuals of other faith traditions. The Catholic Church, as a faithful mother to her children, requires Catholics to exchange consent in a certain way. As has been demonstrated, this is because as the baptized, their commitment to each other impacts their commitments to Christ. They are called to relate to Christ as a couple. Due to challenges in the past, i.e., clandestine marriages, this requirement is taken most seriously. Yet for those who are not in the Catholic Church this can seem a foreign concept. Catholics should seek to better educate themselves and their non-Catholic partners on these practices and help them to understand the reasoning and history behind it. Doing so will only help to make the Sacrament of Marriage a truly grace-filled pathway to richer discipleship in Christ. Perhaps couples who live out their relationships to Christ together, as Pentecostal and Catholic wife and husband, might offer our faith communities the riches of their experiences to give even greater depth to dialogues like this one.

Walter F. Kedjierski (wkedjierski@drvc.org) is Executive Director of the Secretariat for Ecumenical and Interreligious Affairs for the US Conference of Catholic Bishops in Washington, DC, USA.

The definitive history of the Wesleyan movement in the United States

An expansive, substantive history of the Wesleyan tradition in the United States, *Doctrine, Spirit, and Discipline* offers a broad survey of the Methodist movement as it developed and spread throughout America, from the colonial era to the present day.

In the midst of the sweeping changes happening in Methodism and the pan-Wesleyan movement today, Watson shows that the heart of the Wesleyan theological tradition is both more expansive and substantive than any singular denominational identity.

"Promises to be a standard textbook on the history of Methodism for years to come."
TIMOTHY C. TENNENT

"An accessible and engaging account of the history of Methodism in the United States."
SCOTT T. KISKER

"The standard... work for everyone who wants a better understanding of the Wesleyan tradition."
KENNETH G. HODDER

"An insightful and inspirational exposition of our shared Wesleyan heritage."
JO ANN LYON

"What Kevin Watson has achieved here is significant... Highly recommended."
ANDREW C. THOMPSON

LEX ORANDI, LEX SERVIENDI

ROMAN CATHOLIC THEOLOGY OF ORDAINED MINISTRY
IN SELECT TEXTS FROM THE RITES OF ORDINATION

LEONARDO J. GAJARDO

Spiritus 9.2 (2024) 273–294
https://doi.org/10.31380/ 2573-6345.1372
© The Author(s) 2024

Keywords *ordained ministry, ordination, rites of ordination, vocation, Roman Catholic Church, Sacrament of Holy Orders*

Abstract

This article will explore the understanding of ordained ministry within the Roman Catholic Church. The article proceeds by examining the prayer and homily from the rites of ordination for Bishops, Priests, and Deacons in order to observe the biblical foundations of ordained ministry, the role of ordained ministry within salvation history, the functional and ontological dimensions of ordained ministry, the living out of the Sacrament of Holy Orders, and the role of the Holy Spirit in ordained ministry.

Introduction

One of the important tenets of recent Roman Catholic liturgical theology is the principle *lex orandi, lex credendi*.[1] This adage, whose origin can be traced back to Prosper of Aquitaine in the fifth century, can be loosely translated as, "The law of praying [is] the law of believing." Since the time of the liturgical renewal called for by the Second Vatican Ecumenical Council (1962–1965), the axiom *lex orandi, lex credendi* has contributed to a fuller appreciation of the theological meaning and significance of the liturgical rites by which the Christian faithful are sanctified by God and offer themselves as a spiritual worship to God (cf. Rom 12:1).[2]

More recently, some liturgical theologians have expanded the expression *lex orandi, lex credendi* to include a third element, *lex vivendi*, or "the law of living."[3] This extension is meant to highlight the intrinsic connection between what the faithful pray,

---

[1] For a recent and thorough discussion of this principle and its application in the revised rites after Vatican II, see Kevin W. Irwin, *Context and Text: A Method for Liturgical Theology*, rev. ed. (Collegeville, MN: Liturgical Press, 2018), 3–60.

[2] For two examples of this, see Aidan Kavanaugh, *On Liturgical Theology* (New York: Pueblo, 1984); and David W. Fagerberg, *Theologia Prima: What is Liturgical Theology?* 2nd ed. (Chicago: Hillenbrand Books, 2004).

[3] Irwin, *Context and Text*, 81.

believe, and live out. In the spirit of that fuller recognition of the links between worship, belief, and life, this article will examine certain texts from the rites of ordination currently in use in the Roman Catholic Church, in order to enumerate some aspects of current Roman Catholic theology of ordained ministry, or what can be called the *lex serviendi* or "the law of serving."

The rites of ordination of a Bishop, of Priests, and of Deacons[4] are rich and complex liturgical celebrations, containing both ancient elements and recent adaptations.[5] Because these liturgical rites contain so much material that is theologically significant, this article will limit itself to examining and commenting on two elements contained in each of these rites: 1) the model homily and 2) the prayer of ordination. These liturgical texts are particularly important for understanding the nature and purpose of ordained ministry in the Catholic Church.

Following the structure of *De Ordinatione Episcopi, Presbyterorum et Diaconorum*[6] (*Ordination of a Bishop, of Priests, and of Deacons*), the texts from the rite of ordination of a Bishop will be examined first, followed by those from the rite of ordination of Priests, and then the texts from the rite of ordination of Deacons. After the examination of all these texts, five brief observations will be offered on the theology of ordained ministry that emerges from them. These observations will consider the biblical foundations of ordained ministry, the role of ordained ministry within salvation history, the functional and ontological dimensions of ordained ministry, the living out of the Sacrament of Holy Orders, and the role of the Holy Spirit in ordained ministry.

The Rite of Ordination of a Bishop

The Homily

The ritual for the ordination of a Bishop indicates that, immediately after the proclamation of the Gospel, which "constitutes the high point of the Liturgy of the

---

[4] In order to be consistent with the current official English editions of liturgical books, references to Bishops, Priests, and Deacons will be capitalized. Also, the Latin edition of the ritual uses the term "presbyteri" (presbyters) in reference to the second rank of the Sacrament of Holy Orders, while the current official English translations uses the term "Priests." Accordingly, this article will use the term "Priest(s)," rather than "Presbyter(s)."

[5] Antonio Miralles, *Teologia Liturgica dei Sacramenti, vol. 6, Ordine* (Rome: Pontificia Università della Santa Croce, 2010), 111–248. English translations are mine.

[6] *De Ordinatione Episcopi, Presbyterorum et Diaconorum, editio typica altera* (Vatican City: Libreria Editrice Vaticana, 1989). English translations from *Ordination of a Bishop, of Priests, and of Deacons* (Washington: USCCB Publishing, 2021). Hereafter, *OBPD*. When referencing ritual books, the citations given refer to paragraph or section numbers, rather than page numbers.

Word,"[7] the hymn *Veni, Creator Spiritus*, or another suitable hymn, is sung.[8] Then the candidate to be ordained Bishop (Bishop-elect) is presented to the ordaining Bishop. The ordaining Bishop then asks that the mandate from the Apostolic See authorizing the ordination be read. After the reading, all the assembled give their assent to the ordination of the Bishop-elect.[9]

It is then that the ordaining Bishop preaches the homily. Basing himself on the readings from Scripture that have already been proclaimed, the ordaining Bishop may preach a homily that he has composed, he may use the model homily included in the ritual book, or he may combine parts of the model homily with his own words.[10]

The model homily proposed (see Appendix One[11]) is inspired by the teaching on the episcopate proposed in paragraphs 19–27 of the dogmatic constitution *Lumen Gentium* of the Second Vatican Council.[12] The homily is presented in six paragraphs, each developing some aspect of the nature and purpose of episcopal ministry.

The first paragraph grounds episcopal ministry in the ministry of Christ, the gift of the Holy Spirit, and the mission of the apostles. It states that the purpose of the apostles' ministry was the preaching of the Gospel and the gathering of all into one flock, whom they were to sanctify and govern. The apostles chose successors to continue their ministry, laying hands on them so that they might also receive the gift of the Spirit. Through this gift of the Holy Spirit, Bishops receive "the fullness of the Sacrament of Holy Orders."

The second paragraph indicates that, through the person and ministry of the Bishop, surrounded by his Priests, Christ himself is present to the faithful, continually proclaiming the gospel, administering the sacraments, gathering new members, and leading the faithful on their pilgrim journey to the Kingdom. The third paragraph encourages the faithful to receive and honor the Bishop-elect "as a minister of Christ and a steward of the mysteries of God." The task entrusted to the new Bishop is described as "bearing witness to the truth of the Gospel and the ministry of the Spirit and of justice."

In the fourth paragraph, the ordaining Bishop directly addresses the Bishop-elect, reminding him that he has been chosen by the Lord, in order to act on behalf of human beings "in those things that pertain to God." He goes on to say, "For the title of Bishop

---

[7] *General Instruction of the Roman Missal*, 60.

[8] *OBPD*, 35.

[9] *OBPD*, 38.

[10] *OBPD*, 39.

[11] *OBPD*, 39. In each section, the citation from *OBPD* will be footnoted in the reference to the corresponding appendix only. To avoid unnecessary repetition, quotations from the same reference in a particular section will be marked with quotations marks, but they will not include a separate footnote.

[12] Miralles, *Teologia Liturgica dei Sacramenti*, 128–29.

signifies a task, not an honor; a Bishop must strive to benefit others rather than to lord it over them." In the fifth paragraph, the ordaining Bishop exhorts the Bishop-elect to "be a faithful steward, moderator, and guardian of the mysteries of Christ." The Bishop-elect is also urged to "be mindful always of the Good Shepherd, who knows his sheep and is known by them, and who did not hesitate to lay down his life for them."

In the sixth paragraph of the homily, the Bishop-elect is exhorted to have the love of a father and brother for "all those whom God places in [his] care," especially Priests and Deacons, who are his "co-workers in the ministry of Christ." In addition, he should have a special love for the most vulnerable, should collaborate with all the faithful, and should care "for those who are not yet gathered into the one fold of Christ." He is reminded that as a member of the College of Bishops, he should have a concern for all the Churches and for "the whole flock in which the Holy Spirit places [him] to govern the Church of God." He is to do this "in the name of the Father whose image [he] represent[s] in the Church; and in the name of his Son, Jesus Christ, whose office of Teacher, Priest, and Shepherd [he] will discharge, and in the name of the Holy Spirit, who enlivens the Church of Christ and, by his power, strengthens us in our weakness."

The Prayer of Ordination

The General Introduction of *Ordination of a Bishop, of Priests, and of Deacons* states, "Sacred Ordination is conferred by the Bishop's laying on of hands and the Prayer of Ordination by which the Bishop blesses God and calls upon the gift of the Holy Spirit for the fulfillment of ministry."[13] As a result, the Prayer of Ordination is theologically significant for understanding the nature and purpose of ordained ministry in the Catholic Church.

After the homily, the Bishop-elect makes a series of promises with regard to the ministry he is about to assume. The ordaining Bishop then leads all those gathered in the Litany of Supplication, praying for an outpouring of God's grace on the Bishop-elect. The litany concludes with a prayer offered by the ordaining Bishop. Then the Bishop-elect kneels and all the Bishops present lay hands, one by one, without saying anything. When the laying of hands is concluded, two Deacons hold an open Book of the Gospels over the head of the Bishop-elect.[14]

Then, with all Bishops standing near the ordaining Bishop, the latter extends his hands and says or sings the Prayer of Ordination (see Appendix Two[15]). The current Prayer of Ordination is based on the very ancient prayer of ordination contained in the

---

[13] *OBPD*, 6.
[14] *OBPD*, 40–46.
[15] *OBPD*, 47.

Traditio Apostolica, with some minor stylistic changes.[16] The structure of the prayer is that of invocation, anamnesis, epiclesis, and doxology, which is typical of important liturgical prayers.[17]

The prayer begins with the invocation of God the Father, "amplified by two appositions and two relative clauses."[18] The amplifications are all taken from Old and New Testament texts and make general references to the attributes of God. The invocation grounds the entire prayer in the revelation of the mystery of God and of his salvific will. The invocation is further amplified and concretized by the anamnesis, which, in five subordinate clauses, recalls specific events in salvation history in which God provided for the needs of his people through ministers.

Then the ordaining Bishop, together with the other Bishops present, says the epiclesis of the prayer. They ask that God "pour forth upon this chosen one the power that is from you, the governing Spirit, whom you gave to your beloved Son Jesus Christ and whom he gave to the holy Apostles, who established the Church in each place as your sanctuary, to the glory and unfailing praise of your name." These words are essential for the validity of the ordination and highlight that the ministry of the new Bishop is grounded in the Spirit given to Christ and the Apostles. What is asked of God in these words is the bestowal of the Spirit upon the Bishop-elect.[19]

The epiclesis continues with a series of intercessions, which the ordaining Bishop alone says. These intercessions ask for the grace necessary for the new Bishop to exercise faithfully the various aspects of episcopal ministry. These aspects include nourishing God's flock and the exercise of the High Priesthood without reproach, exercising his new authority with meekness and purity of heart.

The whole prayer ends with a doxology, asking that all that has been asked of God the Father may be brought about through Christ and "with the Holy Spirit in the holy Church." That last part highlights what had been mentioned in the homily, namely, that the ordination is not for the sake or honor of the new Bishop, but for the good of the Church and the glory of God.[20]

---

[16] Miralles, *Teologia Liturgica dei Sacramenti*, 140–41.

[17] Miralles, *Teologia Liturgica dei Sacramenti*, 142.

[18] Miralles, *Teologia Liturgica dei Sacramenti*, 143.

[19] Miralles, *Teologia Liturgica dei Sacramenti*, 146.

[20] Miralles, *Teologia Liturgica dei Sacramenti*, 151.

The Rite of Ordination of Priests

The Homily

The ritual for the ordination of Priests indicates that, immediately after the proclamation of the Gospel, the candidates be presented to the ordaining Bishop. The ordaining Bishop then asks that testimony be offered regarding the worthiness of the candidates, and a Priest offers the necessary testimony. The Bishop then accepts the testimony and chooses the candidates for ordination. All the assembled then give their assent to the ordination of the candidates.[21]

As was the case with the rite of ordination for a Bishop, the ordaining Bishop then preaches the homily, either of his own composition, the model one offered in the ritual book, or a combination of the two. The model homily (see Appendix Three[22]) includes themes and expressions taken from *Lumen Gentium,* 28, as well as the decree *Presbyterorum ordinis*, on the ministry and life of Priests, of the Second Vatican Council.[23] It is presented in nine paragraphs, which highlight various aspects of priestly ministry.

The model homily "first affirms the common royal priesthood of all the baptized people of God, relying on 1 Peter 2:9,"[24] but then affirms that "our great High Priest, Jesus Christ, chose certain disciples to exercise in his name" the priestly office in the Church. This refers above all to Bishops, who share in Christ's office of Teacher, Priest, and Shepherd, but that "Priests are established as co-workers of the Order of Bishops with whom they are joined in the priestly office and with whom they are called to the service of the People of God."

In the third paragraph, the homily explains that the candidates are "to be ordained to the Priesthood in the Order of the Presbyterate," and that "[b]y the priestly ministry, [Christ's] Body, that is the Church, is built up and grows into a holy temple, the People of God." The next paragraph indicates that, through ordination, the candidates will "be configured to Christ the eternal High Priest and joined to the Priesthood of the Bishops," as Priests of the New Testament. As such, they will have the responsibility of preaching the Gospel, shepherding God's people, and celebrating the Eucharist and the other sacraments.[25]

---

[21] *OBPD*, 121–22.

[22] *OBPD*, 123.

[23] Miralles, *Teologia Liturgica dei Sacramenti*, 184.

[24] Paul Turner, *Present for God's Call: An Overview of the Rites of Institution and Ordination* (Chicago: Liturgical Training Publications, 2023), 174.

[25] *OBPD*, 123.

As was the case with the homily for the ordination of a Bishop, the ordaining Bishop then addresses the candidates directly. In this case, the Bishop explains how, in Christ, they will exercise the office of teaching, sanctifying, and governing. In each case, the candidates are exhorted to draw ever closer to God and to exercise these functions for the good of the People of God. They are urged to meditate constantly on God's Word, so as to "believe what [they] read, teach what [they] believe, and practice what [they] teach." In addition, in celebrating the sacred mysteries, they are to strive to understand what they do and to imitate what they celebrate, striving "to put to death whatever is sinful within [them] and to walk in newness of life." Finally, they are urged "to gather the faithful together into one family, so that [they] may lead them to God the Father, through Christ, and in the Holy Spirit," always following the example of the Good Shepherd.

The Prayer of Ordination

As was the case in the ordination of a Bishop, after the homily, the candidates to be ordained Priests make a series of promises regarding the ministry they are about to assume. The ordaining Bishop then leads all those gathered in the Litany of Supplication, praying for an outpouring of God's grace on the men to be ordained. The litany concludes with a prayer offered by the ordaining Bishop. Since the essential elements for the valid conferral of the Sacrament of Holy Orders are the laying on of hands and the prayer of ordination, the ordaining Bishop lays hands on each of the candidates in silence, followed by the Priests present, who also lay hands on the candidates in silence.

Then the ordaining Bishop, with the Priests standing alongside him, prays the Prayer of Ordination (see Appendix Four[26]) with outstretched hands.[27] The text of the prayer is substantially the same as has been used in the Roman Church since ancient times, with the only modification being the addition of a request that their preaching may reach the ends of the earth.[28] The prayer "relies heavily on biblical testimony"[29] regarding the role of Priests and is structured in four sections: an invocation, an anamnesis, an epiclesis, and a doxology.

The prayer begins by asking the Father to draw near and then refers to certain attributes of God. It mentions that God, "by the power of the Holy Spirit, in order to form a priestly people, establish[ed] among them ministers of Christ [his] Son in various orders." It then proceeds to the anamnesis, recalling God's action in the Old

---

[26] *OBPD*, 131.
[27] *OBPD*, 130.
[28] Miralles, *Teologia Liturgica dei Sacramenti*, 200.
[29] Turner, *Present for God's Call*, 181.

Testament, including the appointing of Moses and Aaron, the sending of the Spirit on seventy elders to help Moses in his ministry, and the establishment of the Levitical priesthood.

The anamnesis then moves from consideration of priesthood in the Old Testament to that of the New Testament. It recalls, first of all, the sending of Jesus into the world as "Apostle and High Priest of our confession," who, "[t]hrough the Holy Spirit, [. . .] offered himself unblemished to [the Father] and made his Apostles [. . .] sharers in his mission." The prayer then speaks of "companions" whom God gave to the apostles "to proclaim and carry out the work of salvation through all the world."

Then, as Paul Turner explains, "the bishop moves to the purpose of his prayer. Having recalled how God has appointed leaders in both Old and New Testaments, the bishop turns his attention to contemporary needs. As Moses in his weakness required helpers, so does the Church today."[30] The bishop prays the sacramental formula, which is essential for a valid ordination: "Grant, we pray, almighty Father, to these your servants, the dignity of the Priesthood; renew deep within them the Spirit of Holiness; may they hold the office second in order, received from you, O God, and by the example of their manner of life may they inspire right conduct." Miralles notes that "the fact that in the anamnesis the action of the Spirit in the sacrifice of the Cross is recalled makes the epiclesis more meaningful: the Holy Spirit will make the elected participants in the priesthood of Christ exercised on Golgotha."[31]

The last part of the sacramental formulas leads directly to the next part of the prayer, which describes the various ministerial functions of Priests.[32] They are called to be co-workers of Bishops in preaching, guided by "the grace of the Holy Spirit." Together with Bishops, they are to be "faithful stewards of [God's] mysteries," so that the faithful may be renewed by Baptism, refreshed by the Eucharist, reconciled through Penance, and raised up through the Anointing of the Sick. Furthermore, they are to join Bishops in "imploring [God's] mercy for the people entrusted to them and for the whole world."

Before concluding the prayer of ordination, the Bishop indicates that "if God grants this prayer, all the nations may become one people in Christ, a hope that Paul articulated in Romans 11:25."[33] Finally, the Bishop offers a Trinitarian doxology that highlights the mediation of Christ.[34]

---

[30] Turner, *Present for God's Call*, 182.

[31] Miralles, *Teologia Liturgica dei Sacramenti*, 207.

[32] Miralles, *Teologia Liturgica dei Sacramenti*, 207.

[33] Turner, *Present for God's Call*, 182.

[34] Miralles, *Teologia Liturgica dei Sacramenti*, 209.

The Rite of Ordination of Deacons

The Homily

After the proclamation of the Gospel, the rite of ordination of Deacons proceeds similarly as that of Priests, with the presentation of the candidates to the ordaining Bishop, the asking for and giving of testimony regarding the worthiness of the candidates, and the election of the candidates by the Bishop and the assent of the assembly.[35] The ordaining Bishop then preaches the homily, which, as was the case in the two rites already examined, he can compose himself, avail himself of the model homily (see Appendix Five[36]) included in the ritual book, or he can combine parts of the model homily with his own words.

The model homily contained in the ritual book has characteristics similar to those for the ordination of a Bishop and of Priests, with the exception that the one for Deacons also takes into account that some men ordained Deacons are married, while others commit themselves to celibacy.[37] The homily begins with six paragraphs that are applicable to all ordinations of Deacons, then provides three alternative conclusions, depending on whether the group of ordinands includes married and unmarried men, only unmarried men, or only married men.

The homily begins by greeting those present and inviting all to "consider carefully the nature of the ministerial rank to which [the elect] shall be raised." It then "assures all that the Holy Spirit will strengthen these candidates."[38] The homily then says that Deacons "help the Bishop and his Priests in the ministries of the word, of the altar, and of charity, showing themselves to be servants of all." It then expands on the three-fold ministry of word, altar, and charity.

In describing the ministry of the altar, the homily outlines the principal roles of Deacons in the celebration of the Eucharist. Turner observes, "The bishop probably explains [service at Mass] first because the Eucharist is the source and summit of the Christian life."[39] In the next paragraph, the homily explains that "[a]t the Bishop's direction it will be [the Deacons'] duty to exhort believers and unbelievers alike and instruct them in holy doctrine." Another part of their ministry of the word is "to preside over public prayer, administer Baptism, assist at and bless Marriages, bring Viaticum to the dying, and conduct funeral rites." While some of these latter functions are connected to the liturgy and the ministry of the altar, the homily "envisions ministry of

---

[35] *OBPD*, 197–98.
[36] *OBPD*, 199.
[37] Miralles, *Teologia Liturgica dei Sacramenti*, 224.
[38] Turner, *Present for God's Call*, 126.
[39] Turner, *Present for God's Call*, 127.

the Word through instruction and through serving as a leader of prayer outside the celebration of Mass."[40]

The next paragraph focuses on the Deacons' ministry of charity. It begins by asserting that "Deacons derive this consecrated mission of charity directly from the same imposition of hands that binds them more closely to the altar."[41] It goes on to say that "they will carry out a ministry of charity in the name of the Bishop or pastor." It calls on the candidates to carry out the ministry of charity "in such a way that [others] recognize them as disciples of him who did not come to be served but to serve."

The next two paragraphs elaborate on the idea of the example of the Lord Jesus as essential for diaconal ministry. The Bishop, directly addressing those to be ordained, says, "The Lord has given you an example: that, just as he himself has done, so also you should do." He goes on to say that "as Deacons, that is, as ministers of Jesus Christ," they should "serve others with joy as [they] would serve the Lord." He then warns them to "look upon all impurity and greed as the serving of false gods."

It is at that point in the model homily that, as was noted above, the ritual book offers three alternatives, depending on the marital state of those to be ordained. "[I]n reality, there is not a lot of difference [between the three alternatives] because, to the married elect it makes reference to what is common to all and to the celibate ones only a few appropriate references are added."[42] Turner notes, "[t]he conclusion of the suggested homily is the same for all candidates, regardless of their marital status. They are to be planted and grounded in faith."[43] They are urged to live and serve "without blemish and beyond reproach before God and others," holding fast to "the mystery of faith with a clear conscience." They are "to express the Word of God in speech and deed so that the Spirit may bring all people to life"[44] and "to help people become a pure offering to God."[45] If they live and serve in this way, they can hope, on the last day, to hear the Lord say to them, "Well done, good and faithful servant, enter into the joy of your Lord."[46]

The Prayer of Ordination

As with the rites of ordination of both a Bishop and Priests, after the homily, the rite of ordination of Deacons proceeds with a series of promises regarding the ministry they are

---

[40] Turner, *Present for God's Call*, 127.
[41] Turner, *Present for God's Call*, 127.
[42] Miralles, *Teologia Liturgica dei Sacramenti*, 225.
[43] Turner, *Present for God's Call*, 128.
[44] Turner, *Present for God's Call*, 129.
[45] Turner, *Present for God's Call*, 129.
[46] Turner, *Present for God's Call*, 129.

about to assume, and the ordaining Bishop laying hands on the candidates. Unlike those other rites, however, no other clergy lay hands on the ordinands.[47]

The Bishop then prays the prayer of ordination (see Appendix Six[48]). The prayer is based on an ancient prayer for the ordination of Deacons, which has been continually used by the Roman Church since the sixteenth century.[49] The current prayer has been modified, but preserves that original structure of the prayer, namely, an introductory invocation, an anamnesis, an epiclesis, and a doxology.[50] As is the case with the two other prayers of ordination, this prayer "abounds in biblical allusions."[51]

The invocation is similar to the prayer of ordination for Priests, asking God to draw near and then indicating some divine attributes. It then recalls that God is the one "who apportion[s] every order and assign[s] every office." It also mentions that God "make[s] due provision for every age, through your Word, your Power, and your Wisdom, Jesus Christ, your Son, our Lord."

The anamnesis continues by noting how God has provided for the Church, which is "drawn together in the diversity of her members, and united by a wondrous bond through the Holy Spirit," so that it can "grow and spread forth to build up a new temple." The prayer then recalls the service of the sons of Levi in the tabernacle. It then mentions that "in the first days of your Church, your Son's Apostles, led by the Holy Spirit, appointed seven men of good repute to help them in the daily ministry." It also notes that the seven were entrusted this ministry "[b]y prayer and the laying on of hands."

Then, as Turner notes, "[h]aving acknowledged these deeds that God has done, the bishop then makes his request. He asks God to pour out the sevenfold Holy Spirit upon these men."[52] This epicletic request is not made for the benefit of those being ordained, but so that they can "carry out faithfully the work of the ministry." The Bishop goes on to name the evangelical virtues that should abound in new Deacons: "unfeigned love, concern for the sick and the poor, unassuming authority, the purity of innocence, and the observance of spiritual discipline." This is followed by a further description of how they should conduct themselves. The Bishop asks "that their conduct may reflect God's commandments, thus inspiring others."[53] Thus, by following the example of Christ, "who came not to be served but to serve," the Deacons can hope to "be found worthy to reign with [Christ] in heaven."

---

[47] *OBPD*, 207.
[48] *OBPD*, 207.
[49] Miralles, *Teologia Liturgica dei Sacramenti*, 236.
[50] Miralles, *Teologia Liturgica dei Sacramenti*, 236.
[51] Turner, *Present for God's Call*, 136.
[52] Turner, *Present for God's Call*, 136.
[53] Turner, *Present for God's Call*, 137.

The whole prayer ends with the traditional doxology of Roman prayers. Then, the faithful assent to the prayer and make it their own by responding, "Amen."

Observations on the Theology of Ordained Ministry Suggested by the Texts Examined

This cursory examination of the model homilies and prayers of ordination contained in the ritual ordination of a Bishop, of Priests, and of Deacons has tried to highlight the rich and developed theological understanding of ordained ministry of the Roman Catholic Church. Much more could be said about these texts, as well as to the other elements and texts that are part of ordination liturgies. Given the limits of this article, the following observations are offered to encourage and foster dialogue regarding the Roman Catholic theology of ordained ministry.

1. *Roman Catholic theology of ordained ministry is deeply grounded in Scripture.* As was noted in the various sections of this article, the model homilies and prayers examined are thoroughly imbued with scriptural references, including allusions from both the Old Testament and the New Testament. This suggests that any consideration of ordained ministry in the Catholic Church must consider the biblical witness regarding the calling of certain individuals by God to serve in particular offices and ministries. The rites of ordination see in certain ministerial roles of the Old Testament prefigurements of Church offices and ministries established by Christ and the apostles.

2. *Roman Catholic theology understands ordained ministry within the context of salvation history.* Connected to the grounding of ordained ministry within Scripture, the texts examined, especially the prayers of ordination, situate ordained ministry within the larger context of God's relationship with humanity as revealed and lived out in salvation history. Ordained ministry is seen as a way in which God continues to instruct, sanctify, and govern the People of God. In a special way, ordained ministry is a sacramental continuation of the ministry of Jesus Christ, who came into the world to do the will of his Father and continues that work, in part, through those who are ordained. In other words, the roles of Bishop, Priest, and Deacon have their origin in God's will for the building up of the Body of Christ and the salvation of the world.

3. *The Roman Catholic view is that ordained ministry is not only a functional reality, but also an ontological one.* The texts examined in this article make clear that the function of ordained ministers is to continue the mission of the Church in the world and build up the Body of Christ. But they also indicate that ordained ministers do this not merely as deputed functionaries, but as sacramental participants and embodiments of Christ. The model homily for the ordination of Bishop says that Christ himself is

present among the faithful "in the Bishop surrounded by his Priests."[54] The homily for the ordination of Priests says that the candidates "are to be configured to Christ the eternal High Priest and joined to the Priesthood of the Bishops."[55] It also speaks of them as being "consecrated" to preach, govern, and celebrate divine worship. The homily for the ordination of Deacons states, "Consecrated by the laying on of hands passed down from the Apostles and bound more closely to the service of the altar, they will carry out the ministry of charity in the name of the Bishop or pastor."[56] Through their consecration and configuration, Bishops, Priests, and Deacons make Christ the Teacher, Priest, Shephard, and Servant sacramentally present to the Church and the world.

4. *The sacramental configuration and consecration to Christ calls for a lived response from those in Holy Orders.* The model homilies and prayers of ordination make clear that, in being configured and consecrated to Christ, Bishops, Priests, and Deacons assume a particular responsibility of living and acting in a way that incarnates the example of Christ the Good Shepherd. It is the example of Christ, "who knows his sheep and is known by them, and who did not hesitate to lay down his life for them,"[57] that Bishops should strive to live out in their ministry. For their part, Priests are called to "[k]eep always before [their] eyes the example of the Good Shepherd, who did not come to be served but to serve and who came to seek and to save what was lost."[58] Those called to be Deacons are instructed, "The Lord has given you an example: that, just as he himself has done, so also you should do."[59]

5. *The action and grace of the Holy Spirit is essential for the ordination and the living out of the sacrament of Holy Orders.* One thing that all the model homilies and prayers of ordination emphasize is the role of the Holy Spirit in the actual ordination and in the ministry of the ordained. All the homilies make mention of the action of the Spirit in the establishment of the three orders of the sacrament. This is part of the way in which the Spirit builds up the Body of Christ that is the Church. The anamnetic sections of the prayers of ordination for both Priests and Deacons also make mention of the power and guidance of the Spirit in the establishment of those two orders. Of particular importance is that all three sacramental formulas, which are epicletic in nature, make explicit requests for the outpouring of the Spirit on those being ordained, so that they may have the necessary share in the mission and power of Christ. Finally, the homilies

---

[54] *OBPD*, 39.
[55] *OBPD*, 123.
[56] *OBPD*, 199.
[57] *OBPD*, 39.
[58] *OBPD*, 39, 123.
[59] *OBPD*, 199.

and prayers of ordination assert the need for the ongoing grace of the Spirit, so that those in Holy Orders may fulfill their ministry in accordance with the will of God and the need of the Church.

Conclusion

This review of the model homilies and prayers of ordination contained in the ritual ordination of a Bishop, of Priests, and of Deacons has sought to examine how these liturgical texts can help identify dimensions of theological reflection on the nature and purpose of ordained ministry in the Roman Catholic Church today. The observations offered at the end of the article seek to propose some fundamental points that can be discerned from the texts that have been examined, in the hope that they can serve as a starting point for a thoughtful dialogue on ordained ministry as understood by the Roman Catholic Church.

Leonardo J. Gajardo (lgajardo@dcgary.org) is a priest of the Roman Catholic Diocese of Gary, Indiana, USA, and serves as its Director of Diaconate Formation. He has previously taught in seminaries in Baltimore, Maryland, and Washington, DC.

Appendix One: Model Homily for the Ordination of a Bishop

Dearly beloved, consider carefully the nature of the rank in the Church to which our brother is to be raised. Our Lord Jesus Christ, who was sent from the Father to redeem the human race, himself sent twelve Apostles into the world. Filled with the power of the Holy Spirit, they were to preach the Gospel, and gathering all peoples into one flock, they were to sanctify and govern them. In order that this ministry might remain until the end of time, the Apostles in turn chose helpers for themselves. Through the laying on of hands, they passed on to them the gift of the Holy Spirit that they themselves received from Christ. In this way, the fullness of the Sacrament of Holy Orders is conferred. Thus, the tradition handed down from the beginning, through the unbroken succession of Bishops, is preserved from generation to generation, and the work of the Savior continues and grows even to our own times.

Our Lord Jesus Christ, who is High Priest forever, is himself present among you in the Bishop surrounded by his Priests. For through the ministry of the Bishop, Christ himself never ceases to proclaim the Gospel and to administer the Sacraments of faith to those who believe. Through the fatherly office of the Bishop, Christ himself adds and gathers new members to his Body. Through the wisdom and prudence of the Bishop, Christ himself leads you on your earthly pilgrimage toward eternal happiness.

Gladly and gratefully, therefore, please receive our brother whom we, as Bishops, admit into our College through the laying on of hands. Honor him as a minister of Christ and a steward of the mysteries of God. To him have been entrusted both the task of bearing witness to the truth of the Gospel and the ministry of the Spirit and of justice. Remember the words that Christ spoke to the Apostles: "Whoever listens to you listens to me, and whoever rejects you rejects me, and whoever rejects me rejects the one who sent me."

And now, dear brother, you have been chosen by the Lord. Consider that you have been taken from among the people and appointed to act on their behalf in those things that pertain to God. For the title of Bishop signifies a task, not an honor; a Bishop must strive to benefit others rather than to lord it over them. For in keeping with the precept of the Master, let the greater among you be as the younger, and the leader be as one who serves. Preach in season and out of season; reprove with all patience and sound teaching. Whenever you pray and offer sacrifice for the people committed to your care, seek with zeal and devotion to obtain an abundance of grace for them from the fullness of Christ's holiness.

In the Church entrusted to you, be a faithful steward, moderator and guardian of the mysteries of Christ. As one chosen by the Father to govern his family, be mindful always of the Good Shepherd, who knows his sheep and is known by them, and who did not hesitate to lay down his life for them.

With the charity of a father and brother, love all those whom God places in your care, especially the Priests and Deacons, who are your co-workers in the ministry of Christ; but love also the poor and the weak, foreigners and strangers. Exhort the faithful to work with you in your apostolic labors; do not refuse to listen willingly to them. Never tire of caring for those who are not yet gathered into the one fold of Christ; for they too are entrusted to you in the Lord. Never forget that you are joined to the College of Bishops in the Catholic Church, which is unified by the bond of charity; and so, you should have a constant concern for all the Churches and gladly come to the aid of Churches in need. Keep watch, therefore, over the whole flock in which the Holy Spirit places you to govern the Church of God: in the name of the Father, whose image you represent in the Church; and in the name of his Son, Jesus Christ, whose office of Teacher, Priest and Shepherd you will discharge; and in the name of the Holy Spirit, who enlivens the Church of Christ and, by his power, strengthens us in our weakness.

Appendix Two: Prayer of Ordination of a Bishop

God and Father of Our Lord Jesus Christ, Father of mercies and God of all consolation, who dwell on high and look upon the lowly, who know all things before they come to be: it is you who established order in your Church through your gracious word, who from the beginning predestined a righteous people born of Abraham, who instituted rulers and priests and did not leave your sanctuary without ministry, who from the beginning of the world have been pleased to be glorified in those you have chosen.

NOW POUR FORTH UPON THIS CHOSEN ONE THE POWER THAT IS FROM YOU, THE GOVERNING SPIRIT, WHOM YOU GAVE TO YOUR BELOVED SON JESUS CHRIST, AND WHOM HE GAVE TO THE HOLY APOSTLES, WHO ESTABLISHED THE CHURCH IN EACH PLACE AS YOUR SANCTUARY, TO THE GLORY AND UNFAILING PRAISE OF YOUR NAME.

Grant, O Father, knower of all hearts, that this your servant whom you have chosen for the Episcopate may nourish your holy flock and may without reproach exercise before you the High Priesthood, serving you night and day; that he may unceasingly cause your face to shine upon us and offer the gifts of your Holy Church. Grant that by the strength of the Spirit of the high priesthood he may have authority to forgive sins according to your command; that he may apportion offices according to your precept and loosen every bond according to the authority you gave the Apostles; may he be pleasing to you in meekness and purity of heart, offering a sweet fragrance to you through your Son Jesus Christ, through whom glory and power and honor are yours, with the Holy Spirit in the holy Church both now and forever and ever. Amen.

Appendix Three: Model Homily for the Ordination of Several Priests

Dearly beloved; since these men, our sons and your relatives and friends, are soon to be advanced to the Order of Priests, consider carefully the nature of the ministerial rank in the Church to which they shall be raised.

Indeed, the entire holy People of God is made a royal priesthood in Christ. Nevertheless, our great High Priest, Jesus Christ, chose certain of his disciples to exercise in his name, on behalf of the human race, a public priestly office in the Church; for Christ, who was sent from the Father, himself in turn sent the Apostles into the world, that through them and their successors, the Bishops, he might exercise without ceasing his own office of Teacher, Priest, and Shepherd. In addition, Priests are established as co-workers of the Order of Bishops with whom they are joined in the priestly office and with whom they are called to the service of the People of God.

Now that mature deliberation has taken place, these brothers are to be ordained to the Priesthood in the Order of the presbyterate, that they may serve Christ the Teacher, Priest, and Shepherd. By the priestly ministry, his Body, that is the Church, is built up and grows into a holy temple, the People of God.

These men are to be configured to Christ the eternal High Priest and joined to the Priesthood of the Bishops; they will be consecrated as true Priests of the New Testament, in order to preach the Gospel, shepherd God's people, and celebrate divine worship, especially in the Lord's sacrifice.

Now, beloved sons, you are to be raised to the Order of the Priesthood, and for your part, you will exercise in Christ the Teacher the sacred office of teaching. Impart to everyone the Word of God that you yourselves have received with joy. Meditating on the law of the Lord, see that you believe what you read, teach what you believe, and practice what you teach.

And so, let your teaching be nourishment for the People of God, and let the holiness of your life be a pleasing fragrance for Christ's faithful, so that you may build up by word and example that house which is the Church of God.

You will also exercise in Christ the office of sanctifying; for by your ministry the spiritual sacrifice of the faithful will be made perfect: in the celebration of the mysteries, it is united to the Sacrifice of Christ, which is offered, through your hands and in union with them, in an unbloody manner on the altar. Understand, therefore, what you do, and imitate what you celebrate; as celebrants of the mystery of the Lord's Death and Resurrection, may you strive to put to death whatever is sinful within you and to walk in newness of life.

Remember, when you gather men and women into the People of God through Baptism, and in the name of Christ and the Church, forgive sins in the Sacrament of Penance, when you comfort the sick with holy oil and celebrate the sacred rites when you offer praise and thanksgiving through the hours of the day and pray not only for the People of God but for the whole world: always remember that you have been taken from among the people and appointed on their behalf in those things that pertain to God. Fulfill, therefore, the ministry of Christ the Priest with abiding joy and genuine love. Seek not your own concerns but those of Jesus Christ.

Finally, dear sons, united with your Bishop and subject to him, fulfill the office of Christ, head and shepherd, to the best of your ability. Strive to gather the faithful together into one family, so that you may lead them to God the Father, through Christ, and in the Holy Spirit. Keep always before your eyes the example of the Good Shepherd, who did not come to be served but to serve and who came to seek and to save what was lost.

Appendix Four: Prayer of Ordination of Several Priests

Draw near, Lord, holy Father, almighty and eternal God, author of human dignity and bestower of all graces, through whom all things progress, through whom everything is made firm, who, by the power of the Holy Spirit, in order to form a priestly people, establish among them ministers of Christ your Son in various orders.

Already in the earlier covenant there arose offices instituted by mystical rites: so that when you had set Moses and Aaron over your people to govern and sanctify them, you chose men next in order and dignity to join them and assist in their work.

Thus in the desert, you instilled the spirit of Moses in the minds of seventy wise men; with them as helpers he more easily governed your people.

So too, over the sons of Aaron you poured an abundant share of their father's fullness, that the number of priests prescribed by the Law might be sufficient for the sacrifices of the tabernacle, which were a shadow of the good things to come.

But in these last days, holy Father, you sent your Son into the world, Jesus, the Apostle and High Priest of our confession.

Through the Holy Spirit, he offered himself unblemished to you and made his Apostles, who were consecrated in the truth, sharers in his mission; to them you added companions to proclaim and carry out the work of salvation through all the world.

Now, we pray, O Lord, provide also for our weakness these helpers whom we need for the exercise of the Apostolic Priesthood.

GRANT, WE PRAY, ALMIGHTY FATHER, TO THESE YOUR SERVANTS THE DIGNITY OF THE PRIESTHOOD: RENEW DEEP WITHIN THEM THE SPIRIT OF HOLINESS; MAY THEY HOLD THE OFFICE SECOND IN ORDER, RECEIVED FROM YOU, O GOD, AND BY THE EXAMPLE OF THEIR MANNER OF LIFE MAY THEY INSPIRE RIGHT CONDUCT.

May they be trustworthy co-workers with our order, so that by their preaching and through the grace of the Holy Spirit, the words of the Gospel may bear fruit in human hearts and reach even to the ends of the earth.

Together with us, may they be faithful stewards of your mysteries, so that your people may be renewed through the cleansing waters of rebirth and refreshed from your altar, so that sinners may be reconcile and the sick raised up.

May they be joined to us, Lord, in imploring your mercy for the people entrusted to them and for the whole world.

Thus, may the full number of the nations, gathered together in Christ, become your one people, brought to perfection in your kingdom.

Through our Lord Jesus Christ, your Son, who lives and reigns with you in the unity of the Holy Spirit, God, forever and ever. Amen.

Appendix Five: Model Homily for the Ordination of Several Deacons

Dearly beloved brothers and sisters: since these men, our sons and your relatives and friends, are soon to be advanced to the Order of Deacons, consider carefully the nature of the ministerial rank to which they shall be raised.

Strengthened by the gift of the Holy Spirit, they will help the Bishop and his Priests in the ministries of the word, of the altar, and of charity, showing themselves to be servants of all. As ministers of the altar, they will proclaim the Gospel, prepare the sacrifice, and distribute the Body and Blood of the Lord to the faithful.

At the Bishop's direction it will also be their duty to exhort believers and unbelievers alike and instruct them in holy doctrine, to preside over public prayer, administer Baptism, assist at and bless Marriages, bring Viaticum to the dying, and conduct funeral rites.

Consecrated by the laying on of hands passed down from the Apostles and bound more closely to the service of the altar, they will carry out a ministry of charity in the name of the Bishop or pastor. In all these duties, let them act with the help of God in such a way that you recognize them as disciples of him who did not come to be served but to serve.

Now, beloved sons, you are to be raised to the Order of the Diaconate. The Lord has given you an example: that, just as he himself has done, so also you should do.

And so, as Deacons, that is, as ministers of Jesus Christ, who appeared in the midst of the disciples as one who serves, do the will of God in charity from the heart; serve others with joy as you would serve the Lord. Since, in fact, no one can serve two masters, look upon all impurity and greed as the serving of false gods.

Since you present yourselves for the Order of the Diaconate of your own free choice, you must be like those once chosen by the Apostles for the ministry of charity: men of good reputation, full of wisdom and the Holy Spirit.

If both married and unmarried elect are to be ordained, he concludes:

> Those of you who will exercise your ministry in the celibate state must know that celibacy is both a sign of pastoral charity and an incentive to it, as well as a source of spiritual fruitfulness in the world. For, urged on by a sincere love of Christ the Lord and living in this state with total dedication, you will cling more readily to Christ with an undivided heart, you will devote yourselves with greater freedom to the service of God and others, and you will serve single-mindedly the work of spiritual rebirth.
>
> Whether or not you have been called to holy celibacy, be firmly planted and grounded in faith. Show yourselves without blemish and beyond reproach before God and others, as is proper for the ministers of Christ and the stewards of God's mysteries. Do not allow yourselves to be turned away from the hope of the Gospel which you must not only hear but also serve. Hold fast to the mystery of faith with a clear conscience and express by your actions the word of God, which your lips proclaim, so that the Christian people, brought to life by the Spirit, may become a pure offering accepted by God, and so that you yourselves, when you go out to meet the Lord on the last day, may be able to hear him say: "Well done, good and faithful servant, enter into the joy of your Lord."

Or, if only unmarried elect are to be ordained, he concludes:

> Since you present yourselves for the Order of the Diaconate of your own free choice, you must be like those once chosen by the Apostles for the ministry of charity: men of good reputation, full of wisdom and the Holy Spirit.
>
> You will exercise your ministry in the celibate state. Celibacy is both a sign of pastoral charity and an incentive to it, as well as a source of spiritual fruitfulness in the world. For, urged on by a sincere love of Christ the Lord and living in this state with total dedication, you will cling more readily to Christ with an undivided heart, you will devote yourselves with greater freedom to the service of God and others, and you will serve single-mindedly the work of spiritual rebirth. Firmly planted and grounded in faith, show yourselves without blemish and beyond reproach before God and others, as is proper for the ministers of Christ and the stewards of God's mysteries. Do not allow yourselves to be turned away from the hope of the Gospel which you must not only hear but also serve. Hold fast to the mystery of faith with a clear conscience and express by your actions the word of God, which your lips proclaim, so that the Christian people, brought to life by the Spirit, may become a pure offering accepted by God, and so that you yourselves, when you go out to meet the Lord on the last day, may be able to hear him say, "Well done, good and faithful servant, enter into the joy of your Lord."

If only married elect are to be ordained, he concludes:

> You must be like those once chosen by the Apostles for the ministry of charity: men of good reputation, full of wisdom and the Holy Spirit. Firmly planted and grounded in faith, you are to show yourselves without blemish and beyond reproach before God and others, as is proper for the ministers of Christ and the stewards of God's mysteries. Do not allow yourselves to be turned away from the hope of the Gospel which you must not only hear but also serve. Hold fast to the mystery of faith with a clear conscience and express by your actions the word of God, which your lips proclaim, so that the Christian people, brought to life by the Spirit, may become a pure offering accepted by God, and so that you yourselves, when you go out to meet the Lord on the last day, may be able to hear him say, "Well done, good and faithful servant, enter into the joy of your Lord."

Appendix Six: Prayer of Ordination of Several Deacons

Draw near, we pray, almighty God, giver of every grace, who apportion every order and assign every office. While remaining unchanged, you make all things new and, setting all things in order with everlasting providence, you make due provision for every age, through your Word, your Power, and your Wisdom, Jesus Christ, your Son, our Lord.

You grant that your Church, his Body, adorned with manifold heavenly graces, drawn together in the diversity of her members, and united by a wondrous bond through the Holy Spirit, should grow and spread forth to build up a new temple. As once you chose the sons of Levi to minister in the former tabernacle, so now you establish three ranks of ministers in their sacred offices to serve your name.

Thus, in the first days of your Church, your Son's Apostles, led by the Holy Spirit, appointed seven men of good repute to help them in the daily ministry, so that they might devote themselves more fully to prayer and the preaching of the word. By prayer and the laying on of hands they entrusted to these chosen men the ministry of serving at table.

Look favorably also on these your servants, we pray, O Lord, whom we humbly dedicate to serve at your holy altars in the office of the Diaconate.

SEND FORTH THE HOLY SPIRIT UPON THEM, O LORD, WE PRAY, THAT THEY MAY BE STRENGTHENED BY THE GIFT OF YOUR SEVENFOLD GRACE TO CARRY OUT FAITHFULLY THE WORK OF THE MINISTRY.

May every evangelical virtue abound in them: unfeigned love, concern for the sick and the poor, unassuming authority, the purity of innocence, and the observance of spiritual discipline.

May your precepts shine forth in their conduct, that by the example of their manner of life they may inspire the imitation of your holy people. In offering the witness of a good conscience, may they remain firm and steadfast in Christ, so that, imitating your Son on earth, who came not to be served but to serve, they may be found worthy to reign with him in heaven.

Who lives and reigns with you in the unity of the Holy Spirit, God, forever and ever. Amen.

CALLED

A Pentecostal Theology of Vocation

MARTIN W. MITTELSTADT

Keywords *vocation, Pentecost, Fivefold Gospel, prophethood, dreams, Jazzolalia*

Abstract

In this essay, I propose a Pentecostal theology of vocation that extends out of the Full Gospel and prophethood of all believers. Though Pentecostals devote considerable attention to church-related/religious vocations, Pentecostals must reimagine vocational implications for fullness of the Spirit on all believers. All Pentecostals are called to embody the dual impulses of the Fivefold Gospel. They are being saved, sanctified, baptized in the Spirit, healed, and living in eager anticipation of Jesus' return. At the same time, all Pentecostals become saving agents with Christ; they perform holy love; they engage in Spirit-inspired witness; they offer healing balm for a broken world; and they work toward the full consummation of God's kingdom. Prophethood, an extension of Luther's axiom, "priesthood of all believers," concerns the implementation of dreams and visions given by God to the young and old, rich and poor, male and female. Pentecostals live out these vocations daily in their families, workspaces, communities, and churches.

Introduction

Man, if you gotta ask you'd never know.

— Louis Armstrong

In Pentecostal fashion, I begin with a testimony. In July of 2022, I enjoyed perhaps the most fruitful week of teaching in my life as the morning Bible speaker at Manhattan Beach Family Camp at Pelican Lake in Ninette, Manitoba. I first set foot on that hallowed site as a seven-year-old boy in 1972. Fifty years later, I stood in the "tabernacle" pulpit to address the theme of vocation. The crowd represented a panorama of lifelong friendships that included my childhood and teenage Sunday school teachers, camp counselors, youth leaders, and former pastors. Others had sat under my teaching as a Sunday school teacher, pastor, or college professor. The audience also included several former pastoral colleagues from the Manitoba and Northern Ontario District of the Pentecostal Assemblies of Canada. A good number came for the week specifically to hear me. I knew this crowd intimately. These were my people! For one week, whether I deserved it or not, I was their "boy." I grew up with these folks. They were proud of me. I had clout with this group! They leaned into my story.

I had made roughly forty annual pilgrimages to Manhattan Beach Camp for kids camps, youth camps, and family camps. I had walked the grounds in the shoes of a camper, counselor, pastor, and occasional camp speaker. Camp meetings are integral to a Pentecostal story. From early tent revivals to modern posh campgrounds with rented and private cabins, camp meetings continue to shape Pentecostal lives. Pentecostals cherish intimate encounters with God on such hallowed grounds and around tabernacle altars. Those unable to attend summer camps need not worry because Pentecostals carry "camp meetings" in their satchels. Sunday night services, youth meetings, and prayer services bring camp into local churches. Throughout the calendar year, youth and young adult retreats provide a similar venue. Every Pentecostal experiences camp somewhere.

I grew up in a nominal Pentecostal family. We seldom talked about faith at home, but I committed early to my local church. I followed Jesus from a young age and wanted to serve him "to the full." By my teenage years, my faith served as the compass for my life. As I embraced Pentecostal teaching, I wrestled, like many Pentecostals, with questions around vocation. Pentecostals proclaim boldly "the higher calling" to pastoral and missionary vocations. The plea for candidates was direct and subtle, enticing and haunting, daring and frightening at the same time. If God called you to "the ministry," you were a celebrated candidate, but you dare not respond flippantly. I wanted to serve God to the max, but I could not place my finger on a crisis moment where I heard God's voice. Any Pentecostal insider knows this impassioned rhetoric well.

In my final year of high school, I reeled with anxiety. I had come from a broken home. Through no fault of her own, my mother offered little life direction, particularly concerning higher education. Mom migrated to Canada as a young teenager and never went to high school. My first educational interests centered on biology, math, and a burgeoning subject called computer science. As I pondered public university, I was encouraged—even pressured—to attend Central Pentecostal College in Saskatoon, Saskatchewan. The college had recently introduced a one-year discipleship program to prepare students in their transition to adulthood and attendance at public university. In 1982, I enrolled for the longest one year of my life. By the end of that first year, I heard everywhere that God was calling me to the ministry. I responded to this call and graduated with a Bachelor of Theology (BTh) in 1986. I married Evelyn, the love of my life, in 1986, and we embarked on another decade of educational adventure. I completed a Master of Divinity (MDiv) among Mennonites at Providence Seminary in Otterburne, Manitoba, and as I became drawn toward higher education, I completed a PhD in Religious Studies at Marquette University in Milwaukee, Wisconsin. Along the way, I pastored for roughly ten years in my native Winnipeg and southern Manitoba. In 2000, Ev and I moved our young family to Springfield, Missouri, where I accepted the position of Professor of New Testament at Evangel University. The rest is history. My call fulfilled! What a relief! What a testimony! I am a poster story for the call to ministry and that of a Bible professor!

I shared this story intimately in front of my camp crowd. Many of the campers knew the highlights of my story until I pivoted to the counter-testimony. I proceeded to say, "If I had known as a teenager or college student what I know now about 'calling,' I would not be where I am today." My audience leaned in. My revelations captivated them. I showered them with an array of statements that I would unpack over the week: "I no longer believe that pastoral and missionary service are God's highest calling"; "I am convinced that people with such a view led me down a path I would otherwise not have chosen"; "I think I fell prey to erroneous teaching." I slowed down and assured my listeners that I was not bitter. I emphasized that they should not feel responsible for my choice. They could hear joy and passion in my storytelling and teaching. I thanked them for their role in my story. I suggested that my story is a classic Pentecostal story. Everyone hears it. Many wrestle with it. Call stories embody a cherished form of Pentecostal testimony.

As part of this counter-testimony, I ask, "Why do Pentecostals seldom hear testimonies of a calling to other vocations?" I believe the traditional narrative has led many Pentecostal believers toward church-related ministry because of a minimalist theology of the call. Some of these folk, like me, have survived and thrived; others stumbled. Added to this, I have a concern for Pentecostal congregants who never receive the call to church-related ministry. Many struggle to understand why they receive no such call, and many more are left with little instruction and discipleship concerning their day-to-day vocations.

Pentecostals share testimonies as a diagnostic means of rehearsing and developing their theology. Through testimonies, they articulate theology for everyday life. Testimonies of salvation, healing, guidance, and deliverance demonstrate God's hand on their lives. So where are the larger call stories? I suggest that erroneous or undeveloped theologies result in fragmented lives. If this is true, theology must attend to the lives of believers not only for Sunday worship, but to every moment of our weekly calendar.

My testimony—the good, the bad, and the ugly—inspires my interest in a Pentecostal theology of vocation. For over twenty years, I have been teaching a required first-year course that includes an intense unit on vocation. With my department colleagues, we provide roughly fifteen sections of this course annually. I listen to students' stories every day. I see in them the same enthusiasm, adventure, angst, and fright that I experienced before them. Many students sense God's hand on their lives, but others feel lost. Most of them have not reflected theologically about vocation. These students sit in my classroom as the children and grandchildren of the adults I addressed at my beloved camp.

Getting Started

In this essay, I contend that theology inevitably points to Christian vocation. The academy, of which I am part, has produced an invaluable legion of "-ologies." Sadly, most Pentecostal congregants care little about these efforts. I do not blame them. Good theology must not be relegated to ivory towers; instead, it must inspire our material, physical, experiential, affective, social, and vocational lives. Theology must make muster in our homes, on the street, in schools, at the hockey rink, in the marketplace, and in our churches. Theology and vocation cannot be separated. Who are we? Why are we here? What does God require of us? And specifically, how do Pentecostals answer these questions? Pentecostals deserve a theology that offers vocational clarity for their daily lives. Pentecostals deserve a theology that will enrich their lives with deep satisfaction, meaning, and liberation.

Pentecostalism's diversity makes this a daunting conversation. For the sake of this essay, I define Pentecostals broadly. I do so through employment of three common impulses: (1) Pentecostals connect their *raison d'être* to Pentecost; (2) Pentecostals proclaim the *Full Gospel*, an expression also known as the *Fivefold* or *Fourfold Gospel*; and (3) Pentecostals (ought to) embody the axiom "*prophethood of all believers.*" Though average Pentecostals might not know this language, the pervasiveness of these impulses across global Pentecostalism serves as my basis for a Pentecostal theology of vocation. Each impulse begins and ends with Jesus. Pentecost launches the Spirit of Jesus in believers. The Fivefold Gospel captures Jesus' vocation. Prophethood finds its exemplar in Jesus; Pentecostals encounter Jesus as prophet not as professional clergy. Jesus calls believers; Jesus commissions them.[1]

Some Pentecostal Hurdles

Despite their passion for the Holy Spirit, Pentecostals struggle immensely with the meaning of "life in the Spirit." This struggle manifests itself primarily in an erroneous theology of vocation. Why is Sunday so often divorced from Monday through

---

[1] On the difference between the Fivefold Gospel and Fourfold Gospel, see Wolfgang Vondey's *Pentecostal Theology: Living the Full Gospel* (London: T&T Clark, 2018). He states: "Pentecostals hold different views on the place and effect of sanctification in the order of salvation. Most visibly, Pentecostals are divided over the exact reception of sanctification as a work of grace; those following the Wesleyan Holiness tradition speak of sanctification as the experience of a 'second blessing' (subsequent to regeneration) while others follow the Reformed view of progressive sanctification throughout the believer's life" (67–68). This disagreement does not warrant dismissal of fivefold language by fourfold proponents; all Pentecostals emphasize fervently the importance of holiness.

Saturday? Why do many Pentecostal worshippers find little connection between Sunday worship and their weekly duties and activities? Why do Pentecostals experience intimacy with God in worship, prayers, sermons, and service, yet seldom connect these practices to life outside of gatherings? Though they spend the bulk of their lives at work, with families, and in their communities, Pentecostals believe, at least subtly, that what really matters is the time spent in church, in prayer, and in contemplation. I dare say most active Pentecostal churchgoers cannot remember a constructive sermon on the importance of their workplace or community life. Despite good intentions, Pentecostals fail to act out their passion for the Spirit-filled life in their daily lives.

I see three consistent hurdles to a sustainable Pentecostal theology of vocation. First, Pentecostals must address their consistent dive into dualism. They cannot fall prey to compartmentalization, to the trap of sacred versus secular. Second, as I stated in my counter-testimony, Pentecostals must reimagine their erroneous obsession with the vocational superiority of church-related ministry. Third, Pentecostals, like other traditions, must address the significance of calling beyond the workplace. If Pentecostals genuinely cherish terms such as "*life* in the Spirit" or the "Spirit-filled *life*," they must ensure that such a life extends to every moment of their lives for the duration of their lives. What does "life in the Spirit" mean for a child, a teenager, a college student, and a retiree/senior adult?

Jesus

To understand what "life in the Spirit" means for Pentecostal believers, I must turn first to Jesus, the consummate person of the Spirit. At his baptism, Jesus is anointed by the Spirit (Luke 3:22). He emerges full of the Spirit, led by the Spirit (Luke 4:1) and empowered by the Spirit (Luke 4:14). He announces his mission as the fulfilment of Isaiah's prophecy:

> The Spirit of the Lord is upon me
>   because he has anointed me
>   to proclaim good news to the poor.
> He has sent me to proclaim liberty to the captives
>   and recovery of sight to the blind
>   to set at liberty those who are oppressed,
>   to proclaim the year of the Lord's favor (Isa 61:1–2a/Luke 4:18–19).

Jesus boldly states, "Today this Scripture has been fulfilled in your hearing" (Luke 4:21). Near the conclusion of the Third Gospel, when the two Emmaus disciples struggle to recognize Jesus as "a prophet mighty in word and deed" (Luke 24:19), Luke announces that Isaiah's prophecy was emblematic of a grand narrative that "[begins] with Moses and *all* the prophets" and points to Jesus (Luke 24:27).

When Pentecostals turn from the Gospels to Acts, they discover their connection to the prophetic Jesus at Pentecost. Luke transitions with an introductory statement about "all that Jesus began to do and teach" (Acts 1:1). Luke's second volume continues the story of Jesus with unmistakable parallels. Just as Jesus is anointed by the Spirit (Luke 3:22; 4:18), so the disciples will not begin their ministry until they have been baptized with the Spirit (Acts 1:4, 5). As Jesus lives full of the Holy Spirit (Luke 4:1a), so the disciples are filled with the Holy Spirit (Acts 2:4). Just as Jesus is empowered by the Spirit to perform miracles, wonders, and signs (Luke 4:14; Acts 2:22), so also the new people of God perform wonders and signs (Acts 2:43; 5:12; 6:8; 8:6, 13; 14:3). The same prophetic Spirit that enables Jesus' vocation emboldens the life and mission of the new people of God. In terms of the Fivefold Gospel, Jesus' call to conversion sets Pentecostals on a quest for holy love. As Pentecostals conform to the image of Christ, they draw deeper from the well of God's love. As disciples of Christ, they are compelled to witness to the divine love at work in their lives. As Jesus the savior, sanctifier, and Spirit-baptizer transforms their lives, Pentecostals turn their love toward the sick, the needy, the oppressed, and all things near to God's heart.

Pentecost and Pentecostals

With the connection to the prophetic Jesus established, I now turn to Pentecost and its significance for "life in the Spirit." Pentecostals, as their name suggests, trace their origin to Acts 2. They emerged with characteristics described by Grant Wacker as primitivism and pragmatism. Through these impulses, Pentecostals view themselves as recipients of a "last days" deluge of the Spirit that will usher in the return of Jesus in fulfillment of Joel 2:28–32 and Acts 2:17–18:

> In the last days, God says,
> I will pour out my Spirit on all people,
>   Your sons and daughters will prophesy,
>   Your young men will see visions,
>   Your old men will dream dreams,
>   Even on my servants, both men and women,
> I will pour out my Spirit in those days
>   and they will prophesy.

As a restorationist movement, Pentecostals laud the return of charismatic gifts. Within Pentecostalism, the label "primitivist" does not denote a primitive or simple movement; it captures Pentecostals' desire to embody, reenact, and continue the first-century story of Jesus and the Apostles. On one hand, Pentecostals hope to write volume three of Acts (or Acts 29ff.). However, they do not begin at the end of Acts. The inaugural issue of the *Apostolic Faith*, the newsletter of the upstart Apostolic Faith Mission in Los Angeles, signals both the movement's return to and extension of Acts 2. The newsletter's opening headline reads:

> PENTECOST HAS COME
> Los Angeles Being Visited by a Revival of Bible Salvation and
> Pentecost as Recorded in the Book of Acts.[2]

Luke's account of Pentecost serves as more than an event on a first-century calendar. Pentecostals return unashamedly to the Day of Pentecost as a root symbol for an ever-present reality. At the first Pentecost, the resurrected and ascended Jesus becomes the baptizer in the Spirit. Pentecost serves as a "last days" beginning for the first followers of Jesus and for a burgeoning twentieth-century movement.

I cannot overstate the breadth of this Pentecostal conviction. In my office, I have photos of two signs from the tabernacle at my Pentecostal camp. They read, "Be Filled with the Spirit—Ephesians 5:18," and "Jesus is the Same Yesterday, Today, and Forever—Hebrews 13:8." A seasoned Pentecostal worshipper would surely identify these verses with Pentecost. Canadian evangelist Aimee Semple McPherson, the founder of the International Church of the Foursquare Gospel, published a collection of personal experiences and sermons under the title *This is That* (see Acts 2:16).[3] She interprets her life—and subsequent Pentecostal lives—as fulfilment and continuation of Peter's declaration in Acts 2:16 that the Pentecost event realizes Joel's prophecy for a last days outpouring of the Spirit.

Both Joel's and Peter's proclamation of the Spirit's outpouring on "all flesh" has theological implications that carry infinite vocational potential. Nineteenth-century English poet Gerard Manley Hopkins captures well this result: "Christ plays in ten thousand places."[4] As the great equalizer, the Spirit falls upon the young and old, sons and daughters, male and female, servants and free. If the Spirit enlists everyone, patriarchy and hierarchy collapse. The Spirit washes away the sacred and secular divide.

---

[2] "The Apostolic Faith Movement," *Apostolic Faith*, 1:1, September 1906, 1.

[3] Aimie Semple McPherson, *This is That. Personal Experiences, Sermons and Writings* (Los Angeles: The Bridal Call Publishing House, 1919).

[4] Gerard Manley Hopkins, *As Kingfishers Catch Fire* (London, Penguin, 2015), 7. Catholic theologian José Comblin captures a similar link: "There was one Easter; there are millions of Pentecosts" (Cited by Steven J. Land in *Pentecostal Spirituality: A Passion for the Kingdom* [Sheffield: Sheffield Academic Press, 1993], 173).

Though so much more could be said of a barrier-breaking Pentecost, I must turn briefly to Pentecost as a stage for dreamers, visionaries, and prophets.

Dreams and Visions

Peter's affirmation of Joel's prophecy encourages Pentecostals to dream, and even a cursory glance at Pentecostal history reveals consistent tales of visions and dreams. According to the framework at hand, the Holy Spirit stirs believers' imaginations to extend the life of Jesus. Pentecostals affirm that dreams and visions shape their lives whether on a given day or a lifetime. How might Pentecostals carry this worldview toward vocational formation? Though Pentecostals often testify to extraordinary examples such as direct messages through visual, auditory, and physical experiences or through symbols and pictures, they must enlarge their understanding of dreams and visions. Pentecostals cannot expect everyone to dream like Joseph and experience visions like Peter and Paul in Acts. I dare say that most people do not experience such extraordinary revelations. If so, how do we reimagine Spirit-driven dreams and visions? How might Pentecostals imagine their Pentecost-al vocation?

Dreams and visions, whether extraordinary visions or daily reflections, take Pentecostals to an imaginary space. The child in all of us dreams through fantasy or fairytales. "Once upon a time" begins a story that longs for the "day" when dreams come true. Dream stories reveal passions, longing, suffering, and hope, and they demand responsive characters. In these tales, dreamers do not seek escape from this world; they seek its transformation.

Consider the evolution of Martin Luther King's "I Have a Dream" speech. With poetic precision and a S/spirit of improvisation, King performs his dream as hope for a better day. Like Jesus and the prophets of old, King's dream is prophetic. Dreamers do not begin with an answer, but they know something must be done. They do not know the way, but they envision a brighter future. A short rehearsal of biblical dreamers (all prophets are dreamers) like Joseph, Moses, Isaiah, Amos, Micah, John the Baptist, and Jesus demonstrates further that dreamers observe culture. They carefully study their world. They feel need. They experience suffering and abuse. They speak truth to power! This Pentecost-al Spirit creates within them—and us—a visionary zeal. Spirit-inspired dreams move people to live out their vocations with intentionality. Dreamers do not live in the past. King does not say, "I had a dream"; instead, he takes on the role of a prophet. King invites his listeners then and now to ask, "Do you see it?" The Spirit released at Pentecost calls everyone to imagine a better world.

Beyond the extraordinary encounters of Scripture, what about day-to-day life? We dream every day. Quaker scholar Parker Palmer argues that most dreams arise internally;

they emerge slowly, evolve, and remain fluid.[5] The Spirit of Pentecost asks: What do you dream about? How do specific dreams shape your formation, your practices, and your pursuits? The Spirit invites Pentecostals to act out their own "I Have a Dream" speech(es). What would you say? Who would you address? What would compel you to act? How do you turn dream(s) into reality?

Jazzolalia

Along with dreams and visions, Swiss Pentecostal scholar Walter Hollenweger's bid to link Pentecostal roots to black or African-American spiritualities provides further fodder for a theology of vocation.[6] Out of their spiritual songs, African-Americans gave rise to jazz, a genre that serves as a suitable metaphor for Pentecostal life in the Spirit.[7] Pentecostal worship, liturgies, theologies, and—I suggest—vocations do not produce orchestral or symphonic performances; instead, Pentecostals celebrate oral and bodily spontaneity and improvisation. According to Church of God in Christ theologian David Daniels, "Pentecostal sound became a means of constructing an alternative soundscape, social space, and religious culture."[8] For this reason, *jazzolalia* serves as an imaginative extension of first-century glossolalia. Like Louis Armstrong's statement at the outset of this essay, trumpeter Cootie William rejects an invitation to define jazz: "Define it, I'd rather tackle Einstein's theory."[9] If applied to vocation, the aphorism by Nigerian-American Pentecostal scholar Nimi Wariboko resonates well: "It-does-not-make-sense-but-it-makes-spirit."[10]

Pentecostal lives are simultaneously beautiful and messy, rhythmic and complex. They share life together not through stiff and defined parameters but as a dance. Fourth-century theologian Gregory of Nazianzus describes the Trinity with a jazz-like metaphor as a dance of mutuality and reciprocity. Similarly, Pentecostals experience Jesus' love for the Father, and they imitate Jesus' intentionality, freedom, and flexibility. As dreamers and visionaries, Pentecostals play prophetic music in new places. With a jazz consciousness, Pentecostals imagine and improvise God's love and justice.

---

[5] Parker J. Palmer, *Let Your Life Speak* (San Francisco: Jossey-Bass, 1999), 10.

[6] Walter J. Hollenweger, "The Black Roots of Pentecostalism," in *Pentecostals after a Century: Global Perspectives on a Movement in Transition*, eds. Allan Anderson and Walter J. Hollenweger (Sheffield: Sheffield University Press, 1999), 36–43.

[7] Concerning the history of jazz, music historians argue that the improvisation behind African-American spirituals gives rise to genres such as swing, blues, ragtime, soul, and rap.

[8] David Daniels, "'Gotta Moan Sometime': A Sonic Exploration of Earwitnesses to Early Pentecostal Sound in North America," *Pneuma* 30 (2008), 5–32.

[9] William Edgar, *A Supreme Love: The Music of Jazz and the Hope of the Gospel* (Downers Grove: IVP Academic, 2022), 176–77.

[10] Nimi Wariboko, *The Pentecostal Hypothesis: Christ Talks, They Decide* (Eugene: Cascade, 2020), xvi.

Pentecostals should not be preoccupied with vocational certainty but with faithful improvisation; they should not descend into unbridled subjectivity, but they must develop a "listening ear," an ear that responds intimately to the ebb and flow of intense conviction and daily whispers. Like Wariboko's aphorism, the Pentecostal vocation consists of singing, playing, listening, celebrating, suffering, empathizing, sharing, and creating together. All of life involves a call and response. Pentecostal callings, like jazz, are not scripted. Vocations are not mapped out for them. Pentecost invites people to a live performance inspired by love.

On one hand, Pentecostals have an inadequate theology of vocation. On the other hand, I am convinced that they overthink—and overlook—the call of God. If calling looks less like a Mozart score, Pentecostals might do well to refrain from the obligatory search to answer the question, "To what am I called?" If God's call does not come out of a time-sealed vault that reads, "Thus say the Lord, 'Here is your calling!,'" Pentecostals might entertain the metaphor of *jazzolalia*. Imagine the conviction, passion, liberation, and dynamism that accompanies such impulses. The call might be "better felt than telt." In seeking alternative phrases to saying, "I am called," William Klein and David Steiner provide helpful descriptors that reverberate with Wariboko's aphorism:

1. "I desire to pursue . . ." I want to engage in a good thing, I sincerely want to do this.
2. "I feel compelled to . . ." I am wired to do this.
3. "I want to . . ." I am equipped for a task. I have the time and resources. I want to say yes to an inner longing.
4. "I have to do . . ." I am not sure about my passion or interest, but I simply must do it. I cannot wait to see if someone steps up.
5. "I must obey . . ." I must respond to the word of God. I cannot say no.[11]

Perhaps it is better to say that "the love of Christ compels me" (2 Cor 5:14) than "I have found my calling." Perhaps it is better to follow wordless groans (Rom 8:22–27) than to spend a lifetime seeking a template. Finally, I find Hollenweger's poetic articulation of Pentecostal theology applicable:

[it's] not the book, but the parable,
not the thesis, but the testimony,
not the dissertation, but the dance,
not concepts, but banquets,

---

[11] William W. Klein and Daniel J. Steiner, *What Is My Calling? A Biblical and Theological Exploration of Christian Identity* (Grand Rapids: Baker Academic, 2022), 168–70.

not a system of thinking, but stories and songs,
not definitions, but descriptions
not arguments, but transformed lives.[12]
Concerning vocations, I would add "it's not classical music, but *jazzolalia*."

Prophethood of all Believers

A Pentecostal understanding of vocation requires jazz-like improvisation, but the axiom "prophethood of all believers" lies at the heart of the movement's theology of vocation. The phrase "prophethood of all believers" first appeared among Pentecostals in Roger Stronstad's groundbreaking *The Charismatic Theology of St. Luke* in 1984.[13] Stronstad later titles a 1999 work by this axiom.[14] Similarly, and to my knowledge independent of Stronstad, Steven Land argued in his 1993 work *Pentecostal Spirituality: A Passion for the Kingdom* that the time is ripe for Pentecostals to think beyond Luther's theology of the "priesthood of all believers" and to imagine "the prophethood of all believers."[15] Not surprisingly, Stronstad and Land both begin with Pentecost. Where Pentecostals have too often been bogged down on evidential tongues, these authors inspire Pentecostals to turn their attention to prophetic life in the Spirit. Stronstad connects the Spirit in the life of Jesus and Jesus' followers to charismatic (think "prophetic") figures in the Old Testament like Moses, David, or Elijah. Even as these figures serve God's mission, the same Spirit that rests upon them is transferred to their successors, such as Moses to Joshua, Saul to David, and Elijah to Elisha. As the Spirit comes upon and animates Jesus' life, Jesus transfers this same Spirit to his followers on the day of Pentecost.

Peter boldly explains that Pentecost makes the Holy Spirit available "to all flesh" (Acts 2:17 KJV). Where the Spirit in the Old Testament comes upon a select few, Pentecost sets in motion the last days and makes prophethood possible! Pentecostals anticipate this universal potential from the Hebrew Scriptures. In Numbers 11:16–17, after Moses cries out over the burden of leading God's people, God gives Moses seventy elders and grants them the power of the Spirit. Moses responds with a plea "that all the Lord's people were prophets and that the Lord would put his Spirit on them" (Num 11:29). God also promises Ezekiel (like the prophet Joel) that the cleansing, sanctifying, and commissioning Spirit will rest on God's people (Ezek 36:24–32). The Spirit

---

[12] Walter J. Hollenweger, "Pentecostalisms: Article, Research Centers, Bibliographies and Selected Literature," *European Pentecostal Charismatic Research Association*, http://www.epcra.ch/papers.html (6 June 2023).

[13] Roger Stronstad, *The Charismatic Theology of St. Luke*, 2nd ed. (Grand Rapids: Baker Academic, 2012).

[14] Stronstad, *The Prophethood of All Believers: A Study in Luke's Charismatic Theology* (Sheffield: Sheffield Academic Press, 1999).

[15] Land, *Pentecostal Spirituality*, 18.

released at Pentecost invites every person to participate in prophetic fulfilment of God's kingdom. Pentecost makes prophethood a reality.

Pentecostal use of "prophethood of all believers" obviously amplifies Martin Luther's axiomatic "priesthood of all believers." Luther coins this language first in terms of salvation, so that every person has direct access to God without the mediation of a priest. Further, for Luther, the priesthood of all believers makes all vocations equal before God. Sadly, even as I extend Luther's historic advancement of Christian vocation, many Pentecostals are not yet aware of Luther's contributions. To be filled with the Spirit is an initiation into prophetic life. Throughout the book of Acts, and beyond, Luke establishes the people of God as an eschatological community of Spirit-filled prophets, every one of them—and us—called to participate in Christian vocation.

Prophethood requires careful use of language. First, prophethood does not mean every person claims the office or title of a prophet. To the contrary, in an impassioned plea to believers at Corinth, Paul chastises a young congregation for their misuse of utterance gifts during gathered worship (1 Cor 12–14). In order to curb Corinthian pride, Paul provides multiple lists of diverse gifts (or ministries) given to the church for mutual edification. The Apostle asks, "Are all Apostles? Are all prophets? Are all teachers?" (1 Cor 12:29). His questions are rhetorical. Of course not! Not everyone holds the office of apostle, prophet, or teacher. Paul could have gone further. Not everyone serves as a pastor, deacon, or elder. In Ephesians 4:11, Paul describes the ministry of apostles, prophets, evangelists, pastors, and teachers as specific offices given to the church by God, not to all but to specific individuals, for the building up of the church. Just as the priesthood of all believers does not dismiss the specific call to a pastoral office, so also prophethood leaves space for the office of a prophet. So if prophethood does not grant every believer the title and responsibilities for the office of prophet, what might it mean?

A careful rendering of prophethood rescues Pentecostals from dreadful misunderstanding and abuse by those who cheapen the prophetic with their end-time speculations. If Pentecostals truly desire fullness in the Spirit, prophethood gives vocational urgency to everything they say and do. Jesus calls every believer to participate in prophetic Christianity. Like the prophets, Pentecostals seek justice, love, peace, healing, and reconciliation of humanity and God's creation. People of the Spirit must daily take on the mantle of the prophets to stand up and fight, speak out, march, protest, sing, vote, give, hope, love, read, laugh, cry, and do whatever is necessary to fulfill the gospel. Life in the Spirit calls Pentecostals to embody and perform God's vision for humanity.

At an ecclesial level, Pentecostals might draw on the renowned American rabbi Abraham Heschel, who argues that prophets declare the state of a people, whether a nation, community, or workplace. In a world filled with accusations about who is at fault for the state of our world, Heschel states boldly that "no matter who is guilty, all are responsible."[16] Through the Spirit, Pentecostals must dream new dreams within their local churches, denominations, and global networks. In so doing, participants may live out their dreams both individually and collectively.

The Full Gospel: Fivefold Gospel

While the "prophethood of all believers" exists as a key Pentecostal concept, the Fivefold Gospel serves as a plausible structure for Pentecostal theology. The fivefold confession centers on five tenets: Jesus is (1) Savior, (2) Sanctifier, (3) Spirit-baptizer, (4) Healer, and (5) soon-coming King. Even where Pentecostals have not heard or do not employ this specific structure, these historic tenets find space under the large confessional and experiential umbrella that is Pentecostalism. I propose that these tenets offer Pentecostals a solid foundation for a theology of vocation.

These tenets locate the entire—"full"—gospel around Jesus. The connection to Jesus' mission—vocation—cannot be underestimated. Though Pentecostals often restrict these tenets to individual experience, they demand much more. Jesus is not only a personal savior but the redeemer of all things. Jesus calls his followers to holy living and heals our broken bodies, but he is the ultimate sanctifier, healer, and deliverer of every physical and social evil. Jesus the Spirit-baptizer creates space for intimacy and dynamic evangelism, but he opens our world to greater breadth of Spirit. Jesus is "my" king not only in a personal or spiritual dimension, but he launches a new kind of kingdom that decries all injustice and demands a praxis built upon reconciliation in anticipation of new creation.

If Jesus directs and serves as the lead actor of the Full Gospel and if Pentecostals receive the blessings of Jesus' mission, what might be the link between Jesus, the Full Gospel, and vocation? The Spirit-filled Jesus embodies his vocational identity as Savior, Sanctifier, Spirit-baptizer, Healer, and soon-coming King. Jesus' vocation becomes the believer's vocation. Pentecostals not only receive the Full Gospel, but they perform the Full Gospel for the world. Pentecostal vocation is the extension of Jesus' vocation.

Before turning to the specific tenets of the Full Gospel, I want to pull in non-Pentecostal readers. First, the Full Gospel sounds elitist, and Pentecostals have no doubt been guilty of suggesting its superiority. Where Pentecostals have done so, I am saddened and ashamed, and I ask forgiveness. Obviously, the fivefold tenets are not only domain of Pentecostals; they reside fully within orthodox Christianity (another compelling incentive for ecumenism). The Full Gospel provides the necessary language for Pentecostals to construct their identity, theology, experience, and vocations. Even as

---

[16] Abraham Heschel, *The Prophets* (New York: Harper, 1962), 19.

Pentecostals continue to plunge the depths of the Full Gospel, they are not alone in doing so. In *The Secular Age*, Catholic philosopher Charles Taylor describes the human search of happiness as a search for "fullness." While Taylor surely understands the idea of fullness for a Christian worldview, he recognizes that believers and non-believers live their day-to-day lives in routine and drudgery, all the while pursuing greater clarity and fulfilment.[17] Similarly, Pentecostals seek and imagine a *fuller* gospel, a more holistic view of Jesus' life, mission, and commissioning. Indeed, if Jesus is the living Jesus, he continues to speak and act among us. The application of Full Gospel tenets to vocation serves as my attempt to flesh out Pentecostal appropriation of Jesus' call.

Second, though some are tempted to see the Full Gospel as sequential, these tenets are not strictly linear. Salvation is a taste of the end. Healing is integral to salvation. In light of our vocations, we do not seek to fill a tenet, but we participate in a great web of God's work. I also appreciate the words of A. J. Swoboda, who describes the "prophethood of all believers" as the "sixth element of the 'full gospel' message of the earliest Pentecostals."[18] Whether prophethood flows out of the Full Gospel or vice versa, I am not sure. It is not my desire to defend or rehearse this structure, except to locate its importance around vocation.

1. Savior

When outsiders to Pentecostalism (and not a few insiders) describe Pentecostals, they often jump immediately to Pentecostal obsession with Spirit baptism. Pentecostal scholars slow us down. "The Full Gospel," according to Wolfgang Vondey, "is soteriological from beginning to end."[19] Though Pentecostals traditionally celebrate a sudden (or crisis) conversion, an integrated understanding of salvation suggests that Paul's exhortation to "work out your salvation" means people are saved, being saved, and will be saved (Phil 2:12). Similarly, salvation turns our attention not only toward God, but simultaneously toward our neighbor. As Chris E. W. Green puts it, "How God saves us must be inseparable from what God saves us for."[20] Pentecostals are pardoned at salvation, and they begin to proclaim the grace they have received. The call "to be saved" cannot be separated from vocation. Even as conversion turns affections toward God, their experience enlivens a new disposition. To benefit from Christ's sufferings brings an immediate call to suffer with him. As Pentecostals receive God's

---

[17] Charles Taylor, *A Secular Age* (Cambridge: Harvard University Press, 2007), 5.

[18] A. J. Swoboda, *Tongues and Trees: Toward a Pentecostal Ecological Theology* (Dorset, UK: Deo Publishing, 2013), 189.

[19] Vondey, *Pentecostal Theology*, 37

[20] Chris E. W. Green, *Sanctifying Interpretation: Vocation, Holiness, and Scripture* (Cleveland, TN: CPT Press, 2015), 43.

unconditional love, they are invited to forgive those who hurt them. The love of Jesus compels them to avoid bitterness, jealousy, or resentment.

Through salvation, strange as it may sound, "we become like God toward others."[21] In a mysterious but real way, salvation makes Pentecostals saviors with Christ and like him. Some may be surprised by the old Pentecostal hymn "I Am His and He Is Mine." Upon close inspection of the lyrics, the hymnwriter is hardly lost in otherworldly ecstasy with the Divine. Filled with love, he sees a different world:

> Heaven above is softer blue,
> > Earth around is sweet green;
> > Something lives in every hue
> > Christless eyes have never seen.[22]

Similarly, culture critic Steve Turner gives a poignant result of salvation: "We feel differently about trees, leaves, rain, bad housing, animals, food, money, sex, social standing, leisure, poverty."[23] Pentecostals must proclaim that salvation means more than enjoyment of God's love. Jesus the savior calls every person to fulfill this mission.

2. Sanctifier

Salvation offers new believers stirring possibilities for transformation. New believers cast (more or less) their false, messy, and egocentric lives to Jesus in pursuit of a new kind of "fullness." They commit to obey Jesus' commandments and to "walk in the light as he is in the light" (1 John 1:7). They strive to be "imitators of God" and to "walk in love" (Eph 5:1–2). Justification is surely not primary with sanctification as secondary add-on.

Sadly, Pentecostals often reduce sanctification to a list of dos and don'ts. They face a constant temptation to slip toward legalism. Instead, a theology of vocation resists a worldview based on drudgery and plagued by judgment in exchange for the pursuit of God's love and beauty. When "the world is charged with the grandeur of God," holiness ignites a call to discover our truest desires.[24] Food and drink, dance and music, sex and play, work and leisure fulfill God's design. Sanctified people are called not to be drunk with wine, but filled—dare I say "drunk"—with the Spirit (Eph 5:18). Sanctification liberates Pentecostals to enjoy life to the full (John 10:10; Rom 14:13; Gal 5:1).

A further emphasis concerns Paul's call upon the "saints" (literally, "a people set apart"; Rom 1:7; 1 Cor 1:2). Pentecostals declare boldly the call "to be holy as God is

---

[21] Henri Nouwen, *Discernment: Reading the Signs of Daily Life* (San Francisco: HarperOne, 2013), 135–36.

[22] Penned by George Wade Robinson in 1890, many Pentecostal hymnals include this hymn. On its origin, see https://hymnary.org/text/loved_with_everlasting_love (21 June 2023).

[23] Steve Turner, *Imagine: A Vision for Christians in the Arts* (Downers Grove: IVP, 2017), 102.

[24] Hopkins, "God's Grandeur," 5.

holy" (1 Pet 1:14). On one hand, every seasoned Pentecostal knows the call to "come out from among them and be ye separate" (2 Cor 6:17). On the other hand, though Pentecostals take the purity that God demands seriously, an overzealous commitment to separation remains inadequate. Jesus' invitation to a sanctified life means more than sinlessness. Beyond separation and purity, the sanctified people of God are at one and the same time called to the world. Intimacy with Jesus turns Pentecostals toward their neighbor. The great commandment describes holy love turned outward (Matt 22:37–40). God's holy love, enacted in and through Pentecostals, is made manifest through sanctified lives. Holiness becomes a way of laboring in our families, workplaces, schools, and communities (see Gal 5:22–23; Col 3:12–17).

Prophethood commissions every Pentecostal to embody holy reverence and awe with each task. The idea of sacred and secular vocations collapses; every "secular" vocation becomes a "sacred"—a sanctifying—vocation. Prophethood enlists Pentecostals to address moral, social, political, and systemic evils. In so doing, they do not succumb to a message of doom, but they deliver a message of hope. When Pentecostals speak truth to power, the call to sanctification cannot dissolve into debates of who bears guilt. Prophethood makes everyone responsible. Prophetic people imagine spaces filled with divine sanctity, love, and compassion.

Finally, sanctifying vocations with their reordered ambitions, gratitude, and compassion mesh well with Jesus' present and future kingdom. Deeper love for God translates to deeper love for one another and thereby contributes to and creates a yearning for the full consummation of God's kingdom. Like young love between wife and husband, love for God creates longing and unending passion, service, and joy. Our taste of the future creates an insatiable desire for God's perfect love. Living out their sanctifying vocations enables Pentecostals to experience and anticipate the "shalom" promised with the new heaven and earth. Jesus the sanctifier calls Pentecostals to holy living. In a mysterious way, sanctification makes us sanctifiers with him and like him.

3. Spirit-Baptizer

According to Frank Macchia, Spirit baptism is the crown jewel of Pentecostal theology.[25] Although it may be the best known tenet of Pentecostals, Spirit baptism remains difficult to unpack. Many Pentecostals know the refrain, "I'm saved, sanctified, and filled with the Holy Ghost." While classical Pentecostals typically experience Spirit baptism as a crisis experience accompanied by evidential tongues, the larger umbrella of Pentecostalism covers a host of expressions. Charismatic or renewal streams often speak of "fanning the flame" or "actualization of baptismal initiation." In short, though

---

[25] Frank Macchia, *Baptized in the Spirit: A Global Pentecostal Theology* (Grand Rapids: Zondervan, 2006), 20.

Pentecostals debate the reception of the Spirit, all streams agree that life in the Spirit includes current manifestations of spiritual gifts and ongoing pursuit of a deeper, fuller encounter with the Spirit.[26]

I argued earlier that Pentecostals see the Spirit-filled Jesus as exemplar. Sammy Alfaro offers a helpful assessment about Jesus' vocation: "What might be surprising, however, is that to speak of the baptism with the Holy Spirit early Pentecostals began by identifying Jesus as Spirit Baptized," and according to the Gospels, "Jesus did not preach a single sermon or begin his mission in any way until the Holy Spirit had anointed him with power."[27] At the end of Luke's Gospel, Jesus directs the disciples to wait in Jerusalem "until they have been clothed with power from on high" (Luke 24:49; see also Gal 3:26; Col 3:12). Upon his ascension, Jesus the Spirit-baptizer empowers the new people of God to extend his mission. With unending anticipation and in fulfillment of Acts 1:8, Pentecostals sense a divine destiny for their lives. Their participation in the "last days" outpouring compels them to take the gospel to the ends of the earth (see also Acts 2:17). With such urgency, it is no wonder that this zeal leads to the expansion of the movement.

The vocational connection between Spirit baptism and the prophethood of believers should be immediately apparent. Sadly, however, Pentecostals often experience Spirit baptism as a profound encounter with God that fails to impact daily living. Stronstad exhorts—and warns—Pentecostals not to forget its effect. Pentecostals must not reduce Spirit baptism to evangelism (think verbal proclamation). Prophetic people with holy affections speak truth to power. Witnesses testify and advocate for individuals and communities. Spirit-empowered witnesses embody the suffering, stewardship, hospitality, and compassion of God to the world.[28]

Again, where Pentecostals often speak as elitists, the late pastor Jack Hayford offers helpful counsel for insiders and outsiders. The Spirit-baptized life is marked by "a passion for fullness, for *all of Jesus* . . . [to] open me to the Holy Spirit's constant overflow in my life, welcoming His gifts and transcending my limits with His almightiness."[29] I also cling to the words of Pentecostal historian Ronald Kydd, my

---

[26] See my *Reading Luke-Acts in the Pentecostal Tradition* (Cleveland, TN: CPT Press, 2010) and my 2021 SPS presidential address, "A Century in the Making: Receiving the Samaritan Pentecost (Acts 8:4–25) in the Pentecostal and Charismatic Traditions," *Pneuma* 43 (2021), 173–98. In the spirit of ecumenism, see "'Do Not Quench the Spirit': Charisms in the Life and Mission of the Church," the Report of the Sixth Phase of the International Catholic-Pentecostal Dialogue (2011–2015), http://www.christianunity.va/content/unitacristiani/en/dialoghi/sezione-occidentale/pentecostali/dialogo/documenti-di-dialogo/testo-del-documento-in-inglese.html (5 July 2021).

[27] Sammy Alfaro, *Divino Compañero: Toward a Hispanic Pentecostal Christology* (Eugene, OR: Pickwick, 2010), 40–41.

[28] Stronstad, *Charismatic Theology*, 97–98.

[29] S. David Moore, *Pastor Jack: The Authorized Biography of Jack Hayford* (Colorado Springs: David C. Cook, 2020), 241.

college professor, who often stated that "an encounter with God that does not lead to greater intimacy with Jesus is ultimately disappointing." If Pentecostals experience Spirit baptism as an expression of God's love upon them, they will inevitably turn that same love toward the world. The fivefold vocation is increasingly clear: "The fruit of the Spirit [is] the Spirit's work to manifest Christ in the character of the believers. The gifts of the Spirit . . . manifest the power of God in the service of the gospel" to evangelism and edification.[30] Jesus calls every Pentecostal to this life.

4. Healing/Exorcism

Healing plays no small part in Jesus' ministry. Similarly, the new people of God continue his healing ministry. In Acts, disciples heal the sick, grant sight to the blind, and deliver the oppressed in Jesus' name. Paul includes gifts of healing, faith, and miracles among ministries given by God for the common good. James encourages prayer for the sick (Jas 5:13–16). Pentecostals everywhere believe unashamedly that God heals today. That "Jesus Christ [the healer] is the same yesterday, today, and forever" requires little defense among Pentecostals (see Heb 13:8).

Given the outstanding essays on healing by David Han and Andrew Prevot, I draw attention only to links between healing and vocation. In short, a Pentecostal theology of healing must extend further than bodily healing. According to Prevot, healing "may be interpreted in diverse ways and involve features such as emotional comfort, social inclusion, personal empowerment, holistic care, spiritual wellbeing, and lengthy process of change and growth."[31] Healing vocations, formal and informal, attend to economic, social, cultural, political, and environmental dimensions. Similarly, exorcisms include deliverance both from demonic forces tormenting an individual as well as from the systemic evils felt by communities.

Pentecostals must acknowledge and celebrate where they already serve in ministries of healing. They serve in vocations that carry out the ministries that Prevot details above on a regular basis. Though families, local churches, and working communities support and care for one another at a basic level every day, many Pentecostals fail to equate their daily lives with healing. On the other hand, Pentecostals must capture a larger vision for prophetic healing. They must proclaim the convergence of Jesus' announcement of the kingdom with the day of the Lord's favor (Luke 4:19). The ministry of healing calls for Jubilee. In a world filled with corruption, abuse, exploitation, racism, inequality, and bigotry, Pentecostals must reimagine their sphere of influence. As an example, the recent publication of *Open Wide Our Hearts: The Enduring Call to Love,* published by the USCCB in 2018, offers a pastoral appeal to

---

[30] Land, *Pentecostal Spirituality*, 119.

[31] Andrew Prevot, "Varieties of Healing: A Catholic Perspective," *Spiritus* 9:2 (2024), 197.

address racism.³² In the Spirit of Pentecost, Pentecostals must learn from our fellow Christian communities and expand their visions of a better world.

Another implication for vocation concerns the role of those in medical work. Pentecostals pray every day for the physical needs of their fellow congregants and neighbors. Patients yield their lives to physicians, surgeons, nurses, and expansive teams of professionals and workers committed to the common goal of health, recovery, and overall wellbeing. Pentecostals believe intuitively that all healing comes from God, whether extraordinary or ordinary (of course, heart surgeries, knee replacements, and life-saving prescriptions are hardly ordinary). Allow me to share a personal testimony. My audiologist is bi-vocational. During my consultation, Dr. Myers (name adjusted) inquired about my "day job." When he learned that I work as a professor of theology, Myers stated enthusiastically that he pastors a local church. A month after I received my hearing aids, I met Myers for a checkup. When he asked about my adjustment to hearing aids, I told him that I testify joyfully to friends that "God healed my hearing." When I asked Myers if he saw his medical work as healing ministry, his facial response indicated that he had never considered this question. He began to talk of his work as a pastor. Sadly, the majority of Pentecostals do not imagine their work/careers as extensions of Jesus the healer.

5. Soon-Coming King

Early Pentecostals believed that Jesus would return sooner rather than later. While this hope remained strong throughout much of the twentieth century, urgency began to wane. Though later streams did not share the same zeal, all Pentecostal streams remain committed to Jesus' return and the full consummation of his kingdom. I suggest that a theology of vocation provides the necessary impetus to fuel passion and purpose. Whereas early Pentecostals may have been accused of an under-realized (too futuristic) eschatology, contemporary Pentecostals should be on the frontlines of a realized eschatology.³³

Sadly, hymns such as "This World Is Not My Home" and popular choruses like "All Aboard for the Gospel Train" teach a faulty eschatology that marginalizes daily life. Even as Pentecostals engage in end-time evangelical zeal (Matt 9:37/Luke 10:2; Matt 24:14/Mark 13:10; Luke 21:24) and long for the consummation of God's kingdom, they must resist dualism. As the final tenet of the Fivefold Gospel, Pentecostals do not seek escape from this world, but they bring the future into the present. Pentecostals

---

³² *Open Wide Our Hearts: The Enduring Call to Love—A Pastoral Letter Against Racism*, https://www.usccb.org/resources/open-wide-our-hearts-enduring-call-love-pastoral-letter-against-racism (12 June 2023).

³³ Obviously, Pentecostal diversity prevails again. A common thread of the prosperity gospel/Word Faith messengers offers an erroneous and abusive over-realized eschatology.

must proclaim more than "eternal life." The previous tenets of the Full Gospel demonstrate that Jesus steps into his vocation with the announcement that "the kingdom of God is upon us" (Mark 1:14). Paul tells the Ephesians that the promised Holy Spirit is a deposit that guarantees their final inheritance (Eph 1:14). In the fivefold scheme, intimate encounter with Jesus brings a taste of heaven to earth; holiness creates an insatiable passion for love, peace, and joy. Jesus heals the sick, delivers the oppressed, and transforms lives now (Luke 7:22-23)!

The reign of Jesus requires a prophetic response. Not only do Pentecostals reap the benefits of the already kingdom of God, but they join Jesus' vocation as agents of God's kingdom. Contrary to the common images of an endless bliss devoid of work, the rule of Jesus redeems their vocations. Pentecostals' vision for the kingdom renews their commitment as God's agents for co-creation and re-creation. With the prophet Zechariah, Pentecostals imagine a world where people enjoy the fruit of labor and fair compensation (Zech 8:10–12). With Micah, Pentecostals cannot separate their daily "walk with God" from justice and mercy (Mic 6:8). If there is no domain outside of God's rule, Pentecostals must reimagine their politics, business, education, and stewardship. With glossolalic zeal, Pentecostals groan with creation in anticipation of full redemption (Rom 8:28). With prophetic imagination, they extend the rule of God beyond church walls. In so doing, they do not imagine a single politic, but they bring prophethood to every and any kind of *polis*. Through *jazzolalia*, Pentecostals enjoy and anticipate "the kingdom of God . . . [as communities of] righteousness, peace, and joy in the Holy Spirit" (Rom 14:17).

Implications: PCCNA/USCCB Dialogue

Having spent the bulk of this essay developing a framework for a Pentecostal theology of vocation, I turn now to practical considerations. If the Spirit of Pentecost is the great Equalizer and available for everyone and if the Full Gospel promises "fuller" lives and if the prophethood of all believers launches prophetic dreams and visions, where does the rubber meet the road? I invite readers to remember my "Everyman" (and Everywoman) Pentecostal testimony, a tale of hierarchy, angst, and confusion. I invite all Pentecostals to find their place in the call of God. Due to length restrictions, I am limited to the following introductory implications for praxis.

First, as I stated earlier in this essay, a robust theology of vocation addresses Pentecostal proclivities to dualisms. (1) Pentecostals must abandon any obsession with the "spiritual" life. God is not interested in our spiritual lives. Instead, Pentecostals must embrace a spiritual*ity* that does not compartmentalize God's intent for their physical, emotional, sexual, and vocational lives. All humans are created and commissioned wholly by God. Period. (2) Pentecostals must abandon the sacred versus secular divide.

A common mantra at Evangel University is "everyone is called to ministry." The call of God—whatever a student's major—rests on every student that walks on our campus. (3) Pentecostals must not limit their vocation to a career/workplace. Vocation extends to all of life (see below).

Second, Pentecostals must enlarge their theology of vocation to include family, workplace (if applicable), citizen/community, church, friendship, and lifelong learning. I serve at one and the same time as a husband, father, sibling, and son. I serve as a professor, counselor, mentor, and scholar. I am a biblical scholar, a pacifist, an activist (with Missourians for Alternatives to the Death Penalty),[34] and an ecumenist. I worship and teach Sunday School at my local church. I am a Canadian citizen and a permanent resident in the United States. I live in Springfield, Missouri, specifically, the Galloway neighborhood. The list goes on. I wear many hats! Though degrees of consciousness and attentiveness to a specific vocation inevitably vary, I never take off a hat. What a responsibility! What a privilege! God calls every Pentecostal to similar yet unique livelihoods. Imagine the Fivefold Gospel enacted by every daughter and son, young and old, woman and man in every kitchen, bedroom, classroom, factory, city chamber, pew, and cubicle. The list goes on.

As an example, envision our families. The home is the ideal arena to enact the Full Gospel. The home functions as the stage for holy love and ambition, healing, and re-creation. As Luther's priesthood of all believers revolutionizes family life, Pentecost grants every member of every family a call to prophethood. Parents, siblings, and extended family members speak into each other's lives. Eyes and ears are always nearby. When a child states from the back seat of a car, "Mom/Dad, why is that man begging for food?," parents hear the prophets Amos and Micah and our supreme prophet Jesus. Even as parents guide children to their futures, parents receive a call to embody Jesus' fivefold mission. Parents strive to provide quality education, career/workplace guidance, but they also seek to guide their children to faith, to live holy lives, to bring healing, and to raise good citizens and humans. As the decades go by, children often become caregivers for their parents. However, in doing so, children must not deny their aging parents their day of "sageing."[35] Applications are infinite.

Third, I wonder if Pentecostals might reimagine vocation not as a noun (i.e., a call or calling), but as a verb (i.e., called). For this idea, I am indebted to Catholic theologian Kathleen Cahalan.[36] First, we live in an anxious world. As an educator, I see the mental health crisis every day. A consistent concern among young Pentecostal

---

[34] See https://www.madpmo.org (14 June 2023).

[35] See the delightful work by Jewish writer Zalman Schachter-Shalomi, *From Age-ing to Sage-ing: A Profound Vision for Growing Older* (New York: Warner Books, 1995).

[36] Kathleen A. Cahalan, *The Stories We Live: Finding God's Calling All Around Us* (Grand Rapids: Eerdmans, 2017).

students is "what will I do with my life?" and "where is God calling me?" Of course, this anxiety plagues every age group. I propose that an emphasis on "called" rather than "calling" might offer a partial solution to the current crisis. What if Pentecostals would obsess less over an ever-elusive quest to discover an all too often "hidden" calling (and whether they remain in the will of God) in exchange for affirmation and commitment to their current vocations? Every Pentecostal is called. They are called to Jesus, to holy living, to life in the Spirit, to be healers, and to be harbingers of Jesus' return. They are called to prophethood, wherever they live, love, work, and play. Right now! To live such lives constitutes the perfect will of God (Rom 12:1–2).

Fourth, conversations about vocation must recognize the role of privilege. Those of us who ask "what will we do with our lives?" make up a small fraction of the global population. A large percentage of Pentecostals—particularly in the Global South—live daily under socioeconomic duress. Unlike most readers of this essay, the poor of this world invest little energy on a quest for "their callings."[37] Instead, many people care only for daily food, health, and shelter. Many Pentecostals neither choose vocations nor imagine options. This vast need must inspire at least two prophetic possibilities. First, how might a robust theology of the Full Gospel inspire "the rich" to inspire self-worth and vocational value for the poor? Workers nearby and around the world contribute daily to the sustainability of the human project. The world runs on the backs of workers who engage in ordinary and mundane yet essential service; their work must be valued as kingdom work. Second, however, the privileged of this world must use their lives to advocate for and enable the poor. Jesus calls us to employ our resources on behalf of the outcast, the migrant, the incarcerated, and every person desperate for the Day of the Lord's favor (Luke 4:18–19; 11:1–4). Privilege demands prophetic responsibility.

Finally, I believe a major reason for the rising exodus of young people (and older people) out of institutional Christianity stems at least in part from an underdeveloped theology of vocation. I am tired of accusations of laziness and apathy hurled at today's youth. I am saddened by their disdain for church. However, I am convinced that Pentecostal churches do not demand enough from them. Exiled Pentecostals see through siloed living; they are tired of cheap grace. Instead, young adults want to make a difference in their world. If the church does not inspire their efforts, they look elsewhere. What if Pentecostals would reimagine discipleship that turns holiness from legalism and lawlessness to holy ambitions? What if youth would connect their artistic and creative desires to ministries of redemption and healing? Today's youth want to live prophetic lives. Pentecostals must affirm their work.

---

[37] Regardless of tradition, questions about privilege remain scarce in literature on vocation.

Until We Meet Again

Finally, if the prophethood of all believers and the Full Gospel serve as a legitimate foundation for a Pentecostal theology of vocation and if Pentecostals truly aspire to embody the barrier-breaking hospitality of Pentecost, we must represent the call to ecumenism. The Spirit of Pentecost undoubtedly calls Pentecostals to imagine the ecumenicity of the Spirit.[38] Pentecost calls believers to embody and release the cross-traditional recognition of God's work in the life of the "other." A common stated purpose for ecumenical dialogue includes emphasis upon unity and common witness. The world, which is so often characterized by anger, division, and violence, desperately needs prophetic unity and witness. I trust our investment in ecumenism embodies holy love, Spirit-driven witness, and healing. I pray for dreams and visions of a better world. I pray that this exploratory dialogue finds listening ears among my Pentecostal constituents.

Martin W. Mittelstadt (mittelstadtm@evangel.edu) is Professor of New Testament at Evangel University, Springfield, Missouri, USA.

---

[38] See Emilio Alvarez, *Pentecost: A Day of Power for All People* (Downers Grove: IVP, 2023), 36.

BAYLOR UNIVERSITY PRESS

Joy L. Vaughan

Phenomenal Phenomena

Biblical and Multicultural Accounts of Spirits and Exorcism

~~$69.99~~ $48.99 Hardcover | 275 pages | 6 x 9
ISBN 978-1-4813-1836-5

"An excellent compendium of scholarship and an interdisciplinary study of spirit possession in the Gospels and Acts."

—**DANIEL K. DARKO**, *Dean for Global Engagement and Professor of Biblical Studies, Taylor University*

The Holy Spirit and Higher Education
Renewing the Christian University
Amos Yong and Dale M. Coulter
Paperback | ~~$49.99~~ $34.99 | 320 pages | 7 x 10
ISBN 978-1-4813-1814-3

The Holy Spirit before Christianity
John R. Levison
Hardcover | ~~$44.99~~ $31.49 | 272 pages | 6 x 9
ISBN 978-1-4813-1003-1

A Profound Ignorance
Modern Pneumatology and its Anti-modern Redemption
Ephraim Radner
Hardcover | ~~$54.99~~ $38.49 | 463 pages | 6 x 9
ISBN 978-1-4813-4079-6

Receive a 30% discount and free shipping (US addresses)
Use code 17AARSBL23 until 12/31/23 at
www.baylorpress.com | 1.800.848.6224

Response to Martin Mittelstadt

Leonardo J. Gajardo

The experience of participating in our three-year exploratory dialogue was enriching and rewarding for me in several ways. The one that I had anticipated, and that certainly became a reality, was the blessing of learning about Pentecostal theology from Pentecostal brothers and sisters who have been formed by and have formed others in that rich theological tradition. One unexpected way in which I was enriched and rewarded by our three years of dialogue, prayer, and fellowship was that our reflections together afforded me the opportunity to revisit some of the theological tenets and insights of my own Catholic tradition. That was certainly the case with Martin Mittelstadt's paper, "Called: A Pentecostal Theology of Vocation."

In his paper, Mittelstadt frames the question he considers as follows:

> Theology and vocation cannot be separated. Who are we? Why are we here? What does God require of us? And specifically, how do Pentecostals answer these questions? Pentecostals deserve a theology that offers vocational clarity for their lives. Pentecostals deserve a theology that will enrich their lives with deep satisfaction, meaning, and liberation.[1]

He also identifies three consistent hurdles that have made a Pentecostal theology of vocation difficult to develop: 1) the dualism between the sacred and the secular; 2) the erroneous assumption that church-related ministry is vocationally superior to other vocations; and 3) the difficulty of articulating a sense of calling beyond the workplace. According to Mittelstadt, only by overcoming these hurdles will Pentecostals be able to ensure that the "*life* in the Spirit" or the "Spirit-filled *life*," which they cherish so much, "extends to every moment of their lives for the duration of their lives."

While I cannot speak for Pentecostals, I would say that, not just Pentecostals, but all Christians deserve a rich and robust vocational theology, so that they can perceive and respond to the Spirit's call in every aspect of their lives. I also must confess that Catholic theology, imagination, and practice have faced the same hurdles in articulating a theology of vocation that Mittelstadt identifies. But thanks to the questions he raised and the reflections he offered, as well as our rich dialogue, I was led to reflect on what my own Catholic tradition has to say about the vocation of all believers.

As I read Mittelstadt's paper, but even more so during his presentation of the paper and our subsequent discussion, I was struck by the resonance between the

---

[1] Martin W. Mittelstadt, "Called: A Pentecostal Theology of Vocation," *Spiritus* 9:2 (2024), 286.

questions and ideas he raised, and the teaching of the Second Vatican Council (1962–1965) on what the Council fathers called the universal call to holiness. This teaching had been important for me during my ministerial and theological formation, but, in recent years, other theological questions and ideas had caused me to "forget" this important teaching of the Council. I am very grateful to Mittelstadt for helping me to rediscover it and to recognize how it might contribute to the vital work of ecumenism.

The Council's teaching regarding the universal call to holiness in the church is found in the fifth chapter of the Council's dogmatic constitution on the Church, *Lumen Gentium* (*LG*), which was approved by an overwhelming majority of the more than 2,000 bishops present at Vatican II and was officially promulgated by Pope Paul VI in November of 1964. The chapter begins by affirming that God alone is holy, and that through the saving work of Christ, God has sanctified the church and bestowed on it the gift of the Spirit. It then declares:

> For this reason, everyone in the church is called to holiness, whether he belongs to the hierarchy or is cared for by the hierarchy, according to the saying of the apostle: "This is the will of God, your sanctification" (1 Th 4,3; see Eph 1, 4). This holiness of the church is shown continuously, and it should be shown, in those fruits of grace which the Spirit produces in the faithful; it is expressed in many different ways in the lives of those individuals who in their manner of life tend towards the perfection of charity and in so doing are a source of edification for others.[2]

Later in the chapter, the Council fathers declare that "all the faithful, whatever their condition or rank, are called to the fulness of the Christian life and the perfection of charity. And this sanctification is conducive to a more human way of living even in society here on earth."[3] The chapter goes on to describe how all the faithful, each according to his or her own vocation, can live out the universal call to holiness.

The teaching of Vatican II on the universal call to holiness marked a new and decisive, although still not fully appreciated or embodied, effort by the Catholic Church to provide the faithful with the kind of vocational theology that, it seems to me, Mittelstadt suggests that Pentecostals need and deserve. The quotes from *Lumen Gentium* cited suggest how the Council fathers tried to address the very same hurdles that Mittelstadt argues Pentecostal theology confronts as it seeks to articulate a theology of vocation. The Council fathers, grounding their teaching on the holiness of God, affirm that all the members of the Church, whether lay or ordained, are called to live

---

[2] *Lumen Gentium*, 1964, https://www.vatican.va/archive/hist_councils/ii_vatican_council/documents/vat-ii_const_19641121_lumen-gentium_en.html, 39.

[3] *Lumen Gentium*, 40.

the holiness of God, which can in be expressed in "many different ways," and which is meant to bear fruit in the others and in the world.

While Catholics still need to do much reflection on this teaching in order to receive it and reflect it in their concrete lives, my sense from our dialogue is that the universal call to holiness could contrive to a fruitful and mutual enrichment between Pentecostals and Catholics as we seek to discern and articulate a theology of vocation.

ORU PRESS
E21 GNSES Series

THE NEW GENERATION & THE HOLY SPIRIT
BUILDING A SPIRIT-EMPOWERED FUTURE
Wonsuk Ma, Barry Saylor,
Opoku Onyinah, and Rebekah S. Bled

Why is a focus on the new generation so warranted in this time, and how is Spirit-empowerment shaping the conversation about it?

In 2022, an international panel of scholars and practitioners convened in Seoul to discuss how to prepare the new generation with Spirit-empowered faith and leadership. The book begins with biblical, historical, and theological insights and reflections, and leads readers to a large number of contextual case studies from diverse geographical and socio-cultural contexts. Through the various studies, there emerges a unified commitment to the spiritual advancement of the newer generations. The book also urges a collective intergenerational effort towards a stronger future of Spirit-empowered Christianity and its passion for the evangelization of the world.

THE REMAINING TASK OF THE GREAT COMMISSION
& The Spirit-Empowered Movement
Wonsuk Ma and Opoku Onyinah,
Rebekah Bled, Associate Editor

GOOD NEWS TO THE POOR
SPIRIT-EMPOWERED RESPONSES TO POVERTY
Wonsuk Ma and Opoku Onyinah,
Rebekah Bled, Associate Editor

THE PANDEMIC & THE HOLY SPIRIT
FROM LAMENT TO HOPE AND HEALING
Wonsuk Ma and Opoku Onyinah
Rebekah Bled, Associate Editor

PROCLAIMING CHRIST
In the Power of the Holy Spirit
OPPORTUNITIES & CHALLENGES
Wonsuk Ma and Emmanuel Anim,
Rebekah Bled, Associate Editor

HUMAN SEXUALITY
& THE HOLY SPIRIT
SPIRIT-EMPOWERED PERSPECTIVES
Wonsuk Ma and Kathaleen Beld-Martinez,
Annamarie Hamilton, Associate Editor

Check orupress.org

Response to Walter Kedjierski and Leonardo Gajardo

Martin W. Mittelstadt

As a Pentecostal educator, I am seized by an unrelenting mission to address and resist compartmentalization of the Christian life. In my essay, I critiqued a persistent Pentecostal struggle, namely, the dualistic hierarchy promoted for those in church-related vocations. I proposed that the "prophethood of all believers" and "the Fivefold Gospel" provide grounded impetus for prophetic and Full Gospel vocation that resists such a dualistic hierarchy. In my research on vocation, I have found among Catholic scholars a rich and robust theology of religious vocations. Having said this, I felt that the sheer volume of literature on Holy Orders does not adequately address the responsibilities of Catholic laity. Sadly, and stereotypically, I assumed that a Catholic theology of vocation focused too heavily on the Sacrament of Holy Orders to the detriment of lay vocations. Concerning these assumptions, I could not have been more mistaken. Moreover, my fresh understanding of Catholic lay vocation may also prove pivotal for Pentecostals.

I am grateful for God's hand over our 2023 conference theme. I focused on the wide category of vocation, Walter Kedjierski attended to the sacrament of marriage, and Leonardo Gajardo addressed religious vocations. I was particularly struck by the interplay between these respective callings. Kedjierski masterfully displayed the sacrament of marriage (and family) as the extension of the church. Pentecostals resonate naturally with the foundational responsibilities and opportunities to embody the Full Gospel in and through our homes. Concerning religious vocations, Gajardo explored the call and meticulous training for religious vocations. Having said this, I (and my Pentecostal peers) sought further clarity on the vocational lives of Catholic laity.

To do so, my Catholic friends illustrated a "fuller" Catholic understanding of sacrament/al vocation. Following our gathering, I returned to an enduring question: "What do Catholics mean when they say that the church is the 'Body of Christ?'" While Pentecostals typically view Paul's body language as metaphoric (1 Cor 11:29; 12:27), for Catholics, the sacramental bread becomes the Body of Christ and, when understood and experienced correctly, proves integral to a Catholic theology of vocation. At Mass, the presiding priest prepares and offers the eucharistic bread so that he and believers might consume the Body of Christ. The priest may do so only because he serves under the authority of and in continuity with the apostolic community; apostolic succession does not provide a path for historical ancestry but the mysterious and vocational extension of the living Jesus. The Catholic Church under papal authority appoints bishops, who in turn ordain both priests and deacons for parish ministry as well as a wonderful array of sisters and brothers for holy vocations (universities, hospitals, monastic life, etc.). The sacrament of Holy Orders is an extension of the Body of Christ.

At this point, Pentecostals ought to imagine the vocational implications for Catholic parishioners. The (weekly) Mass performs the mysterious and empowering celebration of the Body of Christ within and alongside the sacramental web of succession and ordination. The sacraments enable the church to be the Body of Christ. Believers not only receive the Body of Christ through their officiants, but they in turn are commissioned as the Body of Christ to the world. Kimberly Belcher and Andrew Prevot guided me to several liturgists. According to Lizette Larson-Miller, "Ecclesial sacraments are not static, one-time events with no precedent or ongoing efficacy."[1] Similarly, Kristiaan Depoortere declares a threefold vocational telos for the sacraments:

> [T]hey *authenticate*: "all previous practices of faith related to the sacrament that went before" because it has value and is part of the revelatory character of a sacrament; they *perfect:* "the sacramental act is an epiclesis . . . a performative word that effects what it affirms"; and they *send forth*: "every sacramental seal entails a mission."[2]

The third dimension proves pivotal for Catholic laity. The sacraments bring believers together as the people of God and simultaneously thrust them into the world: "the Church [through its succession, priests, liturgies, and proclamation] makes the Eucharist and the Eucharist makes the church." The Body of Christ (i.e., the church) becomes "sustenance for the planet to engage with our own salvation which is, by the very reality of being part of all things, a transformation of the whole universe into 'a new future in God.'"[3] I am personally drawn to words from the United Methodist communion liturgy: "Pour out your Holy Spirit on us gathered here, and on these gifts of bread and wine. Make them be for us the body and blood of Christ, that we may be for the world the body of Christ, redeemed by his blood."[4] Sacramentality embodies the conviction that the world experiences the full life of God in Christ and the Spirit.

What are the implications for a Pentecostal theology of vocation? What do Pentecostals mean when they claim to be "filled with the Spirit"? Is this filling only a metaphor? Is "fullness" merely functional? Is it sacramental? I proposed that every

---

[1] Lizett Larson-Miller, *Sacramentality Renewed: Contemporary Conversations in Sacramental Theology* (Collegeville, MN: Liturgical Press, 2016), 20.

[2] Khristiaan Depoortere, "From Sacramentality to Sacraments and Vice Versa," in *Contemporary Contours of a God Incarnate*, eds. L. Boeve and L. Leijssen (Peeters: Lueven, 2001), 60.

[3] Larson-Miller, *Sacramentality Renewed*, 53.

[4] "The Brief Great Thanksgiving for General Use," in *The United Methodist Book of Worship* (Nashville, TN: UMC Publishing House, 1992), 36.

Pentecostal commits to the Fivefold Gospel vocation for reception and extension of Jesus the Savior, Sanctifier, Spirit-baptizer, Healer, and Soon-coming King. If Pentecostals believe that the same Spirit that rests upon Jesus now rests on us, pastoral leaders guide their Spirit-filled congregants into their "fuller" vocations.

In light of our Notre Dame gathering, I offer two closing observations. First, we lamented that too many Catholics and Pentecostals are not catechized to understand the extent of their respective vocations. The Catholic Church as the Body of Christ, whether understood or not, is the life of Jesus for the world. Similarly, Pentecostals, whether realized or not, fill up the mission of Jesus. I dream of a day where contemporary disciples would be aware, confident, and intentional in their vocations. I long for a day when discipleship and vocation cannot be separated. Second, if my proposal that Pentecostals must produce a more robust theology of lay vocation is correct, I believe Pentecostal theologians need to reimagine the responsibilities given to those in religious vocations. I encourage Pentecostal theologians and educators to wrestle with the sacramental responsibilities of the Catholic priesthood. Even as every priest vows to feed the Body of Christ, may it be that Pentecostal pastors nurture their congregants toward "fullness." And in turn, may every religious worker—Catholic and Pentecostal—release God's people to a hungry and thirsty world.

REVIEWS

Pentecostal Prophets: Experience in Old Testament Perspective. By Stephen D. Barkley. Eugene, OR: Wipf & Stock. 157 + xii pp.

Stephen D. Barkley is an ordained minister with the Pentecostal Assemblies of Canada and currently serves as Director of Pastoral Leadership and campus pastor at Master's College and Seminary, Peterborough, Ontario, Canada. He completed a Doctor of Practical Theology degree from Master's, and this book is an adaptation of his doctoral dissertation.

The introductory chapter lays out the objective of the book: to probe the coherence between the modern phenomenon of prophecy among Canadian Pentecostals and Old Testament prophecy. The introduction describes prophecy in Pentecostalism and provides definitions of prophecy (7–14). Chapter 1 then presents the author's research tools (methodologies) and plan. Four "lenses" (or approaches) are identified: practical theology, practice-led research, phenomenological perspective, and theological reflection. For each method, the author provides useful definitions and evaluations. The chapter ends with the structure of the book. Chapter 2 takes the discussion of the previous material deeper through a literature review. Divided into theoretical and empirical studies, the former covers the development of prophecy through a long period from the Old Testament (i.e., Jeremiah) to Jesus as the prophet via the intertestamental period. This section also includes modern-day prophecy. The empirical section engages four authors in three aspects of the charismatic prophetic phenomenon. Here, the author's main task is clear: to probe "the coherence between the Old Testament prophets and modern practitioners" (66).

The next three chapters form the main body of the research. Chapter 3 explores the Old Testament prophet's experience (in this case, Jeremiah). Using five programmatic experiences or actions in the prophetic process (69), the author takes the readers through the book of Jeremiah. This analytical reading reveals the inner workings of the prophetic experience in stages: 1) recognizing God's presence; 2) receiving prophetic impulse; 3) discerning the source and message by the Scripture; 4) releasing the message; and 5) experiencing sensations. The discernment stage, for example, analyzes Jeremiah's argument against the false prophets (77–82). Throughout the discussion, the author highlights the emotional and spiritual burden that the prophetic message causes in Jeremiah's life. The author rightly selects the book of Jeremiah, which best reveals the internal process of the prophetic phenomenon.

Chapter 4 then takes us to twenty-first-century Canadian Pentecostal prophets! This qualitative study utilizes phenomenological methodology to describe the prophetic process in modern Pentecostal Christianity. For the "Textural Description" of the Charismatic prophets, the author uses the same five-step analysis of the participating prophets. The "Structural Description" explores three components influencing their prophetic experience. They represent the process of "making of a contemporary prophet": mentoring, location, and prophetic "failure" (114–121). The author concludes the chapter by bringing two descriptions of participant prophets together into a first-person "testimony." I find this two-page recap quite creative. Chapter 5, as anticipated, incorporates the ancient prophetic experience (ch. 3) and the modern one (ch. 4) for comparison to establish the level of coherence. Consistently applying the five-stage framework (but now adding the sixth, "Sacramental Experience"), the author carefully compares the ancient and the modern. In each heading, I appreciate the author's scholarly integrity by not attempting to increase the coherence between the two. After the investigation, the author summarizes, "It is clear from the theological reflection . . . that the experience of modern-day charismatic prophets coheres strongly with the experiences of the Old Testament prophets in many ways" (139). Finally, chapter 6 offers a summary of the study, its limitations in three areas, and new "vistas" for future research. An appendix lists six interview questions.

This book is a fine example of using an ancient text to interpret a contemporary experience, applying different methodologies. This attempted connection between the two eras also influences each other: the modern experience sheds light on the reading of the ancient text, while the Old Testament record serves as a hermeneutical template for the twenty-first-century Charismatic prophets. The author is keenly aware of the limitations of his study: one prophet from many in the Old Testament, and selected Charismatic prophets in Canada (144). But the art of research is the process of delimitation!

Two questions linger after reading the book. The first concerns the agency of the (Holy) Spirit. Chapter 4 includes many voices of modern prophets, and the agency of the Holy Spirit is liberally expressed. They understand the work of the Holy Spirit not only in revealing messages but also in a variety of functions such as "pilot and guide," "inspire," and "flood the soul." (This indicates that they are Pentecostals.) Interestingly, in Jeremiah's experience, it is "God" and the "word," but nowhere is the work of God's Spirit mentioned in the book. In contrast, elsewhere in the Old Testament, the Spirit is often attributed to being the source of revelation, even for a pagan seer Balaam (". . . the Spirit of God came on him, and he spoke his message. . . ," Num 24:2b–3a). I fully understand that Jeremiah best reveals the inner workings of the prophetic vocation, but this would be an interesting issue to explore. The second question is if this comparative study tries to equate Old Testament prophetism with the modern-day prophetic phenomenon. If the author's intention is only to investigate the level of coherence between the two experiences that are millennia apart, he did it well.

Wonsuk Ma (wma@oru.edu) is Distinguished Professor of Global Christianity at Oral Roberts University, Tulsa, Oklahoma, USA.

Phenomenal Phenomena: Biblical and Multicultural Accounts of Spirits and Exorcism. By Joy L. Vaughan. Waco, TX: Baylor University Press, 2023. 265 pp.

Studying exorcism in biblical and theological discourse is not a popular topic. Yet, New Testament interpreters are forced to interpret accounts of exorcism regarding the Synoptic tradition. For many Western scholars, these accounts are problematic to their Western reductionist worldview, and (often influenced by Bultmann) their only option is to explain away the realities of spirit possession as physical, mental, or mythical accounts. At the same time, global anthropological scholars have long accepted spirit possession accounts and have documented the cultural and contextual importance of these phenomena in their analyses. These anthropological insights reveal much about the worldview of cultural contexts unhindered by Western reductionist paradigms. However, very few studies have sought to engage the continuity of both. In *Phenomenal Phenomena*, Joy L. Vaughan seeks to do just that by using insights into modern spirit possession accounts in global contexts to shed light on biblical spirit possession accounts. In this way, Vaughan hopes not only to allow these multicultural perspectives to illuminate these ancient texts but also demonstrate that the ancient worldview has more in common with the global contextual worldview than seen in Western NT scholarship.

In Chapter One, Vaughan lays out a comprehensive history of the interpretation of exorcism in the New Testament, pointing out that while scholars widely recognize Jesus as an exorcist, scholars have debated the interpretation of these passages (8). From legendary tales in Bultmann to psychological conditions for modern anthropologists, most of these methods for interpreting spirit possession disavow the historicity of the accounts to "disallow the genuine existence of modern experiences of possession and exorcism" (17). At the same time, modern anthropological studies of spirit possession recognize the value of cultural accounts yet do not use these insights to read back into the first-century worldview. Vaughan argues in Chapter Two that anthropological studies also fall into the trap of analyzing the spirit-worldview as either customs or religious practices without engaging the validity of these experiences. They occupy the worldview but do not necessarily represent reality. This, too, is a Western paradigm. Instead, in Chapter Three, Vaughan presents a methodology of interpretation that allows the biblical author's historical account to be compared to contemporary cultural phenomena and asks "if they are historically plausible" accounts to provide some sense of validity to the supernatural biblical data (75).

The second section is the heart of her contribution to this task. In Chapter Four, she explores how spirit possession is related to the cause of sickness. She demonstrates that spirit and illness are widely experienced phenomena globally. With these insights, she looks at various Gospel texts where possession is linked to diseases and disability, and exorcism is a method of cure. She then compares this text to accounts from many different regions of the world, including Asia, Africa, South America, and Europe. She uses these insights to show that Bultmannian interpretations of the supernatural as "myth" are "not an allowable premise" in light of these realities (133). In Chapter Five, she explores spirit-possession's impact on human strength in various biblical accounts. Again, her comparison to multicultural, global accounts seeks to establish lines of continuity to validate ancient biblical accounts. In Chapter Six, she looks at spirit possession and its effects on speech, voice inflection phenomena, and ocular alteration, finding anthropological parallels in global accounts.

Chapter Seven concludes with the findings of her research. She argues, "The collection of evidence above demonstrates that there are many reports of possession experience that are characteristically analogous to the stories of Jesus and those who suffered ailments" (206). These insights counter a history of biblical studies that offered non-spiritual explanations of such biblical phenomena. The fact that global contexts have documented multicultural phenomena should give biblical interpreters pause before making such reductionistic claims. In this way, Vaughan rightfully "narrows the gap" between the "Jesus of history and the historical Jesus" (209).

To finish the final chapter, Vaughan, a professor at Asbury University, takes up the legacy of "deliverance ministry" in the Pentecostal and Charismatic tradition. She notes that healing and spirit possession were a reality in the Healing Movement with ministers like Oral Roberts and William Branham. Later, Charismatic ministers also embraced healing and deliverance as interconnected. She notes that some of this possession worldview expanded into end-times prophecy teaching and demonology-based fictional literature. The strength of the Spirit-empowered traditions is that there is no disconnect between the spirit-worldview of the New Testament and their ministry phenomena. For Vaughan, the totality of global, ancient, and Spirit-oriented contexts confirm that supernatural phenomenon and spirit possession is an ontological reality that all biblical interpreters must take seriously.

Vaughan's engagement with the subject of exorcism contributes to both biblical interpretation and critiques of Western enlightenment anti-supernatural assumptions that have shaped the church and its worldview. By connecting the ancient biblical accounts with modern phenomena, her work should be viewed by those in the Spirit-empowered tradition as a new way to support the supernatural worldview that comes with its embedded theology of healing, miracles, and the supernatural. Though it is uncertain whether Vaughan would include herself in the Pentecostal academy, this study should undoubtedly be elevated to prominence in the canon of Pentecostal-Charismatic scholarship not just for biblical interpretation but for its contribution to documenting the global phenomena of healing and the supernatural. Additionally, its contribution to epistemology is consistent with the Pentecostal hermeneutic that elevates the experience of phenomena in interpreting Scripture. While the average believer may get lost in the rich documentary research, this text would be perfect for any graduate or post-graduate course looking at Pentecostal hermeneutics or global contextual readings of Scripture. It will undoubtedly spur new discussions of demonology, deliverance, and Pentecostal phenomenology in general.

Daniel D. Isgrigg (disgrigg@oru.edu) is an Associate Professor of the History of Spirit-empowered Christianity at Oral Roberts University, Tulsa, Oklahoma, USA.

Christ Centered: The Evangelical Nature of Pentecostal Theology. By Robert Menzies. Eugene, OR: Cascade, 2020. 190 pp.

It is unanimously accepted that Christology is an indispensable theological tenet of Pentecostal theology. Thus, the title of Robert Menzies book, *Christ Centered*, has historical ties to origins of early Pentecostal theological expressions rooted in the Full Gospel. Yet it is the decidedly more divisive subtitle of the text, *The Evangelical Nature of Pentecostal Theology*, that provides the scaffolding for the text. Menzies' objective is to tether Pentecostal theology to a narrow subsection of religious expression commonly labeled Evangelicalism. In the opening pages of the text, he laments that the strong Evangelical convictions of Pentecostalism are being forgotten (xv). Further into the Introduction he presses the issues further claiming those who do not affirm the Evangelical origins of Pentecostal theology ". . . do not understand the Pentecostal movement or seek to transform it into an image of their creation" (xvii). Menzies' strong assertions provide the reader with a clear understanding of his stance regarding his views on the relationship between Pentecostalism and Evangelicalism.

Given the strong assertions in the Introduction, Menzies' appeal to R. A. Torrey as historical evidence for the Evangelical origins of Pentecostal theology should not come as a surprise to those familiar with early Pentecostal history. Unlike Charles Parham, whose reputation has been called into question under historical scrutiny, the historical record regarding Torrey is favorable. Further, Torrey provides a direct connection to the Keswick Movement, which played a larger role in shaping Evangelical sensibilities than the Wesleyan roots of William Seymour. Torrey, whom Menzies suggests is the "father of Fundamentalism" (3), provides the historical ties necessary for Menzies to assert the Evangelical origins of Pentecostalism. While he does not explicitly make the claim, those familiar with the historical underpinnings of Pentecostalism will note that Menzies is essentially shifting the primary influence of Pentecostalism from Azusa Street to the Keswick Movement in his appeal to Torrey as the father of Pentecostalism (4), despite Parham and Seymour having the strongest historical consensus. Considerably more historical scrutiny must be conducted prior to validating Menzies' assertions regarding Torrey as the "father of Pentecostalism." While the influences of the Keswick and Higher Life movements upon Pentecostalism have been historically documented, the attempt to position the Keswick Movement as the primary influence of early Pentecostalism requires more than the condensed biographical sketch provided by Menzies.

Part II transitions towards a theological argument in favor of the Evangelical origins of Pentecostalism. The opening pages anticipate the absence of Azusa Street from the previous historical defense by devaluing the role of Azusa Street. Citing his father, a renowned historian, Menzies insinuates that the Evangelical origins of Pentecostalism protected the Pentecostal Movement from being cast to the periphery, which he claims has been the fate of over twenty charismatic movements documented in the history of the church. Conveniently, the discussion of Azusa Street and its most influential characters, Parham and Seymour, is only mentioned in passing as evidence for the Evangelical nature of Pentecostal theology. The remaining portion of Part II addresses the three key theological themes of baptism in the Spirit, glossolalia, and signs/wonders in three separate chapters. Menzies' choice of these three specific theological themes is anticipated as they are historically the most commonly rejected among Evangelical/fundamentalist theological systems. The argument that Pentecostal theology has its Evangelical root hinges upon being able to justify these three theological themes within the theological systems of Evangelicalism. Menzies leans heavily on the works of James Dunn and Max Turner, whose influence is evident in the numerous citations to their works within the chapters. Notably absent are works from influential Evangelical theologians such as John Frame, Wayne Grudem, Louis Berkhof, or Millard Erickson, who have produced works of systematic theology. The fact that Menzies is unable to make direct connections between prominent Evangelical theologians and these key doctrinal issues suggests the relationship between Evangelicals and Pentecostals may be more tremulous than he is willing to admit.

In the next section of the text, Menzies shifts the dialogue from theology to spirituality. The section contains chapters on the necessity of a personal relationship with Jesus Christ and missions. Ignoring the pietist influences of the Reformation, Menzies advances his argument for the Evangelical origins of Pentecostalism by appealing to the Reformer Martin Luther. Bypassing the pietist influences Menzies is relieved of addressing the theological differences between the magisterial reformers and pietist movements regarding religious experience. As a renowned historian Menzies is no doubt aware of the abundant historical documentation concerning the influence of Wesleyan/Holiness religious expression upon Pentecostalism, which suggests the omission was intentional. The omission raises questions concerning the strength of Menzies' argumentative ability to withstand alternative historical and theological proposals.

The fourth and final section enters into dialogue with two of the premier contemporary Pentecostal theologians: Veli-Matti Kärkkäinen and Amos Yong. Menzies specifically addresses an article written by Kärkkäinen for the book titled *The Spirit in the World*. He rebuffs the idea that the diversity of Pentecostalism makes it difficult to construct a set of unifying theological principles. Menzies attempts to parlay what is a valid critique of Kärkkäinen to promote the Evangelical origins of Pentecostal theology. This attempt is only viable if the origins of early Pentecostal theology are shifted away from Azusa Street and relocated to the Keswick Movement. Such an attempt runs upstream against the consensus of Azusa Street as the defining event of modern Pentecostalism. Menzies continues his critique of Kärkkäinen, questioning the primacy of spirituality over theology within the Pentecostal tradition. This positions Menzies to argue that Kärkkäinen is "dissatisfied with the simple focus on the Bible as the source of our theology" (124). Menzies' argument is one that has been leveled by fundamentalists since the days of Azusa Street. Having registered his critique of Kärkkäinen, Menzies now turns his attention to Yong. He takes issue with Yong's assertion that other religions may be "instruments of the Holy Spirit working out the Divine purposes in the world" (131). Menzies argues that Yong has elevated pneumatology at the expense of Christology, lamenting that Yong's exhortations "sound more like a product of contemporary Western and liberal culture than the apostolic mandate" (132). Again, Menzies raises valid concerns about the views of Yong that must be critically examined. Yet, Menzies forgoes such critical examination in favor of casting Yong as outside the Pentecostal Movement. The attempts by Menzies to position two prominent Pentecostal scholars outside acceptable parameters of Pentecostalism weakens his argument for the Evangelical origins of Pentecostalism.

Since the acceptance of the Assembly of God into the National Association of Evangelicals in 1942, the origins of Pentecostalism have been disputed. Menzies is among the minority of Pentecostal scholars in the academy who advocate for the Evangelical origins of Pentecostal theology. He should be commended for reminding Pentecostals of the deep influences that Evangelicalism has asserted upon Pentecostal theology. The tendency of Pentecostal scholarship to downplay these influences needed to be corrected. Menzies' work attempts to provide such a correction. The challenge for Menzies is his assumption that such influences are grounds for locating the origins of Pentecostal theology in Evangelicalism. The latter is much more difficult to justify historically and theologically. It requires repositioning the historical origins of Pentecostalism from Azusa Street to the Keswick Movement, ignoring the pietistic influence of the Wesleyan/Holiness Movement and reworking key theological themes within Pentecostalism to fit within fundamentalist theological systems. Despite the difficulty in claiming the Evangelical origins of Pentecostalism, Pentecostals should not dismiss the claims of Menzies. Rather, Pentecostals should see Menzies' book as an opportunity to engage in critical dialogue around the areas of continuity and discontinuity with Evangelical theology. Such ecumenical dialogue will allow for Pentecostals to come out of the shadows of Evangelicalism and begin to establish and articulate itself as a unique theological tradition.

Michael Young (mdyoung@seu.edu) is Adjunct Professor of Theology and Leadership for Pacific Rim University, Honolulu, Hawaii, USA.

Follow the Healer: Biblical Foundations for Healing Ministry. By Stephen Seamands. Grand Rapids: Zondervan, 2023. 176 pp.

In *Follow the Healer*, Stephen Seamands examines the subject of divine healing, surveying the biblical and theological foundations of Jesus' healing ministry to inspire his readers to continue this ministry in the church today. Although he writes from an admittedly Wesleyan perspective, his primary concern is to encourage all Christians to be engaged in the healing ministry. His influences range from John and Charles Wesley, A. B. Simpson, and Smith Wigglesworth to Randy Clark, Jack Deere, and John Wimber. This is reflected in his wide appreciation of the diverse contributions of various schools of healing throughout the history of the church.

Seamands argues that when followers of Christ engage in the healing ministry, they join Jesus' continuing ministry through the church today. Jesus gave us a threefold pattern of ministry that his followers participate in—*incarnation, crucifixion, and resurrection*. Undergirding Jesus' healing ministry is his love and compassion. This motivation should determine our purpose and shape our practice of the healing ministry, encouraging us to be patient and persistent when faced with challenges. Seamands presents five ways Jesus heals today: 1. through supernatural healing and miracles; 2. through doctors and medicine; 3. through the human body's healing power—the miracle of nature; 4. through bestowing grace in suffering; and 5. through victorious dying. He also examines the relationship between healing and the image of God. He shows that Jesus' healing encompasses all four dimensions of the broken divine image—spiritual, social, physical, and psychological.

The relationship between healing and the kingdom of God is also explored. By showing that Jesus inaugurated the kingdom of God, the author lays the foundation for understanding one aspect of the mystery of the kingdom: the *already/not yet* dual nature of the kingdom. He maintains that this "radical middle" perspective is foundational for understanding healing in this age. Toward the end of the book, he builds upon this foundation and encourages his readers to embrace the mystery of the kingdom. He illustrates that several truths in Christian theology (e.g., the Trinity, incarnation, divine sovereignty, and human free will) contain aspects of mystery that must be maintained. He then attempts to present a balanced view of two debated topics in healing: the relationship between atonement and physical healing and the role of faith in healing. The issue of theodicy is also addressed within the context of physical healing. He holds that any helpful answers in this area need to emphasize that God fully identifies with human suffering through the life and death of Christ. In turn, those involved in the ministry of healing are wounded healers who allow their "radiant scars" to propel them to the ministry of healing to others in need. In the last chapter, Seamands clarifies the relationship between healing and the Holy Spirit. While many books on this subject focus on the role of the gifts of the Spirit in the healing ministry, the author stresses the crucial role of the fruit of the Spirit working in tandem with the charismata.

Overall, *Follow the Healer* is an excellent resource that bridges the gap between academic theology and praxis. The author has the unique vantage point of being involved in both worlds, which is evident in his writing. His involvement in formal theological education, as well as his decades of experience in the healing ministry, add a valuable overarching dimension to his contribution. His treatment of the topic does not come across as aloof from the real-world challenges associated with this particular ministry. If anything, it affirms the widespread experience of many and provides biblical and practical insights on how to advance toward effectiveness in ministering healing today.

His treatment of key biblical and theological concepts related to the healing ministry are all aimed at helping his readers gain a foundational understanding of divine healing. Therein lies the value of this work to those interested in engaging in the healing ministry. It answers many pertinent questions related to this subject in a balanced, nuanced, and straightforward way. Its direct approach makes it accessible to academic students and practitioners in the church alike. His theological/biblical presentation in this work lays down a solid foundation for the healing ministry today.

In his attempt to cover the core issues relating to divine healing from a theological/biblical standpoint, Seamands' work may come across as less practical to some who are familiar with other authors in this field. Some leading writers in the past, like John Wimber and Francis MacNutt, provided sections in their books that walked the reader step-by-step on how to minister healing to others, offering various field-tested models. Still, it may not have been Seamands' intention to write an exhaustive book on healing covering every related aspect, so this point does not necessarily take away from this excellent, concise treatment of healing.

Seamands presents nuanced theological concepts in a simple and straightforward way that is easy to absorb by a wide variety of audiences, even those in the church who may lack seminary training but nevertheless have been gifted by God in the healing ministry. His articulation of such concepts as *already/not yet* of the kingdom will introduce many readers to this New Testament theological principle in a clear and approachable manner. One of the more challenging topics related to divine healing is the question of why some are not healed. Seamands' approach to this question is both pastorally sensitive and theologically adept. He refrains from providing petty answers and maintains the tension of mystery that runs through several biblical doctrines. At the same time, his approach provides a helpful model that encourages believers to persist in praying for healing and walk compassionately alongside those who are still waiting for their prayers to be answered. He does not shy away from dealing with the complex questions of theodicy. His treatment is a commendable approach that provides a helpful, workable model for anyone involved in Christian ministry.

Sam M. Barsoum (sbarsoum@oru.edu) is Director of the Bible Institute at Oral Roberts University, Tulsa, Oklahoma, USA.

The Kaleidoscopic City: Hong Kong, Mission, and the Evolution of Global Pentecostalism. By Alex R. Mayfield. Waco, TX: Baylor University Press, 2023. 269 pp.

Studies of the Pentecostal Movement have proved the existence of many forms of Pentecostalism, with the various permutations of Pentecostalism practiced in different places, thus causing the emergence of the term "Pentecostalisms." Hong Kong is no exception to the rule; since its earliest days, the Pentecostalism in that colonial city took shape by "a kaleidoscopic mix of people with competing ideas and practices" (p. 4). The form of Pentecostalism that took root in Hong Kong was influenced by missionaries and preachers from various originations, networks, institutions, and nations, carrying opposing ideas at times. However, this smorgasbord of ideas and creeds took a new form by engaging with the local Chinese culture and the message of modern Pentecost. Alex Mayfield, in *The Kaleidoscopic City*, pens the mission history of Pentecostalism in Hong Kong between 1907 and 1942. Using Foucault's conception of discourse, Mayfield describes the Pentecostal discourse on this island as "the product of global interconnections, sustained through a bevy of international revival centers, periodicals, and eventually—denominations" (p. 4). In this convincing discourse, Mayfield highlights the effect of globalization on the Pentecostal Movement in this city and how the global-local exchange transformed the form of Pentecostalism embraced and merged in Hong Kong.

In his attempt to explore the development of Pentecostalism in the early twentieth century, Mayfield employs an often-neglected methodology of spatial analysis using a combination of qualitative and quantitative data. In this discursive spatial approach, he examines the development of the Pentecostal movement in Hong Kong as a local expression while considering the multivalent nature of the global Pentecostal movement. Using 1,072 articles referencing Hong Kong in Pentecostal periodicals along with other available historical records, Pentecostalism in Hong Kong is treated as a diverse yet singular network as well as a part of the global Pentecostal network. In this transnational network discourse, one will find the interactions among local missionaries and institutions and how the global Pentecostal networks influenced it through publications, conferences, and interpersonal relations.

In five chapters, Mayfield explores a distinct face of Pentecostalism in each chapter. Chapter one treats Hong Kong as a gateway city to the region, focusing on its struggle for a center. In chapter two, he delves into denominational identity and Pentecostal mission structures. He tells readers about the move from faith mission models of the Pentecostal norm to the denominational models as denominations were formed in the homelands of the missionaries. With the shift in the mission model comes a shift in the aims, identities, and missional approach of Pentecostals in Hong Kong, looking like Pentecostals at one moment and like evangelicals at other times.

Chapter three portrays Hong Kong as a soul-saving city sharing the soul-saving, Spirit-filled education offered by Pentecostal missionaries and evangelistic institutions. He points out that Pentecostal evangelistic practices look "un-Pentecostal" as they see education, colportage, and Sunday schools as the most effective means to evangelize this colonial city. Chapter four focuses on Pentecostal spirituality, where the Pentecostals compete in Hong Kong's religious market. Chapter five discusses the role of female missionaries, the acceptance of the evangelical missionary wife model, and the vital role of the local Chinese Bible women in the spread of the Pentecostal message. As the book is named, these five chapters show the kaleidoscopic view of Hong Kong's Pentecostal movement in five distinct themes.

Mayfield's *The Kaleidoscopic City* is a thematic examination of Pentecostalism in Hong Kong using a discursive spatial approach. In this impressive work, he manages to capture the development of Pentecostalism that is being transformed by globalization and the local culture where it is planted. His approach vastly differs from the traditional Pentecostal historiography drawn by three patterns rooted in different historiographies. Unlike the historical discourses of Vinson Synan, Walter Hollenweger, and Allan Anderson, who structured their work on the origins of Pentecostalism, Mayfield's emphasis is on the transformation of Pentecostalism and the form of Pentecostalism that emerged in Hong Kong.

One of the contributions of Mayfield to the study of global Pentecostalism is his inclusion of historical data omitted in Anderson's *Introduction to Pentecostalism*, which mainly focuses on the early part of the Pentecostal history, as Anderson intends to point to the multiple origins of global Pentecostalism. Thus, while the revival centers and pioneer Western missionaries are included in Anderson's work, it ends with the indigenous leader, Mok Lai Chi, excluding the development of Hong Kong's Pentecostalism in later decades. Mayfield's work fills out the denominational histories from 1925 until 1942. His account includes the Chinese leaders who worked alongside the Western missionaries and the impact of social and ideological changes in global Pentecostalism on its local expression.

His choice of method is effective in handling the vast amount of historical data in a manageable way, and the use of the kaleidoscope analogy fits a city like Hong Kong that played many vital roles in the region. Moreover, viewing Pentecostalism in Hong Kong as part of a transnational spatially specific discourse provides a broader and more nuanced description of the Pentecostal mission in the city. However, the thematic approach has drawbacks as some other important facts are omitted. As the author acknowledges, his method of pulling out meta trends using charts and figures is not self-explanatory and is challenging for making sense without added narrative. One should be mindful of the biased nature of historical discourses as this project relies heavily on periodicals that are, in fact, official narratives. One should be open to the possibility of non-official narratives that can be somewhat contrary to what is included in this project.

Overall, this book provides the readers with a better understanding of the history of the early Pentecostal mission in Hong Kong and the evolution of global Pentecostalism in the early twentieth century. It is an excellent book for students who study Pentecostalism, Asian Pentecostal history, and scholars of global Christianity.

Van Hnuai Kim (vkim@oru.edu) is a PhD candidate at Oral Roberts University, Tulsa, Oklahoma, USA.

Soon and Very Soon: A Biblical and Theological Study of the Events Surrounding Jesus Christ's Second Coming. By David K. Hebert. Tulsa: Word and Spirit Press, 2019. 193 pp.

As a youth it was intriguing to hear messages from preachers about the end times. People called it *prophecy*. Through the years as a pastor if I inquired of lay people what their favorite book of the Bible was I either received one of two answers: Psalms or Revelation. I am sure that the late gospel singer Andraé Crouch's song "Soon and Very Soon" was the inspiration for the title of Hebert's inquiry.

Soon and Very Soon is a collection of numerous ideas on eschatology and end times models from the past 150 years. The author's motivation comes from his early days as a Christian in the 1970s when the Jesus People and the Charismatic Renewal were in full swing. This time in his life provided the impetus behind the research.

He commences in chapter one by asking the question, "What does the term *end times* mean?" Many people quote Joel 2:28–32 as a basis for what the last days entail, that God will pour out the Spirit on all flesh and the great and terrible Day of the Lord will come. Yet, we are still waiting for that Day and many ideas abound about what will occur. Herbert states he is speaking of the "Perfect/Complete Gospel of Both Comings of Jesus Christ," as he terms it. Providing a definition to this phrase, he writes that the "concept cohesively unifies Jesus' first coming (for redemption, reconciliation, and restoration) with His second coming (the Rapture and Resurrection of the Body of Christ) into the complete salvation of the Body of Christ (both corporately and individually)" (5). This Perfect/Complete Gospel, which he believes Christ related to his disciples (Matt 24; Mark 13; Luke 17), will constitute the entirety of his investigation.

In chapter two he defines Bible prophecy. The concept is set into two paradigms, *forthtelling* and *foretelling*. Forthtelling states it "like it is" in today's terms, such as in preaching, while foretelling speaks of the future. The book contains much of the second term, *foretelling*. The author's writing concludes with defining the distinctive eschatological interpretations of Revelation—preterist, idealist, historical, and futurist.

Hebert's understanding of time, utilizing the Greek words *kairos* and *chronos*, is presented in chapter three. In essence, *kairos* is linear and *chronos* sequential time. He supports both ideas of time with scriptural references, leading to a discussion of salvation history through Jesus Christ. Carrying the chapter to its summation, he speaks about a gap of time named the "time of the Gentiles" (Dan 9:26). This period ranges between the beginning of the church and the rapture (33).

These thoughts flow directly into the next chapter with a discussion of the kingdom of Heaven and kingdom of God. He believes both phrases "are synonymously, biblically, and theologically meaning the same thing" (39). Noting the kingship of Christ in Scripture and the mystery of the kingdom in Jesus' parables, these thoughts lead to a short discussion of dispensationalism and replacement theology.

Chapter five concerns the second coming of Christ or what we call the *parousia*. With numerous scriptural references, Hebert seeks to define the two comings of Christ—his first advent and second coming. These thoughts lead to his opinion of the idea of the Perfect/Complete Gospel. As he sees the timeline in Scripture develop, he notes the next event on the prophetic calendar, the millennium.

In chapter six Hebert defines three major views of the millennial kingdom—premillennial, postmillennial, and amillennial. He remarks that the millennial ideas are more controversial than the second coming beliefs for Christians. Delving into the church fathers and church history, he presents the wide range of ideas and thoughts about the millennium through the centuries. Because the presuppositions of the author are premillennial, he moves directly into chapter seven with the Old Testament idea of the Day of the Lord.

Observing numerous references to the Day of the Lord (Yahweh) in Isaiah, Jeremiah, and Joel, the author believes this idea leads into the book of Acts with Peter's utterance of Joel 2 in the apostle's first sermon (Acts 2). He notes that the Day of the Lord predicts judgment to the world systems as never before experienced. Linking the Day of the Lord to the tribulation in Revelation, Hebert states it will be an "unprecedented" time of wrath (88).

In chapter eight he tackles the famed rapture theory. Jumping between partial rapture theories and the like, he concludes with the idea that the pretribulation rapture fits deftly into his idea of the Perfect/Complete Gospel.

Moving into other areas of eschatology, chapter nine is about the intermediate state, eternal state, and resurrection/judgment. As well, he writes of annihilationism and the Roman Catholic views of purgatory. However, his conclusions, drawn from his reading of Scripture, do not accept these two prior interpretations.

Finally, chapter ten speaks of the "signs of the times." Bringing together all he has written to this point, he concludes with an appeal to preach the gospel to all the world (143). His Perfect/Complete Comings of Christ leads to "such a time as this" and an urgency to take the gospel to the world.

There are two observations I would offer of Hebert's research. Number one, he is not writing an analysis of end times speculations. Each chapter essentially lists the various topics from a premillennial dispensationalist point of view. The author shares research about other views; however, his thinking fundamentally comes back to the pretribulation rapture model. Secondly, coming from my own studies of eschatology and as a pastor in churches, I know there are a number of other concepts on what Christ's second coming means to Christian people. There are pastors who do not believe in a literal second coming. As one minister told me in seminary, Christ comes a second time when we worship or when we feed the poor (Matt 25). These impressions are not addressed in his research. In short, *Soon and Very Soon* is a good resource for lay people who believe in a premillennial rapture and literal millennium, but a number of other interpretations are not examined in his study.

Cletus L. Hull, III (chull@oru.edu) is an Assistant Adjunct Professor of Biblical Studies, Oral Roberts University, Tulsa, Oklahoma, USA. He also pastors Trinity United Christian Church as the Senior Minister in Lower Burrell, Pennsylvania, USA.

www.ingramcontent.com/pod-product-compliance
Lightning Source LLC
Chambersburg PA
CBHW070126080526
44586CB00015B/1577